distributed
by
INDIANA
UNIVERSITY PRESS

FILM ON FOUR

1982/1991

A SURVEY

Moonlighting: Jeremy Irons

FILM ON FOUR

1982/1991

A SURVEY

by
JOHN PYM

credit collaborator
MARKKU SALMI

BFI Publishing

First published in 1992 by the
British Film Institute
21 Stephen Street
London W1P 1PL

British Library Cataloguing in Publication Data
Pym, John
Film on Four
I. Title
791.4375
ISBN 0-85170-345-3

Designed by Edwin Taylor

Set in Melior by
Rowland Phototypesetting Ltd
and printed in Great Britain by
St Edmundsbury Press Ltd, Bury St Edmunds, Suffolk

CONTENTS

To
KENNY McBAIN

INTRODUCTION

T HIS BOOK IS a personal survey. It covers 136 fiction films 'commissioned' by the drama department of Channel 4 Television
(London) – see note page 9 – and transmitted in the slot 'Film
on Four' between 2 November 1982 and 31 December 1991. During this
period, the department was headed by David Rose and Karin Bamborough and their associates Walter Donohue and Peter Ansorge. The 136
films are a mix. (All were shown complete, except for *Praying Mantis*,
which was transmitted over two evenings.) Some, *Paris, Texas* and *Voyage to Cythera*, for example, are unmistakably scaled for cinema – the
larger the theatre the better – and their effect is undoubtedly diminished
on television, though not entirely diminished. Others, such as *Moonlighting* and *Prick Up Your Ears*, are at home equally in a cinema or on
television. Others still, such as *Walter* and *Wild Flowers*, benefit from
being seen on television. And some exist in a visual no man's land.

When three years ago, Renee Goddard of the European Script Fund
insisted (as only a producer can insist) that a book on David Rose and
Channel 4 must be written, it struck me that here was an opportunity
to identify the difference, if one existed, between a television and a
cinema film. Having reviewed all 136 films described in the following
pages, I came to the conclusion, however, that my first impulse was
wrong. The fundamental question about television-backed fiction films
– that is, films regarded by their makers as principally theatrical features
– is not whether they work better, or differently, in the cinema or on
television, but whether they work at all in either medium.

If a film has something to say, it will make its voice heard in the
stalls or the living-room. The rest, in short, is largely a matter of degree.
And in any event, no film-maker today can afford to disdain television
and the money it disburses. Eleven years ago, Richard Roud, the film
critic and then director of the New York Film Festival, reflected on the
future. 'We have to reckon that soon everything is going to be on cassette

INTRODUCTION

or disc, and it is no longer going to be simply a matter of showing films [at festivals], but of showing the best print in the best possible way. It is going to be like hardback and paperback. Paperback will be the cassettes. But there will always be people who will want to see the film properly: the festivals will be for them . . .'

Discerning viewers will always favour the 'hardback' *Comrades*, *Another Time, Another Place* or *The Sacrifice.* But as the director Kenneth Loach asserted, when asked in 1991 if he considered his *Riff-Raff* (a Film on Four outside the scope of this book) a film-film or a television-film: 'Today *everything* is on television.' The 'paperback' – the film as seen on television – is an inescapable reality. And the hairsplitting arguments over what constitutes an authentic new theatrical feature seem increasingly inconsequential. This book, I hope, is chiefly about substance, what these 136 films have to say, not style. Which of the hardbacks will merit a retrospective festival screening? Which of the paperbacks will be signed out, in expectation, from some as yet uninvented library of the twenty-first century?

It is often asked, in debating-shops, whether Channel 4 gave a life-saving transfusion to the British film industry in the 1980s. It gave a transfusion, certainly – witness the careers of Stephen Frears, Peter Greenaway and Colin Gregg – but whether the patient has the strength to quit his sickbed and produce a substantial amount of worthwhile work only the next ten years will reveal. The Channel's policy for fiction films, tested on the Continent but untried in Britain before November 1982, was to encourage new (and not so new) independent film-makers by offering them not only money, but the chance (if a distributor could be found) to exhibit their work in the cinema, where it might gain a reputation and an identity, before its television transmission. That was Channel 4's novel achievement – the modest, elegant idea was put to David Rose in a few sentences by the Channel's first chief executive,

INTRODUCTION

Jeremy Isaacs, in December 1980 – and its first fruits are the subject of this survey. It took the BBC, it may be noted, some eight years to follow suit with the release of its first theatrical co-production, *Dancin' Thru the Dark*.

Channel 4, unlike BBC TV, is no studio, quite the reverse. It was created to commission the work of independent programme-makers, to act as a 'visual publishing house' to which ideas as well as wares could be brought. During his time as senior commissioning editor for fiction (1982–90), David Rose and his associates helped to 'enable' these 136 films. They are not uniform 'Channel 4' product, nor were they intended to be. The level of the Channel's investment has, after all, ranged from two to 100 per cent (see Appendix A). The film-makers were, for the most part, mavericks, not company men. How many of these co-ventures would ever have been made had it not been for Channel 4? Impossible to say. But very many would not, and for that assuredly we would have been the poorer.

NOTE: This book does not cover every Film on Four transmitted between 1982 and 1991. It is limited to those films (of feature or near-feature length) commissioned by the Channel 4 drama department. With one exception, all were shot on film. Other fiction films have been commissioned by other Channel 4 departments for other slots. Very occasionally these films have found their way on to Film on Four (for example Mira Nair's documentary-fiction *Salaam Bombay!*). I have omitted, too, all films of both British and overseas origin acquired after their completion: these include the majority of Film on Four's sister slot (for subtitled work) 'Film on Four International'. The survey covers only those films which Channel 4 commissioned outright, co-commissioned or pre-purchased before or during production; films which, it can be said, it helped when help was most needed.

October 1982 Parade in London for victory in Falklands Campaign.
November President Brezhnev of the USSR dies; Yuri Andropov succeeds.
January 1983 Franks Report clears Mrs Thatcher of lacking foresight
over the Falklands invasion. **February** Klaus Barbie,
'Butcher of Lyon', jailed in France for wartime atrocities.
Theft of 'Shergar', winner of the 1981 Derby.
March Famine in Ethiopia. **April** Maiden voyage of the US space shuttle
Challenger. 'Hitler Diaries' exposed. *Gandhi* wins eight Oscars.
May People's Express offers London–New York flight for £99. **June** Mrs Thatcher
elected for a second term; 144 Tory majority in the General Election.
July End of martial law in Poland. **August** Philippines opposition leader
Benigno Aquino assassinated at Manila airport. **September** Soviet jet
shoots down South Korean passenger plane. **October** Neil Kinnock

elected leader of the Labour Party. United States invades Grenada.
November Denis Nilsen jailed for 25 years for six murders. £26m Heathrow
airport bullion theft, Britain's largest-ever robbery.
December Provisional IRA bombs Harrods store, six die.

CHAPTER 1

WHERE ARE YOU, PIGEON?

1982/1983

FILM ON FOUR announced itself on Channel 4's first night (2 November 1982) with the wintry tale of a mentally handicapped man. WALTER, directed by Stephen Frears, was sixty-five minutes long. Its setting was straitened postwar England but the action, filtered through the limbo of Walter's mind, floated disconcertingly outside time and place. Its approach was unemphasised realism, yet a realism shockingly enlivened by scenes of operatic violence and emotion. The tone was composed and dispassionate; and the performance of Ian McKellen as Walter most remarkable perhaps for its lack of sentimental special pleading. It is hard to forget Walter's face, his oversized cap, his eyes, his teeth too large for his mouth.

The film was in colour but could equally (perhaps better) have been in black and white; and it unfolded through spare vignettes, one fading into the next. Walter was cared for at home by his strict, anxious mother (Barbara Jefford). At the storeroom where he swept up he was first mocked then bullied. His silent father, slumped in a chair, was incapable of action; he kept pigeons and bequeathed Walter an affection for the birds. After the death of his parents, Walter is placed in an institution where he will remain for the rest of his life.

At a Christmas party Walter informs an orderly (Jim Broadbent) that he would like a baby. The orderly scans the hall: Walter, he says, doesn't really want a baby; he, the orderly, has all these children and only Walter to help him and by rights Walter should not be there at all. A sequel, WALTER & JUNE (26 May 1983), hooked on to this theme. (Both films were taken from novels by David Cook.) Twenty-one years have passed; the paint has brightened but nothing essential has changed. Walter runs away with a fellow patient (Sarah Miles), an unwed mother, and together they keep house in a London squat. She abandons him, takes up with another man, dies in a fall. She leaves a pathetic message intended for Walter: 'Where are you, Pigeon?' Had everything been different they could perhaps . . . The films have no moral except to show us as we are.

P'TANG, YANG, KIPPERBANG, transmitted on Channel 4's second evening (3 November 1982), struck a different note. It was the first of seven films produced by David Puttnam's company Enigma under the title 'First Love'. Unlike Walter's world, the postwar London in which 14-year-old Alan Duckworth is comfortably at home could only be re-imagined in sunshine and colour. (The series logo was a red heart on which an unseen hand chalked '1st'.) Alan's well-appointed state secondary school has a bright-eyed groundsman, Tommy. The boys take organised runs. Despite a streak of hypocrisy the cane-happy headmaster is a figure of authority. Things work, there is order, solidity, tradition; and the required tone of voice for the school slang-phrase 'P'Tang, Yang, Kipperbang' signifies a weary, if meaningless, acceptance of this.

Written by the series' story editor Jack Rosenthal, author of the award-winning BBC TV play *Bar Mitzvah Boy* (1976), the film is an indulgent comedy (with a dash of bitters) about a first kiss. Having fluffed his chance in the school play, Alan comes to realise (with relief) that his emotional confusion has been for nothing. John Arlott punctuates the action with commentary on a Test Match in which Duckworth is forever winning (or losing) the day for England. *P'Tang, Yang, Kipperbang*, directed by Michael Apted, knows exactly what it is doing. It deals in real feelings but glancingly. Its world is specific and circumscribed. And its plot and subplot – Alan's teacher Estelle is pregnant by Tommy after the adult equivalent of a first kiss – run on lines which are not so much predictable as cheerfully unpretentious.

Of the twenty-seven films transmitted by Film on Four between November 1982 and the end of 1983, fifteen were set in England, five in Scotland and two in France; with one each in Wales, Northern Ireland, the Republic of Ireland, Poland and the Soviet Union. Twelve take place in the present but only six, *Giro City, Angel, Moonlighting, The Ploughman's Lunch, Meantime* and *Accounts*, focused on the contemporary state of the United Kingdom and of these only *Giro City* and *The Ploughman's Lunch* drew a bead on specific political issues. Nine featured people who were in some sense on the run; and two, *Ill Fares the Land* and *Another Time, Another Place*, concerned the perils of living in remote spots. Of the first twenty-seven only two cut their cloth direct from history – *Red Monarch*, a black farce on Stalin's enormities, and *A Flame to the Phoenix*, a doomed tale of Poland on the brink of the Second World War. In the early 1980s the producers, directors and scriptwriters backed by Film on Four favoured the past over the present, the personal over the public, separation over connection.

In three of the five Scottish films, landscape – the specific sense of an exact location – plays a governing role in the action. The most fully realised of the three, **ANOTHER TIME, ANOTHER PLACE** (10 November 1983), is set on the Black Isle, the peninsula north of Inverness, and the leading character Janie (Phyllis Logan) seems sometimes an almost tangible feature of the enveloping Highland landscape. The story by Jessie Kesson, adapted and directed by Michael Radford, is a small tragedy about frustration and the mistaken actions which flow from it. Three Italian prisoners of war are billeted on a watchful farmer in autumn 1944. His young wife Janie longs for something other. She imagines romance with the carpenter Paolo but it is Luigi (Giovanni Mauriello), a sensual homesick Neapolitan, who finally has her. Later, after Luigi is falsely accused of raping a local girl, Janie sacrifices everything in a vain attempt to save him. The film then halts, and the rest must be imagined. Janie says most when the camera simply rests on her, as she brushes straw from her breasts, twirls at a dance or watches her husband count the heavy, important coins they have saved.

The film is flecked with the comedy of observation and an occasional dry aside ('*Never* possible!' Janie tells Luigi with a Scots finality softened by the echo of his broken English). It is, however, soaked with real if buried feelings which are treated as if they matter. Without the breadth and emptiness of the landscape (the shot for instance of a figure stumbling across a ploughed field with news of the armistice) and without a pace which mirrors the countryside and seasons, the events depicted and the tangible absence of another, warmer, southern landscape would be diminished.

Landscape features even more immediately in two other films, both of which ask: What price must we pay to remain attached to that which we choose to call home? **ILL FARES THE LAND** (19 May 1983), a first feature written and directed by Bill Bryden (known chiefly for his theatre work), is the recollected story of the last thirty-six inhabitants of Hirta, the largest of the islands constituting St Kilda in the Hebrides, and their decision reached in 1930 after two years of argument and debate to quit the island for the mainland. The prospect is of irrevocable loss. The cropped barrenness of Hirta, the cliffs down which boys are lowered to catch puffin and fulmar and the turbulent immensity of the surrounding ocean are effectively caught; but the film as a whole is marked by a tone of somewhat willed desolation and a tendency to tell rather than show.

ACCOUNTS (22 December 1983), conversely, is about the optimism of the fresh start. Mary Mawson and her two teenage sons cross the border from Allendale, Northumberland, to Kelso, Roxburgh, and set themselves to work, no longer tenant farmers but freeholders. The film is accurate in telling details: a stock-catalogue quiz, an evening entertainment as natural as watching television; the boys' pride in a new milking parlour; a crow shoot which bursts a bubble of tension. And it has throughout a refreshing openness; as if the Borders were the whole of life. It is brought most sharply into focus, however, by the performances of the Newcastle actors Robert Smeaton and Michael McNally. They are as noisy and restless as Phyllis Logan in *Another Time, Another Place* is quiet and self-composed. Like Janie, though, the Mawson boys are bonded to the landscape: they stride across it with confidence.

Accounts, adapted from a play by Michael Wilcox, is a small film happily embracing its regionalism. Some elements, such as the attraction of one boy to the family friend who advises on the farm accounts, are handled a little awkwardly. But there are several scenes, such as a confrontation composed of extended silences where the incipient homosexuality of the younger brother is acknowledged and accepted, which slip clear of the script and into a wider world.

In 1975 Jack Gold directed *The Naked Civil Servant* (Thames Television), the dramatised autobiography of Quentin Crisp. The film, written by Philip Mackie, struck a popular chord and made a star of its amused, honest protagonist, a gay (in every sense of the word) crusader who, like any true believer, suffered his knocks without complaint. The team of Gold and Mackie subsequently made another (somewhat less telling) camp entertainment, PRAYING MANTIS, a 'thriller' adapted from a novel by Hubert Monteilheit. The film was shown in two parts (17/24 November 1982) and is as yet the only commission of Film on Four shown over more than one evening. When it was repeated in November 1984, Part 2 drew the highest viewing figures of any 1982–83 film transmitted by Film on Four (see the tables at the end of each chapter).

The plot turns on the life-insurance policy of Professor Canova, an unsuspecting Egyptologist living in a chateau near Rouen. He has acquired two predatory women: a second wife (Carmen du Sautoy) and a promiscuous secretary (Cherie Lunghi). Which will decapitate him first? Both actresses play up to the melodrama. The patsy, it transpires, is the professor's fumbling assistant Christian (Jonathan Pryce). The film crosscuts between scenes ending with a question mark; and the result (everyone dies) is not a great deal more than a diversion brightened by snatches of comic implausibility. In league with the vampish Mrs Canova but by now married to the secretary, Christian trembles at the sound of a secret tape-recording of his villainy while his wife affects to hear nothing . . .

A more arresting thriller (but one which also teased) was **THE DISAPPEARANCE OF HARRY** (8 December 1982), written by Howard Wakeling and the director Joseph Despins. Until her husband vanishes, Lizzie Webster, a textile worker, is as trim as the bright bland pattern on her loom. There is little sense of a real (or even cinematic) France outside the gates of Professor Canova's chateau. But the Nottingham into which Lizzie ventures in search of her husband pulses with believable if only half-explained mysteries: the echo of Luddite outrages; an eighteenth-century watch engraved with a non-existent date; a plot to explode a bomb among the licensed fools of Goose Fair. For all its dark secrets, however, the film stands up best (and with pleasing modesty) as a study of middle-class fortitude. Lizzie (Annette Crosbie) falters then regains her composure as the certainties of life one by one dissolve. And by the end she has learnt about herself, if not what became of Harry.

Nottingham is conjured; the depth of its manufacturing roots suggested. If the picture has a fault it is perhaps to have underestimated the danger of leaving a thriller (even a paranoid one) unsolved. A similar shortcoming cannot be found in **ANGEL** (28 April 1983), a first feature written and directed by the novelist Neil Jordan, who was to make two other well-regarded films co-financed by Film on Four, *The Company of Wolves* (1984) and *Mona Lisa* (1986). *The Disappearance of Harry* is an academic exercise in mystery-spinning; *Angel* on the other hand drives hard and cuts corners to reach its climax.

Crouched in a drainage pipe, Danny, a showband saxophonist, watches the mute girl to whom he has just made love shot dead by a lame man and the Dreamland dancehall where he has just performed consumed in a dull blast and a whoosh of flame. There follows a revenge plot as callous and compelling if not as polished and developed as John Boorman's *Point Blank* (1967). (Boorman was executive producer of

Angel.) The script uses the Troubles as its backdrop; but the politics of Northern Ireland are not its concern. The story of protection money, exemplary murder and a rotten detective might have occurred in Amsterdam or Atlantic City; and there is too a seedy universality about a lone man running ahead of the killer he must kill.

Angel nevertheless reverberates with a truly Irish desolation, the sense of an empty countryside (a wide strand where a murder can take place unobserved) and a peculiarly Irish rural desperation (a farmer's widow shoots herself – Danny's order that she cut his hair and give him her husband's clothes and her failure to stab him with a kitchen knife being the final straw in an impossible life). In *The Company of Wolves* fastidious elaboration sometimes drains the life from a scene; but in *Angel* Neil Jordan had the instinctive confidence to use – and get away with using – a song such as 'Danny Boy' for bold and touching emotional effect. Sustained by the hangdog Stephen Rea as Danny, 'the Stan Getz of South Armagh', and Honor Heffernan as Deirdre, the band's tough-tender singer, *Angel* comes straight from the heart and like a number of good-bad B-pictures is enhanced by the authentic roughness of its edges.

THE DRAUGHTSMAN'S CONTRACT (30 June 1983), written and directed by Peter Greenaway, is an English country-house mystery set in the seventeenth century in which it sometimes seems the position of every blade of grass has been considered with refined disinterest. Mr Neville (Anthony Higgins), a fastidious artist, is commissioned by Mrs Herbert (Janet Suzman) to draw the twelve elevations of her husband's elegant house (it came to Mr Herbert through his wife's father). Mrs Herbert invites Mr Neville to her bed (this is his bonus). Who will inherit the house? Louis Talmann, Mr Herbert's impotent German son-in-law? Or will Talmann's wife Sarah (an only child) produce an heir? She too has called on Mr Neville's services. Or perhaps Mrs Herbert will at last give birth to a son? And what of Noyes, the estate manager once promised to Mrs Herbert, or even self-assured Mr Neville himself . . . ? In due course Mr Herbert's body turns up in the moat.

Who tossed him in the water is not revealed (a live statue grins mischievously); and the absence of a solution is by contrast with *The Disappearance of Harry* turned to good effect. (Mr Herbert had declined to have the moat cleared: he did not like to see the carp, they lived too long and reminded him of Catholics.) The contract offers a clue: everything in life and art depends on the position of the easel. Costumed and mounted with scrupulous care, the film mocks the vanity of its characters with a lack of pity equal to their own. The couplings (some comically formal) register with the titillating but distanced effect of full-dress pornography. Witty, symmetrical and conjuring a half-real England wholly its own, *The Draughtsman's Contract* is a game more sophisticated than Cluedo but in its own way just as vivid and clearly delineated.

The form devised by Charles Wood for the script of **RED MONARCH** (16 June 1983) was more robust and less ambiguous. Stalin (Colin Blakely) is a ghastly paranoid prankster; and Beria (David Suchet), his lecherous Chief of Police, survives by rolling with the jokes and, like a jester, abusing himself when his master seems about to dispense with his services. Had Beria ever stopped talking, it seems, the trap door would have dropped. Based on the stories of Yuri Krotkov, a well-placed collector of anecdotes about Stalin, Jack Gold's film differs from *Praying Mantis* in that here the jumpy pace accurately reflects the nervousness of the antagonists. The film has an assured, compelling tone: bold red intertitles tag the secondary characters like museum specimens.

Nothing perhaps is so chilling as a cruel joke told seriously. On a whim Stalin pardons his old comrade Sergo, once Deputy Minister of Foreign Affairs. Sergo and his wife Sopha have spent thirteen years in a camp. Stalin clasps them to his bosom. Perplexity. Out of the blue the dictator announces he was once an informer for the Tsarist police; Napoleon too started as an informer. He simply betrayed Sergo. Gaunt, dignified, on guard against a double bluff, Sergo insists that this cannot be true. Stalin loses his temper and threatens to reimprison Sergo unless he will admit that he *believes* Stalin betrayed him. Sergo acquiesces.

Distinguished by its central quicksilver double act (the two Georgians are represented as distrustful Ulstermen), *Red Monarch* runs up and down the comic scale: from the deadpan of Sergo's humiliation; through the absurdism of Mao Tse-tung's visit to the Kremlin on Stalin's 70th birthday (unable to communicate, the two dictators stuff themselves on hard-boiled eggs); to the macabre finale when the Politburo gathers outside Stalin's door hoping against hope that he may be dead (opening his eyes to see his marionettes jigging for joy, the tyrant spits out the one word 'Idiot!' – a judgment on himself perhaps – before Beria sinks to his knees and throttles him). The film ends with a line from Yevtushenko: the poet will never feel safe until Stalin's heirs cease to occupy the Kremlin.

A FLAME TO THE PHOENIX (15 December 1983) memorialises the Polish army whose officers Stalin later exterminated and its attempt to stay the

Walter: Ian McKellen

Meantime: Tim Roth (left), Gary Oldman

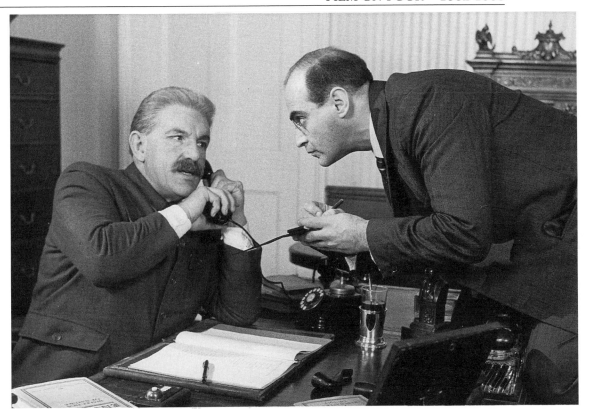

Red Monarch: Colin Blakely (left), David Suchet

Experience Preferred But Not Essential: Elizabeth Edmonds

German invasion of September 1939 with a valiant cavalry charge. Made by the Granada Television team of the detective series *Strangers* (1980–82), the film jumps hither and thither as the Poles attempt to alert the world while simultaneously resigning themselves to fate. The action centres on a country house where a final boar hunt is in preparation and where the regal owner (Ann Firbank) gives herself with a half-smile to her son's handsome young friend. The budget allows for no wide-screen cavalry charge, but the performance of Frederick Treves as the retired General Pradzynski lends the drama a measured dignity.

Film on Four transmitted three other 'First Love' films in its first fourteen months, *Experience Preferred But Not Essential*, *Secrets* and *Those Glory Glory Days*. The scriptwriters were respectively June Roberts, a television drama producer; Noella Smith, a former programme-maker for the Open University (both first-timers); and Julie Welch, football reporter for the *Observer*. The stories were set in the early 60s and concerned girls as unformed (but not as timid) as Alan Duckworth in *P'Tang, Yang, Kipperbang*.

The most striking film, partly because it focused on a school-leaver taking her first adult steps and not on a harum-scarum 13-year-old, was Peter Duffell's **EXPERIENCE PREFERRED BUT NOT ESSENTIAL** (22 December 1982). In the summer before going to college, Annie from Billingham, Cleveland, becomes a maid at a Welsh seaside hotel. She arrives dressed in serious black and sporting a CND badge. Mike the chef, an ex-seaman from Paisley, lays siege; she succumbs, but in her own time. In *Caught on a Train* (BBC TV, 1980) Peter Duffell memorably demonstrated how with the right actors (Peggy Ashcroft and Michael Kitchen: she on this occasion deftly laying siege to him) and the right script (by Stephen Poliakoff) dramatic action need not be constricted by a confining space (a train compartment). In *Experience Preferred But Not Essential* the action is more diffuse and predictable; but the strong sense of another confining space (which also binds strangers with its rituals) is effectively and sometimes movingly conveyed.

Backstairs life at the hotel is uncarpeted, cheerful, overemotional; nothing requires experience, everything works out after a fashion. And in the autumn Annie leaves with a parting gift from the worldly receptionist, her first proper frock. To have lost her virginity was a relief; but the frock meant (or would mean) something. The players form an agreeable sympathetic ensemble. Ivan the wine waiter sleepwalks; but his predictable naked presence in the maids' attic causes no great stir.

There is real feeling here, sympathetically touched on. It is hard, though, to summon up the absent worlds of Billingham and Paisley, or to imagine what will become of these transient people. The fate of Janie and Luigi in *Another Time, Another Place* matters in a way which, fundamentally, that of Mike and Annie does not.

Gavin Millar's SECRETS (12 May 1983) and Philip Saville's THOSE GLORY GLORY DAYS (17 November 1988) are, like *P'Tang, Yang, Kipperbang*, more overt comedies. The first (and more subtle) is set in a Wiltshire boarding-school where Jane, Sidney, Trottie and their leader Louise (Anna Campbell-Jones) attempt to exorcise a supposed masonic curse. ('Why *Benenden*?' asks Louise's mother, baffled and slightly hurt by the Queen's choice of school for Princess Anne.) And the second, a knockabout escapade cast as a nostalgic recollection of a burning childhood moment, is centred on White Hart Lane, North London, where the uncouth Tub, Toni, Jailbird and their leader Julia (Zoe Nathenson) scheme to see Tottenham Hotspur take on Leicester in the 1961 FA Cup Final (the year Spurs won the Double).

In *Secrets* the first love is imagined. Louise is not, as her mother fears, smitten (or worse): she is simply scared stiff by her late father's book of masonic lore; and she is also puzzled by his silver box of prophylactic sheaths. And in *Those Glory Glory Days* the first love is disappointed. Julia (alias 'Danny') is prevented from attending the Cup Final: she is stopped at the gate by her father, from whose wallet (all else having failed) she was forced to steal the sacred tickets. And it is not until her first assignment as a professional sports reporter that she finally meets her footballing hero, the now retired and sober-suited Mr Blanchflower. Gavin Millar has a gift with children and catches the tone of Louise and her chums with detached and kind amusement; Philip Saville, though, tends to give the merry Tottenham girls their head, with the result that they sometimes run off out of control, taking the picture with them.

That perennial British concern, the deadman's grip of the boys' boarding-school, is the subject of GOOD AND BAD AT GAMES (8 December 1983), the third of four films directed by Jack Gold for Film on Four. William Boyd's story, interleaving past and present, is triangular: Cox, who was bullied at school, becomes an investigative journalist; he plans revenge on Mount, his persecutor, now an Army officer serving in Northern Ireland; between them is Niles, a weak-willed salesman of motor parts who was only saved from ostracism at school (or worse) by being good at games. At the climax, an old boys' cricket match, Niles cannot prevent himself saving the supercilious Mount by hurling a ball at the head of Cox, who is preparing to despatch Mount with his own pistol. Moral: nothing changes.

Secrets, Those Glory Glory Days and *Good and Bad at Games* are pent by their scripts. The secondary characters are agents of clear literal stories and are governed by what (not who) they are: Louise's mother (Helen Lindsay) epitomises abstracted motherhood; Julia's parents (Peter Tilbury and Julia McKenzie) are cut-out models of frenzied propriety and undisguised indifference; and Niles (Martyn Stanbridge) is little more than shirking, contemptible cowardice. Deirdre, the band singer of *Angel*, on the other hand could have found a home in any number of quite different stories.

A number of fragmentary, quite different stories, mixed together and only at the end coming together (for a moment) in a violent inconclusive club brawl, make up Colin Gregg's vivid and melancholy REMEMBRANCE (10 November 1982). The film, written by Hugh Stoddart, concerns the rituals of leave-taking as much as the effort of recalling and fixing the past. Set in Plymouth over two nights and a day, it follows the individual members of a group of ratings preparing for six months at sea on a NATO exercise. The impermanence, foul weather and salty language of a naval town is precisely caught, as the young sailors (whose identities and lives the viewer must strain to pick up as the action unfolds) make their accommodations with families, wives and girlfriends.

The film is at its best conjuring moods of awkwardness and unease: Douglas (Timothy Spall) and his pregnant wife Christine (Kim Taylforth) betwixt and between in a cold hotel room with only a view of the kitchen (she has a backache, he takes a solitary walk along the front), where there is nothing to do and everything to say, and the one anticipation is an Indian meal to which in the event she is unable to do justice. Another commonplace service marriage, another commonplace parting? Up to a point. But these two, despite the view, her backache and the unpalatable rich meal, enjoy a visible affection, hardly emphasised, but emphasised enough.

The manner in which individual lives touch without intersecting, and the significance of remembering even the most transitory encounter, become part of the film's central thread: the search by Mark (David John), the most innocent of the ratings, for the identity of a man, Daniel (Gary Oldman), beaten and fatally injured outside a club in which they had both been drinking on the first night. The mystery is finally solved – Daniel, absent without leave from the Army, his regiment about to go to Belfast, is the brother of another rating – but the haunting question of why exactly he came to Plymouth remains unanswered and genuinely unanswerable.

In its first fourteen months Film on Four transmitted two back-to-front puzzle-pictures: *Nelly's Version*, directed by Maurice Hatton from a novel by Eva Figes; and *The Bad Sister*, directed by Laura Mulvey and Peter Wollen from a novel by Emma Tennant (the latter the only commission by Film on Four shot entirely on videotape). It also transmitted two equally individual (and equally isolated) period pictures: Pascal Ortega's *Bad Hats*, about two soldiers, French and British, who desert an unseen battlefield in 1917 and attempt to sail to Ireland; and Barney Platts-Mills's *Hero*, a subtitled, 'Gaelic'-language version of the legend of Dermid and Grannia (here set in Scotland not Ireland) and their flight from the cuckolded Finn MacCumhaill.

NELLY'S VERSION (9 June 1983) begins with a woman (Eileen Atkins) registering at a hotel as 'Mrs Nelly Dean', opening a suitcase full of £10 notes and then visiting a papershop (where she is recognised by the suspicious owner: 'You always were a liar!') to buy a notebook in order to write down 'the facts' and give them some coherence. The facts appear to be that Nelly has a dutiful grown-up son and an impatient unfaithful husband and that she has suffered some sort of mental collapse: there are worrying coincidences (the papershop woman is assaulted, an empty house which Nelly visited burns down) and the police are forever turning up and asking polite insistent questions.

Can we believe what we see? Is there some deeper reality? Who is sane? The film dances round these questions while Nelly's troubled face tries in vain to unravel what has or has not happened. Susannah York offers a voice-over commentary. Tangled perception is also the subject of THE BAD SISTER (23 June 1983), although here, with two editors analysing clips from the 'audio diary' of the protagonist, the tricks and techniques of film (or video) storytelling seem equally to be the matter in hand.

Who slashed to death Ishbel Dalzell, and who a few days before killed her unreliable father? And why was Ishbel separated as a child from her sister Jane? The viewer is taken on a tortuous journey from London to Scotland (with supernatural interludes: one reason, the makers asserted, for employing video) before an answer is furnished. Along the way Jane, who lives with a struggling film-maker, takes down a copy of Peter Wollen's *Signs and Meaning in the Cinema* (1969): a word to the wise, perhaps, that *The Bad Sister* itself should be read as an additional chapter in some future edition of that book.

BAD HATS (15 December 1982), co-written by the actor Mick Ford, who plays the English soldier, more legibly prints its moral that there is no running away from the consequences of war. The British tearaway and the stolid French family man (Marcel Bozzuffi) form an uneasy alliance and settle in a wood where a young widow (with no time for mourning) determines to conceive a child by both of them. The Somme is only the rumble of distant gunfire, but the cocoon the three create for themselves (running races, balancing on a tightrope) has a palpably endangered fragility.

Opening with a scrawled blood-spattered title, **HERO** (29 December 1982) radiates a slapdash vigour, often trying but sometimes diverting. The special effects are rudimentary (a sword falls, a doll's head bounces), not video-generated; and the performers (excepting Grannia and Finn), a misfit troupe of barefoot amateurs from Drumchapel, Glasgow, assembled by the director in a fraught attempt at green-field community enterprise. Barney Platts-Mills's *Bronco Bullfrog* (1969), about a group of London boys drifting into petty crime (also performed by an unknown cast), was executed with more sensitivity and control; both films, however, are streaked with a commitment (brave or misguided) to allow the players-cum-characters to speak up for themselves.

Hero is spotted with a humour all its own, some childish (a gust lifts the smock of a runner scrambling up a hill to reveal a white bottom) and some surprisingly delicate (Grannia, the apprentice of a magician, throws a trout on the ground and up jumps a pageboy; later the page appears with four fish on a stick, and since the fugitives need a little extra help the princess conjures a second boy). The predominant tone, though, is set by the minstrel 'O'Shin' (Finn's son Ossian): in this version of the great legend he is a drunk with few delusions about the heroes he is supposed to be commemorating.

Glaswegian spirit and wit was memorialised with more restraint and greater effect in **LIVING APART TOGETHER** (2 June 1983), written and directed by Charles Gormley: a run of impressionist episodes from the life of a rock musician, Ritchie Hannah (B. A. Robertson), on his return home from the South to attend a friend's funeral and face his own unsatisfactory personal affairs. In 1986 Charles Gormley made *Heavenly Pursuits* for Film on Four, a picture less spread out than this but one in which perhaps the shaggy comedy was more consciously spread on. *Living Apart Together* comes from the school of the early Bill Forsyth

(Gormley's former documentary partner), though here the subject is adults with childlike propensities, not worldly-wise schoolboys. As with the Border country of *Accounts*, Glasgow is all the film's world, not boastfully or insistently but just as an unremarkable fact of the matter. And it is this unstrained self-confidence as much as the details of Ritchie's picaresque attempts to run to earth his weary, intelligent wife Evie (Barbara Kellerman) which most indelibly marks the film.

Desmond Davis made his debut as a feature director in 1963 with a version of *Girl with Green Eyes*, the second of the three bestselling novels in which Edna O'Brien evoked her childhood in the West of Ireland and her escape to freedom in England. The first part of Caithleen Brady's story – her scholarship ('third place in all Ireland') to St Joseph's Convent, Galway; her fall from grace and expulsion from school; her life in Dublin as a grocer's assistant with her rambunctious friend Baba – was subsequently told in Davis's **THE COUNTRY GIRLS** (24 November 1983).

Adapted by Edna O'Brien, the film is more literary than cinematic: the recollection of Cait's development (the central episode being her calf love for the ill-named Mr Gentleman) unfolds leisurely, its pace at first that of Scariff, County Clare, where farmers eventually return home drunk to their suffering wives and professional men throw moonstruck looks at teenage girls. But Cait and Baba (Maeve Germaine and Jill Doyle) are filled with vigour and enthusiasm, and go more than halfway towards routing the prevailing sleepiness. Beria in *Red Monarch* kept talking to save his life; Baba, one feels, babbles on not only to keep warm but to remind herself that she is truly alive. *The Country Girls* may lack the essential drive of (say) *Angel*, but it is scented with the genuine (if nostalgic) atmosphere of Ireland – and not least by the wistful foursquare theatrical quality of some of the acting, by Niall Toibin and John Kavanagh in particular, in the supporting roles.

GIRO CITY (1 December 1982), written and directed by Karl Francis, and **THE PLOUGHMAN'S LUNCH** (3 November 1983), written by Ian McEwan and directed by Richard Eyre, both concern commonplace corruption (the partiality of news management). The first, from a sometime current affairs programme-maker, is raw, direct and functional. It follows Sophie (Glenda Jackson), an independent TV current-affairs programme-maker tracking two stories, one about an intransigent Welsh farmer and a land-hungry corporation in the nuclear-waste business, and the other about a clandestine interview in Dublin with an IRA commander which is broadcast but not in the unedited manner stipulated.

The second, from a novelist and a theatre director, employs an emollient form of irony. In his rise to BBC radio news editor, James Penfield (Jonathan Pryce) has left behind his humble origins. He determines to rise even higher (to join the assured intellectual middle class) by writing a real book on the Suez Crisis. He is duped by his media colleagues, his closest friend, a gossip-writer (Tim Curry), and a well-connected cold-hearted TV researcher (Charlie Dore), and finally learns the dispiriting lesson of the 'ploughman's lunch', that in Mrs Thatcher's Britain (and James listens to the rabble-rousing of the 1982 Tory conference) the adman rules and that his pre-eminence is symbolised by being able to market even the patently bogus.

That the adman (Frank Finlay) is a socialist and quite happy for Penfield to service his assured, intellectual, middle-class wife adds a further bitter twist. Neither film, however, completely closes the door on its leading character: the programme-maker Sophie, a wiser woman, wearily accepts another assignment; and James, told he must cast his account of Suez in the form of a textbook for American students, nevertheless buckles down to composition. Sophie is principled, James less so, but neither is a quitter. Both films leave the aftertaste of disillusion.

The real 'giro city', a world of subsistence-level state benefits (forever), is conjured in more compelling dramatic terms in Mike Leigh's MEANTIME (1 December 1983). The argumentative Pollock family – Mavis (Pam Ferris), the bovine mother; Frank (Jeff Robert), the weak malcontent father; and their teenage sons, the feral, needling Mark (Phil Daniels) and the slow Colin (Tim Roth), gazing at the world through a pair of crooked taped-up spectacles – possesses a power to transfix and horrify (and ultimately to affect) the viewer unequalled by any other film transmitted by Film on Four in its opening fourteen months. The concerns of *Giro City* and *The Ploughman's Lunch* were authentic and legitimate but the manner in which they were framed lacked the crucial concentration, brevity and heart-sinking inevitability of Mike Leigh's indictment of the way we lived then and still live now.

The story is simple. Mavis's sister Barbara (Marion Bailey) has risen from the underclass, from London E2 to Chigwell, and offers to employ Colin to help redecorate her bedroom. Outraged by this condescension, Mark prevails upon his brother to walk away from the bogus job. The film is a melange of comic vituperation as the two mercilessly caricatured families say (or suppress saying) what they feel about each other; and as the sheer hopelessness and degradation of the Pollocks' situation becomes increasingly apparent. Beneath the maelstrom, however, resides a simple unalloyed moral – that human beings, come what may, must defend their dignity – suggested throughout and finally encapsulated in a remarkable, unexpected metaphor.

After walking out on Barbara, Colin skulks home, the fur-fringed hood of his jacket pulled up. He refuses to explain himself and goes to sleep in his clothes. Next morning Mark, who has until now mocked Colin with a litany of names ('Dobbin', 'Muppet', 'Kermit'), gently pushes back the hood to reveal a skinhead haircut. The boys' friend Coxy (Gary Oldman), a posturing rude boy, sports a similarly shaved head; but the significance of Colin's haircut is that it has nothing to do with Coxy, it is the first thing he has ever done for himself. Mark puts a hand on Colin's head and there is the curious satisfying sound of sandpaper being rubbed. Colin, in disgrace, went to bed without his tea. 'What you having – bald egg?' Mark asks with a smile. They are his first kind words. Muppet will henceforth be Mark's ally 'Kojak'. The moment cracks like a pistol shot.

Jerzy Skolimowski's **MOONLIGHTING** (5 May 1983) displayed a sovereign quality lacking in all the other twenty-six films transmitted in the first fourteen months of Film on Four. It fizzed with compulsion: it was about something (the imposition of martial law in Skolimowski's native Poland in December 1981) which demanded immediate comment. The filmmakers' skill was to proceed through indirection.

Nowak (Jeremy Irons), intelligent, paranoid and cunning, is sent to London from Warsaw to supervise and spur along the reconstruction of a house belonging to a zloty millionaire. Are you a member of Solidarity, he is asked at customs. No – and then in voice-over, 'That was the only true answer I gave.' He is trapped every which way: by a shortage of funds, by apprehensions about his wife Anna and the unseen 'boss' whose mock-Tudor house they are gentrifying, by the cussed, baffling habits of the British (an Indian shopkeeper tears the plug from the flex of a second-hand television set Nowak has bought for £40), and by the necessity of keeping his three fellow workers at their task until it is finished – only then will he dare reveal what has happened at home. Executed with grace, brevity and exactitude, the film is perfectly balanced between comedy and tragedy; and for once a true tragedy in that Nowak, the only one who understands English, knows what is happening, is himself implicated in it and yet can do nothing about it.

The beauty and merit of *Moonlighting* is that it may be taken as a parable – the paymaster 'boss' being the hidden hand of Moscow;

Nowak, the Polish government, bending with the wind, trying to control his rebellious subjects, hoping somehow to make a profit for himself – or as a turned and finished story in its own right. The secondary characters – the neighbour (Denis Holmes) who cannot contain his fury at the incessant din; the supermarket manager and supervisor (David Calder and Judy Gridley), thwarted in their efforts to catch Nowak shoplifting – are caricatures to be sure, but living caricatures who dovetail into the plot rather than drawing attention to its artificiality. Misfortune makes the greatest comedy, and *Moonlighting* has several sinking moments (the new plumbing system leaks at every joint and a ceiling about to collapse is gallantly propped up by a cardboard box held aloft). There are, too, some sublime moments of silent comedy. One of the workmen, Banaszak, seizes a live wire while painting a windowsill from a stepladder; he is transfixed until Nowak emerges from the front door, kicks the ladder, and Banaszak topples like a colossus to the pavement.

Nowak's men finally finish the job. But not before Nowak has come to realise the truth about himself. He enters the confessional of the Polish church and we hear his thoughts. 'I don't want to confess, I don't believe in God. I am here to find my self-respect. I chose those men because they were stupid. I thought I could control them, but I can't – I am weaker than they are.' At night the police arrive (summoned perhaps by the neighbour) but their lights find only an empty, sterile, immaculately decorated house. Nowak and his men, each with a supermarket trolley loaded with meagre spoils, make their way to Heathrow: a six-hour walk with only five pence between them. Then Nowak breaks the news. The men are caught in a haunting long-shot, pummelling Nowak, their trolleys rolling away towards the camera.

◆

VIEWING FIGURES
1982/1983

	1st TX '000s	2nd TX '000s
WALTER	*2 Nov 82* **3,737**	*19 Sep 85* **1,944**
P'TANG, YANG, KIPPERBANG	*3 Nov 82* **3,097**	*9 Jul 87* **3,478**
REMEMBRANCE	*10 Nov 82* **2,499**	*18 Jul 85* **2,549**
PRAYING MANTIS 1/2	*17 Nov 82* **2,376**	*7 Nov 84* **3,893**

PRAYING MANTIS 2/2	*24 Nov 82* **3,027**	*8 Nov 84* **4,953**
GIRO CITY	*1 Dec 82* **1,796**	*27 Jun 85* **2,519**
THE DISAPPEARANCE OF HARRY	*8 Dec 82* **2,686**	
BAD HATS	*15 Dec 82* **1,386**	*14 Nov 85* **1,678**
EXPERIENCE PREFERRED BUT NOT ESSENTIAL	*22 Dec 82* **2,640**	*22 Nov 84* **4,868**
HERO	*29 Dec 82* **0,382**	
ANGEL	*28 Apr 83* **2,842**	*15 Nov 84* **1,757**
MOONLIGHTING	*5 May 83* **2,733**	*13 Dec 84* **2,322**
SECRETS	*12 May 83* **4,314**	*16 Jul 87* **2,893**
ILL FARES THE LAND	*19 May 83* **2,069**	*23 Jan 86* **3,416**
WALTER & JUNE	*26 May 83* **3,708**	
LIVING APART TOGETHER	*2 Jun 83* **2,261**	*6 Dec 84* **2,583**
NELLY'S VERSION	*9 Jun 83* **1,339**	*21 Nov 85* **3,156**
RED MONARCH	*16 Jun 83* **1,311**	*16 Jan 86* **1,678**
THE BAD SISTER	*23 Jun 83* **2,341**	
THE DRAUGHTSMAN'S CONTRACT	*30 Jun 83* **2,132**	*29 Nov 84* **2,121**
THE PLOUGHMAN'S LUNCH	*3 Nov 83* **1,682**	*25 Jul 85* **1,527**
ANOTHER TIME, ANOTHER PLACE	*10 Nov 83* **3,780**	*4 Jul 85* **3,384**
THOSE GLORY GLORY DAYS	*17 Nov 83* **1,878**	*11 Jul 85* **2,917**
THE COUNTRY GIRLS	*24 Nov 83* **4,230**	*20 Jun 85* **3,084**
MEANTIME	*1 Dec 83* **2,875**	*28 Nov 85* **3,166**
GOOD AND BAD AT GAMES	*8 Dec 83* **2,525**	*30 Jan 86* **4,383**
A FLAME TO THE PHOENIX	*15 Dec 83* **3,166**	
ACCOUNTS	*22 Dec 83* **2,027**	*6 Feb 86* **4,481**

Source: BARB

February 1984 President Andropov of the USSR dies; Konstantin Chernenko succeeds. **March** Miners strike over pit closures. **April** WPC Fletcher shot dead outside Libyan People's Bureau, London. **June** 250 Sikhs die when troops storm Golden Temple, Amritsar. **July** Robert Maxwell buys Mirror newspapers for £113.4m. **September** Second son for Princess of Wales. **October** IRA bombs Brighton hotel during Tory conference; 5 killed, 32 injured, Mrs Thatcher unharmed. Indira Gandhi, PM of India, assassinated by Sikh bodyguards; son Rajiv succeeds. **November** Ronald Reagan re-elected President of the United States. **December** 400 die in gas leak at a pesticide plant at Bhopal, Madhya Pradesh. **January 1985** First live House of Lords TV broadcast. **February** Reagan seeks tripled spending on 'Star Wars' space weapon research. **March** Pit strike ends without settlement. Mikhail Gorbachev becomes Soviet leader on death of Chernenko.

April Soviet moratorium on missile deployment in Europe. **May** Liverpool fans riot at Heysel stadium, Belgium; 38 die; Europe bans English football clubs. **October** PC Blakelock killed in North London riot; racial disorder in Birmingham and Brixton. Palestinian guerrillas hijack Italian cruise liner. **November** US–Soviet summit concludes nuclear war can never be won, must never be fought.

CHAPTER 2

◆

PLAYING ON THE SEA-SHORE

1984/1985

◆

MAROONED IN SOUTHWEST London in December 1981, Nowak, the gang foreman of *Moonlighting*, borrows a copy of *The Times* from a neighbour's letterbox and reads of the military crackdown in his native Poland. Later he looks through a shop window at television footage of Polish tanks. **SQUARING THE CIRCLE** (31 May 1984), written by the dramatist Tom Stoppard and directed by Mike Hodges, also treats the events leading to the December 1981 crisis, but from a different angle, from inside Poland and the Soviet Union, and in a different style, as a history lesson cast as a piece of seaside theatre.

An American narrator (Richard Crenna) debates with stock secondary characters. He identifies the real-life principals and elucidates the action. 'Between August of 1980 and December of 1981 an attempt was made in Poland to put together two ideas which would not fit. The idea of freedom, as it is understood in the West, and the idea of socialism, as it is understood in the Soviet empire. The attempt failed because it was impossible, in the same sense as it is impossible in geometry to turn a circle into a square with the same area – not because no one has found out how to do it, but because it can't be done.'

The scaffold propping the scenery is visible; and the double meaning underlined by the scene in which a painted flat of leatherbound books – representing a real painted flat of leatherbound books, the backdrop to a television broadcast by the Polish Party boss Edward Gierek – topples to reveal two shadowy men waiting and listening. The film opens with a piece of Chopin, the self-conscious resignation of which would not have been out of place in *A Flame to the Phoenix*.

But fatalism is not this film's undertone. The hero is the tough, deceptively artless Lech Walesa, given a few extra inches by Bernard Hill and photographed in the monumental style of Soviet Realism. He deals shrewdly with both the intellectuals of Solidarity, some of whom such as Kuron wanted to square the circle, and the Polish government, all of whom twisted to avoid the wrath of President Brezhnev. To its credit the script is awake to the dilemma of Poland's administrators, who in December 1981 were faced with the threat of imminent Soviet invasion.

This historical digest allows for nuances absent from *Red Monarch*, the satire on Brezhnev's forebear Stalin. The final effect, though, is something of a rush of momentous events. Walesa is, it seems, the one person with a level head; but in the end he too is forced into autocracy. *Squaring the Circle* has an urgency, in the sense that a current affairs programme on a distant not immediately threatening upheaval has an urgency. But *Moonlighting*, set on our doorstep, with its alienated, imperfect, human protagonist, leaves the viewer with a sharper appreciation of what it actually felt like to be a Pole caught at Christmas 1981 between the ungraspable freedom of the West and the disintegrating socialism of the Soviet Union.

Film on Four transmitted seventeen new films in 1984–85; and Film on Four, Take Two repeated seventeen from the first fourteen months. Three-quarters of the new films were set in the British Isles, nine in England and three in southern Ireland. *Squaring the Circle* took place on an English studio beach mocked up as Warsaw, Gdansk and Moscow. And four other films spread themselves variously between Lisbon and an unnamed city on the Rhine; West Berlin; Basle, Milan and London; and Guatemala, Mexico and California. Thirteen films were set in the approximate present and two in the specific past. One was divided between past and present, and another set in an indeterminate rural Ireland of ghosts and superstition.

Apart from *Squaring the Circle*, no new film directly focused on history or politics. Two films, however – *El Norte*, about a pair of Guatemalan villagers on a quest north, and *Christmas Present*, a parable on charity (after Dickens) – concluded with forthright morals; and another, *A Song for Europe*, about the consequences of 'whistle-blowing', wagged a finger at injustice. Among the seventeen new films the perils of isolation were less apparent than in the 1982–83 films; nevertheless, there was a current – in *A Song for Europe, Runners, Flight to Berlin, El Norte* and *Sacred Hearts* – of individuals either on the run or trapped in situations from which they felt compelled to escape. Six films were love stories, two ending in death and one in unresolved unhappiness.

A SONG FOR EUROPE (23 May 1985), directed by John Goldschmidt, had a mission to explain; but its method, unlike *Squaring the Circle*, with a foreign correspondent addressing the camera, was clinical re-enactment. The well-made script was by Peter Prince, author of the 1981 BBC TV series on the nuclear physicist Robert Oppenheimer; and the subject a cautionary tale based on the true experiences of Stanley Adams, a one-time employee of the pharmaceutical corporation Hoffmann La Roche.

Steven Dyer, the nervous hero, is a Maltese-born Englishman who discovers a conspiracy among vitamin manufacturers involving his own company Schumann-Fougère, of Basle. Before resigning his position, and beginning afresh as a pig farmer in Italy, he delivers up Schumann-Fougère to a team of EC investigators. The corporation drops on Dyer like an eagle. He is denied a lawyer and charged with industrial espionage. His wife Maddy kills herself. The investigators temporise. Exoneration finally comes, but grudgingly and not before Dyer has lost everything.

Polished and respectable, Steven Dyer (David Suchet) has not a spoonful of worldly cunning. He assumes that honesty will be acknowledged and that because he is rich now (a Fortnum & Mason cake arrives for Maddy's birthday) he will be secure and untroubled forever. The refrain of this traditional song is that of course the powerful behave as they please. But what gives it an edge is the suggestion that when national pride is at stake the Swiss are second to none in ruthlessly closing ranks. The film unfolds with a downplayed smoothness in keeping with setting and subject; and despite touches of melodrama is stamped with a telling indignation.

One of the best sequences is Dyer's arrest at the Swiss frontier as he returns from Italy to spend Christmas with his wife's family. The polite insistence of the guard, the family all alone in an expensive car beside a calm silent lake and a sense of the gathering disaster are exactly caught.

FLIGHT TO BERLIN (21 June 1984), directed and co-written by the former film critic Christopher Petit, starts with another interrogation, but one familiar from a hundred police movies. There follows, however, a deliberately aborted thriller about an escape from responsibility. Shot by Martin Schäfer and produced by Chris Sievernich, partner of the German director Wim Wenders, this resolutely disengaged film is marked by the flat arid tone of the old divided capital.

An Englishwoman, Susannah, arrives in Berlin and seeks her German sister Julie, a photographer. There has been an unexplained death in England. Julie's young lover Jack seduces the English sister ('Thank you, I needed that,' she says, as though she has just had a nice cup of tea). Susannah's husband, who is going blind, turns up in fretful pursuit. Jack's employer Edouard, the shady husband from whom Julie is separated, offers to spirit Susannah out of Berlin . . . The last image is the Wall. The film is less knotted than *The Bad Sister*, Film on Four's previous tale of two women parted at childhood, although its chief concern is to establish a similar abstract mood of restless possibility. It suggests a mystery capable of explanation but which due to the flux of events is never unravelled and in the end simply set aside.

Flight to Berlin is peopled with lived-in faces, Tusse Silberg, Ewan Stewart, Lisa Kreuzer; and it contains scenes of individuality, such as one with the sisters on a bleak rooftop, when a gust of wind flicks a family photograph from Susannah's hand. A false note, however, is struck by the talkative American actor Eddie Constantine. He appears as himself and draws attention to a lost tradition of old Hollywood rather than New German cinema to which this film pays a passing, somewhat contradictory tribute.

RUNNERS (17 May 1984) is about unravelling a mystery, not sidestepping it. A girl from Nottingham vanishes and her father (James Fox), for whom she is an unshakeable obsession, assumes she must be in London and sets out to find her. The theme is runaways. (In the early 80s, however, children who fled their parents did not automatically end up dossing on the streets.) The more affecting subtext, though, is the loneliness and anxiety of individuals, like the father Tom Lindsay, waiting for something, anything to happen.

Written by Stephen Poliakoff and directed by Charles Sturridge (co-director of Granada TV's *Brideshead Revisited*, 1981), *Runners* contains unconscious echoes of Film on Four's other Nottingham mystery, *The Disappearance of Harry*. The world into which its ordinary protagonist ventures is again alive with threatening, suspicious, eccentric people. And again the mystery is unresolved. The girl (Kate Hardie) is eventually run to earth, but she will not, perhaps cannot, tell her father what lay at the heart of her actions.

EL NORTE (13 June 1985), directed by Gregory Nava, an American of Mexican–Basque parentage, is also about running away, but running towards something as well, the golden north where enterprise is rewarded. Tom Lindsay was penned in a railway hotel overlooking a teeming concourse. The action was hints and feints; the pursuit of clues and the abstracted help of other parents abandoned by their children. *El Norte*, the essence of directness, though sometimes lured into swooning lyricism, begins with a massacre and ends after a vivid odyssey with the stark silhouette of a severed head hanging from a tree. The film has a sweep and confidence, and a sense that things must be spoken boldly, even at the risk of naivety, which separates it from previous Films on Four.

The devoted siblings Rosa and Enrique flee their village in Guatemala, spurred by the memory of their father's political murder. They reach California and begin life for themselves: he as a kitchen hand, she as a maid (laying out clothes on the lawn because the dryer is a mystery). But the bubble bursts and Enrique is tempted to desert his sister for money and responsibility in Chicago. He is stopped by news of Rosa's illness. She dies of typhoid contracted from rat bites received in a sewage pipe under the US–Mexican border. Her brother then realises that the outsider is worth only his day labour and that protest is pointless. Steven Dyer, the whistle-blower of *A Song for Europe*, learnt something similar.

Alain Tanner's **IN THE WHITE CITY** (28 June 1984) is set in Lisbon; and no other Film on Four succeeds in conjuring so evocatively the spirit of a city. Paul, a Swiss mechanic, jumps ship and takes a room above a bar. He then simply waits, contemplates life, writes letters to a woman (his wife perhaps) in an unnamed northern city, clean and well-ordered. Periodically he sends the woman packets of ciné film, shots of himself, the city, his room, nothing in particular. He begins an affair with the barmaid Rosa (Teresa Madruga), a spirited girl who wants to quit Lisbon for the wider world of France. She calls him an axolotl, a salamander. One day Paul is robbed, pawns his watch and continues to do nothing. Later, spotting one of the thieves, he tracks the man to his home and is stabbed for his trouble. By the time he emerges from hospital, Rosa, who thinks he has disappeared, has herself left for France. He boards a train for home.

The film sustains its mood with hypnotic skill from the opening title shot looking down on the suspension bridge across the wide green Tagus, with Paul's tanker cutting across the shadow of the bridge and a mournful saxophone solo breaking the distant silence, to the last moment on the train with Paul seated opposite a beautiful girl in whose face he sees a reflection of Rosa's features. Acácio de Almeida's fluid natural camerawork records everything it settles on – a tram creaking

Squaring the Circle: Bernard Hill (right)

Last Day of Summer: Annette Badland

In the White City: Bruno Ganz

Sacred Hearts: Oona Kirsch

up a narrow cobbled street; a soccer match on a TV in a spacious dark bar with the traffic flashing by outside – with absolute authenticity. The notion of a passage of time in which nothing happens and nothing has to happen, and where for Paul (Bruno Ganz) to do absolutely nothing is perfectly acceptable to all around him, is also magically conjured. Everything in this film, from Paul and Rosa's lovemaking to Paul's questioning of Rosa's peasant parents, rings true. It absorbs the viewer as blotting-paper absorbs ink.

Four 'First Love' films were transmitted in 1984–85. Like *P'Tang, Yang, Kipperbang*, each was identified by a cheerful lack of pretension, though none perhaps was entirely free of sentimentality. The least sentimental, in part because it was a portrait of an authentic curmudgeon, was **ARTHUR'S HALLOWED GROUND** (30 August 1984). The cameraman Freddie Young (b. 1902) was the first-time director; and the complete variety performer Jimmy Jewel (b. 1912) starred as the North Country groundsman Arthur Chapman, who after forty-five years of having his own way still refuses to adapt his wicket to the advantage of the home team.

Written by Peter Gibbs, a former Derbyshire cricketer, the film is at its best observing Arthur at work, drilling stump holes, attending to the top-dressing, surveying the contents of his shed: a man at home in his landscape. The plot is slight: the players and an upstart committee man (Michael Elphick) want rid of the groundsman, but he demurs, or rather simply ignores them. In exchange for a new auto-seeder, however, Arthur accepts an assistant. The relationship between the distrustful old man and the solemn boy from the Youth Opportunity Programme (Vas Blackwood) is neatly developed and economically played. At heart, though, the film is not a great deal more than a frame for Jimmy Jewel to cruise through his repertoire. 'Well, you've managed it at last,' Arthur's wife (Jean Boht) observes, crawling into the tent her husband has put up to defend the ground, 'you've finally got into bed with the pitch.'

A bad-tempered guru and a young, though this time importunate disciple reappear in **SHARMA AND BEYOND** (24 May 1984). Stephen Archer (Michael Maloney), a would-be author who makes ends meet by teaching English to foreigners, winkles his way into the country home of the reclusive novelist Evan Gorley-Peters (Robert Urquhart, the headmaster of *P'Tang, Yang, Kipperbang*). But this 'Shakespeare of science fiction' from whom Stephen hopes to gain enlightenment is needling and tiresome, and just as much the crusty ham-actor as Arthur

Chapman. The film traces Stephen's descent from the clouds of hero-worship into the practical arms of Natasha, the guru's daughter (Suzanne Burden). She proves a much more helpful critic than her father. Lay off the mythology, Natasha advises, cheer up and try using the experience of the language school. The film, a first feature written and directed by National Film School graduate Brian Gilbert, avoids the pitfalls of palpable sincerity; and Robert Urquhart's cynicism adds a welcome squirt of lemon.

WINTER FLIGHT (20 December 1984), written by Alan Janes and directed by Roy Battersby (co-founder of BBC TV's *Tomorrow's World*), is partly about the sanctioned brutality of service life. One evening at a bar on an RAF base, the pink-cheeked hero, Mal Stanton, an airforce bird-spotter, is ducked in a bucket of witch's brew (urine, beer, fag-ends) by the unstable Hooker (Sean Bean). The reason? His face for some reason does not fit, just as Daniel White's face did not fit in the Plymouth club from which he was dragged at the start of *Remembrance*. The counterpoint to the violence here, however, is a teenage love story marked by the bright innocence of *Sharma and Beyond*.

Mal (Reece Dinsdale) is taken home and tidied up by the sparrowlike barmaid Angie (Nicola Cowper). Like Natasha, Angie has lost her mother and learnt to shift for herself without fuss. A bond forms. But Angie is pregnant by another man, now departed. Mal offers marriage, pleased that his mates, when they learn the reason, will at last think him a man. She accepts, then balks. The baby is put up for adoption. But Mal, who will not desist from kindness even though Angie has refused to marry him, calls at the hospital and is allowed to see the child. That the baby is black and so cannot be passed off as his own only strengthens Mal's love. The camera pulls back from a reconciliation scene.

The couples in *Sharma and Beyond* and *Winter Flight* are guileless and a little naive, but also honest, resilient and forthright. FOREVER YOUNG (6 June 1985) on the other hand is about two men whose friendship was broken by a boyhood betrayal. It is fuelled by knotted motives and suppressed desires. The director was David Drury, whose documentary credits included a film on the boxer Alan Minter; and the writer was the journalist Ray Connolly, who in the early 1970s scripted the pop movies *That'll Be the Day* and *Stardust* for David Puttnam, First Love's executive producer.

Whereas Mal and Angie are genuinely childlike, James and Father Michael, the antagonists of *Forever Young*, have never grown up. The pop music of the 1950s is still their first love; but their obsessive

Runners: James Fox, Kate Hardie

reverence fails to convince. Michael when young seduced James's girl. Twenty years on, chance reunites the men. Michael is now a parish priest and James comes to town to deliver an Eng. Lit. lecture series. Consciously or not, James squares the score by seducing Mary, a wholesome nurse separated from her husband, whose son Paul dotes on Michael as a surrogate father. Alec McCowen potters eccentrically as an older priest who tolerates Michael's weekly guitar-strumming fund-raisers.

The hippies of the riverside commune in **LAST DAY OF SUMMER** (7 June 1984) are another faintly embarrassing throwback. Adapted by Ian Mc-Ewan from a story in his book *First Love, Last Rites* (1976), this brief impressionistic film, directed by Derek Banham, an experienced commercials man, is also centred on a solemn boy watching the caperings of his elders. This story, however, is told from the child's point of view. Tom, aged 12, and his older, monotonously soft-spoken brother Peter have been orphaned by a car crash. The family home has become a hopeless pot-den. Tom, though, is neat and capable and delighted to go to school in uniform. Jenny (Annette Badland), a cheerful, overweight ex-teacher, answers an advertisement for the spare room in the com-

Flight to Berlin: Tusse Silberg

mune. She looks to the boy's needs and his exuberant friendship brings her a kind of passive contentment. Their idyll is played out chiefly on the river in Tom's rowing-boat at the end of the summer holidays.

The film is composed of moods, overheard indistinct voices, and particularly a sense of false security and impending tragedy. The action proceeds in an effective, almost hypnotic state of slowed time until the long-delayed moment when the boat capsizes and Jenny drowns. **SACRED HEARTS** (16 May 1985) also features Annette Badland. Here she plays a nun expelled from an East Anglian girls' orphanage at the beginning of the Second World War for showing her charges, in an exuberant fit of pride, photographs of East African natives before and after their conversion to Christianity. Written and directed by Barbara Rennie, this auto-biographical film echoes Gavin Millar's *Secrets*. In the earlier film the mystery was fantastical but the girls treated it seriously; here the mystery is serious (one girl, Doris, must hide the fact that she is Jewish) but the approach more cheerfully knockabout.

The rituals of the convent – those who wet their beds must walk the grounds draped in the offending sheet – are guyed; and Anna Massey as the martinet in charge is every bit as intransigently tyrannical as Helen Lindsay, the mother in *Secrets*, was flutteringly abstracted. Caricature is carried further in Tony Bicât's **CHRISTMAS PRESENT** (19 December 1985), in which Sir Percy Hammond (Bill Fraser), chairman of the family bank, dispatches Nigel Playfayre (Peter Chelsom), young, upwardly mobile, insufferable, to present the traditional Christmas cheque to a family of the deserving poor. An Indian family are somewhat improbably the latter-day Cratchits of Camden Town. Nigel succeeds in losing the cheque and the address to which he is to deliver it: failure spells dismissal from the bank. Meanwhile Mary and Joseph, in biblical regalia, wander the city's mean streets searching for somewhere to stay.

SINGLETON'S PLUCK (12 December 1985), directed by Richard Eyre from a script by Brian Glover, was a more robust and less fanciful Christmas tale. Infuriated by the strike of his plucking team, Ben Singleton (Ian Holm), an irascible farmer fast losing the sympathy of his family, fixes on the ancient remedy of walking his flock of geese from Norfolk to Smithfield. Of the 1984–85 films, this one, photographed by Clive Tickner, gives the clearest sense of a story firmly connected to a specific landscape. From the moment that Ben tars the feet of his birds and walks them through sand, preparatory to setting out, the monotonous trek becomes authentic.

The mud, cold and general uncertain misery of agricultural life strikes home, and remarkably so because this is a broad comedy, with yokels both canny (Bill Owen) and clodlike (Richard Hope), and not without its sentimental patches. Ben Singleton's consistent bad temper is not, though, the play-acting of Evan Gorley-Peters in *Sharma and Beyond* or the practised music-hall routine of Arthur Chapman in *Arthur's Hallowed Ground*, but the real thing, and designed to drive his wife (Penelope Wilton) to the edge of distraction.

The crawl through the tunnel in *El Norte* is gripping enough and the fugitives' encounter with the swarm of rats appropriately spine-tingling; but the geese, liable to wander off and sail into the middle of inviting ponds, are proper creatures. In *Accounts*, the story of the trials of farming in the Borders, one of the Mawson brothers skins a dead lamb and pulls the fleece over a live lamb which has lost its mother. These are animals with value; and the same is true of Ben Singleton's geese.

Of the three Irish films of 1984–85, two were period pieces, one a full-dress literary adaptation, the other a raggedy peasant fantasy. Directed and co-written by the documentary-maker Paul Joyce, **SUMMER LIGHT-NING** (30 May 1985) was taken from Turgenev's *First Love*. It begins with a voice-over in an ancient library. Old Sir Robert Clarke (Paul Scofield) recalls his first betrayal. When he was 14, during a summer in Wicklow, he discovered that his father (Tom Bell), a hard-faced Dublin lawyer, was the lover of the coquette (Leonie Mellinger) who had toyed with his own affections . . . The film abounds with forced gaiety and somewhat starched settings. Like Scofield's voice, the tone is reverential. But the action fails to establish Louise's captivating spirit; and her entourage (including David Warner and Donal McCann) seem in the end rather desperate suitors.

THE OUTCASTS (14 June 1984), conceived by Robert Wynne-Simmons, is about another sort of captivation. A wild fiddler, Scarf Michael (Mick Lally), finds a soulmate in the half-crazed Maura (Mary Ryan), the youngest of three sisters and the butt of the village. The natural and the devilishly supernatural slide into one another: the cruelty meted out to Maura is no worse and no less plausible, for instance, than the prank played by Scarf Michael on one of the village girls, Roisín, who suddenly finds herself copulating not with a man but a goat.

Maura has no fear of the fiddler in a straw mask who plays at Janey her pregnant sister's wedding. 'You're only a man,' she says, telling him to remove his mask. 'Yes, only that,' he replies. He was, he says, once wrapped in sailcloth and nearly murdered. Now he is a man returned from the dead. He and Maura spend the night together and she wakes next day in a graveyard covered in snow. The film makes a strange and powerful case for the tragic self-perpetuation of the outcast's lot.

'I do not know what I may appear to the world, but to myself I seem to have been only like a boy playing on the sea-shore, and diverting myself in now and then finding a smoother pebble or a prettier shell than ordinary, whilst the great ocean of truth lay all undiscovered before me.' REFLECTIONS (5 July 1984), directed by Kevin Billington, begins and ends with Sir Isaac Newton's famous summary. What occurs between in John Banville's masterly adaptation of his own novella *The Newton Letter* is an arresting illustration of the melancholy deceptiveness of appearances.

The smoother pebble with which the Dublin historian William Masters (Gabriel Byrne) is diverting himself when he rents the lodge of a country house near the town where he grew up is an unfinished book on Newton; and the prettier shell the niece of the house, Ottilie Grainger (Harriet Walter). The great ocean is until the very end what Masters has in fact been unable to apprehend: that the small boy wandering in the grounds of the house is not in fact Ottilie's child, and that the love he has come gradually to acknowledge for Lottie (Fionnula Flanagan),

Ottilie's obscurely put-upon aunt, is based on a multitude of false assumptions. Most movingly and tragically, Masters is finally brought to an understanding of how he appears to the world, to Ottilie, and how immense and unreachable is the great ocean of human experience.

Beautifully played by the entire cast – and not least by Donal McCann as Lottie's unhappy, bitterly eaten-away husband Edward Lawless – the film is full of glinting, sustained, fully written scenes. Before a tea party Edward hooks William round the neck with a hurling stick and, standing in the yard, fills him full of whiskey while expatiating on his own life – but failing to reveal the one secret (that he is dying) which would for William have explained everything. Later Ottilie tears into William for his blindness at not realising that she was a virgin when she first came to him and that she gave herself because she loved him. At the film's climax, or anti-climax, William at last finds the moment, with Edward sprawled in the vacant hall in drunken incapacity, to make plain his love for Lottie, only to find that her sedated eyes and brain have seen and understood nothing he has said.

◆

VIEWING FIGURES
1984/1985

	1st TX '000s	2nd TX '000s
RUNNERS	17 May 84 **3,713**	7 Nov 85 **3,985**
SHARMA AND BEYOND	24 May 84 **1,764**	9 Jan 86 **3,510**
SQUARING THE CIRCLE	31 May 84 **0,908**	22 Jan 87 **1,227**
LAST DAY OF SUMMER	7 Jun 84 **3,095**	5 Dec 85 **3,501**
THE OUTCASTS	14 Jun 84 **1,741**	21 Jan 88 **2,689**
FLIGHT TO BERLIN	21 Jun 84 **1,908**	8 Jan 87 **3,424**
IN THE WHITE CITY	28 Jun 84 **1,403**	
REFLECTIONS	5 Jul 84 **1,978**	29 Jan 87 **3,222**
ARTHUR'S HALLOWED GROUND	30 Aug 84 **3,341**	27 Aug 87 **2,018**
WINTER FLIGHT	20 Dec 84 **5,762**	23 Jul 87 **3,825**

SACRED HEARTS	*16 May 85* **5,638**	*5 Feb 87* **4,775**
A SONG FOR EUROPE	*23 May 85* **3,120**	*15 Jan 87* **3,163**
SUMMER LIGHTNING	*30 May 85* **3,151**	*17 Aug 89* **1,470**
FOREVER YOUNG	*6 Jun 85* **4,189**	*20 Aug 87* **1,443**
EL NORTE	*13 Jun 85* **2,231**	*2 Aug 90* **0,748**
SINGLETON'S PLUCK	*12 Dec 85* **4,172**	*8 Dec 88* **2,858**
CHRISTMAS PRESENT	*19 Dec 85* **3,487**	*14 Dec 86* **2,766**

Source: BARB

January 1986 Space shuttle explodes on take-off. **February** Channel Tunnel treaty signed. Olof Palme, PM of Sweden, assassinated. **March** Abolition of Greater London Council. **April** US bombs 'terrorist bases' in Tripoli and Benghazi. Chernobyl nuclear accident. **June** Kurt Waldheim elected President of Austria despite his suspect war record. Patrick Magee jailed for 1984 Brighton bombing. **July** Corporal punishment abolished in state schools. **August** 25th anniversary of Berlin Wall. **September** Biggest one-day fall in Wall Street share prices since 1929. **October** 'Big Bang', London stock exchange computerised. **December** Earl of Stockton (Harold Macmillan), PM 1957–63, dies at 92. **January 1987** Terry Waite, envoy of the Archbishop of Canterbury, kidnapped in Lebanon. **March** Ferry capsizes off Zeebrugge; 187 die. Van Gogh's *Sunflowers* sold for £22.5m. **April** Mikhail Gorbachev

offers to dismantle all European short-range nuclear weapons. **May** Matthias Rust of FGR lands plane in Red Square. **June** Mrs Thatcher elected for third term; 101 Tory majority in the General Election. **August** Rudolf Hess, Hitler's deputy, commits suicide in Spandau jail. **September** Liberals vote to merge with Social Democrats. **October** SE England struck by its worst storm in 300 years. Dow Jones index falls 23%. **November** 70th anniversary of Bolshevik Revolution. Moscow CP chief Boris Yeltsin dismissed for advocating faster reforms. Thirty die in King's Cross fire.

CHAPTER 3

THAT'S HER IN A MOVIE

1986/1987

At the beginning of **PARIS, TEXAS** (29 May 1986) a hawk looks down on a man. Travis Anderson (Harry Dean Stanton) stumbles out of the South Texas wilderness after an unexplained absence of four years. But the director Wim Wenders does not have a cold eye or a lofty viewpoint. Travis recovers himself and reunites Hunter, the now seven-year-old son he abandoned, with Jane (Nastassja Kinski), the wife with whom he could not live. But this redemptive act is double-edged. Travis is forced to punish not only himself but his kindly brother Walt (Dean Stockwell) and Walt's wife Anne (Aurore Clément) who have raised Hunter as their own. The last scene echoes the first. In an empty parking lot at dusk Travis gazes up at a window behind which Hunter clings to his mother in the tightest of mutual embraces. Travis then drives into the sunset.

Like a latter-day Western, majestically photographed by Robby Müller, *Paris, Texas* addresses the theme of a lone man returning to fulfil a hard duty. Each long sequence counts and the action advances in operatic bounds. The emotion is poured neat; notably in the scene which introduces Jane. As Walt projects a home movie taken by the ocean, Travis sits transfixed by the silent fleeting images while Hunter, to avoid his father's eye, drags his fingers across a fish tank. The title alludes to a vacant lot purchased by Travis. Here he hoped to create a real family. Travis's father, it transpires, met his wife in 'Paris': a story he enjoyed telling, particularly for the reaction of his audience in the pause before he added '. . . Texas'.

This large-hearted film, written by Sam Shepard, is much more than a disguised Western dipped in the melancholy of past unhappiness. It has a sanding of natural humour: 'That's not *her*,' Hunter informs Travis after the film show, 'that's her in a movie' – with a smile – 'a long time ago in a galaxy far far away.' And there is, too, an uncanny sense of the mingling of the natural and the man-made (a sense of what an outsider sees): a house overlooking a freeway which might be a swift river; a pristine billboard of a bisected girl advertising bottled water; and on either side of the rock-faces of a drive-in city bank, Hunter and Travis lying in wait for Jane, redskins with walkie-talkies.

The climax, instinctively acted, simple and unforgettable, occurs in a booth divided by a two-way mirror in a cavernous whorehouse. On one side of the glass, slumped in the dark, a telephone crooked to his ear, is Travis; on the other, like a beautiful, brightly lit tropical fish, Jane. As Travis begins hesitantly to describe what became of their marriage, recognition is one of a dozen feelings which break slowly across Jane's face. *Paris, Texas* is justly dedicated to the film historian Lotte Eisner.

The Indian and British characters of **HEAT AND DUST** (22 May 1986) are parted by a barrier as deceptive (if not as tangible) as the two-way mirror in the Texas whorehouse. Directed by James Ivory and adapted by his established collaborator Ruth Prawer Jhabvala from her prizewinning novel, the film interleaves two reflecting stories. One, set in an Indian princely state in 1922, contains the central mystery. Olivia (Greta Scacchi), the eager young wife of an assistant collector, is entranced and overwhelmed by the country in which she finds herself. She is surrounded by the servants of the Raj for whom duty is armour against experience.

Olivia becomes pregnant (through mischance rather than intention) and flies to her seducer, the corrupt, undeniable Nawab of Khatm (Shashi Kapoor). Time passes; the scandal is no longer mentioned. She stays on, installed in a house in Kashmir, separated from her own people, content with the Nawab's occasional visits. In the other, present-day story, Anne (Julie Christie), a BBC researcher, sets out to discover the source of her great-aunt Olivia's contentment. Olivia resorted to an abortionist; but Anne, who has yielded to her insistent host Inder Lal (the tabla-player Zakir Hussain), decides to keep her baby and, maybe, to raise it in India.

Olivia could no more have remained with her earnest pipe-smoking husband than Travis could have remained with Jane. In the dry expanse of both South Texas and South India time ceases to matter, four years or sixty, the same rules apply: duty must be done, but the duty of the heart. And in both places the defeat of inertia – Travis's catatonia, Olivia's suffocation – requires a heroic effort of will. But the chief strength of *Heat and Dust* is the variety of its humour and the lightness, the deceptive lightness, with which it treats Olivia's fate. At the close, her contentment remains her secret.

Immaculately photographed by Walter Lassally, the film has much to say about friendship and about loyalty which has nothing to do with duty. 'I know I'm a monster egoist, or a plain monster,' the Nawab tells Harry (Nickolas Grace), the companion who seems about to leave him. 'But, my goodness, for a monster I do grow fond of people. I miss them when they leave me. Now, you see, you say nothing.' And Harry looks shamefaced. For the Nawab, friendship is for life; and one may imagine that for earnest chain-smoking Walt even Travis's flight with Hunter to find Jane will in the end be a pardonable betrayal.

The geographical spread of the twenty-two new films transmitted on Film on Four in 1986–87 was greater than in previous years. In addition to those from the United States and India, six films were set on the European mainland, in France (two), Spain, Italy, Greece and the Netherlands. Another used a French jail to represent one in Uruguay. Eleven films were located in England: four in London, two each in Liverpool and Yorkshire, one in the Forest of Dean, another in the Lake District and one in a menacing fairytale wood at Shepperton studios. There were no films from Scotland or Wales and only one from Ireland.

Eleven films were rooted in the real present and five in a present tinged to some extent by fantasy. Four were set in the past, and two were divided between past and present. The first three films from 1986, *The Eyes of Birds* (*Les Yeux des Oiseaux*), *Strawberry Fields* (*Die doppelte Welt*) and *The King and the Queen* (*El Rey y la Reina*), were tagged respectively Film on Four from France, Germany and Spain. Subtitled films were, however, later transmitted under the heading 'Film on Four International' (distinct from 'Film Four International', the Channel 4 sales arm and after 1984 the Channel's standard production credit). The first FoFI with pre-completion money from Channel 4 was Agnès Varda's *Vagabonde* (*Sans toit ni loi*) in June 1987; though purists will note that the first subtitled Film on Four was Alain Tanner's *In the White City* (*Dans la ville blanche*), transmitted three years earlier.

The scrambled principles of West German terrorists, the legacy of the Greek Civil War, the routine barbarities of a South American jail, class conflict during the Spanish Civil War, and the ostracism of a modern beggar girl wandering through the Languedoc, were treated in five films. All were from overseas, though one, *Strawberry Fields*, was adapted from a play by Stephen Poliakoff. Also examined were the toils of the artist Caravaggio, the process of animal decay, and a vengeful conspiracy in wartime Lyon.

Of the films set in England, three, *No Surrender*, *My Beautiful Laundrette* and *Wetherby*, felt the nation's pulse. Two others, *The Company of Wolves* and *Success Is the Best Revenge*, probed (respectively) the dream of a fevered girl and the nightmare of artistic compromise. And four were more or less conventional dramas – comedies, *The Chain* and *She'll Be Wearing Pink Pyjamas*, and nostalgia pictures, *The Innocent* and *The Assam Garden*. There was, too, a hard-driving musical, *Billy the Kid and the Green Baize Vampire*, and a rough-edged Liverpool love story, *Letter to Brezhnev*.

Unlike the explosive tyrant of *Squaring the Circle*, the President of the USSR glimpsed in **LETTER TO BREZHNEV** (7 May 1987) is a bald functionary ('Take a letter, Miss Jones'), a cut-out Ivan happy to further Anglo-Soviet détente. One desperate Friday night in Liverpool, Teresa and Elaine (Margi Clarke and Alexandra Pigg) pick up two sailors, the forward Sergei from Leningrad (Alfred Molina) and the sensitive Peter from the Black Sea (Peter Firth). Love blossoms in adjoining hotel rooms, and when next day the goodwill visitors return to their ship Elaine and Peter swear they will somehow meet again. Enter Brezhnev – how could he refuse a plea from Liverpool? – and presto! an uncertain Elaine is being seen on to a plane to the Soviet Union. Teresa is in tears, knowing that *she* will never escape from Merseyside.

The impact of this play-to-film, written by Frank Clarke and directed by Chris Bernard, derives from its makeshift transposition (cf. *Hero*) and the cockiness of the young Liverpudlian cast. 'Food first, filth later,' Teresa declares, typically. It mixes basic effects (a painted sky, a star to wish on) with ingenious sentimentality (Elaine's rapture is as exaggerated as Teresa's ecstasy). But its pace flies over improbability. The story balances on the edge of fantasy, but is pulled back to reality – Elaine and Teresa work in a chicken factory – by a stream of unabashed backchat.

The tone of *Letter to Brezhnev* is set when Teresa, her pay packet burning a hole in her purse, swoops Elaine from a taxi to a club and then carelessly lifts the wallet of a middle-aged punter who thinks he has struck lucky. Less insouciant clublife is the subject of **NO SURRENDER**

(19 March 1987), directed by Peter Smith from a script by Alan Bleasdale. 'A normal night out / (these days) / Liverpool, New Year's Eve,' a title reads. Here, though, an ironic fantasy tips into a surreal chasm. On his first evening at the Charleston Club, a hangar on a backlot, the manager Mike Moriarty (Michael Angelis) faces a double-booking, a Roman Catholic pensioners' club (in fancy dress) and a branch of the Orange Lodge (whose former grandmaster, Billy McRacken, is harbouring a fleeing gunman).

Behind the scenes, the club owner, a gangster, is bloodily settling scores. On the surface, the film piles on the mayhem with sometimes frantic desperation: added to the warring factions is a party of the mentally handicapped. Underneath, in a calmer voice, it makes two points. Billy (Ray McAnally) turned from violence years ago. Now he is under duress. He has been estranged from his daughter since her marriage to a Roman Catholic. But unless he helps the gunman, something unpleasant may happen to her. At the end, with the gunman dead in the club lavatory, Billy sits down in the half-light and calmly places a call to Belfast to wish his son-in-law a happy New Year.

The second point is about what it takes to retain a job. Knocking on the club door, his dinner jacket slung over his shoulder, Mike is conned by a gang of boys playing outside and then sent away, like a child, for arriving too early. He is, it seems, no more than the sap hired to clear up the mess left by his malicious predecessor. Mike survives by compliant stealth until an opportunity arises to better the gangster in his torture chamber. He succeeds, but the victory is incomplete. He will doubtless have to fight for his job again tomorrow. And as a sign of his surrender to this truth, that the future is not a secure investment, Mike the married man submits with a resigned shrug to the casual proposition of the club singer (Joanne Whalley). This is the moral of a night out in Liverpool in 1985.

The shadow of a gunman, but an IRA gunman, falls over the name-character in CAL (26 February 1987), the first of two adaptations from his own books by the novelist Bernard MacLaverty. The script was developed for the modest 'First Love' series but later upgraded. Stuart Craig, the production designer, also acted as co-producer, and the film, directed by Pat O'Connor, has a confidence which sets it apart from David Puttnam's other Channel 4 films. Of all the 136 films transmitted by Film on Four in its first nine years this is the only one to have tackled head-on the present cycle of Irish Troubles.

Cal (John Lynch) is a Roman Catholic living with his father Shamie

(Donal McCann), a peace-loving widower, on a Protestant estate in Belfast. Shamie works in an abattoir and the film begins with striking, unemphasised scenes of evisceration. The real slaughter, the IRA's job, has already occurred. Cal has been the unwilling driver on a night operation which ended with the shooting of a Protestant policeman. Riven with guilt, he is drawn back to the policeman's widow, Marcella (Helen Mirren), a fellow Catholic, living miserably on the farm kept by her husband's mother. The farm manager (Ray McAnally) fixes a very sharp eye on him. Cal brings wood to the farm and then finds himself with a regular job lifting potatoes.

Love, or rather a mutual desperate attraction, begins to form. But Cal cannot tell Marcella who he is and what he has done; and the IRA needs him for just one more job. Bernard MacLaverty's stark moral tale is transposed with blunt conviction. The soldiers have the air of men with live ammunition in their rifles and the tight Protestant atmosphere of the farm has a chilling truth. Cal and Shamie are eventually burned out of their home. Cal moves into an outhouse on the farm, in the false hope that this is the start of his life. One Sunday he visits Shamie, who is lodging with an older man. Shamie has lost the will to live and sits in an old neglected chair picking and picking away at the stuffing of the arm.

Bettering a smooth drug-pusher and keeping a job – and more, making something of yourself – is the theme of **MY BEAUTIFUL LAUNDRETTE** (19 February 1987), written by Hanif Kureishi and directed by Stephen Frears. Since the suicide of his wife, Omar's father has sacrificed his liberal principles to the bottle. But young Omar (Gordon Warnecke) has an Uncle Nasser (Saeed Jaffrey), a businessman who has prospered in Thatcher's England; and Nasser offers Omar the management of a decrepit South London launderette, gives him, in short, his chance. Corruption, violence and complacency are everywhere; but also a certain sort of opportunity. On the streets, as in *Meantime*, the foot-soldiers of the National Front kick their heels. By swindling Nasser's cousin Salim, Omar transforms the launderette into a paradise: neon over the door, a glowing fish tank, yellow walls with a motif of breaking waves. Mike Moriarty, even had he wanted to, could never have performed a miracle like this on the Charleston Club.

The first quality of *My Beautiful Laundrette* is its ability to surprise. The subject is fresh, the style quicksilver, from naturalism though make-believe to full-blown surrealism. Nasser and his family are not the humble Indians of *Christmas Present* but untroubled entrepreneurs.

Nasser has a white mistress, Rachel (Shirley Anne Field), and Omar a white boyfriend, Johnny: both Rachel and Johnny are pieces of property, bought and paid for, but both are also oddly cherished. They nevertheless suffer the consequences of a sort of reverse racism. Rachel is blistered from the spells of Nasser's wife and Johnny receives a bloody face from defending the launderette against his former skinhead friends. Daniel Day Lewis is memorable as the mysterious Johnny, his jaunty bleached quiff a complement to his open lecherous smile.

There are striking performances too in the potpourri musical **BILLY THE KID AND THE GREEN BAIZE VAMPIRE** (2 April 1987), written by George Fenton (music) and Trevor Preston (lyrics): from Phil Daniels, the needling Mark Pollock of *Meantime*, as the Cockney contender for the snooker championship of the world; and from Alun Armstrong as the Bradford 'Vampire' Maxwell Randall, the ticklish veteran from whom Billy Kid aims to take the title. A parody of hustling and blood-sucking movies, *Billy the Kid* is nevertheless spare and unselfconscious. 'Do you concur, father?' the Vampire asks; and father signals his approval of Maxwell taking on the whippersnapper by firing balls across the baize top of his interior-lit glass coffin.

Directed by Alan Clarke (*Scum*, 1979), the film is a studio fantasy, strikingly designed by Jamie Leonard, swathed in billowing stage smoke and marked by such audible songs as 'The One' (performed by Billy's manager, Bruce Payne) with the signal quality of enriching rather than halting the action. The climactic tournament, which occurs in a steep-sided gladiatorial well, has an unshakeable grip despite the predictable outcome (the Vampire freezes Billy's winning ball on the lip of the pocket, but to no avail). This is not snooker as seen on TV at inordinate length with hushed voice-over, but more the fast and dangerous click of balls from the opening moments of Martin Scorsese's *The Last Waltz*.

For Teresa in *Letter to Brezhnev* a good 'going-over' was a natural end to Friday night; but for the eight women on the Lakeland survival course in **SHE'LL BE WEARING PINK PYJAMAS** (12 March 1987), sex trouble is the dormitory talking point. A lack of self-pity stiffened Teresa and even mordant Mike Moriarty, but these mainly middle-class women are champion worriers. The Alps played a significant if minor role in *A Song for Europe*, the director John Goldschmidt's earlier Film on Four; the peaks of Cumberland, however, although real enough, often seem a challenge more to the actors than their characters. The journalist Eva Hardy wrote the script, from experience; and Julie Walters played

Fran, the group's noisiest member, with familiar locker-room gusto.

THE CHAIN (12 February 1987), directed by Jack Gold, features another assortment of individuals linked in trying circumstances. A chain of Londoners moves home and nice distinctions are made (for London viewers) between Tufnell Park and Willesden, Hampstead and Hammersmith. Like *P'Tang, Yang, Kipperbang*, also written by Jack Rosenthal, this modern 'ronde' is comfortable within its limits: a folksy, dovetailed comedy of humours – obsessive meanness (Nigel Hawthorne), highly coloured grief (Billie Whitelaw), bossy selfishness (Maurice Denham) – drawing the best from a string of name players in essentially cameo roles. Bamber (Warren Mitchell), a night-school philosopher full of soothing advice, heads the removal team which connects the episodes. Moral: trade up by all means, but death waits patiently.

Property, debt and the ghost of an Indian tea-planter are the ingredients of Mary McMurray's THE ASSAM GARDEN (16 April 1987). Helen Graham, a determined widow, transplanted to Gloucestershire, ignores ominous letters from the solicitor. Her one concern is that her husband Arthur's garden, a nostalgic corner of the Brahmaputra valley, should be fit for inclusion in the book *Great British Gardens*. She finds an ally in her obliging, somewhat vague neighbour Mrs Lal (Madhur Jaffrey, the Nawab's suspicious mother in *Heat and Dust*). Two assured middle-class cultures bump up against each other. The garden is trimmed, watered and made ready; and perhaps something may in time flourish between the women. In the end, though, Mrs Lal is granted her wish to return to India with her ailing husband; and the solicitor arrives in person with the news that Mrs Graham is living beyond her means. Elisabeth Bond's miniature story has an appropriate dying fall; and Deborah Kerr, as the widow, hits the exact note of unintentional but inflexible rudeness.

LETTERS TO AN UNKNOWN LOVER (5 June 1986), directed by Peter Duffell, is a pair with the melodrama *Praying Mantis*. Both films starred Cherie Lunghi and were produced by Ian Warren; and both were adapted from French novels, here *Les Louves* ('The She-Wolves') by Pierre Boileau and Jean Narcejac, featuring monstrous women and elaborate deceptions. During the war two Frenchmen flee the Germans. After Bernard dies, legs amputated in a Lyon shunting yard, Gervais (Yves Beneyton) shelters with the woman Bernard had been writing to from prison. But why, he puzzles, does the woman, a piano-teacher, insist on believing he is Bernard? She and her vampish sister are gold-diggers and Bernard, it transpires, had expectations.

Like its companion, the story ends in a snowstorm of improbability.

Seriousness, solemn and moody, is the watchword of two films set in Yorkshire. THE INNOCENT (19 June 1986), directed by John MacKenzie from a novel, *The Aura and the Kingfisher*, by Tom Hart, is about the growing pains of an epileptic 11-year-old to whom no one has troubled to explain anything. The 1930s, the mill is shut and the boy's father (Tom Bell) unemployed. Meanwhile, a poet with an independent income (Liam Neeson) is romancing a neighbour (Miranda Richardson) encumbered with a violent husband. The boy becomes the go-between. The tone is suggestive – what occurred in the First World War between the poet and the boy's father? what bright hope is symbolised by the doomed kingfisher the boy observes? – but the effect on the whole heavy-shod.

In WETHERBY (12 June 1986), written and directed by David Hare, schoolmistress Jean Travers (Vanessa Redgrave) is haunted by the death of her lover Jim Mortimer, an airman, in the Malayan war. Would their marriage have lasted? Jean made small impression on her future in-laws: 'Did you bake it yourself?' she asks Jim's mother about a Battenburg cake. 'Don't be *daft!*' the father explodes. Such levity is uncommon. Like *The Innocent*, though in a different register, elusive suggestions predominate. The film's unanswered questions are not, however, the dramatic mysteries of *Runners* and *The Disappearance of Harry*, but more the abstract conundrums of *The Bad Sister* and *Nelly's Version*. Can we believe what we see, must we repeat the past, shall we ever know what drives a person to self-destruction?

The town of the title is the home of the northern branch of the British Library. And it is to the library that John Morgan (Tim McInnerny), a PhD student at the University of Essex, comes to do research. One evening he is standing at the door when the librarian, Marcia Pilborough (Judi Dench), arrives for dinner with her friend Jean. Both women think the young man belongs to the other. During the meal, Morgan follows Jean upstairs. They sense perhaps that they are soulmates and fall into each other's arms. Next day Morgan returns to Jean's cottage, puts a pistol in his mouth and pulls the trigger. Young Jim died not in action but with his throat slashed in a gambling den. All of which is executed, somewhat in the manner of *The Ploughman's Lunch*, with a cool certitude about the way the educated middle class behaves.

If *Wetherby* had a fault, it is that coolness turns to chilliness. John Morgan was informed that he could not actually borrow books from the British Library; and the film, with its flashbacks and inversions, also

Paris, Texas: Nastassja Kinski

Letter to Brezhnev: Alexandra Pigg

Vagabonde: Sandrine Bonnaire

The Company of Wolves: Micha Bergese

requires the viewer (ideally a bookish viewer) to absorb everything on the premises. The characters' passions, a reflection of the times, are tamped down and incomplete. Ian Holm, for example, as Marcia's husband, is all wry discontent: he shows none of the forthright anger of Ben in *Singleton's Pluck*. But the mystery of Jean Travers is fundamentally an arm's length mystery. We are not made to care about her, made to care because the film-maker has the confidence to speak with straightforward simplicity.

Directed by the French documentary-maker Gabriel Auer (co-producer of Alain Tanner's *The Salamander*, 1971), THE EYES OF BIRDS (13 March 1986) is nothing if not unambiguous. Using a quasi-documentary format, it addresses a burning question, the abuse and murder of prisoners in Uruguay's model Libertad jail. Indignation and a streak of melancholy resignation are evident; but the film weakens its attack by sentimental special pleading. The title alludes to the crazy but indicative prohibition of any picture entering the jail which shows a live creature with 'eyes'. The pretty young daughter of one prisoner makes a nonsense of this by giving her father a painting of a tree containing not birds but simply 'les yeux des oiseaux'.

The film alleges that the jailers secretly recorded prisoners' confidential complaints to a Red Cross team. This allegation, it was claimed, led to a real-life ban on future Red Cross visits; but also, thanks to repeated screenings of the film in Uruguay and in twenty-one other countries, to the release in March 1985 of all the Libertad inmates. The film is flecked with incidents which ring true (the separate interrogation, for instance, of two men caught talking in the yard and each confessing to the same innocuous topic of conversation down to the smallest detail). Less persuasive are the flatly dramatised exchanges among the Red Cross team and the cynical villainy of the somewhat Ruritanian prison authorities.

Equally stark, though cast not as agitprop but as a down-played three-hander, STRAWBERRY FIELDS (20 March 1986) considers another manifestation of extreme rightwing behaviour. Charlotte is a serious bespectacled young woman, her companion Karl a ranting hippie who is slowly losing his sight: both belong to the neo-Nazi National Volksfront, dedicated, it seems, to saving Germany from drowning in a sea of filth. On their way to collect weapons from a town in north Germany, the couple pick up the clear-sighted Nicki; he attempts to puncture their contradictory beliefs, but is undone by his attraction to Charlotte. The rendezvous goes wrong, a policeman is shot and the trio flee, only to be surrounded on the idyllic Lorelei Rock. Charlotte despatches Nicki with a bullet through the back of the head, and the camera pulls back into the sky from a line of antlike policemen closing on the fugitives. Kristian Kühn directs this adaptation of Stephen Poliakoff's play with flat deliberateness; and the dominant tone echoes the enervation of the two deluded terrorists.

THE KING AND THE QUEEN (27 March 1986), drawn from a novel by Ramón J. Sender and starring Nuria Espert as the Duchess of Alquezar and Omero Antonutti as her watchful retainer Rómulo, sets about its period reconstruction with more élan. The pistol-flourishing, boiler-suited Republicans who requisition the Duchess's mansion at the start of the Spanish Civil War are, however, as caricatured as the shaven prisoners of Libertad jail and the angry automatons waiting their fate on the Lorelei Rock. The film, written and directed by José Antonio Paramo, begins as it will go on with the sublimely aristocratic Duchess receiving Rómulo, who has come to deliver a letter, in her bath.

To the Duchess the servants are invisible and insensible. But Rómulo flares with desire, and matters only worsen when he is compelled to keep the Duchess's continued presence in a wing of her own home (a well-appointed tower) secret from the occupiers. The melodrama is worked out with not much more probability than the other tale of sex and wartime captivity, *Letters to an Unknown Lover.* The Duchess continues to receive her husband and her lover, the Marquis of Irati, and also to tease the faithful but now patently besotted Rómulo. When fighting starts in earnest, Rómulo, who seems doomed to have vainly prostituted his honour in the Duchess's service, departs for the front and is wounded for the Republic. He returns in due course and the Duchess pours out her love before expiring in his arms.

VAGABONDE (4 June 1987) begins with the discovery of the corpse of the beggar girl Mona in a vineyard ditch in the south of France. An unseen interviewer, the director Agnès Varda, then picks up the pieces of the last months of Mona's life. The film has ice in its bones. When in *Runners* Stephen Poliakoff addressed the subject of a girl who ran away from home for no apparent reason, he cast the story as a dramatic mystery. Agnès Varda adds only touches of dramatic narrative. These, however, have an off-the-cuff crudity which when mixed with the fragments of documentary reportage give the film as a whole a peculiarly disorienting and disquieting impact. Of all the unsolved mysteries proposed in Film on Four, Mona

Bergeron's is perhaps the most harrowing and most fiercely intractable.

The Eyes of Birds, which also mixed drama and documentary, had the limited scope of a political harangue. *Vagabonde*, however, is dangerously unpredictable. The viewer, like Mona herself, is never sure who or what the heroine will encounter: two somnolent goatherds, a woman at a water-pump, a prostitute by the roadside, a wild man in a wood. There is a moral, no less crude perhaps than that of *The Eyes of Birds*, but slipped in like a knife. Mona is befriended by a university lecturer (Macha Méril), a specialist in a cancerous disease which attacks plane-trees. She lectures Mona. The disease took twenty-five years to identify; it came to France in 1944 in weapon crates abandoned by the Americans. In thirty years every plane-tree in the country will be infected. Stupid, Mona observes. Not stopping it, the scientist counters, is even more stupid.

This bald statement, against shots of the falling rotten trees and insinuated among episodes of Mona's fleeting encounters, strikes with the force of unmistakable originality. The film draws its muscularity from its non-professional 'witnesses', small farmers, mechanics, North African labourers, and also from its exact sense of the hard land from which they make a living, but mostly from the ragged, sullen performance of Sandrine Bonnaire. Mona is by almost any reckoning dislikable: idle, ungrateful, unmotivated, boneheaded. And yet she is not; she is unquestionably free; and her freedom stamps her death with tragedy.

VOYAGE TO CYTHERA (18 June 1987) is the tragedy of an old man, a former Communist partisan, returning to Greece after thirty-two years' exile in the Soviet Union. The hard duty which Spyros (Manos Katrakis) must perform, after his years in the wilderness, is not that of Travis in *Paris, Texas* to return his son to his mother, but in a sense to return himself to the wife and children he was compelled to abandon. In the case of his son Alexandros, an anxious film director (Julio Brogi), and his daughter Voula, who no longer believes in anything, Spyros fails; at the end, though, and by now thoroughly out of sorts with everything to do with a Greece which wants nothing to do with him, Spyros is joined by his wife Katerina on a raft cast adrift in Piraeus harbour bound for the island of Cythera, birthplace of Aphrodite, the goddess of love and regeneration.

Theo Angelopoulos's long film is, particularly in its first half, infused with the melancholy of both past and present unhappiness. Like *Paris, Texas*, it is punctuated with moments of neat emotion: the return to Spyros's native village, for instance, when the erect old man gets out of the car and hears a distinctive birdsong, the old outlaw's language. Angelopoulos and his cameraman Giorgios Arvanitis are masters of the sequence shot, and in no other Film on Four, with the exception of Andrei Tarkovsky's *Sacrifice* (see Chapter 4), is the sense of confident visual composition, of the movement of characters within a shot, so distinct or so imbued with narrative significance.

Voyage to Cythera is marked by the director's familiar motifs, a troupe of travelling players (here an amateur company of dockers), a gleaming, sterile petrol station, a bare hotel room alive with associations, but also in the mid-section by an overwhelming sense of the Greek countryside, its barren beauty, and its apparent uselessness for anything worthwhile. The old man is taken back to his village in order to agree the sale of his section of the surrounding land for a winter sports centre. He refuses and, in a marvellous long-shot, vents his anger by beating a mattock on the unbreakable ground. The film has a double-dyed bitterness; but a bitterness transformed by the clarity of its images and a sense of the healing power of art.

At the beginning, Alexandros goes to work at the studio and listens to a line of old men auditioning for a part. Each utters the same line. 'It's me – It's me – It's me.' Again and again, one after the other. In desperation the director goes for a coffee and sees in the bar the perfect old man, a lavender-seller. He follows the man into the street, on to a train and out to Piraeus. Here Alexandros meets his irritable sister; he is, it seems, always late for everything. They have come to collect their father. A ship docks with majestic calm. An old man, all alone, a violin case in his hand, descends from the vast MV *Ukrania*. The three of them stand looking at each other. Angelopoulos holds the moment. 'It's me,' the old man says. The spell is broken and Alexandros goes forward to take his bag. But he has forgotten something. 'Aren't you going to kiss me?' his father asks.

SUCCESS IS THE BEST REVENGE (26 June 1986) makes a pair, two years on, with the director Jerzy Skolimowski's previous Film on Four, *Moonlighting*. The Kensington house which the Polish builders were illegally renovating (Skolimowski's own house) is now the home of an honoured émigré director, Aleksander Rodak (Michael York), his long-suffering wife (Skolimowski's own wife, Joanna Szczerbic) and their two awkward sons (the Skolimowskis' sons; one of whom, Michael Lyndon, is the film's co-author). The house is again being done over (the jokes this time at the expense of London building regulations); and the task now facing the hero, another wily Pole far from home and on another non-existent budget, is the production of an elaborate 'happening', a mirror of the student protests then taking place in Warsaw.

Both films were made at urgent speed. But, unlike *Moonlighting*, the second substitutes concentrated exactitude for scattershot freneticism, the madness in short of trying to raise production money before the immutably fixed first day of principal photography. At the end of *Moonlighting*, Nowak leads his men, with their trolleys of Western produce, back to Heathrow and a flight home; *Success* ends with the director bringing off his happening (and thus becoming a dissident barred from Poland) and his son Adam (Michael Lyndon) selling the video camera Aleksander gave him for his sixteenth birthday and buying a ticket to Warsaw. 'I want to have real friends and enemies,' Adam writes to his father, 'to go to Warsaw Cathedral, to play football for Poland and help them win.'

Success Is the Best Revenge is marked most effectively perhaps by its asides: a bank manager (Jane Asher) very dubious about a loan for a car, discomfited when Rodak notices she is warming her stockinged feet on a leaking hot-water bottle; a history lesson on the division of Europe after 1945 with the boys applying Tipp-Ex to their atlases. **THE COMPANY OF WOLVES** (5 March 1987), adapted by the novelist Angela Carter from her own work, is also full of asides: a story of a girl's fitful dream of a granny recounting a cautionary tale within a cautionary tale... Designed by Anton Furst, Neil Jordan's lycanthropic studio fantasy is most notable perhaps – once a path has been cut through the tangled sexuality of the teenager's dream – for a tone of melancholy sympathy for the ravening wolf.

At the core is a reworked version of Little Red Riding Hood. 'What have you done with my granddaughter?' granny demands. 'Nothing she didn't want,' the wolf (the dancer Micha Bergese) replies. A fight ensues which ends with granny decapitated and the wolf killed by the girl he has wooed. The girl, it seems, subsequently becomes a wolf herself and must be saved by mother from her father's gun. The film delights in its effects (designed by Christopher Tucker): a wedding party, for instance, at which the pompadoured guests turn into wolves, smash the crockery and hare away in their trailing frocks. But it is Angela Lansbury who has the last word, playing up to the role of sage granny (beware men whose eyebrows meet in the middle) with a gusto so delightful it makes the viewer momentarily doubt the film-makers' wholly serious intent.

A ZED & TWO NOUGHTS (30 April 1987), written and directed by Peter

Greenaway, is another restless fantasy. *The Draughtsman's Contract*, Greenaway's earlier Film on Four, was kept within bounds by the elegant symmetry of its story. Here delirious free association abounds. The setting is a zoo, although the deconstructed word of the title may also spark associations with the twins (the brothers Deuce) who have lost their wives in a motor accident and are now drawn to one-legged Alba Bewick (who, to make the alphabetical association clear, has a daughter Beta . . .). But the film is also about another sort of deconstruction: the time-lapse photography of dead creatures. The story ends with the naked brothers contentedly lying down to die: the record of their own disintegration is foiled, however, by snails crawling over the carefully prepared equipment and shorting the lights.

The film is never dull and often droll (if somewhat heartless): one brother attempts suicide by eating the diamonds of glass from the windscreen of the car which killed his wife; 'I'm having breakfast,' he observes. The film also explores its maker's preoccupation with pornography, and in particular the art of pornographic storytelling. 'There used to be a bed at the back of the vulture's cage,' the zoo's harlot (Frances Barber) informs the establishment's director (Joss Ackland). Dazzling, singular, undeniable; but also, sometimes, not unlike a great fantastical machine spinning out of its creator's control.

Van Meegeren, the faker of Vermeers, appears in *A Zed & Two Noughts* to underline the notion that repetition in art is perhaps more than deceptive fakery. Is the zoo's zebra a black creature with white stripes or a white creature with . . . ? **CARAVAGGIO** (14 May 1987), on the other hand, which begins with the wonderfully evocative sound of layer upon layer of black paint being applied to a canvas, concerns the struggle of an earlier artist not to palm off his work but to find his own visual language. Derek Jarman's meditation on a life in art, told as a flashback from Caravaggio's deathbed in Porto Ercole, is another studio-bound fantasy with a great deal to say about fevered sexual matters. In *The Company of Wolves* the paint was as it were squeezed thick from the tube on to the scenery. Here Christopher Hobbs's clean elegant sets are filled with only the wholly sufficient essentials. The soundtrack, especially in the room in Porto Ercole with the sea just out of eyesight, is marvellously modulated; and the lighting, often echoing Caravaggio's use of chiaroscuro, gives the whole a unity which no Hollywood budget could ever have purchased.

The film concerns the price the artist pays for the privilege of patronage. But it is as a work devoted to the celebration of artistic creation –

the mixing of pigments, the arrangement of models, the thought which precedes the first brush-stroke – that *Caravaggio* comes into its own. Aleksander Rodak in *Success Is the Best Revenge* brings his momentous happening to life, but as he reads his son's letter he senses that the baton of commitment (artistic or political, it makes no odds) has been passed to the next generation. As Caravaggio (Nigel Terry), attended by his mute assistant Jerusaleme, considers his life, he recalls the dictum of his first patron, Cardinal Del Monte, that the task is simplicity, repeating old truths in new language. And the dying artist drew some satisfaction perhaps from the knowledge that he had not shirked that duty.

VIEWING FIGURES
1986/1987

	1st TX '000s	2nd TX '000s
THE EYES OF BIRDS	*13 Mar 86* **2,013**	*9 May 88* **1,208**
STRAWBERRY FIELDS	*20 Mar 86* **2,488**	
THE KING AND THE QUEEN	*27 Mar 86* **1,409**	
HEAT AND DUST	*22 May 86* **3,628**	*7 Jan 88* **3,426**
PARIS, TEXAS	*29 May 86* **3,703**	*11 Feb 88* **2,894**
LETTERS TO AN UNKNOWN LOVER	*5 Jun 86* **2,502**	*28 Jan 88* **2,944**
WETHERBY	*12 Jun 86* **2,947**	*14 Jan 88* **3,429**
THE INNOCENT	*19 Jun 86* **4,489**	*24 Aug 89* **3,544**
SUCCESS IS THE BEST REVENGE	*26 Jun 86* **1,307**	*31 Aug 89* **1,101**
THE CHAIN	*12 Feb 87* **5,240**	*8 Jun 89* **3,725**
MY BEAUTIFUL LAUNDRETTE	*19 Feb 87* **4,336**	*10 Apr 88* **3,550**
CAL	*26 Feb 87* **3,737**	*1 Jun 89* **3,072**
THE COMPANY OF WOLVES	*5 Mar 87* **5,789**	*15 Jun 89* **3,387**
SHE'LL BE WEARING PINK PYJAMAS	*12 Mar 87* **7,585**	*29 Jun 89* **4,959**

NO SURRENDER	*19 Mar 87* **5,357**	*6 Jul 89* **2,914**
BILLY THE KID AND THE GREEN BAIZE VAMPIRE	*2 Apr 87* **1,513**	*14 Sep 89* **0,882**
THE ASSAM GARDEN	*16 Apr 87* **3,921**	*21 Sep 89* **2,014**
A ZED & TWO NOUGHTS	*30 Apr 87* **1,885**	*7 Sep 89* **1,409**
LETTER TO BREZHNEV	*7 May 87* **5,107**	*25 May 89* **2,859**
CARAVAGGIO	*14 May 87* **1,824**	*27 Jul 89* **0,842**
VAGABONDE	*4 Jun 87* **2,012**	*2 Mar 90* **0,838**
VOYAGE TO CYTHERA	*18 Jun 87* **0,732**	*29 Mar 90* **0,163**

Source: BARB

March 1988 Three IRA soldiers killed by the SAS on Gibraltar.
May Soviet forces begin withdrawal from Afghanistan. Poll tax passes
the Lords. **July** Iranian airliner shot down by US warship in the
Gulf. Paddy Ashdown becomes first leader of Social and Liberal Democrats.
October Mikhail Gorbachev elected executive President of the USSR.
Broadcast ban on Sinn Fein and Loyalist officials. **November** George Bush
elected President of the United States. **December** Bomb explodes
on Pan Am jet over Lockerbie. **February 1989** Rupert Murdoch launches
UK's first satellite TV station. Ayatollah Khomeini of Iran sentences
author Salman Rushdie to death for alleged blasphemy. **April** 95 die in
crush at Hillsborough football ground. Solidarity legalised.
May Mrs Thatcher the longest continuously serving British PM since Lord
Liverpool. **June** Troops quell mass protest in Tiananmen Square,

Beijing; thousands believed killed. Ayatollah Khomeini dies.
July Israelis kidnap Sheik Obeid the spiritual leader of
the pro-Iranian Hizbollah militia. **November** East Germany opens
its border with West. Berlin Wall demolished. **December** Cold War ends.
President Noriega of Panama taken to the US to face drug charges.
Romanian revolution; President Ceausescu and his wife executed.
Playwright Vaclav Havel elected first non-Communist
president of Czechoslovakia in forty-one years.

CHAPTER 4

OFF THE RATION

1988/1989

A SAILOR DANCES on an open-air stage for a group of Dorset farm-workers. Hard times in the 1830s. The audience is captivated by the dancer's elegance. This is one of two themes in Bill Douglas's COMRADES (27 April 1989): that art and chiefly the art of light – the hand-shadow of a dog's head, a peepshow of Eve in the Garden of Eden, a face on an unfixed glassplate – dignifies humankind and transforms the mean into the noble. The film, 'a Lanternist's account of the Tolpuddle Martyrs and what became of them', is a moral epic as clearly incised as the Giant of Cerne Abbas seen in its opening sequence.

The other theme is comradeship itself: the remembrance of who you are and where you came from. Allied to which is the belief, sustained by Christian faith, that no workman should accept six shillings a week when promised eight. A hundred and fifty years later, in the godless London of *Meantime*, Colin Pollock absorbed a similar lesson. Douglas's method is not the sequence shot of *Voyage to Cythera*, another epic on the price of exile, but the distilled emblematic moment (a piece of bread on a table; a pay clerk pushing away coins as if he feared his fingers might be bitten), and spare juxtaposition (the lashing of a prisoner; a display of whip-work; and a diagonal of blood on earth).

A famished man unearths a turnip and bites into it, then carefully replants the stolen remains. In no other Film on Four is surprise – the touch of the comic, sentimental and heart-stopping – so varied. An English country courtship with two labourers vaulting a fence for the benefit of the girls is as unaffected as a scene from D. W. Griffith; later, in the Australian outback, a prison guard is pickaxed to death in the act of bestiality. Photographed in widescreen by Gale Tattersall, and running some three hours, the film commands its landscape: from the curves of the Dorset downs to a shimmering Australian valley extending to the dry horizon.

Comrades is less concerned with vistas, however, than with the lanternist's intimate art, the ability to conjure something from nothing. The Martyrs' voyage to Australia is depicted by a horizontal roller screen, the stormy journey home by a series of circular glass pictures: unadorned, evocative and correct – no fancy modern animation here but reliance on the integrity of nineteenth-century image-making. The film echoes and reverberates. The workers propose to create a friendly society and for a banner their leader George Loveless (Robin Soans) copies a skeleton from a bookplate; later another comrade, Old Stanfield (Stephen Bateman), finds himself lecturing on serfdom to Aborigines decorated with skeletal lines.

The film is memorable for its held moments: a fleeting look, a young woman gazing down an empty road along which six men in chains have just passed; or an unforgettable gesture, a child placing a small coin got by her own efforts between the toes of her sleeping sister. Like many long films, this one should perhaps have been even longer: there are several missed connections. It can be accused, too, of attacking strawmen: the landowner Frampton (Robert Stephens) is a villain straight from melodrama. But its vision is touched by the utopianism of the poet. Only *Moonlighting* fizzed with similar compulsion; and no other Film on Four has spoken with such confident sincerity.

The Taviani brothers' **GOOD MORNING BABYLON** (6 April 1989) also focused on comradeship (the universal brotherhood of craftsmen) and the continuity of art. *Comrades* paid tribute to the Diorama showman, the photographer with his steam-engine camera, the inventor of the spinning disc which put a bird inside its cage; and by celebrating their work on film confirmed the continuity of their achievements. *Good Morning Babylon*, a fictional tribute to the Tuscan masons who built the elephants for Griffith's silent epic *Intolerance*, attempts something similar. Here, though, the tone is marked by a curious and in some ways perhaps deliberate flatness. The Romanesque church which the film's heroes, two brothers from a dynasty of craftsmen, are first seen restoring is merely a facade; and Charles Dance's Griffith has a sort of lazy, aristocratic indifference even when contemplating the great dream of *Intolerance*.

In Bill Douglas's film the dirt beneath the nails is real, and even the most artificial confrontation is animated by an almost electric intensity. The climax of *Good Morning Babylon* is a double wedding hosted by Griffith before the Babylonian steps flanked at the top by the rampant elephants. The father of the brothers (Omero Antonutti) comes from Italy for the occasion and one master craftsman (rather uneasily) greets another. What we see, though, is a reconstruction of an approximation of an original (now non-existent) work of art, and the effect is inevitably somewhat anticlimactic. The spinning disc with its bird and cage is precision-scaled: the art is there, magically, before our eyes.

Twenty-eight new films were transmitted in 1988–89. Ten took place wholly in England (London predominating) and one each in Scotland and the Republic of Ireland. Two films were divided between England and Australia; and four travelled, respectively, from Ireland to London and back again; from Florence to the Home Counties; from London to Turkey; and from East Berlin to West Berlin to Cambridge. One film went from Jamaica to Toronto and back, and another from Italy to Hollywood and then to a battlefield in the First World War. There were films set in Sweden, Greece, India, Spain, Poland, Italy, Germany and the United States. Eight took place in the past and nineteen in the present; and one was divided between the two.

Seven films were adapted from novels: Janni Howker's *The Nature of the Beast*, Samaresh Basu's *Genesis*, Ernest J. Gaines's *A Gathering of Old Men*, Peter Prince's *The Good Father*, Bernard MacLaverty's *Lamb*, Vladimir Nabokov's *Maschenka* and E. M. Forster's *A Room with a View*. There was too a Hungarian version of Lorca's *Yerma* with the German actress Gudrun Landgrebe. Two British films, *Dance with a Stranger* and *Prick Up Your Ears*, ended with the untidy, melancholy deaths of their leading characters. A comic thread ran to some extent through eight of the 1988–89 films. There were two fantasies, *Shadey* and *Born of Fire*; two films, *Fatherland* and *Leave to Remain*, which addressed current political issues; and two, *The Belly of an Architect* and *The Sacrifice*, which began with birthday parties and developed, respectively, into meditations on disintegration and the apocalypse.

Written and directed by Charles Gormley, **HEAVENLY PURSUITS** (17 March 1988) is a tale of providential happenings at a mixed secondary school in Glasgow. A liberal teacher, the agnostic Vic Mathews (Tom Conti) is attempting to romance the forthright Roman Catholic music mistress

Ruth Chancellor (Helen Mirren); in the background the pious head-master (Dave Anderson) is negotiating delicately for the beatification of the school's patron, the Blessed Edith Semple. Vic faints in the street. An X-ray reveals a shadow on the brain. He has not long to live, a doctor concludes, why trouble him with the news. Then Vic's record-player starts up by itself . . .

The plot ultimately fizzles and the miracles fall a little too profusely (the shadow clears); but the droll comedy – few other films could raise a laugh from the words 'cheesey biscuits' – is consistently amiable. And although the flavour of Glasgow is not perhaps quite as pronounced as in Gormley's previous Film on Four, *Living Apart Together* (1983), the relaxed sparring double-act is attractively played and the prevailing tone is of kindliness unspoiled by sentimentality. The film has a delightful beginning, with the school's dishevelled priest (Brian Pettifer), clutching his folder of miraculous proofs, pattering into the Vatican, like some vague but determined Scottie, there to nip the heels of a sleekly dubious American monsignor.

Another shaggy comedy, **EAT THE PEACH** (7 April 1988), was set on the flat expanse of the Bog of Allen near the border with Northern Ireland. Directed and co-authored by Peter Ormrod, the film is about two perennial dreamers (Stephen Brennan and Eamon Morrissey) who, inspired by Elvis Presley's *Roustabout*, conceive the notion of building a motorcycle Wall of Death. Vinnie's wife Nora (Catherine Byrne) looks on aghast, but not surprised.

Heavenly Pursuits is marked by some agreeable flights of fancy (the dull boy in Vic's class astonishes himself by suddenly spouting a list of motorcycle manufacturers); but here the crazy (though quite plausible) central notion is sustained with the confidence exhibited by the men themselves as, pole by pole and plank by plank, they erect their rickety edifice. The plot is buttressed by conventional shenanigans (madcap cross-border smuggling) and some stock secondary characters, but the sense of something real being built – a sense lacking in *Good Morning Babylon*, even during the brothers' construction of a prototype papier-mâché elephant – is movingly conveyed. The doomed, heroic futility of the rattling Wall is emphasised by the vast peat-cutters which roll past in silent indifference.

A ROOM WITH A VIEW (13 April 1989) is a comedy of manners beginning in the warm South with a stolen kiss in a cornfield near Florence. *Heat and Dust* (1982), James Ivory and Ruth Prawer Jhabvala's previous Film on Four, had at its centre a young woman far from home who decides to leave her husband and follow her heart. Forster's story opens with another young woman, Lucy Honeychurch (Helena Bonham Carter), far but not that far from home, on holiday in Italy under the sharp eye of her Aunt Charlotte. Then comes the kiss. Everything changes and, back in the blowy Home Counties, Lucy too eventually finds the courage to break for freedom. As Olivia succumbed to the experience of India, so Lucy, not yet married but soon to be engaged, succumbed to Italy – a handsome Englishman in a linen suit shapes a question mark from the vegetables on his dinner plate; a dark Italian is stabbed to death, a murder of passion, in the Piazza della Signoria; a packet of unwritten bloodstained postcards is consigned to the swollen Arno . . .

The first strength of *A Room with a View* derives from its performers, none of whom puts a foot wrong: from Simon Callow, as the plump Reverend Beebe casting himself into Forster's 'Sacred Lake' with his excited young friends; through Maggie Smith, as Lucy's spinster aunt fiddling helplessly with her change purse when it is time to pay the cabman; and Patrick Godfrey, as Mr Eager, chaplain of the Anglican Church of Florence, lecturing with pinched propriety to a group of tourists in Santa Croce ('Observe how Giotto in these frescoes – now unhappily ruined by restoration – is untroubled by the snares of anatomy and perspective'); to Daniel Day Lewis, as the storklike Cecil, Lucy's fiancé, the mother's boy of all mother's boys, with his monocle, his broken wrist and his reptilian superciliousness.

Its second strength, perhaps, is its determination not to be downhearted. Even Cecil, after his rejection, and after shaking hands with Lucy, does not allow himself that indulgence. The film made a star of its leading lady and transformed two Puccini arias if not into pop songs then at least into tunes familiar to thousands who had never entered an opera house. Things work out at the end of *A Room with a View*. There are no teasingly unresolved mysteries, no glum prospects. The film is infused with an optimism not often encountered in Film on Four: it sets out to touch the heart, not wring it.

London's underbelly was explored in two puzzle films, **HIDDEN CITY** (9 March 1989) and **PING PONG** (23 March 1989). In the first, written and directed by Stephen Poliakoff, a statistician (Charles Dance) is led on a caper through the rubbish tips, industrial incinerators and secret tunnels of the capital by a young woman, a lowly film librarian, who believes she has discovered clues to a wartime kidnapping hidden in actuality footage edited into innocent instructional films on animal husbandry and hop-picking. In the second, directed by Po Chih Leong (Liverpool-born and previously active in Hong Kong features), a novice solicitor, Elaine Choi (Lucy Sheen), is set to follow another thread, through an extended squabbling Chinese family, the will of whose patriarch, Sam Wong, she has been assigned to execute.

Both films are at their best when dwelling on the unfamiliar. The tunnels of *Hidden City* are stuffed with yellowing papers and rusty film cans and guarded by equally forgotten young men as brusque as White Rabbits. And the Gerrard Street of *Ping Pong* is home not only to a hatchet-waving cook but also, less predictably, to an old man who jumped ship years ago, never registered on any official list and has as a result himself become another forgotten subterranean secret. At Sam Wong's wake the holymen argue about the wrong ceremonial tile having been broken. Both films are touched by fantasy. There is something of 1984 in Poliakoff's London where children, it seems, learn everything from screens. And broad-shouldered Elaine, with her Cockney manner and uncertain grasp of Chinese, becomes in the end a Warrior Woman from a kung-fu potboiler.

The two full-blown fantasies, **SHADEY** (28 April 1988) and **BORN OF FIRE** (14 April 1988), were on less certain ground. The first, directed by Philip Saville from a script by the playwright Snoo Wilson, is a camp entertainment about the fastidious manager of a body-repair shop (Anthony Sher) with the power to photograph other people's thoughts. He attempts, quiveringly, to sell his gift to finance a sex-change operation. The second, by Pakistani-born Jamil Dehlavi, concerns a seductive djinn and a naked devil and the virtuoso English flautist (Peter Firth) who is drawn to Turkey to confront them in order to learn the secret of his father's death. Raficq Abdullah's script is encased in mystical quotations. Hocus-pocus aside, however, the film uses an eerie mountain location with jagged caves and calcified rock-pools to considerable effect.

Striking a less sententious note was the Anglo-Australian film **THE FIRST KANGAROOS** (21 April 1988), about the formation of the NSW Rugby League and its first ramshackle tour of England in 1908. Written by the novelist Nigel Williams and directed by the documentarist Frank Cvitanovich (a former US pro-footballer), this somewhat overstretched comedy is most notable for the sympathy it extends to the aging star of Hunslet, Albert Goldthorpe (Dennis Waterman), who spends much of the film seated in the stands with the two morose members of his management committee contemplating the imminence of his defeat. The puppyish Australians, whose leading player is still tied to his mother's apron strings, are agreeably stoical. As the money trickles away they are cajoled into accepting more and more pinched conditions (they stoke the furnaces of the liner taking them to England). And much innocent fun is had at the expense of everything concerning Yorkshire.

PLAYING AWAY (4 May 1989), directed by Horace Ové, takes a bickering team of West Indian cricketers from Brixton to a friendly match, the climax of an African Famine Week, in the depths of Suffolk. The Londoners find themselves the butt of condescension and abuse, while the captain's daughter only narrowly escapes gang rape. Written by the playwright and novelist Caryl Phillips, the film concludes that each side has its share of personal difficulties. The match is won by the visitors thanks to some eccentric umpiring from a touched old colonial (Robert Urquhart). The relationship in *Arthur's Hallowed Ground* between the ill-tempered groundsman and the quiet black youth assigned to help him was a less pumped-up racial encounter.

Set on the island of Rhodes, **HIGH SEASON** (2 March 1989) was another comedy which incidentally pitched one culture against another. Modern Greece is again good for nothing but tourism; and Penelope (Irene Papas), the fiery widow of a resistance hero, will have none of it, even though her son Yanni insists on turning the family shop into the 'Lord Byron' minimarket. Co-written by Mark Peploe (*The Last Emperor*, 1987) and his sister, the director Clare Peploe, the film makes much of its location but less of its mare's nest of plot threads. Matters centre on an aging homosexual spy, Basil Sharp (Sebastian Shaw), who is about to be unmasked. To the island comes young Rick Lamb of the FO (Kenneth Branagh), whose task it will be to escort Basil, an art historian, to retirement in the East. Rick has a wife, Carol, who, naturally enough, Yanni regards as a sign that the Lord Byron will prosper . . . There is a commotion over an ancient vase and the plot climaxes with the unveiling of a statue to the Unknown Tourist in the village square, the final straw for poor Penelope.

THE NATURE OF THE BEAST (30 March 1989), directed by Franco Rosso, is set in a Lancashire town where the mill is under threat and an unseen creature stalks the surrounding moorland. Adapted by Janni Howker from her prizewinning novel, the film sketches a bleak sympathetic portrait of a motherless boy living with his father and grandfather on an anonymous estate. The beast is real enough, it makes short work of grandpa Chunder's hens; but (in a departure from the novel) it may also

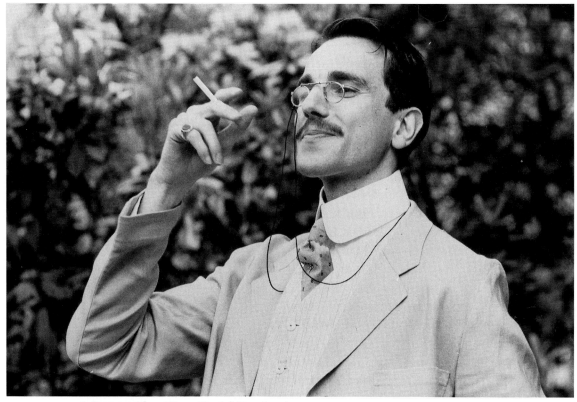

A Room with a View: Daniel Day Lewis

Prick Up Your Ears: Gary Oldman

Comrades: Philip Davis

Dance with a Stranger: Miranda Richardson, Rupert Everett

be a malevolent cousin of the unseen force menacing the mill. The film is less authentic and raw than *Vagabonde*, the story of a lost and angry beggar girl, but at times one feels a gust of the same chill realism.

Walter's moment of truth arrived when a policeman entered his parents' bedroom. His mother had been dead for several days and her body was covered in pigeon droppings. Walter had let loose his father's birds to keep her company. Stephen Frears's third Film on Four, PRICK UP YOUR EARS (16 March 1989), begins with another policeman ('Dear, oh dear, somebody here's been playing silly buggers!') coming upon another scene of Grand Guignol. Kenneth Halliwell lies beside the corpse of the playwright Joe (formerly John) Orton on the floor of their Islington bedsit.

The film was adapted by Alan Bennett from Orton's biography and like Orton's comedies set out to entertain with a cheek more innocent than shocking. Performed with brio by Gary Oldman and, particularly, Alfred Molina as the bald, longfaced, angrily frustrated Halliwell, it is equally powerful as a pen-portrait of London in the 50s and early 60s. The literary agent Peggy Ramsay (Vanessa Redgrave, happier here than as the schoolmistress in *Wetherby*) diligently explains to the American author John Lahr (and his angrily frustrated wife) the facts of Orton's life. 'The Festival of Britain?' Lahr queries. 'That's when it all came off the ration,' Peggy says. Everything, and notably sex.

The film is packed with sex, in public lavatories, on a beach in Morocco, on a spiral staircase in the London Underground, but not in the Islington bedsit. Here, imprisoned by walls overlaid with pictures stolen from library books, live an old married couple, one on the up-and-up, the other blighted by his total eclipse. The film is embellished with Bennett's characteristic asides: 'Get some clothes on!' Orton's mother (Julie Walters) yells at her son, adding – 'walking round like Sabu.' Beneath the volleying repartee, however, lies a tragedy of carefree self-destruction.

The fascination of Orton stems from the coldness of his heart. And the film underlines this with an absence of sentimentality apparent from the opening scene. Peggy Ramsay takes a breath, directs a queasy constable to the kitchen for a brandy, then lifts the officer's helmet, dabs at a spot of blood and places Orton's diary beneath her coat. Later, when Orton's prim brother-in-law from Leicester deprecates John's morals, his wife Leonie (Frances Barber) smartly pulls him up – the family, she says, never objected to Joe's royalties.

Buried inside **MONA LISA** (23 February 1989), directed by Neil Jordan, lies another tragedy, about a prostitute, Simone, secretly obsessed with a girl she once befriended and seemingly betrayed. It too ends in an eruption of violence, with the prostitute (Cathy Tyson) shooting Mortwell, the gangster who destroyed her girlfriend. Mortwell (Michael Caine) falls leaving a skidmark of blood on the wall of an airy Brighton hotel room; a white rabbit jumps from his arms and hops delicately across the carpet. Simone's chauffeur George, the hero, stands horror-struck. This is not the end, however. George (Bob Hoskins) returns to London, tells the story to his kindly friend Thomas and then finds consolation in the love of his own daughter (Zoe Nathenson). Thomas, George and the girl are last seen in a park, tripping away from the camera in an impromptu danceline.

Hidden City begins with a skimming shot along the dead water of an anonymous canal; *Mona Lisa* with George marching across Waterloo Bridge at sunrise to the accompaniment of Nat 'King' Cole. Photographed by Roger Pratt and co-scripted by David Leland, *Mona Lisa* has an oiled action and a smooth finish reminiscent of *The Company of Wolves*. The film has, however, a matter-of-fact way with violence and touches of human rather than fantastic poetry (notably in Robbie Coltrane's Thomas with his taste for the twists of pulp thrillers) which place it more securely in the territory of Neil Jordan's first feature, *Angel*, with its equally attractive but less spirited no-hope hero.

Mike Newell directed two films for Film on Four in 1988–89. In 50s Britain homosexuality merited imprisonment and murder the gallows. **DANCE WITH A STRANGER** (3 March 1988), written by Shelagh Delaney, was drawn from the true story of Ruth Ellis, who was hanged in Holloway jail on 13 July 1955. She had shot her inconstant lover David Blakely outside a Hampstead pub and then shot him again as he lay on the ground. Ruth fired less ostentatiously than Simone, but with the same impetuous indifference.

Prick Up Your Ears evoked an England returning to life: couples tossing under blankets on the Embankment; a famous literary agent addressing a louche stranger in tee-shirt and army-surplus cap with unforced affection. *Dance with a Stranger* dealt vividly with another side of English life: the milieu of spivs; the tired, rather forced glamour of the motor-racing circuit; the dusty, buttoned-up middle classes. Ruth Ellis manages a vulgar overdecorated club. And she has a manner useful for dealing with drunks. She will sleep with anyone, habit having turned to compulsion, but shows no real enthusiasm for the act of love. Joe

Orton was a greyhound in the slips when it came to sex.

The film ends simply and eloquently with Ruth's voice reading a letter to Blakely's mother. And here, as throughout, Miranda Richardson gives an exact inflection to every syllable. She displays neither fear nor remorse, but beneath the distant conventional language, a curious acceptance of what has happened and what awaits her. Joe Orton's death was a tragedy. Why didn't Halliwell read his diary, Orton asked repeatedly, as if willing his friend to jealousy; it contained all his sexual escapades. For a manipulative woman, Ruth it seemed understood little and controlled nothing; but her life is moving and pitiful thanks to the restraint and dispassion with which it is anatomised.

Mike Newell's second film, **THE GOOD FATHER** (12 May 1988), adapted by Christopher Hampton from Peter Prince's novel, is about a man, Bill Hooper, who becomes obsessed with the wife he has left and the son he has lost. Bill takes vicarious revenge by persuading an acquaintance, Roger, to use the majesty of the law to punish his own errant wife. Anthony Hopkins plays the knotted, vengeful Bill and Jim Broadbent his meek ally. *Dance with a Stranger* imposed nothing on its story. To see Ruth and the owner of the drinking club (Stratford Johns) counting the night's takings in a mean room in a domestic house was to experience the uncertain falsity of the club and those who patronised it. In *The Good Father*, Roger reads an article published by his wife in 'the quarterly bulletin of the Crouch End Women's Collective'. The mockery reflects badly on Roger; but the subtext does little to blunt the obviousness of the assault. The film boils with Bill's unfocused indignation, but boils perhaps a little too relentlessly. Simon Callow makes a meal of his role as a cynical barrister, delighted at the speed with which he can bring Roger's case before a suitably misogynist judge; and Miriam Margolyes, at the other extreme, offers a caricature of self-righteous feminism. In the end it turns out it was their son who had come between Bill and his wife . . .

Of greater subtlety, though in its own way no less forthright, was Colin Gregg's **LAMB** (24 March 1988), adapted by Bernard MacLaverty from his own novel. After the death of his father, Brother Sebastian, a teacher, becomes obsessed with one of his pupils, a mistreated epileptic boy. On impulse and with an advance on his modest inheritance, Sebastian (Liam Neeson) takes the boy Owen (Hugh O'Conor) from the blighted school where they are both imprisoned on the clean windswept coast of Galway. Their flight ends in London, and here with slow, agonising inevitability the priest is forced to confront the implications of what he has done. They return to Ireland and Sebastian drowns Owen in a terrible misguided act of love. He can drown the boy, but he cannot of course drown himself.

The focus of Colin Gregg's first Film on Four, *Remembrance*, was Daniel White (Gary Oldman, memorable in an almost invisible part) and his flight from the Army to avoid a posting to Northern Ireland. The fragmentation of the earlier film has been avoided here in favour of a plain narrative. The tone of melancholy, however – of the priest and the boy trapped in a rooming-house quite as desolate as the cold Plymouth hotel which confined the naval rating and his pregnant wife – is equally enveloping. *Lamb* contains a memorably bitten-back performance by Ian Bannen as the calloused headmaster Brother Benedict. At one point he is called on to give Sebastian a cursory lecture. This is not, one imagines, the first young man to have sat in the headmaster's study and confessed to a loss of faith; and as he delivers his strictures Brother Benedict gets on with the practical (insulting) business of trimming his toenails. The significance of this scene is that Sebastian is treated as a child, which of course he is. His attempt to become a man, the good father to an unbiddable boy, is doomed from the start.

Four 1988–89 films dealt with immigration. **MILK AND HONEY** (18 May 1989) was an Anglo-Canadian production, directed and co-produced by the married couple Glen Salzman and Rebecca Yates, about a young woman, Joanna, who leaves her son in Jamaica in the care of his grandmother and travels to Toronto to work as a nanny. The script, developed at Robert Redford's Sundance Institute, was by Salzman and the Jamaican playwright Trevor Rhone. The result, not unlike *El Norte*, is a broad unambiguous story about exploitation and subterfuge. The nanny is quiet, strong and believable; though Josette Simon's performance seems at odds sometimes with the stock melodrama. Matters end with the Canadian headmaster who has seduced Joanna and, it seems, betrayed her to the immigration authorities, splashing across a stream in Jamaica, the true land of milk and honey, and falling happily into his loved one's arms.

The other three films had perhaps a more convincingly downbeat European tone. **LEAVE TO REMAIN** (11 May 1989), written by Rob Ritchie and Iraj Jannatie Ataie and directed by Les Blair, concerns the troubles of an Iranian student, Shahin (Meda Kidem), who contracts a marriage of convenience with an English oaf when the mullahs prevent the transfer of family money from Tehran. The film, set in London, has two strengths: its snapshots of English bureaucracy and its shadowy hints of the frozen world of Muslim fanaticism. Shahin and her husband present themselves to a sharp but ineffably weary Dover official who pokes about in Shahin's life much as the customs man in *Moonlighting* poked inside the bag of Polish hammers and cold chisels. In the end, raped and to her relief abandoned by her husband, Shahin accepts that there is no escape from politics and, like a soldier of the counter-revolution, prepares for her first protest demonstration.

Leave to Remain was produced in 1988 by Irving Teitelbaum. Two years earlier Teitelbaum had been executive producer on another film, FATHERLAND (20 April 1989), written by Trevor Griffiths and directed by Kenneth Loach, which propounded a more cynical view of the efficacy of protest and the dangers of compromise. This was something of a puzzle picture too. An East German singer, Klaus Drittemann (Gerulf Pannach), crosses to the West to sign a recording contract. His mother is a senior Party official and has been able perhaps to ease his escape from what a title identifies as 'actually existing socialism'. Drittemann has few illusions about the land of cocaine. The puzzle is his father, a former classical musician, now living a secret life in Cambridge. During the Spanish Civil War he was turned by the Nazis and during the Second World War had been responsible for the deaths of Dutch resistance fighters. All of which is uncovered by Drittemann with the help of a French journalist (Fabienne Babe) who turns out to be a covert Nazi-hunter. The father dies – suicide or murder? – before the journalist can get to him.

The interest of the film is not Trevor Griffiths's by-blows. Accepting his visa from an emollient West German culture minister, Drittemann makes plain his own position: 'What use is freedom if you can't get published? At least in the GDR they applauded my criticism.' And when he arrives in England a group of secondary-pickets is being harassed by the police. More arresting is Kenneth Loach's precise eye and low-key approach. The scene between Drittemann and his erect mother, her bleak office exactly registering her status and authority, speaks volumes. And there can be few more chilling examples of rapacious professional womanhood than Cristine Rose's Lucy Bernstein, the record-company executive who meets Drittemann at the West Berlin checkpoint and attempts without success to get him to sign her company's contract.

A Flame to the Phoenix ended with a Polish cavalry charge in September 1939. THE ROAD HOME (15 April 1989) begins in Germany at the end of the Second World War with young Jerzy being returned by the

The Belly of an Architect: Brian Dennehy

Red Cross to his mother Maria and his paternal grandparents living not uncomfortably in a large house near the Black Forest. The Polish Western Territory was then under the jurisdiction of the Red Army. Jerzy's father Stanislaw, a Polish cavalryman, disappeared in 1939. A flame is kept burning at night to guide him home ... Stanislaw is of course dead; but he does manifest himself (in the person of the English-born writer-director Jerzy Kaszubowski) in his son's dreams.

The Road Home, an Anglo-Polish production, with a Polish cast speaking German and Polish, focuses tight in on its historical moment, on a section of Poland sandwiched between its past, Germany, and its future, the Soviet Union. The film is heavily symbolic, with a threatening eagle making several appearances, and a white horse cantering about the countryside, the same horse perhaps on which Stanislaw was riding when glimpsed by Jerzy in a cinema newsreel on prewar Poland. The film ends with Jerzy and his stepfather Edward, a Polish government placeman, wandering in the forest after their lorry has been ambushed by partisans. Edward is terrified for his life. On several occasions Jerzy has imagined killing Edward; now is his opportunity. But the boy throws aside Edward's pistol. The white horse passes.

MASCHENKA (31 March 1988), directed by John Goldschmidt and adapted by John Mortimer from Vladimir Nabokov's first novel, is set in a Berlin boarding-house in the 1920s. But for the hero Ganin (Cary Elwes) reality resides in pre-Revolutionary Russia on the now lost family estate near St Petersburg where as a teenager he first fell in love. Ganin is dismayed to learn that the girl Maschenka (Irina Brook), to whom he failed to surrender his virginity, married the boorish mathematician Alfyrov, a fellow guest at the boarding-house, and that she is arriving shortly in Berlin.

The pension in *A Room with a View* with the Cockney Signora standing guard at the dining-room door was brought to life with a few strokes. Frau Dorn's Berlin establishment, with its gaggle of refugees, has an inanimate air; and the idyllic life of the past has something of the imposed feel of *Summer Lightning*, Film on Four's other adaptation from a Russian novel. As they are about to depart into exile, Ganin's father (Michael Gough) enquires of the butler, 'Oh, Yasha, perhaps you could arrange some caviar sandwiches.'

The echoes of feudalism are again heard, though with more conviction, in the adaptation of another novel, **A GATHERING OF OLD MEN** (19 May 1988), set in present-day Louisiana. A white farmer hollering murder chases Charlie, a black man, into the shack of Old Mathu. A shotgun pokes through the crack in the door and the white man, Beau Boutan, is unceremoniously shot dead. But before the Boutan clan organise a lynching, young Candy Marshall (Holly Hunter in full throat) assembles all the other ancient blacks living (as she sees it) under her protection. They are ordered to bring with them discharged shotguns. Then, inspired by Candy's example, each man confesses to the murder. Sheriff Mapes (Richard Widmark) settles down outside Mathu's shack to await developments.

The film, directed by Volker Schlöndorff, is a concise vignette about a stand-off. Mathu's porch is clustered with an array of distinguished actors – Louis Gossett Jr, Woody Strode, Tiger Haynes, Julius Harris – who take impassivity to the limit. The evocation of a hot day with nothing to do but go fishing, of a shack in front of which a large white man of no great consequence lies spreadeagled on his back, and of an imperturbable sheriff who having discovered that half-hearted intimidation has got him nowhere happily shares food with those he is about to arrest, is executed with an appropriate lack of display.

Directed by Imre Gyöngyössy and Barna Kabay, **YERMA** (8 April 1989) begins with the naked shepherds of San Isidro manhandling their flock across a fast stream. And a fit sense of communal fecundity is the key-note of this version of Lorca's tragedy of barrenness and fidelity. In *The King and the Queen*, at the beginning of the Spanish Civil War, the Duchess of Alquezar was penned in a tower to which her husband and suitor came for sexual gratification. Her servant Rómulo burned inwardly. Gudrun Landgrebe as Yerma has a somewhat cool and distant northern manner and it is hard to believe, as one believed of Nuria Espert's Duchess, that sensuality, either sexual or maternal, is the well of her being. She nevertheless embodies the heroine's contained misery with sometimes moving simplicity. 'I want to drink but there is no water.'

THE BELLY OF AN ARCHITECT (16 February 1989), Peter Greenaway's third contribution to Film on Four, also discourses on the theme of fecundity and barrenness, of grand buildings conceived but never built and ancient buildings preserved, guarded and floodlit but inexorably crumbling away. At the heart of the film is a real architect, the inspirational Etienne-Louis Boullée (1728–99), in tribute to whom another (fictional) architect, Stourley Kracklite of Chicago, is mounting an expensive, long-planned, immensely ambitious exhibition.

The exhibition, in the Victor Emmanuel building, Rome, is being co-ordinated by another architect, the Italian Io Speckler. But Speckler's son Caspasian, yet another architect, is diverting funds intended for the glorification of Boullée to the restoration of Mussolini's Foro Italico stadium. Kracklite, cuckolded by Caspasian and afflicted by terminal stomach pains, finally, after nine months, loses control of the exhibition, and at its opening, as his wife gives birth to their son, falls backwards to his death through a fanlight in the dome of the Vittoriano. There was a certain brittleness (and inhumanity) about the Draughtsman and the brothers Deuce, but in Stourley Kracklite (Brian Dennehy), over whose stomach a photocopy of the heroic abdomen of the Emperor Augustus is at one point laid, Peter Greenaway created perhaps the most complete and human, yet authentically larger-than-life character so far seen in Film on Four.

Kracklite has wit, authority, physical presence, and is placed, in his fifty-fifth year at the turning-point of his personal and professional life, in a situation filled with intrigue, comedy and passion which tests and tempers him to the very limit. The subject, in short, is a great one and is matched by the nobility of Sacha Vierny's photography, of the archi-tecture of Rome, naturally, but also of the punctuating personal set pieces, the opening birthday party against the backdrop of the Pantheon and later Kracklite's walk along an airy hospital gallery flanked by busts of the Emperors during which he is gently given his death warrant.

The film opens with Stourley and his young wife Louisa (Chloe Webb) making love, silhouetted against the large window of a speeding train carrying them across the Italian frontier to Rome: a cinema screen within another screen, the framed screen itself in motion in a stateless limbo. There is a cut to a travelling shot along a line of marble memorial plaques. The simplicity and density of this opening – here are contained the themes of generation and death, passing in a few seconds of self-referential cinematic time – is carried into the film as a whole with its swooping magical connections between the contours of architecture and those of the human body, the poisoned stomach and the fertile womb.

Greenaway's skills are arrayed with exhilarating energy in the birth-day scene. Kracklite's darting wit is on full display. The duplicity of the Italians is foreshadowed. A cake of white icing is produced, a copy of Boullée's memorial building to Isaac Newton, inspired by the Pantheon. 'In England,' Kracklite says, 'architects are respected. Sir Christopher Wren, complete with his portrait, buildings and plans, appears on the English fifty-pound note – architects are expensive – but . . . Sir Isaac Newton, the subject of this cake, is in every Englishman's wallet . . . he's on the English one-pound note. I always carry one for good luck. A man who discovered gravity and thus successfully secured our feet to the ground is a good companion. In fixing us to the earth, he enabled us – with equanimity – to permit our heads to remain in the clouds.'

Kracklite challenges his hosts to find the reference to gravity on his good-luck charm. They fail and he points to a delicate apple-blossom: from the majesty of the Pantheon to an engraved detail on a banknote. Kracklite later loses his one-pound note. He will not perhaps be able to get another, for they are (and Greenaway can never resist a pun) drop-ping out of circulation. Then there among the ruins of the cake, the guests having departed, is the burning worthless banknote with its tiny elegant laconic English detail soon to vanish forever.

Mrinal Sen's **GENESIS** (18 March 1989) is set in a ruined isolated village in Bengal. Here the buildings were never much in the first place. A nameless Farmer and Weaver flee from servitude and set to work on their own account; a brightly robed Trader, his camel hung with bells, acts as the middleman to their needs. But then a Woman, a destitute young widow, arrives, and the harmony, as the Trader predicted, is broken. The Woman (Shabana Azmi) becomes pregnant. But which of the men is the father? The film ends with the village overrun by the servants of its absentee landlord and an immense earthmover coming to create something – though one can hardly believe it will be a second Rome. This stark parable is as distant from *The Belly of an Architect* as the Pantheon is from an apple-blossom; but it speaks from the other side of the world with the same undeniable urgency.

At the beginning of **THE SACRIFICE** (18 February 1989), written and directed by the Russian émigré Andrei Tarkovsky, Alexander (Erland Josephson), a successful man of letters, plants a leafless tree by the seashore to mark his fiftieth birthday. With faith and patience, and daily watering, he tells his young son, the tree may blossom. At the end of the film, on the following morning, Alexander fulfils the pact he made with God during the night and burns down his house. The important thing, it seems to Alexander, in this moment of both clarity and madness, is not the cherished wooden house in which his son was born, and an exact model of which the boy aimed to give his father, but the pitiful tree, propped with large smooth stones but still tipping, which may one day become something – part perhaps of a more enduring house than the one consumed in flames.

Shot on the island of Gotland, *The Sacrifice* is a parable on faith. The Farmer and the Weaver existed on nothing and had at the start only disinterred skulls for company. Alexander and his family, who have also it seems retired from the world, live not exactly on nothing but with a tasteful lack of ostentation. One of Alexander's birthday presents is, however, a seventeenth-century map of the world, a framed original. Alexander reprimands the giver, Otto, for such a valuable present. A present should be a sacrifice, Otto the postman replies. The map of the world is destroyed with the house, a sacrificial thanksgiving, perhaps, that Europe itself has not been destroyed. In the night a nuclear catastrophe threatened and it was this which drove Alexander to his knees to make his pact with God.

The Sacrifice lacks the rounded finish of *The Belly of an Architect*; and Andrei Tarkovsky is not as unambiguous a moralist as Mrinal Sen. But this monumental film, Tarkovsky's last, has three marvellous distinguishing features. Its use of the long unbroken take, the uncanny effect of which is to make the spectator a participant in the action; its demonstration that sound – from the St Matthew Passion to regional Swedish cattle-calls – is as significant to the complete film-maker as vision; and its proof that the symbolic and the mystical can be made as 'real' as the natural.

The long takes used for Alexander's first walk from the shore to his house, with Otto riding beside him on a bicycle and his son weaving between them and finally playing a joke on the postman, and for the final sequence of the burning of the house, the return of the family from a walk and the capture of Alexander by ambulance men, are astonishing achievements. Similarly, the sound of Bach's exhortation to pity combined with a snaking shot up the thin tree at the centre of Leonardo's dark unfinished *Adoration of the Kings* has a commanding authority.

In the middle of the night, Otto urges Alexander to go to their neighbour Maria, a strange Icelandic woman, and to lie with her in order to save them all. The unexplained incongruity of this request becomes almost ludicrous when Alexander, on his way to the woman's house, falls off Otto's bicycle. But once inside the house, and once Maria has washed Alexander's hands and dried them on a folded linen towel, and they are locked in an embrace suspended in mid-air several feet above the bed, the strangeness evaporates in a moment of the purest and most entrancing mystery.

VIEWING FIGURES
1988/1989

	1st TX '000s	2nd TX '000s
DANCE WITH A STRANGER	*3 Mar 88* **6,017**	*7 Jun 90* **3,399**
HEAVENLY PURSUITS	*17 Mar 88* **5,531**	*21 Jun 90* **2,799**
LAMB	*24 Mar 88* **3,956**	*28 Jun 90* **2,807**
MASCHENKA	*31 Mar 88* **2,253**	*5 Jul 90* **1,374**
EAT THE PEACH	*7 Apr 88* **3,331**	*12 Jul 90* **1,997**
BORN OF FIRE	*14 Apr 88* **2,658**	*19 Jul 90* **1,456**
THE FIRST KANGAROOS	*21 Apr 88* **3,144**	
SHADEY	*28 Apr 88* **3,936**	*16 May 91* **2,435**
THE GOOD FATHER	*12 May 88* **3,735**	*10 Nov 88* **2,845**

A GATHERING OF OLD MEN	*19 May 88* **4,530**	*9 May 91* **1,874**
THE BELLY OF AN ARCHITECT	*16 Feb 89* **2,140**	*15 Aug 91* **1,357**
THE SACRIFICE	*18 Feb 89* **0,456**	
MONA LISA	*23 Feb 89* **7,818**	*30 May 91* **4,699**
HIGH SEASON	*2 Mar 89* **4,303**	*12 Sep 91* **2,552**
HIDDEN CITY	*9 Mar 89* **4,015**	*29 Aug 91* **3,007**
PRICK UP YOUR EARS	*16 Mar 89* **2,637**	*1 Aug 91* **1,412**
GENESIS	*18 Mar 89* **0,511**	
PING PONG	*23 Mar 89* **2,829**	
THE NATURE OF THE BEAST	*30 Mar 89* **4,161**	*23 May 91* **2,866**
GOOD MORNING BABYLON	*6 Apr 89* **2,782**	*5 Sep 91* **1,118**
YERMA	*8 Apr 89* **0,960**	
A ROOM WITH A VIEW	*13 Apr 89* **4,039**	*25 Jul 91* **2,313**
THE ROAD HOME	*15 Apr 89* **0,949**	
FATHERLAND	*20 Apr 89* **1,153**	*22 Aug 91* **0,619**
COMRADES	*27 Apr 89* **1,925**	*23 Dec 91* **1,309**
PLAYING AWAY	*4 May 89* **3,121**	*8 Aug 91* **2,023**
LEAVE TO REMAIN	*11 May 89* **1,650**	
MILK AND HONEY	*18 May 89* **3,575**	*19 Sep 91* **2,989**

Source: BARB

February 1990 Nelson Mandela, leader of the African National Congress, freed from jail. March Lithuania declares independence. Four hundred injured in poll-tax riot. April USSR accepts responsibility for the murder of 15,000 Polish officers at Katyn in 1940. Strangeways jail siege. May Latvia and Estonia declare independence. Boris Yeltsin elected President of the Russian Federation. June British Social Democratic Party disbands. July Yeltsin resigns from the CPSU. George Carey appointed Archbishop of Canterbury. August Iraq invades Kuwait. October German reunification. President Gorbachev awarded the Nobel Peace Prize. November Mary Robinson elected first woman President of Ireland. Mrs Thatcher resigns; John Major becomes PM. December Channel Tunnel breakthrough. Lech Walesa elected President of Poland. January 1991 Gulf War. February IRA mortar attack on Downing Street; Cabinet unharmed. Iraq driven from Kuwait. March Birmingham Six cleared. April Poll tax to be scrapped. May Rajiv Gandhi, PM of India, assassinated by Tamil

suicide bomber. June Civil war in Yugoslavia. August Soviet coup fails; effective power passes to the Russian Federation. November Beirut hostage Terry Waite freed. December Robert Maxwell dies and his business empire collapses. President Gorbachev resigns; Soviet Union dissolves.

CHAPTER 5

❖

THANK YOU, ADOLF!

1990/1991

❖

DURING A HISTORY lesson in *Success Is the Best Revenge* (1984) pupils at a London secondary school paint the map of Europe 1945 with white correction fluid. In **HOPE AND GLORY** (28 April 1991), which begins on 3 September 1939, a teacher points at a linen roller-map of the world. 'Pink – pink – pink. What are the pink bits, Rohan?' 'They're ours, Miss,' replies the hero (Sebastian Rice Edwards). 'Yes, the British Empire,' the teacher says. 'And what fraction of the earth's surface is British?' A girl answers. 'Yes, two-fifths. *Ours*. And that's what the war is all about. Men are fighting and dying to save all the pink bits for you ungrateful little twerps.'

The pink bits could not be saved. But for Bill Rohan aged eight (a light self-portrait of the director John Boorman) the war was more about collecting shrapnel and smashing things up. That is, until his own home in suburban Rosehill Avenue caught fire – an accident while the family was at the beach – and a gang of ungrateful little twerps went scavenging among his possessions. All Bill saved, or rather the only thing he saved, was a box of lead soldiers with Merlin fused to King Arthur.

The film is notable for its sense of people doing their duty; of Bill's mother Grace, for instance, accepting the unhappiness of her marriage. Grace (Sarah Miles) and her sisters – Faith, Hope and Charity – have disappointed their tactless, irascible father, and he in turn misses no chance to discomfort them. But the idea that this might fracture the family never crosses anyone's mind. The film is also about the joyfulness and preposterousness (from a boy's point of view) of an island under siege: of a stray bomb landing in the river and providing a feast for tea; of reciting the nine times table in a gas mask ideal for blowing raspberries. 'We never used to sing much before the war, did we?' observes Grace's friend Molly (Susan Wooldridge). 'Not in the daytime anyway.'

Love should not be shut out, Grace tells her daughter Dawn, who is pregnant by a Canadian corporal. And the mother's voice is both urgent and angry. The melancholy at the film's heart is coloured, however, by streaks of peculiarly touching comedy. The caricatures are executed with style. Bill's headmaster (Gerald James) is a Welsh fire-breather: 'Guide Mr Churchill's hand in the cunning of war. Let our righteous shells smite down the Messerschmitts and the Fokkers. Lord, send troublesome dreams to Herr Hitler . . .'

But in Ian Bannen's grandfather, in whose house by the Thames the Rohans seek refuge after the fire, caricature is made to highlight and deepen the significance of family life. One morning grandfather calls for his gun to despatch a rat he has spotted eating his Brussels sprouts. He misses and there is an uneasy silence at the breakfast table. Then Bill finds the correct words. 'I think you hit him, Grandpa. He was limping when he ran off.' Deference surrenders to laughter.

The tone of *Hope and Glory* is expressed in the cry 'Thank you, Adolf!' Bill's school has taken a direct hit and for a moment anarchy reigns in the playground. The tone of **THE DRESSMAKER** (26 May 1991), however, is stifled and sometimes bitter. The script is by John McGrath from a novel by Beryl Bainbridge set on the outskirts of Liverpool in 1944; direction by Jim O'Brien (*The Jewel in the Crown*, Granada TV, 1984). Two sisters, Nellie, a ruling spinster (Joan Plowright), and Margo, a vivacious widow (Billie Whitelaw), have charge of their brother's orphaned niece, Rita (Jane Horrocks). The family home, where they sleep three to a bed, is cluttered with sacred ancestral furniture.

But here, it seems, love is best shut out. The shy niece takes up with Wesley, an American corporal. But Rita is no Dawn, who made her brother ink a stocking-seam on her bare leg. During an outing to the sea, Rita buries her mother's pearls in the sand. Wesley notices, says nothing and discreetly digs them up. (Before the fire which destroyed all her heirlooms, Grace Rohan found she could still perform handstands on the beach.) In the end, however, Wesley wearies of Rita's rebuffs and seeks comfort with aunt Margo. Nellie comes upon them and the unfortunate soldier ends up dead at the foot of the stairs. Nellie, a capable dressmaker, stitches him into a shroud and has Jack, her butcher brother, tip the corpse in Bootle dock.

Jack, with his slicked hair and leg-of-mutton features, was played by Peter Postlethwaite. In **DISTANT VOICES, STILL LIVES** (4 August 1991), also about family life in wartime Liverpool, Postlethwaite plays the father who dominated the childhood and youth of the director Terence Davies. *Hope and Glory* and *The Dressmaker* were ordered reminiscences; Davies's vivid memoir is, in a sense, a slideshow minus commentary. Time as an agent of change is meaningless in this brief, distilled film, made in two consecutive parts (*Distant Voices* and *Still Lives*) which were then joined. Events are ordered subconsciously, however, by the influence of Tommy, the volcanic father – in life, on his deathbed and long afterwards.

In *Letter to Brezhnev*, the Liverpool girls Teresa and Elaine, the grandchildren of Tommy Davies's generation, chatter their way through life. Their parents accept their waywardness. Tommy, however, is a real tyrant. Film on Four has produced no other quite like him. He thumps his frail wife (Freda Dowie) with a broom handle and tries to squeeze the life from his daughters (Angela Walsh and Lorraine Ashbourne) and his son (Dean Williams). But he cannot prevent them singing. They sing wherever they happen to be. And whoever happens to be there joins in. Everyone knows the words: they mean something and have a transforming power. Through this singing Tommy is defeated. Liverpool girls of the 40s and 50s were as forward as those of the 80s. But here they stand straight, and come straight off the screen.

Nothing extraordinary happens in *Distant Voices, Still Lives*. There are births, deaths and marriages. The father suddenly demolishes a table laid for tea; his son, now in khaki, squares the account. But the particularity of one house, its narrow flight of stairs and its front-door opening on to a pavement, is exactly caught. The rituals may be universal but this is a community of individuals (women to the front) who know who they are and where they came from. The film reveals no more than we need to know, less perhaps. (The father at the end remains a threatening mystery who lives on in the ghostly presence of his looming brother.) But it disturbs and moves us by its mastery of the tableau and the exactitude of its editing.

In 1990–91 Channel 4 transmitted forty-two new films on Film on Four. Twenty-three were set in the present and fifteen in the past; two were outside time and two were divided between past and present. Twenty films were located in England: three in the South, spread between Sussex, Suffolk, Wiltshire and Cambridge; eight chiefly or exclusively in London; and nine in the North, two each in Liverpool, Manchester and the Yorkshire countryside, and one each in Bradford, North Shields (with a bucketing excursion into the North Sea) and on the Northumberland moors. Three films were set in the Republic of Ireland, two in Scotland and two in Wales. Fifteen films took place outside the British Isles: in Greece and Portugal (two each), France, West Germany, Switzerland, Spain, the Netherlands, Denmark, Norway, Canada, the United States, Kenya and South Africa.

In addition to *The Dressmaker*, twelve films were adapted from novels, stories or plays: Bruce Chatwin's *On the Black Hill*, Ruth Rendell's *Tree of Hands*, Barry Unsworth's *Pascali's Island*, Lars Molin's *The Bomb*, E. M. Forster's *Maurice*, J. R. Ackerley's *We Think the World of You*, J. L. Carr's *A Month in the Country*, James Joyce's *The Dead*, Osman Sahin's *The White Ox* (*The Mirror*), Herman Bang's *Along the Road* (*Katinka*), Manfred Karge's *Conquest of the South Pole* and Andrea Dunbar's *Rita, Sue and Bob too*. The plots of fifteen of the forty-two films were fuelled by violence, political intrigue, a desire to run away or an inability to escape. Two films, *A World Apart* and *Lorca – Death of a Poet*, centred on real people in real places at critical moments in history, South Africa in the 60s and Granada at the beginning of the Spanish Civil War; another, *The Kitchen Toto*, looked at a moment of British colonial history through the eyes of a fictional Kikuyu servant boy; and a fourth, *The Dream*, dramatised a judicial scandal in North Friesland in the 1890s.

Two films, the comedy *High Hopes* and the psychodrama *Conquest of the South Pole*, considered how to survive the wintry economic climate of London and Leith. The problems of winning a film role in Canada and mounting a one-man show in Paris were treated in *Speaking Parts* and *Hôtel du Paradis*; and the disposal of husbands (with the help of a moonstruck coroner) was one theme of Peter Greenaway's *Drowning by Numbers*. Four films were frostbitten love stories: *Maurice*, *We Think the World of You*, *A Month in the Country* and *Wild Flowers*; and two, *Katinka* and *The Dead*, concerned love's denial and love's endurance. As well as the domestic stories of *Hope and Glory*, *The Dressmaker* and *Distant Voices*, there were two Welsh family sagas: *Angry Earth*, the story of an indomitable miner's wife, and *On the Black Hill*, about identical twins who never shift from the farm on which they were born.

In Karl Francis's first Film on Four, *Giro City* (1982), modern big business attempts to turn a Welsh farmer from his land. In his second, **ANGRY**

EARTH (22 September 1991), hard-faced mine-owners repossess the home of a widow and her children. A woman, Gwen (Sue Roderick), lies quietly in hospital. She is a hundred years old, but the cameras and the fuss have come too late. Her mind runs to the past. When she needed real help, a pension for the service her husbands had given the nation, she received nothing. Both her men died in the mines before the First World War. 'Solomon in all his glory was not arrayed as one of these,' says Evan, her second husband, as a group of miners is lowered underground. *Angry Earth* ends with a shot of headstones to those who died in the Senghenydd colliery explosion of 14 October 1913.

The world is divided between us and them. The miners – the Welsh miners – are on the side of the angels. Anyone who stands against them deserves everything he gets. An English soldier rapes Gwen on a hillside; but before submitting she lays her baby on the grass beside her; later Gwen's son Guto lures the assailant into an animal trap and throws in beside him a bag containing a large venomous snake. ON THE BLACK HILL (3 May 1990), written and directed by Andrew Grieve, is also about the right to security of tenure. Amos Jones, a tenant farmer (Bob Peck), feuds with his neighbour. Lambs are killed, cattle are eviscerated, a barn is burned. On the death of the landlord, Amos bids to purchase his farm, 'The Vision'. But Watkins, his enemy, forces up the price only to drop out with a smirk when the damage has been done. Amos is at times a man possessed. 'I want none of your *filthy* Indian food,' he cries, flinging his wife's meal on the floor. The daughter of an English clergyman, she has seen a wider world. Amos is resolutely chapel.

Welsh suspicions about what the English may try to serve them is evident in both these uneven, impassioned films. During the First World War, Benjamin, one of Amos's twin sons, is double-crossed by an Englishman and taken in chains to Hereford barracks where he is beaten on the parade ground. When their parents die, the twins (Mike and Robert Gwilym) cleave to their inheritance. Neither marries. Like Nellie and Margo in *The Dressmaker*, they sleep in the same bed. They remain cocooned until the very end, when they are saved from themselves by an outsider, their nephew, someone on whom they can lavish affection and to whom they can leave The Vision. The film's abiding image, however, is of queer, backward-looking distrust.

WILD FLOWERS (15 March 1990) begins with an old woman washing her daughter's corpse. Suddenly she administers a resounding slap. 'Ma hands itched to do that!' When, after her first husband's death, Gwen took the job of undertaker's assistant, she washed the dead and released their bowels with loving reverence. Robert Smith's film, however, set in a tight Scottish coastal community, concerns the necessity of irreverence. Annie (Colette O'Neil), a woman who loves women, is daggers drawn with her widowed mother Marguerite (Sheila Keith), who in her own way is as terrifying and unforgiving as Tommy in *Distant Voices, Still Lives*. Annie was a child of her mother's middle age; Marguerite has laid out all four of Annie's brothers. At the centre of this intense, unexpected film, scripted by Sharman Macdonald and handsomely photographed by Witold Stok, is Annie's son Angus (Stevan Rimkus), who has returned home on a visit with his friend Sadie from Edinburgh.

But Angus lacks mettle. He adores nothing so much as the sweet sound of his own singing voice. And Annie finds herself compelled to save Sadie (Beatie Edney), a fellow free spirit, from this fastidious young man. The film acts like a measure of neat whisky and has a keen nose for the odour of Scotch propriety. Adapted from a German play and transposed to Leith docks, **CONQUEST OF THE SOUTH POLE** (26 April 1990) has, likewise, no time for propriety. With nothing to do and no prospects, Sloopianek (Stevan Rimkus, now decisiveness itself) persuades four friends to re-enact Roald Amundsen's great adventure of 1911. I read a book, Sloopianek tells 'Penguin', who has a rope round his neck and intends to jump to his death because he has no job, about a group of Frenchmen suffering from an affliction called '*lenny*'.

Penguin jumps, but the rope breaks. And what follows is a vigorous, doomed but sometimes joltingly tender attempt by the young men to banish boredom and regain the will to live. Gillies MacKinnon's first feature is full of rough humour. Poor Penguin (Ewen Bremner) with his blue strip of upright hair is sat upon after his botched suicide and compelled to eat a quantity of fortifying hard-boiled eggs. The journey to the Pole is inventively staged amid billowing white sheets on a clothes-line and in the fissures between the tables of a chip shop. Penguin takes the role of Bjaaland, the champion skier. When he falls into a crevasse someone shouts, 'What's it like?' 'Bottomless,' he replies. The final conquest, after many setbacks, is upon Arthur's Seat.

The hero of Mike Leigh's second Film on Four, **HIGH HOPES** (1 March 1990), is Cyril Bender (Philip Davis), a kindhearted motorcycle despatch-rider. He is the spirit of armchair republicanism: 'The day they machine-gun the Royal Family I'll cut my hair and put a tie on.' He lives with Shirley (Ruth Sheen), a hardworking council gardener, but will not father a child until some modest demands have been met. 'I want everyone to have enough to eat, places to live, jobs.' His sincerity is undeniable, but his absolutism, as Shirley finally convinces him, is daft. They possess a huge cactus named 'Fatcher'. 'It pricks your bum every time you pass it.' Their pleasures are at this uncomplicated level. Absurdities amuse them.

Pitted against them are Cyril's sister Valerie (Heather Tobias), a shrieking hysteric, and her suffering husband Martin Burke (Philip Jackson), a lewd motor-salesman in a sheepskin jacket, and another appalling couple, the wealthy Boothe-Braines (Lesley Manville and David Bamber), who live in a gentrified terrace house next to Cyril's mother (Edna Doré), the street's last council tenant. 'Chop-chop!' orders put-upon Mrs Boothe-Braine as old Mrs Bender, who has forgotten her keys, hobbles up the front steps to telephone for help. Even more than *Meantime* (1983), Mike Leigh's first Film on Four, *High Hopes* is a potent mix of unforgiving caricature, natural tenderness and splenetic farce. Its energy is exhausting; but its gallery of grotesques, just as much as its quiet, unvarnished humanism, is impossible to ignore.

The couple at the centre of **SAMMY AND ROSIE GET LAID** (8 March 1990), written by Hanif Kureishi and directed by Stephen Frears, have nothing in common with Cyril and Shirley. They are middle-class, philandering, indifferent. Rosie (Frances Barber) is a bloodless social worker, Sammy (Ayub Khan Din) a successful accountant. 'I can't always mother you, baby,' Rosie tells Sammy with tender, withering pity as she departs for a night out with someone else. Johnny and Omar, the streetwise lovers who made something of the beautiful laundrette, had an innocence which Sammy and Rosie would neither have recognised nor valued.

King's Cross and Highgate Cemetery are home to Cyril and Shirley. The park where she works is worth tending. But Notting Hill and the squatters' camp under the Westway flyover, the unreal territory through which Sammy and Rosie move, shakes with incessant, surreal street-fighting. 'We've got a big job to do in some of those inner cities,' Mrs Thatcher declares over the opening desolate cityscape. And the film rather sledgehammers the message home.

Sammy's father Rafi (Shashi Kapoor), a charming but spectacularly corrupt Indian politician in flight from his enemies, comes to London to revisit an old flame, Alice (Claire Bloom), and to reassure himself that the England he loved as a student still exists. Alice, a beneficiary of the Thatcher years, lives in cool, leafy prosperity. Rafi cannot, however, close his eyes to the inner city, or to Sammy and Rosie's morals – and their naivety. The riots, Rosie says, are an affirmation of the human spirit. 'A kind of justice is being done.' At the end, Rafi hangs himself and Sammy and Rosie are jolted back (for a moment at least) into each other's arms.

Ribaldry is the keynote of **RITA, SUE AND BOB TOO** (10 May 1990), directed by Alan Clarke from an adaptation of two plays by Andrea Dunbar. The setting is a Bradford housing estate where high hopes are unknown. Two schoolgirls take up with Bob, a married man, who one night, instead of driving them straight home from babysitting, detours to a moorland parking spot and complacently takes down his trousers. Who will be first? The brassy girls later fall out when fair shares is taken off the menu. Driving to his mother-in-law's seventieth birthday party, Martin Burke calls on his forlorn inadequate girlfriend. She is distraught that he can only stay a moment and is unbuttoning his shirt the moment the door is shut. Bob is a cousin of Martin. Their functions, though, are quite different. Rita and Sue see Bob for what he is, a means to their pleasure, a ridiculous figure – giggled at behind his back – who finds their adolescent demands something of an uphill run.

When, in **WISH YOU WERE HERE** (15 February 1990), young Dave the bus conductor goes to bed with the heroine, Lynda Mansell, he cries out in almost immediate ecstasy, 'Any more fares, please!' And from then on Lynda has trouble taking any man seriously. For Rita and Sue sex is a lark; for Lynda it is silly (if necessary) and summed up by the image of a Jack Russell trotting along a respectable pavement in a seaside town with a spent condom in its teeth. Shirley in *High Hopes* longed for a baby and in the end was probably going to have one. Lynda has a baby by accident. Anxiety turns to delight. It is all hers, and most important – as she marches along the esplanade – one in the eye for all the useless, hypocritical men who all her life had pushed her about.

Personal Services (1987), written by David Leland, was freely based on the experiences of Cynthia Payne, England's most famous, and most workaday, modern brothel-keeper. *Wish You Were Here*, written and directed by Leland, was based, equally freely, on Mrs Payne's early life. The year is 1951 – the Festival of Britain – when sex came off the ration. And the film, designed by Caroline Amies (also responsible for the slightly earlier settings of *The Dressmaker*), has a powerful, if faintly theatrical, sense of the period. It is not perhaps as vividly theatrical as Anthony Pratt's main set for *Hope and Glory*, where Rosehill Avenue was complete with everything from gas-works to barrage balloons; but it does convey the atmosphere of an unheated garret above a flaking resort cinema and the bogus refinement of a 'Paris' tearoom where all the waitresses have learned their lines but might at any moment slip out of character.

Rita and Sue (Siobhan Finneran and Michelle Holmes) answer back with lumpish self-assurance. But Lynda (Emily Lloyd) betters the older generation, and men particularly, with subtle delight. A psychiatrist (Heathcote Williams), bowed, dishevelled and covered in cigarette-ash, faces Lynda across a desk and fails to extract from this bright teenager with her tossing locks an admission that she knows anything more than the standard nursery list of rude words. They are playing alphabet association and have reached the sixth letter. 'You must be one of the last people on God's earth who doesn't know,' the psychiatrist says irritably. 'Everyone knows a swear word beginning with the letter F.' 'Then what are you asking me for?' Lynda counters. 'Because I want to hear you say it.' '*You dirty old bugger!*'

THE BOMB (29 September 1990), written and directed by Helmut Christian Görlitz, is a multi-national film, which looks forward to the day when, in the wake of the new world order, nuclear proliferation is put on the agenda by a cracked but principled individual with access to enriched plutonium. The film – a dreadful warning – is set in the main square in Hamburg and shaped as a cliffhanger. Will the madman holding the world to ransom with his Heath Robinson device respond to his wife's pleas? Can the authorities, the greyest of grey German bureaucrats, prevent him from learning of the city's evacuation? The story ends as the timer ticks to zero. The city is evacuated and the bomb-maker, handcuffed in a hotel room overlooking the square, is to be the only symbolic martyr – this time.

In SHOOTING STARS (17 May 1990), three tykes kidnap a professional soccer player, Calvin Clarke (Gary McDonald), who has just been sold to Hamburg FC for £3 million. The esprit which marked *Letter to Brezhnev*, Chris Bernard's first Film on Four, wears somewhat thin in this follow-up, written by Barry Hines (*Kes*, 1969). Gary (Chris Hargreaves), leader of the trio, is a petty thief tipped into the big time by accident. His girlfriend wins a radio quiz for which the prize is a night out with Calvin at the Millionaire Club. Neither is accustomed to this artificial glamour, and Calvin's thoughts are occupied by his unwilling transfer. Outside the club, Gary is unable to contain his jealousy. Calvin is knocked down and – 'Why not, we've got nothing to lose' – bundled off to a disused flat.

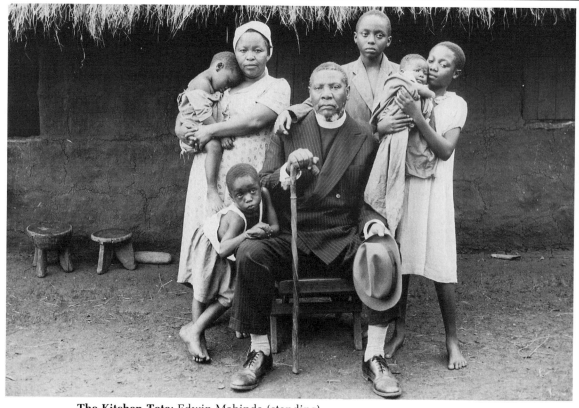

The Kitchen Toto: Edwin Mahinda (standing)

Distant Voices, Still Lives: Angela Walsh

The Dead: Donal McCann (centre)

We Think the World of You: Gary Oldman (left), Alan Bates

The twist is that Calvin is no class traitor. The soul of patience, he even gives the youngest kidnapper some ball practice. But for soccer, he might have been Gary, earning pocket-money hawking video-cameras to a fence. The escapade ends in chaos. Calvin, though, lacks the heart to turn in the boys. The three kidnappers, it seems, know what is right: they were prepared to squeeze City football club; but when it comes to real money – from Calvin's pocket – which bought them all a Chinese take-away, they are scrupulous in returning the change.

Another bizarre kidnapping takes place in TREE OF HANDS (2 June 1991), directed by Giles Foster from an adaptation by Gordon Williams of a Ruth Rendell mystery. The manic depressive Marsha (Lauren Bacall) pays an inconvenient call on her daughter Benet (Helen Shaver), the author of a new book, *The Marriage Knot*, and a single mother who has recently moved house to Hampstead. Benet's young son dies unexpectedly, after going into hospital with suspected croup, and Marsha, to her daughter's dismay, picks up a replacement child in the park. Marsha then has a fit of the vapours and announces she is flying home to Florida. The new little boy, whose real mother (Kate Hardie) is in the habit of holding a pistol to her lover's head, seems content with his new home, and Benet is caught in a moral and emotional bind when she misses the first opportunity to confess Marsha's crime. The film ends in a melodramatic hail of bullets and, as in *Shooting Stars*, conventional justice is ironically turned on its head.

Two more conventional small-scale thrillers were SMACK AND THISTLE (19 May 1991), written and directed by Tunde Ikoli, and THE FINAL FRAME (12 April 1990), directed by Paul Oremland and written by Howard Wakeling (co-author of *The Disappearance of Harry*). The first concerns Abel (Charlie Caine), a black ex-con with the bearing of a self-confident male model who is determined to start a new life as a plumber. Through a chain of circumstances, involving a stolen briefcase containing the papers of a compromising business deal, he falls in with the upper-crust Elizabeth (Rosalind Bennett), a drug-addict too confused to know where she is going. They take to the road and find themselves. The second film is about a freelance video-reporter who sees a pop star killed by a bomb at an animal-rights concert and goes down a twisting trail which ends in his own death.

All three thrillers have a touch of the fantastical, but what they lack, since each tests credibility to the limit – and what a similarly unreal thriller such as *Mona Lisa* does have – is a twist of ironic humour. The fantastical is put to the test, too, in VROOM (22 March 1990), written by

Jim Cartwright and directed by Beeban Kidron. This is a whimsical picture about following your dreams. Jake (Clive Owen), a handsome young Lancastrian, as pleased with his looks as Angus in *Wild Flowers* was pleased with his voice, falls in love with Susan (Diana Quick), a separated *femme fatale.* 'They might think I'm your mother taking you on an outing,' Susan says when Jake asks her on a date to Blackpool. But this only whets his appetite.

Jake and his friend Ringe have for four years been secretly refurbishing a large pink-and-chrome motorcar. Here is an opportunity worthy of the machine. The car is in a garage in the countryside: a pull on a rope and the walls and roof collapse outwards. The magic carpet is revealed and off – away from everything – the three of them happily roar. After a number of small adventures, Susan concludes that this cannot go on. Her house, she learns, is being sold off. Jake is furious at this betrayal. 'I can't catch up to you, Jake,' Susan confesses. At which Jake and the pink chariot takes off into the sky . . .

LADDER OF SWORDS (11 August 1991) ends with the hero, Don Demarco (Martin Shaw), a circus performer named the 'Shogun Warrior', shooting an arrow at a box – the sides of which collapse like the garage in *Vroom* – and releasing a flock of doves. The whimsy in Norman Hull's first feature is, however, a counterpoint to a solidly grounded story set in the Northumberland countryside. At the start, Demarco is not the Shogun Warrior, but one of the 'Three Dees', the others being his explosive, unreliable wife, Denise (Eleanor David), and an omnivorous bear called Daley.

The film's strength is its ability to mix convincingly the real – the chill of the moor and a foursquare character such as Alice Howard (Juliet Stevenson), the woman with whom Don takes up after Denise's departure and Daley's death – with the elegantly off-centre – the policeman Atherton (Bob Peck), obsessed with nailing the ex-con Demarco, becomes the butt of the squad-room when he digs up the moor looking for Denise's body only to find the remains of poor Daley. Neil Clarke's script does not perhaps add up to much more than an honest wish to entertain. But like the best circus acts, it exemplifies the art of exiting on a cymbal clash.

BEARSKIN (29 September 1991), by Ann and Eduardo Guedes, is subtitled 'an urban fairytale'. Johnny Fortune (Damon Lowry), a hustler fleeing an angry gambler, hooks up with Silva (Tom Waits), a boxer who faked his death in Los Angeles and has restarted life in London as a Punch-

and-Judy man. Johnny, encased in a bearskin, performs Silva's warm-up routine. Silva's mute partner, Laura (Julia Britton), is the daughter of the mournful Mrs J. – for 'Jackdaw' (Isabel Ruth) – with whom Johnny has taken refuge. Mrs J. presides over an immense warehouse (one of Film on Four's most striking set-pieces) filled with costumes. They are never hired, but like a miser's useless horde must forever be counted and re-counted. Mrs J., it seems, has been in decline since Laura left her for Silva.

Photographed by Michael Coulter, the film is a revenge drama encased in a fastidious, velvety shadow-play on camouflage and role-playing. Maurice Hatton's political thriller **AMERICAN ROULETTE** (18 August 1991) has a more playful tone and contains a less coded message. Carlos (Andy Garcia) is the president-in-exile of an oppressed South American nation. He is in London, a step ahead of the assassins, to receive a donation from well-wishers. In his black tie, white shirt and double-breasted suit he is the image of cool responsibility. But he is unsure if he can sustain the role. He has a second vocation as a poet (his lines are borrowed from the Chilean Pablo Neruda). But in the end, after a bloodless coup, Carlos opts for politics over poetry. The English love-interest (Kitty Aldridge) softens the blow. She promises to visit him. But, she adds, 'I pay my own way, remember.'

After years of less cushioned exile, the American James 'Doc' Matter (Paul McIsaac) finds himself in a riverside shack in Lisbon. He begins his annual letter to Rozzie, his former wife. **DOC'S KINGDOM** (13 October 1990), written and directed by Robert Kramer, then leads us – cinéma-vérité style – back into the past. Doc's kingdom has been the world. And the film is redolent of the 60s when meandering reminiscence was sanctified. Indeed, Doc might well have been a character in *Milestones* (1975), Kramer's long documentary fiction about 60s American activism.

He worked in a weedkiller plant; was jailed; left the organisation (the political underground); spent time in Africa in a 'permanent war zone'; contracted a disease which was never diagnosed. Now, aged forty-six (his face showing the hammering of experience), he has created a new identity as a hospital doctor. From New York comes Jimmy, the son he has never seen. He was conceived while Doc was in jail – in the chaplain's office. Jimmy brings news of Rozzie's death. Their meeting settles only that they need never meet again.

Alain Tanner's **NO MAN'S LAND** (15 February 1990) is set on the Franco-Swiss frontier, in another odd moment of dead time. The shaggy story concerns a group of amateur smugglers who trail back and forth between the two countries, often by the slow local bus. Like Tanner's first Film on Four, *In the White City* (1983), about a Swiss ship's engineer trapped in Lisbon and somehow unable to make a move, *No Man's Land* is about the grip of habit and the effort of change.

The smugglers – a cowman, an Algerian girl, a couple who run a club with a small dance-floor – would all like to be elsewhere, to do something new. But they cannot. It is as if they are bewitched. In the end, death breaks the spell. They are asked to do something out of the ordinary – something more – to smuggle gold rather than the odd necklace or the odd hardworking Arab. The film lacks the unity and concentration of *In the White City*, but it has a feel for landscape and geography, and a genuine sense of a group of tentative, slightly oddball characters carrying their hopes into a world outside the loose confines of the plot.

At the end of *Voyage to Cythera* (1984), Theo Angelopoulos's previous Film on Four, an elderly couple – a man who has spent thirty-two years in exile and the wife from whom he has become estranged – cut loose from the Greek mainland and drift on a raft towards the island of Cythera. At the beginning of Angelopoulos's LANDSCAPE IN THE MIST (28 April 1990), a girl, Voula, and her small brother, Alexandros, find the courage to board an express train in an unnamed Greek city and begin a long journey to find the father they believe is living across the frontier – a metaphorical frontier – in Germany.

Voyage to Cythera was told from the point of view of another Alexandros, a small boy seen in the prologue running through deserted streets and knocking a baton from the hands of a German soldier. This Alexandros grows up and becomes a film director, and must now welcome back from the Soviet Union the father he has never known. The themes of Angelopoulos's work are the strands of a single carpet. But what perhaps makes *Landscape in the Mist* a more satisfactory and more fully realised work than *Voyage to Cythera* is that it concerns the young, not the old, and is motivated by the will to achievement, to find something, to go somewhere, rather than the necessity of saving something from the wreckage, of simply not surrendering.

Spyros, the old resistance fighter in *Voyage to Cythera*, can only beat a mattock on the unbreakable ancestral ground outside his village; Voula, holding tight to her brother's hand, is prepared to do and suffer anything – to run away from the police, to submit to rape, to offer herself to a soldier for the price of a train ticket – to obtain her goal. And what is this goal? To find a father who does not exist, who is simply the convenient fiction of the children's mother? No, it is to celebrate the transforming power of cinema – and notably wide-screen cinema.

In *Landscape in the Mist*, the travelling players, who for Angelopoulos represent a noble but dying art, are still trying to find somewhere to perform *Golfo the Shepherdess*, still wandering in circles on a grey empty beach testifying in broken fragments to the disappointments and betrayals of modern Greek history. But here on a windswept quay, they are at last forced to sell their costumes. And Orestes, their youngest member, must sell his motorcycle and play the role of a soldier.

The future lies with the indomitable children, the only ones capable of movement when, escaping from the police, they run through a town, coated unexpectedly with snow, whose inhabitants stand frozen in mute astonishment. When Voula and Alexandros cross the frontier and emerge from the mist, there before them is a distant tree. They run forward and embrace it. It is the tree, it may be supposed, on the fragment of discarded film which Orestes saved from a rubbish bin and gave the children as a talisman.

Three of the 1990–91 films dealt in contrasting styles with the perils of the sea – and, in *Drowning by Numbers*, the perils of bathwater, too. **THE DIVE** (15 September 1991), an Anglo-Norwegian production directed by Tristan de Vere Cole, was composed of tested ingredients. Two Norwegians, the experienced Gunnar and the novice Rolf, take a quick, 'bounce' dive to inspect a valve on a North Sea oil pipe snagged by a fishing net. Their diving-bell becomes trapped and the umbilical cord breaks. The weather turns foul and there is no oxygen in the bell's emergency tanks. The rescue inches along; and everyone, on the whole, keeps calm. Gunnar's old partner, Bricks (Michael Kitchen), perishes in a successful solo dive to reconnect the lifeline. His corpse, unnervingly, lies for a while on the floor of the bell.

The film furnishes suitably graphic details. Rolf, for instance, is ordered to pierce the eardrums of the stricken, decompressed Gunnar with an instrument 'no longer than a biro' – and the wire on his portable music-system comes in handy. **IN FADING LIGHT** (31 May 1990), produced by the Newcastle workshop Amber Films, takes place chiefly on a rusting fishing vessel which puts out from North Shields for what the skipper Alfie (Dave Hill) fears may be her last voyage. Life on the Norwegian diving ship with her shining white helicopter pad and fluorescent control-panel is purringly hi-tech: on the little *Sally* with her tipping galley, tiny wheelhouse and defunct winching gear, everything is uncertain, freezing and potentially deadly. The skipper drinks and no wonder. One of Alfie's crewmen loses the top of his finger in an accident with a spinning chain; but no one – the victim included – thinks to make much of this.

In Fading Light, written by Tom Hadaway, is a lightly dramatised portrait of a shamefully beleaguered industry. And it is notable chiefly, beneath the foul language and explosive outbursts of the crew, for the evenness of its tone and the authenticity of the ensemble acting. As Bricks, in *The Dive*, prepares for his fatal descent, one sees him for a moment, a tiny figure in a chopping, menacing well of oily water. Every scene of *In Fading Light*, however, leaves the taste of stinging spray. No other Film on Four has celebrated working people at their tasks with such a keen and sympathetic eye.

DROWNING BY NUMBERS (5 May 1991), written and directed by Peter Greenaway and set on the Suffolk coast, concerns three women named Cissie Colpitts – grandmother (Joan Plowright), mother (Juliet Stevenson) and daughter (Joely Richardson). Each in turn disposes of her husband. In *The Dressmaker*, Joan Plowright's Nellie made a tremulous stab at a sex-starved soldier with a pair of scissors, whereupon he took a fatal tumble down a flight of stairs. In Greenaway's film, Cissie Colpitts 1 is more decisive. Her husband of thirty-four years (Bryan Pringle), an old goat, is drowned in a tin bath. Why, her granddaughter asks. 'Because . . .' says Cissie 1, as if from somewhere far far away. 'Because he'd stopped washing his feet . . . because he wouldn't cut his beard . . . because he had a hairy backside.'

The territory of this film is fantastical, like the menagerie of *A Zed & Two Noughts* (1985), rather than solid and identifiably human, like the Roman buildings of *The Belly of an Architect* (1987). The film – perhaps Greenaway's most consistently funny – delights in heartless chop-logic, lists, number puzzles and games involving tethered sheep and the turn of the tide. Lynda in *Wish You Were Here* did not rate men very highly; and neither do the three Cissies. Lynda had her sad, oily, self-confident cinema projectionist; the Cissies have their husbands, but also Henry Madgett (Bernard Hill), the local coroner, melancholy and made queasy by death, who yearns for all three of them – and will, in consequence, fix the paperwork. Sex makes men ridiculous; and women must bear the consequences, as best they can.

A WORLD APART (21 April 1991) was written by Shawn Slovo, the daughter of Joe Slovo, the leading South African Communist, and his wife, the journalist Ruth First, who was assassinated in Mozambique on 17

Wild Flowers: Sheila Keith

August 1982. The director was Chris Menges, cameraman on *Walter* (1982), Channel 4's first Film on Four. *A World Apart* begins in June 1963, the month that South Africa's 90-Day Detention Act became law. It is hard to remain unmoved by this cool, careful, autobiographical story – not so much by the injustice it touches on, but by Shawn Slovo's torn, ambiguous feelings for the central character, Diana Roth (Barbara Hershey), her principled, preoccupied and neglectful mother.

Ruth First was held in solitary confinement for one hundred and seventeen days, and attempted suicide. *A World Apart* covers this harrowing time. The film wears its ribbons on its chest. The members of the banned African National Congress are heroes and heroines, noble, wronged and unbowed. But to sturdy thirteen-year-old Molly Roth (Jodhi May) – Shawn Slovo – they are separate and unbridgeably different. Spanish dancing classes are important to her. She has her own, conventional, middle-class life. The revolution has taken her mother and left an awkward void.

The Roths' maid Elsie (Linda Mvusi) invites Molly to a meal at her family home. Elsie, a member of the ANC, is a bosom member of her employers' household. One evening she quietly shows Molly a photograph album of her absent children. 'Are you sad?' Molly asks. 'Yes, I am

Ladder of Swords: Bob Peck (left), Martin Shaw

sad,' Elsie replies quietly. They could not be closer. But in the township, seated at a table surrounded by the proud, welcoming faces of Elsie's family, Molly cannot eat the delicacy in her soup plate, a long chicken foot. Laughter, and it is taken away. This is the other world apart.

Like *Distant Voices, Still Lives*, but in a different register, *A World Apart* has a singular virtue. Its first impulse was the urgent necessity to tell a particular story. Harry Hook's **THE KITCHEN TOTO** (29 March 1990) was set in Kenya in 1950 as the armed struggle for independence was beginning. A black priest is murdered for refusing to co-operate with the clandestine Kikuyu insurgents. His son Mwangi (Edwin Mahinda), aged twelve, is employed by John Graham, the district police chief (Bob Peck), as the family's kitchen servant. He is given a fez and 12 shillings a month. Graham's son Edward, aged eleven, is a repellent child: a midget colonialist with smarmed hair. He likes nothing better than killing and cutting up animals. At one point he slits open a long snake and gleefully extracts the rat in its gullet.

The insurgents come at night to win over Graham's servants. The cook is forced to take the oath and so is Mwangi. On the radio, as though the sun will never set on the pink bits of the British Empire, Elizabeth Bowen gives a talk on books. Graham is casually unfaithful to his abstracted wife (Phyllis Logan). The eventual attack on the police chief's house occurs one teatime. Graham is away on an assignation. Edward is left to defend the homestead. He shoots dead an attacker with his father's pistol and then, horrifyingly, his mother. His baby sister is kidnapped. Later, Mwangi remembers his humanity and rescues the girl. Carrying her home, he is shot dead by one of Graham's Samburu policemen. A title reminds us that eighty Europeans and 14,000 Africans were killed in the Mau Mau rising which led to Kenya's independence in 1963.

PASCALI'S ISLAND (8 September 1991), written and directed by James Dearden, sees the end of another colonial era, the Ottoman Empire. In 1908, on a Greek island in the Aegean occupied by the Turks, Basil Pascali (Ben Kingsley), the bastard son of an acrobat mother, has for twenty years been a faithful spy for the last Sultan. Envelopes of money have appeared under his door, but his reports have never been acknowledged. *A World Apart* and *The Kitchen Toto* are attractively modest films. Emotions are tamped-down and domestic: when Diana goes to jail, her mother (Yvonne Bryceland) – who bites her lip when it comes to her daughter's politics – takes over the care of Molly and her two younger sisters; when Graham hires Mwangi, his wife remonstrates mildly at the invasion of her territory. *Pascali's Island*, in which the spy attempts to bring his life's work to a head by exposing a British treasure-seeker (Charles Dance), springs from a more lush tradition, of vistas and sunsets, and acting where looks, gestures and a very British sort of intensity count for more than plain speaking.

WE THINK THE WORLD OF YOU (12 May 1991) concerns the proper treatment of a large dog. Johnny (Gary Oldman), cunning as only the weak can be, controls the admiring, generous Frank Meadows (Alan Bates) by the novel method of neglecting Evie, his own boisterous Alsatian. Frank, a single man, works for a London publisher; Johnny, married to the sluttish, suspicious Megan (Frances Barber), is in jail for housebreaking; and Evie, who lives temporarily with Johnny's mother (Liz Smith) and her grumbling second husband (Max Wall), is miserable for lack of exercise. Frank grows beside himself with frustration. He wants to help everyone – Johnny with books, Johnny's mother with discreet handouts, Evie by throwing a stick into the Thames – but somehow, obscurely, everyone is against him.

On his release from jail, Johnny grows indifferent to the dog. He stole in order to buy her. She was, he tells Frank, in his customary maudlin tone, a reminder of a dog in his youth. Frank can buy her now; Johnny does not care – life with Megan, it seems, stretches limitlessly before him. Once the dog becomes Frank's property, Evie transforms into a capricious, unbiddable mistress. But Frank, of course, continues to love her. And one day, walking the dog, he meets Johnny in a park. 'I reckon you had the best of the bargain,' Johnny says.

Hugh Stoddart's adaptation of J. R. Ackerley's novel is concise and elliptical. And the film, handsomely designed by Jamie Leonard with the correct touch of slightly heightened reality, is marked by an ironic, literary humour not found in the director Colin Gregg's previous work for Film on Four, *Remembrance* (1982), on which Stoddart and Leonard also collaborated, and *Lamb* (1985). The humour is bone-dry and, above all, grown-up. That Frank is a willing partner in his humiliation at the hands of Johnny's grotesque family seems (as it should) a wholly unexceptional fact of life.

James Ivory's **MAURICE** (5 April 1990), adapted from E. M. Forster's posthumous novel, contains a theme present in both *Heat and Dust* (1982) and *A Room with a View* (1985) – that the world belongs to those with the courage to break with convention and be true to their hearts. 'Omit the unspeakable vice of the Greeks,' orders the Dean (Barry Foster), without raising his eyes from the book. And the young man translating a classical text meekly obeys. But this is modern Cambridge, 1909, and Maurice Hall (James Wilby) has no intention of pretending things do not exist when quite plainly they do. Among the other, sophisticated and somewhat arch undergraduates, Maurice stands out for his frank enthusiasm. He falls in love and roars off into the fens on his motorcycle with Clive Durham (Hugh Grant) in the pillion. The Dean spots them cutting a lecture and Maurice is sent down. But he refuses to write the requisite letter of apology.

The years pass and, for the sake of propriety, Clive chooses to marry. Viscount Risley, a fellow Cambridge man, is arrested in an alley with a guardsman and sent to prison, Clive having declined to speak for him at the trial. Maurice, meanwhile, wrestles with his emotions. The family doctor sends him to Lasker-Jones (Ben Kingsley), a quack hypnotist, who recommends that he stroll around with a gun. Maurice calls at Pendersleigh, Clive's country home, and there Alec Scudder, the under-keeper, recognises him for what he is and what he wants. Alec climbs a ladder at night into Maurice's room. Maurice gives up the pretence and finds happiness. The final scene shows the pursed butler Simcox (Patrick Godfrey) locking up Pendersleigh, and Clive, trapped in the matrimonial bedroom, looking out into the night.

James Moon (Kenneth Branagh) – from the same class and about the same age as Maurice Hall, but a quick wit – spent the last six months of the 1914–18 war in jail, found guilty of the same 'crime' committed by Maurice and Scudder. **A MONTH IN THE COUNTRY** (19 April 1990), adapted by Simon Gray from the novel by J. L. Carr, is set in Yorkshire soon after the war. Moon and another young man, Tom Birkin (Colin Firth), are reassembling the pieces of their lives through working, slowly and methodically, with their hands. Moon is hunting for a buried Saxon chapel in the grounds of a church, under the guise of searching for the bones of the forebear of a local beneficiary; and Birkin is restoring a fifteenth-century 'Judgment' on the wall of the church nave.

The significance of both these tasks has perhaps more literary than cinematic punch, but the evocation of summer days with time not pressing and of two men becoming friends and of one of them almost allowing the vicar's neglected wife (Natasha Richardson) to develop a tenderness for him is admirably achieved. The director Pat O'Connor displayed a similar confidence in *Cal* (1984) with the evocation of the working life of a Protestant farm in Northern Ireland.

A Month in the Country is embellished with rather obviously quirky minor characters; but it has, too, several finely judged comic moments. A sister and brother enter the church one day and play Birkin a gramophone record, 'Angels ever bright and fair/Take, O take me in your care.' The girl has brought a nourishing rabbit-pie from her mother. 'My dad said you were an opportunity that mightn't come again in a spot like this,' she says, 'watching an artist at work.' 'Ah, but I'm not an artist,' Birkin replies. 'I'm the labourer who cleans up after artists.'

LORCA – DEATH OF A POET (4 August 1990), directed by J. A. Bardem, is a two-hour film created from a television series, and the result is slow and unbalanced – the pace, in short, of a serial drama. Nickolas Grace, however, plays the gaunt poet with composure: dressed in dinner clothes in a prison cell he does not appear unduly out of sorts. The action begins on 13 July 1936 with reports of the triumph of *The House of Bernarda Alba* (though Nuria Espert, as Margarita Xirgú, does not appear in this version of the film) and then moves, via several operatic battle scenes, to Granada where Lorca's brother-in-law was mayor and where the poet attempts to shelter with his honourable Falangist friends the Rosales. Shortly afterwards, at dawn, he is shot in the back as he walks calmly up a winding hill road. The reasons for this crime are unexplained. 'When I die, bury me if you like in the weather vane.'

A more melodramatic death occurs at the end of **VERTIGES** (15 March 1990), written and directed by Christine Laurent, when on the first night of a fraught production of *The Marriage of Figaro* the Count (Henri Serre) shoots dead Figaro (Thierry Bosc) with the actor Kirkmayer's own pearl-handled pistol. This is no more than Kirkmayer deserves since he has throughout rehearsals tormented the conductor with hints of some old injustice. The conductor, meanwhile, has been growing increasingly obsessed with the memory of his former mistress, La Gradiva, and her perfect voice. One of the singers (Krystyna Janda) loses her voice. 'You have to be a *real* diva to lose your voice,' the conductor's current mistress says, comfortingly. News arrives of La Gradiva's retirement. The conductor swoons and expires. The Countess swears vengeance; and the Count, in the event, acts the gentleman. Vertigo, indeed.

SPEAKING PARTS (1 September 1991), written and directed by Atom Egoyan, is a fantasy also concerned with the confusion of art and reality. In some future world dominated by moving images, instead of visiting a graveyard, the bereaved sit reverently in a video mausoleum. An aspiring actor, working as a hotel cleaner, comes upon a script and lands his first speaking part in a film in which a woman writer memorialises the dead brother who saved her life. In due course, the script is changed so that the hero donates a lung to his *brother*, not his sister. Not that much has changed.

In Jana Bokóva's **HÔTEL DU PARADIS** (24 May 1990), Joseph (Fernando Rey) checks into his favourite Paris hotel and begins the more ancient ritual of finding a venue and the money to mount his one-man show based on Camus' *The Fall*. Meanwhile, Arthur (Fabrice Luchini), another of the hotel's agreeably oddball denizens, contrives to press one of his film scripts on Mme Bresson. The man who may put on Joseph's show is in difficulties and prevails upon Joseph, a Lithuanian Jew, to impersonate an American producer at a meal arranged to impress the bank manager.

On the wall of the primitive windswept house of Zelihan and her husband Necmettin, in Erden Kiral's **THE MIRROR** (8 March 1990), is a faded picture of God staying the hand of Abraham. This Anglo-German production of a Turkish film shot in Greece is notable for its complete absence of superfluous detail. The couple have few possessions – a red eiderdown, an enamel bowl with a painted iris – and their livelihood depends on a white ox. The creature's bower is the other half of their house. The young Aga to whom Necmettin is beholden comes courting Zelihan. In mournful silence he leaves her gifts: money under a stone, daffodils, a small round mirror – she has, perhaps, never seen her face. Necmettin lures the young Aga to his hut, stabs him in the heart and buries his remains in the ox's bower. The restless beast pores the earth; Zelihan, remembering her mirror, begins to pine; in impotent rage, her husband sacrifices the ox.

Max von Sydow's first film as director, KATINKA (26 May 1990), based on a turn-of-the-century novel, *Along the Road*, by the Danish author Herman Bang, centres on the home of a boorish station master whose wife, Katinka (Tammi Øst), longs for something other – not a mirror, but a spark of life. She becomes friends with Huus, a newly arrived foreman (Kurt Ravn), but nothing occurs. He gives her a blue shawl, a pair to one which her husband never noticed was torn. At a carnival, they look at a peepshow of the Jungfrau and the Bay of Naples. There is one passionate kiss, then Huus goes away – on her orders – and Katinka takes to her bed and dies.

THE DREAM (15 September 1990), directed by Pieter Verhoeff, is a vigorous costume picture conjuring the turbulent atmosphere of North Friesland in the 1890s when the cry 'Hunger knows no laws' led to a rash of pillage and assault. The authorities bear down on the police to make an arrest. The story unpicks the events – villainy, misunderstanding and perjury – which led to the notorious false conviction of three brothers for the violent attack on a farmhouse and the subsequent efforts of a schoolmaster to reach the truth. The case against Wiebren Hogerhuis (Peter Tuinman), the most vociferous of the brothers, turns on the evidence of the woman with whom he was having an affair, Iemkje (Joke Tjalsma), the housekeeper at the farm which was attacked. What turned Wiebren against his lover was a seed of doubt; and what turned Iemkje against him was the sight of him dancing with another woman.

Two of the three Irish films transmitted by Film on Four in 1990–91 contained couples on the run. The more fractured of the two was Joe Comerford's REEFER AND THE MODEL (25 August 1991) about a bearlike ex-con and one-time Republican who skippers a Galway Bay trawler, the *Reef*, quite as grimy and unreliable as the North Shields fishing boat from *In Fading Light*. Reefer (Ian McElhinney) takes up with a prostitute, the Model (Carol Scanlan), and they are soon pitched into a picaresque adventure, robbing banks and trading shots with the guards. The film, notable for its immediacy, ends with a display of uncompromising melodrama. In the wheelhouse of the *Reef*, the Model gives birth to a baby; the vessel, meanwhile, churns towards the rowing boat in which Reefer hopes to escape from the law.

JOYRIDERS (6 October 1991), directed by Aisling Walsh, has a less ferocious bite, but nevertheless catches with sometimes moving sympathy another aspect of life in the West of Ireland – the sense of a passed-by place where middle-aged men will, it seems, never find wives at the hotel tea-dance, The couple of the title find each other in a Dublin pub and then take off for Kilkenny, to the hotel where she spent her honeymoon. Later they stop off at the farm of a widower. 'Four years,' the old man says of the time he has been alone, 'it's longer than the rest of me life put together.'

THE DEAD (22 February 1990), as smooth as ivory where the other two Irish films were splintered and unfinished, was the director John Huston's last film. The year is 1904 and the setting a Dublin house kept by two maiden sisters who every year on the Feast of the Epiphany give a dinner for their friends and relations. There is dancing, recitation, singing. A couple, the Conroys, have come from Munster, as they always do. Gabriel Conroy (Donal McCann), the sisters' nephew, and their favourite, carves the goose and makes an elegant speech of thanks.

The conversation – real conversation, formal, complete, conducted in turned sentences – flows with delightful ease. The tipsy Freddy, who has forgotten the pledge he recently took, somehow misses out on the port. The world of nearly ninety years ago rises before our eyes. One of the party, a shining-eyed Irishwoman, who burns for the coming nation, slips away to hear James Connolly speak at Liberty Hall. The talk, which has moved to the subject of singing, comes alive with a new animation. One of the sisters, Miss Julia, had earlier given a quavering rendition of Bellini's 'Arrayed for the Bridal' – 'from her concert days'. Everyone remembers his favourite singer, and in remembering somehow makes us hear an echo of those voices. Miss Kate, the other sister, recalls the nonpareil of singers – a pure English tenor – and by her tone she was perhaps in love with him.

As the party breaks up Mr Bartell D'Arcy, the celebrated tenor, who has not deigned to give the company a taste of his quality, can be heard singing 'The Lass of Aughrim' to one of the young ladies. Gabriel's wife Gretta (Anjelica Huston) stands listening on the stairs. When the Conroys reach their room at the Gresham Hotel, Gretta is moved for the first time to tell the story of Michael Fury. When she was a girl in Galway living with her grandmother, Michael Fury sang and paid court to her. He died, having caught a chill singing at night outside her window. All down the years, Gretta has kept a place in her heart for Michael. At which, Gabriel realises he has never known his wife. And the screen fills with a succession of images of snow-covered countryside.

VIEWING FIGURES
1990/1991

	1st Tx '000s
WISH YOU WERE HERE	*15 Feb 90* **6,667**
NO MAN'S LAND	*15 Feb 90* **0,644**
THE DEAD	*22 Feb 90* **2,298**
HIGH HOPES	*1 Mar 90* **3,043**
SAMMY AND ROSIE GET LAID	*8 Mar 90* **3,061**
THE MIRROR	*8 Mar 90* **0,625**
WILD FLOWERS	*15 Mar 90* **2,241**
VERTIGES	*15 Mar 90* **0,285**
VROOM	*22 Mar 90* **3,494**
THE KITCHEN TOTO	*29 Mar 90* **2,537**
MAURICE	*5 Apr 90* **2,185**
THE FINAL FRAME	*12 Apr 90* **2,467**
A MONTH IN THE COUNTRY	*19 Apr 90* **2,591**
CONQUEST OF THE SOUTH POLE	*26 Apr 90* **1,243**
LANDSCAPE IN THE MIST	*28 Apr 90* **0,420**
ON THE BLACK HILL	*3 May 90* **3,118**
RITA, SUE AND BOB TOO	*10 May 90* **5,756**
SHOOTING STARS	*17 May 90* **2,095**
HÔTEL DU PARADIS	*24 May 90* **1,023**

KATINKA	*26 May 90* **0,697**
IN FADING LIGHT	*31 May 90* **2,810**
LORCA — DEATH OF A POET	*4 Aug 90* **0,236**
THE DREAM	*15 Sep 90* **0,449**
THE BOMB	*29 Sep 90* **0,376**
DOC'S KINGDOM	*13 Oct 90* **0,436**
A WORLD APART	*21 Apr 91* **2,345**
HOPE AND GLORY	*28 Apr 91* **4,584**
DROWNING BY NUMBERS	*5 May 91* **2,773**
WE THINK THE WORLD OF YOU	*12 May 91* **1,636**
SMACK AND THISTLE	*19 May 91* **2,129**
THE DRESSMAKER	*26 May 91* **2,856**
TREE OF HANDS	*2 Jun 91* **2,675**
DISTANT VOICES, STILL LIVES	*4 Aug 91* **1,268**
LADDER OF SWORDS	*11 Aug 91* **3,250**
AMERICAN ROULETTE	*18 Aug 91* **1,662**
REEFER AND THE MODEL	*25 Aug 91* **1,765**
SPEAKING PARTS	*1 Sep 91* **0,861**
PASCALI'S ISLAND	*8 Sep 91* **2,435**
THE DIVE	*15 Sep 91* **2,408**
ANGRY EARTH	*22 Sep 91* **0,986**
BEARSKIN	*29 Sep 91* **1,132**
JOYRIDERS	*6 Sep 91* **2,779**

Source: BARB

Note: Figures from 11 August 1991 are 'consolidated'
(that is, including off-air video recordings).

APPENDIX A

BUDGETS

TITLE (© YEAR)	BUDGET	C4 INPUT	
	£'000s	£'000s	
ABOVE £5M			
HOPE AND GLORY (1987)..	[$9,100]		
	5,564.............	325	(6%)
ABOVE £3M			
COMRADES (1986)	3,014.............	1,000	(33%)
ABOVE £2M			
BILLY THE KID AND THE			
GREEN BAIZE VAMPIRE (1985)	2,700.............	350	(13%)
A WORLD APART (1987)..	2,675.............	275	(10%)
MONA LISA (1986)...	2,400.............	225	(9%)
THE COMPANY OF WOLVES (1984)...........................	2,400.............	200	(8%)
NO SURRENDER (1985)..	2,337.............	600	(26%)
PASCALI'S ISLAND (1988)...	2,261.............	275	(12%)
A ROOM WITH A VIEW (1985)	2,259.............	235	(10%)
THE DEAD (1987)...	2,259.............	175	(8%)
A GATHERING OF OLD MEN (1987)	[$3,500]		
	2,140.............	50	(2%)
ABOVE £1M			
TREE OF HANDS (1988)	[2,000]...........	275	(14%)
MASCHENKA (1986)	2,000.............	300	(15%)
CAL (1984)...	[1,933]	325	(17%)
HIGH SEASON (1987)	1,902.............	350	(18%)
PRICK UP YOUR EARS (1987)....................................	1,900.............	300	(16%)
THE SACRIFICE (1986)	1,831.............	275	(15%)
THE BELLY OF AN ARCHITECT (1987)......................	1,800.............	630	(35%)
THE DIVE (1989)	1,800.............	275	(15%)
THE KITCHEN TOTO (1987).......................................	1,767.............	332	(19%)
MAURICE (1987)..	1,577.............	375	(24%)

THE FIRST KANGAROOS (1988)	1,433	558	(39%)
DANCE WITH A STRANGER (1984)	1,400	283	(20%)
EAT THE PEACH (1986)	1,387	517	(37%)
SAMMY AND ROSIE GET LAID (1987)	1,370	400	(29%)
WE THINK THE WORLD OF YOU (1988)	1,357	550	(41%)
VROOM (1988)	1,356	949	(70%)
BEARSKIN (1989)	1,310	895	(68%)
LADDER OF SWORDS (1989)	1,300	882	(68%)
JOYRIDERS (1988)	[1,300]	100	(8%)
MILK AND HONEY (1988)	[Can$2,800]		
	1,299	40	(3%)
THE DRESSMAKER (1988)	1,276	827	(65%)
HIGH HOPES (1988)	1,276	745	(58%)
LAMB (1985)	1,260	605	(48%)
AMERICAN ROULETTE (1988)	1,223	640	(52%)
PARIS, TEXAS (1984)	1,162	250	(22%)
LETTERS TO AN UNKNOWN LOVER (1985)	1,153	600	(52%)
HEAVENLY PURSUITS (1986)	1,150	748	(65%)
THE CHAIN (1984)	1,150	363	(32%)
WISH YOU WERE HERE (1987)	1,132	849	(75%)
WETHERBY (1985)	1,125	750	(67%)
HEAT AND DUST (1982)	[1,100]	115	(10%)
A MONTH IN THE COUNTRY (1987)	1,075	678	(63%)
HIDDEN CITY (1987)	1,068	1,068	(100%)
REEFER AND THE MODEL (1988)	1,052	250	(24%)
SQUARING THE CIRCLE (1984)	1,029	330	(32%)
DROWNING BY NUMBERS (1988)	1,023	450	(44%)
THE NATURE OF THE BEAST (1988)	1,022	702	(69%)
SHE'LL BE WEARING PINK PYJAMAS (1984)	1,005	955	(95%)

ABOVE £900K

THE INNOCENT (1984)	1,000	300	(30%)
RITA, SUE AND BOB TOO (1986)	993	726	(73%)
SUCCESS IS THE BEST REVENGE (1984)	983	280	(28%)
SMACK AND THISTLE (1990)	978	873	(89%)
SHADEY (1985)	959	959	(100%)
PLAYING AWAY (1986)	924	924	(100%)
RUNNERS (1983)	913	354	(39%)
LANDSCAPE IN THE MIST (1988)	912	50	(5%)

ABOVE £800K

LEAVE TO REMAIN (1988)	900	900	(100%)
A SONG FOR EUROPE (1985)	898	454	(51%)
FATHERLAND (1986)	884	459	(52%)
BORN OF FIRE (1986)	854	755	(88%)
RED MONARCH (1983)	811	350	(43%)

ABOVE £700K

KATINKA (1988)	?800	45	
THE ROAD HOME (1987)	800	400	(50%)
SHOOTING STARS (1990)	800	350	(44%)
THE COUNTRY GIRLS (1983)	770	330	(43%)
THE GOOD FATHER (1986)	764	764	(100%)
SINGLETON'S PLUCK (1984)	750	715	(95%)
HÔTEL DU PARADIS (1986)	704	459	(65%)

DISTANT VOICES, STILL LIVES (1988)....................... 703............. 375 (53%)

ABOVE £600K

PRAYING MANTIS (I and II) (1982)	680.............	450	(66%)
PING PONG (1986)	650.............	650	(100%)
MY BEAUTIFUL LAUNDRETTE (1985)......................	650.............	650	(100%)
ON THE BLACK HILL (1987)	639.............	122	(19%)
A ZED & TWO NOUGHTS (1985).............................	635.............	250	(39%)
ILL FARES THE LAND (1982)	628.............	300	(48%)
WINTER FLIGHT (1984)	[606]............	275	(45%)
SACRED HEARTS (1984)	601.............	559	(93%)

ABOVE £500K

THE ASSAM GARDEN (1984)	600.............	200	(33%)
SPEAKING PARTS (1989)......................................	600.............	75	(13%)
THE PLOUGHMAN'S LUNCH (1983)........................	599.............	300	(50%)
THE DREAM (1985)	[$800]		
	596.............	17	(3%)
MOONLIGHTING (1982)...	596.............	298	(50%)
BAD HATS (1982)	586.............	387	(66%)
THOSE GLORY GLORY DAYS (1983)	581.............	200	(34%)
ANOTHER TIME, ANOTHER PLACE (1983)...............	580.............	300	(52%)
CHRISTMAS PRESENT (1985)	567.............	567	(100%)
WILD FLOWERS (1989)...	560.............	560	(100%)
ANGRY EARTH (1989)..	558.............	246	(44%)
SHARMA AND BEYOND (1984)..............................	529.............	240	(45%)
FLIGHT TO BERLIN (1983)	525.............	332	(63%)
FOREVER YOUNG (1983)	506.............	240	(47%)
EXPERIENCE PREFERRED BUT			
NOT ESSENTIAL (1982).................................	505.............	200	(40%)
REFLECTIONS (1983)	502.............	462	(92%)

ABOVE £400K

VAGABONDE (1985)...	500.............	36	(7%)
SECRETS (1982)	486.............	200	(41%)
LIVING APART TOGETHER (1983).........................	485.............	393	(81%)
CARAVAGGIO (1986)..	[475]	250	(54%)
ANGEL (1982)..	469.............	384	(82%)
GOOD AND BAD AT GAMES (1983)	468.............	355	(76%)
THE FINAL FRAME (1989).....................................	?450............	?450	(100%)
THE KING AND THE QUEEN (1985)	?450............	50	
ARTHUR'S HALLOWED GROUND (1984)	[445]	240	(53%)
ACCOUNTS (1983)..	444.............	397	(89%)
GIRO CITY (1982)	441.............	185	(42%)
NELLY'S VERSION (1983)	440.............	400	(91%)
A FLAME TO THE PHOENIX (1983)........................	[440]............	300	(68%)
THE BAD SISTER (1983).......................................	418.............	318	(76%)
THE DISAPPEARANCE OF HARRY (1982)................	413.............	403	(98%)

ABOVE £300K

P'TANG, YANG, KIPPERBANG (1982)	395.............	200	(51%)
LETTER TO BREZHNEV (1985)...............................	379.............	231	(61%)
HERO (1982)	363.............	363	(100%)
EL NORTE (1983)	361.............	25	(7%)
THE DRAUGHTSMAN'S CONTRACT (1982)...............	360.............	180	(50%)

MEANTIME (1983)	357	307	(86%)
VOYAGE TO CYTHERA (1984)	350	50	(14%)
REMEMBRANCE (1982)	338	338	(100%)
WALTER (1982)	325	250	(77%)
WALTER & JUNE (1982)	325	250	(77%)
IN FADING LIGHT (1989)	310	310	(100%)

ABOVE £200K

CONQUEST OF THE SOUTH POLE (1989)	300	300	(100%)
LAST DAY OF SUMMER (1983)	209	160	(77%)
SUMMER LIGHTNING (1984)	201	126	(63%)

ABOVE £100K

THE EYES OF BIRDS (1982)	?200	36	
THE MIRROR (1984)	?150	50	
STRAWBERRY FIELDS (1984)	125	25	(20%)
THE OUTCASTS (1982)	112	47	(42%)

BUDGETS NOT KNOWN

GOOD MORNING BABYLON (1986)	?	125
LORCA – DEATH OF A POET (1987)	?	75
THE BOMB (1987)	?	75
NO MAN'S LAND (1985)	?	50
YERMA (1985)	?	26
IN THE WHITE CITY (1983)	?	25
DOC'S KINGDOM (1987)	?	?
GENESIS (1986)	?	?
VERTIGES (1985)	?	?

See p. 121, note 4 for source of figures in square brackets.
All other figures: Channel 4.

CREDITS

COMMISSION **c ed** commissioning editor Channel 4 (DR David Rose; KB Karin Bamborough; WD Walter Donohue; PA Peter Ansorge). **no** Film on Four commission number

PRODUCTION **p** producer. **exec p** executive producer. **exec i/c p** executive in charge of production. **co-p** co-producer. **line p** line producer. **assoc p** associate producer. **p sup** production supervisor. **p co-ord** production co-ordinator. **p admin** production administrator. **p man** production manager. **unit man** unit manager

DIRECTION **d** director. **asst d** assistant director. **2nd unit d** 2nd unit director. **sc sup** script supervisor. **sc girl** script girl. **casting d** casting director. **dialect d** dialect director

SCRIPT **sc** script. **sc ed** script editor. **story ed** story editor. **creative adv** creative adviser. **sc adapt** script adaptation. **story adapt** story adaptation. **sc assoc** script associate. **sc collab** script collaboration. **sc cons** script consultant. **dial** dialogue

PHOTOGRAPHY **ph** director of photography. **addit ph** additional photography. **stunt ph** stunt photography. **cam op** camera operator. **2nd unit ph** 2nd unit photography. **2nd unit cam** 2nd unit camera. **underwater cam** underwater camera. **rostrum cam** rostrum camera. **sp ph** special photography. **video op** video operator. **video co-ord** video co-ordinator

MUSIC **m** music. **m prod** music producer. **m sup** music supervisor. **m co-ord** music co-ordinator. **addit m** additional music. **md** musical director. **cond** conductor. **orch d** orchestral director. **orch** orchestration. **m arr** musical arranger. **m perf** music performed by

MOVEMENT **choreo** choreography

EDITING **ed** film editor. **co-ed** co-editor. **sup ed** supervising film editor. **collab ed** collaborating editor

DESIGN **pd** production designer. **des** designer. **ad** art director. **set des** set designer

COSTUMES/MAKE-UP **cost/ward des** costume/wardrobe designer. **cost/ward** costume/wardrobe. **cost/ward sup** costume/wardrobe supervisor. **cost/ward mist** costume/wardrobe mistress. **sp eff make-up** special effects make-up. **sup hair** supervising hairdresser. **hair** hairdresser

EFFECTS **d vis eff** director of visual effects. **sp eff sup** special effects supervisor. **sp eff des** special effects design. **sp eff** special effects

STUNTS **stunt arr** stunt arranger. **stunt co-ord** stunt co-ordinator. **stunt perf** stunt performer

GRAPHICS **graphic des** graphic design. **title des** titles designer

SOUND **sd sup** sound supervisor. **sd rec** sound recordist. **sd mix** sound mixer. **sd ed** sound editor. **dub ed** dubbing editor. **sd re-rec** sound re-recordist. **dub mix** dubbing mixer. **sd eff** sound effects. **eff ed** effects editor

TV TRANSMISSION **1st tx** date of first Channel 4 transmission. FF Film on Four. FFI Film on Four International (subtitled films)

REVIEWS **MFB** *Monthly Film Bulletin*. **SS** *Sight and Sound* (incorporating *MFB* from May 1991). **V** *Variety*

AWARDS A/As award/s. F/Fs film/s. P/Ps prize/s

NOTES

1 Running times are given as far as possible at a projection rate of 24 frames per second.

2 Production credits to Channel 4 vary ('Channel Four', 'Film on Four', 'Film Four International'). Here the credit has been standardised to 'Channel 4'. The copyright credit follows the wording on the print. After 1984 Channel 4 used the credit 'Film Four International' on all films in which it had invested.

3 An **MFB** review signals a UK theatrical release. Films which were reviewed as 'television films' in *Sight and Sound* after May 1991 may not, however, have had a theatrical release.

4 **Budget** figures show the cash investment in a film's production costs. Names in square brackets indicate a source of information other than Channel 4.

5 **C4 input** shows the total Channel 4 contribution to a budget through cash investment (i) and/or the pre-purchase of a film's TV licence fee (lf) (source: Channel 4).

◆

ACCOUNTS
UK, 100 mins, colour
Partners in Production for Channel 4.
© 1983

c ed DR/WD. **no** 16
p TOM SACHS. **p man** John C. Wilcox
d MICHAEL DARLOW. **casting** Jose Scott
sc MICHAEL WILCOX
ph CHARLES STEWART
m FRANCIS SHAW
ed BERYL WILKINS
ad TONY ABBOTT
ward DONALD MOTHERSILL. **make-up** Ann Buchanan
sd rec DEREK WILLIAMS. **dub mix** Colin Martin
cast Elspeth Charlton (*Mary Mawson*), Jonathan Newth (*James Ridley Bowes*), Anthony Roper (*John Duff*), Robert Smeaton (*Andy Mawson*), Michael McNally (*Donald Mawson*), Charles Kearney (*auctioneer*)
shooting Kelso
budget £444,000. **C4 input** £397,000 (lf/i) (89%)
1st tx 22 Dec 83 (FF)
festivals American F Festival 86

AMERICAN ROULETTE
UK, 102 mins, colour
Roulette Productions for Mandemar Group, British Screen and Channel 4. © Roulette Productions 1988

c ed DR/KB. **no** 103
p GRAHAM EASTON. **exec p** VERITY LAMBERT. **p man** Laura Julian. **p co-ord** Cate Arbeid
d MAURICE HATTON. **asst d** Gino Marotta, (2nd) Paul Lowin. **sc sup** Andrea Fontaine. **casting d** Sheila Trezise
sc MAURICE HATTON. Carlos's poetry from Pablo Neruda's *Selected Poems*
ph TONY IMI. **cam op** John Campbell. **stills** Frank Connor
m MICHAEL GIBBS
ed BARRY PETERS
pd AUSTEN SPRIGGS. **ad** Peta Button
cost des LOUISE STJERNSWARD. **make-up** Magdalen Gaffney. **hair** Jane Hope-Kavanagh
sp eff TERRY GLASS
sd rec DAVID CROZIER, JOHN MIDGLEY. **sd ed** Graham Harris. **sup re-rec mix** Bill Rowe. **re-rec mix** Ray Merrin
cast Andy Garcia (*Carlos Quintas*), Kitty Aldridge (*Kate Webber*), Guy Bertrand (*Ruben*), Ricardo Sibelo (*Miguel*), Lino Omoboni (*Alfonso*), Ben Onwukwe (*hijacked van driver*), Peter Guinness (*policeman*), Sheila Burrell (*Raul's neighbour*), Alfredo Michelsen (*Ramón*), Carola Palacios (*Inez*), Adolpho Cozzi (*Paco*), Gloria Romo (*Raul's widow*), Yves Aubert (*reporter at ICA*), Robert Stephens (*Gerald Screech*), Juanita Waterman (*Zoe*), Kate McKenzie (*Ms van Doorn*), Christopher Rozycki (*Vladimir*), Boris Isarov (*Nickolai*), Rosalind Bennett (*Pickwick*), Al Matthews (*Morrisey*), Jayne Irving (*TV interviewer*), Yolande Vasquez (*Isabella*), Sayo Inaba (*Japanese reporter*),

Accounts

American Roulette

Darcy Flynn (*American TV reporter*), Steve Weston (*Ricks*), Mike Mungarvan (*embassy policeman*), Francisco Morales (*embassy official*), Mel Calman, Christopher Logue, Susannah York (*themselves*)
   shooting Aug–Sep 87. London
   budget £1,223,000. **C4 input** £640,000 (lf/i) (52%)
   1st tx 18 Aug 91 (FF)
   SS Sep 91. **V** 25 May 88
   festivals Montreal, Ghent, London 88; New Delhi, Los Angeles, Moscow, Edinburgh 89

L'AMOUR FUGITIF *see* **BAD HATS**

AND NOTHING BUT THE TRUTH *see* **GIRO CITY**

ANGEL
UK/Eire, 92 mins, colour
The Motion Picture Company of Ireland with the Irish Film Board for Channel 4. © The Motion Picture Company of Ireland 1982
   c ed DR/WD. **no** 5
   p BARRY BLACKMORE. **exec p** JOHN BOORMAN. **p man** Seamus Byrne
   d NEIL JORDAN. **asst d** Barry Blackmore, Martin O'Malley, John Lawlor. **continuity** Jean Skinner
   sc NEIL JORDAN
   ph CHRIS MENGES. **stills** Tom Collins
   saxophone solos KEITH DONALD. **original songs** Paddy Meegan
   ed PAT DUFFNER
   pd JOHN LUCAS
   ward mist JANET O'LEARY. **make-up** Rosie Blackmore. **hair** Joanna Lennox
   sp eff GERRY JOHNSTON

   sd rec KIERAN HORGAN. **sd ed** Ron Davis. **dub mix** Doug Turner
   cast Veronica Quilligan (*Annie*), Stephen Rea (*Danny*), Alan Devlin (*Bill*), Peter Caffrey (*Ray*), Honor Heffernan (*Deirdre*), Lise-Ann McLaughlin (*bride*), Ian McElhinney (*bridegroom*), Derek Lord (*best man*), Ray McAnally (*Bloom*), Donal McCann (*Bonner*), Marie Kean (*Aunt Mae*), Don Foley (*bouncer*), Gerald McSorley (*assistant*), Liz Bono (*girl assistant*), Tom Collins (*photographer*), Tony Rohr (*George*), Anita Reeves (*Beth*), Sorcha Cusack (*Mary*), Michael Lally (*uncle*), Macrea Clarke (*Francie*)
   shooting Eire
   budget £469,000. **C4 input** £384,000 (lf/i) (82%)
   1st tx 28 Apr 83 (FF)
   MFB Nov 82. **V** 26 May 82
   awards Best 1st Feature, Durban 82. Jury P, Antwerp 83. Most Promising Newcomer (Neil Jordan), Best Technical Achievement (Chris Menges), *Standard* F As 83
   festivals Durban, Edinburgh 82; Antwerp 83; Hong Kong, Tokyo, Jerusalem 84; Madrid 85; Reggio nell'Emilia, Sorrento 86; Le Touquet 88; Antenna 89

ANGRY EARTH
UK, 107 mins, colour
Cine Cymru/Bloom Street Productions for S4C with Channel 4. © Cine Cymru/Bloom Street Productions 1989
   c ed DR/KB. **no** 132
   p RUTH KENLEY. **p man** Marc Munden. **p co-ord** Angharad Francis
   d KARL FRANCIS. **asst d** Maurice Hunter; Cheryl Davies, Dewi Griffiths. **casting** (cons) Suzy Korel

Angel

Angry Earth

sc KARL FRANCIS
ph ROGER PUGH EVANS. **stills** Anthony Haughey, Ceri Norman
m KEN HOWARD. **m arr** John Altman
ed CHRIS LAWRENCE
pd FRANCIS PUGH
cost des KATIE PEGG. **make-up/hair** Sabrina Low. **old Gwen's make-up** Penny Smith
sp eff DAVID WILLIAMS
sd SIMON BISHOP. **dub mix** John Cross
cast Sue Roderick (*Gwen*), Mark Lewis Jones (*Guto Ellis*), Maria Pride (*Siwan*), Dafydd Hywel (*Evan Evans, Gwen's 2nd husband*), Robert Pugh (*Emlyn Ellis, Gwen's husband*), Gareth Skelding (*Twm Ellis*), Catrin Elisa (*Mair Ellis*), Jack Shepherd (*Dr Price*), Phyllis Logan (*Mary Penry-Jones*), Anne Valery (*Mrs Penry-Jones*), Donna Edwards (*Nurse Davies*), Ruth Sheen (*Nurse Berry*), Charlotte West-Oram (*Sister Jackson*), Keith Allen (*photographer*), Meredith Edwards (*Professor Evan Wynn James*), Crispin Letts (*Andrew*), Dominic Letts (*1st soldier*), Kevin Allen (*2nd soldier*), Ian Rowlands (*Jack*), Jack Walters (*Shoni Mawr*), Alan Devlin (*Grant*), Robin Griffiths (*Mr Thomas*), Emyr Llŷr (*Dai*), Siwan Jones (*Margaret*), Olive Michael (*Ann*), Sharon Morgan (*Dai's mother*), Hubert Rees (*mayor*), Simon Coady (*Dick James, TV director*), Boyd Clack (*master of ceremonies*), Caroline Stubbs (*nurse*)
shooting Bedwas, Gwent; Bedlinog, Mid-Glamorgan; Brechfa, Dyfed
budget £558,000. **C4 input** £246,000 (lf) (44%)
1st tx 22 Sep 91 (FF)
SS Oct 91. **V** 13 Sep 89

ANOTHER TIME, ANOTHER PLACE
UK, 102 mins, colour
Umbrella Films with Rediffusion Films, Channel 4 and the Scottish Arts Council.
© Rediffusion Films 1983
c ed WD/DR. **no** 23
p SIMON PERRY. **exec p** TIMOTHY BURRILL. **assoc p** Paul Cowan
d MICHAEL RADFORD. **asst d** Ian Madden, (2nd) Gus MacLean. **continuity** Margaret Waldie
sc MICHAEL RADFORD from the novel by Jessie Kesson. **script assistance/Italian co-ordinator** John Francis Lane
ph/cam op ROGER DEAKINS. **stills** Tom Hilton
m/cond JOHN MCLEOD. **Neapolitan musical arrangers** Corrado Sfogli, Giovanni Mauriello
choreo PEARL SINCLAIR
ed TOM PRIESTLEY
ad HAYDEN PEARCE
cost des LOUISE FROGLEY. **make-up** Yvonne Coppard. **hair** Anne McFadyen
sd rec DIANA RUSTON. **dub ed** Nicolas Gaster. **dub mix** Tony Anscombe
cast Phyllis Logan (*Janie*), Giovanni Mauriello (*Luigi*), Gian Luca Favilla (*Umberto*), Claudio Rosini (*Paolo*), Paul Young (*Dougal*), Gregor Fisher (*Beel*), Tom Watson (*Finlay*), Jennifer Piercey (*Kirsty*), Denise Coffey (*Meg*), Yvonne Gilan (*Jess*), Carol Ann Crawford (*Else*), Ray Jeffries (*Alick*), Scott Johnston (*Jeems*), Corrado Sfogli (*Raffaello*), Nadio Fortune (*Antonio*), Peter Finlay (*officer*), David Mowat (*Randy Rob*), Stephen Gressieux (*POW*), Joyce McBrinn (*postmistress*), Nicholas McArdle (*grocer*), Colin Campbell (*accordionist*), James Alexander (*fiddler*), John Francis Lane

Another Time, Another Place

Arthur's Hallowed Ground

(*farmer*), Claire Campbell (*Ella*), Sandy Grey, Hugh Macdonald, John Henderson (*men at threshing mill*)
  shooting Sep–Oct 82. Ross & Cromarty; Inverness
  budget £580,000. **C4 input** £300,000 (lf) (52%)
  1st tx 10 Nov 83 (FF)
  MFB Aug 83. **V** 25 May 83
  awards Best Actor (Giovanni Mauriello), Best Actress (Phyllis Logan), Taormina 83. Best Actress (Phyllis Logan), *Standard* F As 83. Most Outstanding Newcomer (Phyllis Logan), BAFTA F As 84
  festivals Cannes, Taormina 83

ARTHUR'S HALLOWED GROUND
UK, 80 mins, colour
Enigma Television/Goldcrest Films & Television for Channel 4. © Techno Sunley Leisure 1984
  c ed DR. **no**. 42
  p CHRIS GRIFFIN. **exec p** DAVID PUTTNAM. **assoc p** David Bill. **p man** Dominic Fulford. **p co-ord** Mo Coppitters
  d FREDDIE YOUNG. **asst d** Ken Baker; Russell Lodge, Peter Bennett. **continuity** Penny Daniels. **casting d** Simone Reynolds
  sc PETER GIBBS. **sc ed** Jack Rosenthal
  ph CHICK ANSTISS. **cam op** Trevor Coop. **stills** Robert Marshall
  m DAVID EARL
  ed CHRIS RIDSDALE
  ad SIMON WATERS
  cost des TUDOR GEORGE. **make-up** Madeleine Masters
  sd rec DAVID CROZIER. **sd ed** Ron Davis. **dub mix** Gerry Humphreys
  cast Jimmy Jewel (*Arthur Chapman*), Michael Elphick (*Len Draycott*), David Swift

(*Lionel*), Vas Blackwood (*Henry*), Bernard Gallagher (*George*), Jean Boht (*Betty Chapman*), Derek Benfield (*Eric*), John Flanagan (*Norman*), Sam Kelly (*sales representative*), Al Ashton (*Billy*), Mark Drewry (*Kev*), Paul McLean (*young Arthur*), Ron Forfar (*foreman*)
  shooting May 83
  budget £445,093 [David Puttnam].
C4 input £240,000 (lf) (53%)
  1st tx 30 Aug 84 (FF: 'First Love')
  V 5 Feb 86

THE ASSAM GARDEN
UK, 90 mins, colour
The Moving Picture Company. © 'The Assam Garden' Moving Picture Company Films 1984
  c ed KB/DR. **no** 57
  p NIGEL STAFFORD-CLARK. **assoc p** Peter Jaques. **p co-ord** Clare St John
  d MARY MCMURRAY **asst d** Micky Finch, (2nd) Jerry Daly. **continuity** Phyllis Townshend. **casting d** Simone Reynolds
  sc ELISABETH BOND
  ph BRYAN LOFTUS. **cam op** Mike Proudfoot. **stills** Daniel Meadows
  m RICHARD HARVEY. **solo viola** Roger Chase
  ed RODNEY HOLLAND
  ad JANE MARTIN
  cost des CATHY COOK. **make-up** Patricia Kirkman. **hair** Paula Gillespie
  titles Robert Ellis
  sd mix TONY JACKSON. **sd ed** 'Budge' Tremlett. **dub mix** Paul Carr
  cast Deborah Kerr (*Helen Graham*), Ronald Russell (*Mr Grace*), Daisy Bell (*Elsie Edison*), Peggy Ann Wood (*Mrs Grace*), Iain Cuthbertson (*Arthur Graham*), Simon Hedger

The Assam Garden

Bad Hats

(*boy*), Paul Bown (*water board man*), Madhur Jaffrey (*Ruxmani Lal*), Paula Jacobs (*Carol, fish lady*), Maiser Asghar (*Meena*), Waseem Aziz (*Vijay*), Zia Mohyeddin (*Mr Lal*), Dev Sagoo (*Raju Lal*), Tara Shaw (*Sushi Lal*), Alec McCowen (*James Philpott*), Anton Lesser (*Mr Sutton*), Denys Hawthorne (*radio announcer*)
  shooting Aug–Sep 84. Forest of Dean
  budget £600,000. **C4 input** £200,000 (lf) (33%)
  1st tx 16 Apr 87 (FF)
  MFB Aug 85. **V** 24 Jul 85

AYNA *see* **THE MIRROR**

BAD HATS
UK/France, 95 mins, colour
Les Productions Audiovisuelles (Paris) and Skreba Films (London) for Channel 4.
© Channel 4 Television Co 1982
  c ed WD/DR. **no** 11
  p BERNARD LORAIN, PIERRE HEROS. **exec p** ANN SKINNER. **p man** Bernard Lorain
  d PASCAL ORTEGA. **asst d** Xavier Castano, (2nd) Philippe Roussel. **continuity** Ené Watts
  sc MICK FORD, ROBERT HICKSON
  ph GERARD STERIN. **stills** Jean-Philippe Reverdot
  m JEFF COHEN
  ed CHRISTOPHER KELLY
  set des CLAUDE CHEVANT
  cost des CHRISTIAN GASC. **make-up** Florence Fouquier
  sp eff GUY TRIELLI
  sd mix LAURENT QUAGLIO. **dub ed** Martin Evans. **dub mix** Trevor Pyke
  cast Marcel Bozzuffi (*Henri Rouchon*), Mick Ford (*Harold Chapin*), Catherine Lachens (*Catherine Desagnaux*), Laure

Duthilleul (*lady on beach*), Robert Hickson (*officer on beach*), Gilles Girardin (*French officer*), Xavier Castano (*corporal*), Frederick Schlicklin (*private in café*), Guy di Rigo (*fisherman*)
  shooting Northern France
  budget £586,000. **C4 input** £387,000 (lf/i) (66%)
  1st tx 15 Dec 82 (FF)
  V 29 Jun 83
  French release title *L'Amour Fugitif*

THE BAD SISTER
UK, 90 mins, colour
The Moving Picture Company for Channel 4 with Modelmark. Assisted by the National Film Development Fund. © Channel 4 1983
  c ed DR. **no** 21
  p NIGEL STAFFORD-CLARK. **assoc p** Peter Jaques. **p man** Andrew Barratt
  d LAURA MULVEY, PETER WOLLEN. **asst d** Deborah Kingsland, (2nd) Monica Hyde.
  continuity Phyllis Townshend. **casting d** Susie Figgis
  sc LAURA MULVEY, PETER WOLLEN from the novel by Emma Tennant
  ph (video) DIANE TAMMES. **stills** Johanna Tranberg
  m/m perf KARL JENKINS, MIKE RATLEDGE
  ed BOB GOW, ANDY KEMP
  ad HILDEGARD BECHTLER
  cost des CARLA WILLSHER. **make-up** Gordon Kay. **hair** Paula Gillespie
  d vis eff A. J. MITCHELL. **glass paintings** Marguerite Nix
  sd mix PETER GLOSSOP. **dub mix** Peter Maxwell
  extracts *The Loveless*, *King Blank*
  cast Dawn Archibald (*Jane*), Isabel Dean (*Mrs Marten*), Kevin McNally (*Tony Marten*),

The Bad Sister

Bearskin

Matyelock Gibbs (*Meg*), Hugh Millais (*Michael Dalzell/Mr Aldridge*), Neil Cunningham (*Rev Stephen Pauling*), Clive Merrison (*Paul*), Marty Cruickshank (*Mary/ Marie*), Libba Davies (*Kathy*), Emma Jacobs (*Miranda*), Bill Denniston (*Luke*), Maeve Watt (*Louise Dalzell*), Ian Stewart (*Mr Elliot*), A. S. Ross (*interviewer*), Allan Mitchell (*doctor*), Annilee Kuukka (*Jane, girl*), Harriet Laidlaw (*Ishbel Dalzell*)
  shooting Sep–Nov 82. London; Scotland
  budget £418,000. **C4 input** £318,000 (lf) (76%)
  1st tx 23 Jun 83 (FF)

BEARSKIN
An Urban Fairytale
UK/Portugal, 95 mins, colour
Cinema Action (London) for Channel 4 and British Screen with the Portuguese Cinema Institute (Lisbon) and RTP (Lisbon).
© Channel 4 Television Company. 1989
  c ed KB. **no** 137
  p EDUARDO GUEDES, LEONTINE RUETTE. **p man** Alison Barnett, (Portugal) João Pedro Benard. **p co-ord** Diane Chittell, (Portugal) João da Ponte, (post-) Britt Harrison
  d ANN & EDUARDO GUEDES. **asst d** Ray Corbett, (2nd) Andrew Wood, (2nd, Portugal) Rui Cunha. **sc sup** Marian Fowles. **casting** Marilyn Johnson
    sc ANN & EDUARDO GUEDES
    ph MICHAEL COULTER. **cam op** Nigel Willoughby. **stills** Christine Parry
    m MICHAEL MCEVOY. **song** Tom Waits
    ed EDWARD MARNIER
    ad JOCK SCOTT, LUIS MONTEIRO
    cost des MICHAEL JEFFREY. **cost** (bearskin) Alice Power. **make-up** Sula Loizou. **hair** Maureen Hetherington.

    sp eff sup ARTHUR BEAVIS
    stunt arr TIP TIPPING
    sd rec JOAQUIM PINTO. **sd ed** Shirley Shaw. **dub mix** Peter Maxwell
    cast Tom Waits (*Silva*), Damon Lowry (*Johnny Fortune*), Julia Britton (*Laura*), Isabel Ruth (*Mrs J*), Charlotte Coleman (*Kate*), Bill Paterson (*Jordan*), Alex Norton (*Harry*), Mark Arden (*George*), Ian Dury (*Charlie*), Pip Torrens (*Gold-Cufflinks*), David Gant (*Broker*), Karl Collins (*Edison*), Russell Lee (*Mite*), Phil Atkinson (*bouncer*), Tom Thompson (*performer*), Glyn Grimstead (*1st policeman*), Robert Warner (*2nd policeman*), Joe Abdo (*stockbroker*), Arthur Whybrow (*captain*)
    shooting May–Jul 89. London; Portugal
    budget £1,310,000. **C4 input** £895,000 (i) (68%)
    1st tx 29 Sept 91 (FF)
    SS Sep 91. **V** 20 Dec 89
    festivals London 89; San Sebastián, Dinard, Flanders, Leeds, São Paulo, Barcelona 90; Würzburg, Avoriaz, Montecatini Terme, Warsaw 91

THE BELLY OF AN ARCHITECT
UK/Italy, 118 mins, colour
Mondial (London) and Tangram Films (Rome) for The Callender Company (London) with Hemdale (London), SACIS (Rome) and British Screen for Channel 4. © Mondial/ Tangram Films 1987
  c ed DR. **no** 83
  p COLIN CALLENDER, WALTER DONOHUE.
  assoc p Conchita Airoldi, Dino Di Dionisio.
  p/post-p co-ord Irene Jay
  d PETER GREENAWAY. **asst d** Fabio Jephcott. **continuity** Anita Borgiotti. **casting** (Rome) Rita Forzano, (New York) Ellen

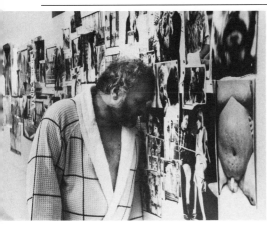

The Belly of an Architect

Billy the Kid and the Green Baize Vampire

Lewis, (Los Angeles) Vickie Thomas, (London) Simone Reynolds
　SC PETER GREENAWAY
　ph SACHA VIERNY. **cam op** Agnès Godard.
stills Sergio Strizzi, Ermano Serto
　m WIM MERTENS. **addit m** Glenn Branca.
m perf The London Sinfonietta, leader Joan
Atherton, conductor Paul Daniel. **fiddle
player** Peter Cooper
　ed JOHN WILSON
　ad LUCIANA VEDOVELLI. **Flavia's
photographs** Steve Pyke
　cost des MAURIZIO MILLENOTTI. **make-up**
Franco Corridoni. **hair** Alberta Giuliani
　sd rec PETER GLOSSOP. **sd ed** Matthew
Whiteman, (dial) Sarah Vickers. **dub mix**
Peter Maxwell
　cast Brian Dennehy (*Stourley Kracklite*),
Chloe Webb (*Louisa Kracklite*), Lambert
Wilson (*Caspasian Speckler*), Sergio
Fantoni (*Io Speckler*), Stefania Casini (*Flavia
Speckler*), Vanni Corbellini (*Frederico
Boccini*), Alfredo Varelli (*Julio Ficcone*),
Geoffrey Copleston (*Antonio Caspetti*),
Francesco Carnelutti (*Pastarri*), Marino Mase
(*Trettorio*), Marne Maitland (*Salvatore
Battistino*), Claudio Spadaro (*Mori*), Rate
Furlan (*violinist*), Julian Jenkins (*old
doctor*), Enrica Maria Scrivano (*mother*),
Riccardo Ussani (*little boy*), Stefano
Gragnani (*the nose man*), Andrea Prodan
(*young doctor*), Fabio Sartor (*policeman*)
　shooting Jul–Aug 86. Rome
　budget £1,800,000. **C4 input** £630,000
(lf/i) (35%)
　1st tx 16 Feb 89 (FF)
　MFB Oct 87. **V** 6 May 87
　festivals Cannes 87

THE BIG SURPRISE *see* **WINTER FLIGHT**

**BILLY THE KID AND
THE GREEN BAIZE VAMPIRE**
UK, 93 mins, colour
Zenith Productions with ITC Entertainment.
© ITC Entertainment 1985
　c ed DR. **no** 70
　p SIMON MALLIN. **p sup** Bill Kirk. **p co-ord**
Kathy Sykes
　d ALAN CLARKE. **asst d** Peter Waller,
Kieron Phipps, Tony Aherne. **continuity**
Francine Brown. **casting d** Beth Charkham
　SC TREVOR PRESTON
　ph CLIVE TICKNER **cam op** Nigel
Willoughby. **stills** Simon Mein
　m/md GEORGE FENTON. **lyrics** TREVOR
PRESTON. **m perf** Ray Russell (guitar), Don
Weller (saxophone), Neil Wilkinson
(drums), Mo Foster (bass), Gavyn Wright
(violin), Jess Bailey (synthesizer), George
Fenton (piano)
　ed STEPHEN SINGLETON
　pd JAMIE LEONARD. **ad** Andy Harris
　cost des TUDOR GEORGE. **make-up** Jenny
Shircore, Lesley Rouvray-Lawson. **hair** Liz
Michie, Patti Smith
　titles Peter Govey
　floor sd mix ANDREW BOULTON. **dub ed**
Anthony Sloman, (dial) Sarah Vickers. **dub
mix** Paul Carr
　cast Phil Daniels (*Billy Kid*), Alun
Armstrong (*Maxwell Randall, The Vampire*),
Bruce Payne (*T.O., The One*), Louise Gold
(*Miss Sullivan*), Eve Ferret (*Mrs Randall*),
Richard Ridings (*Egypt*), Don Henderson
(*The Wednesday Man*), Neil McCaul (*Big
Jack Jay*), Zoot Money (*Supersonic Sam*),
David Foxxe (*The Spook*), Johnny Dennis
(*Charlie Clegg, referee*), Trevor Laird
(*Floyd*), Daniel Webb (*TV director*), Ben Cole,
Paul Cooke, Trevor Cooper, Chrissie

The Bomb

Born of Fire

Cotterill, Sarah Crowden, Ricky Diamond, Teresa Garraway, Peter Geeves, Glyn Grimstead, Tracie Hart, Sam Howard, Gareth Kirkland, Edwina Lawrie, Claire Lewis, Kevin Lloyd, Sarah London, Christina Matthews, Liz Morton, Paul Mulrennan, Clive Panto, Robert Pereno, Caroline Quentin, Nick Revell, George Rossi, Liza Sadovy, Roger Tebb, Claire Toeman, Tim Withnall, Justin Case, Tony Chinn, Joe Fordham, Lisa Hart, Johnny Irving, Arnold Lee, Lindsay Neil, Joan Rhodes, Fiona Sloman, Gillian De Terville
　shooting Twickenham studios
　budget £2,700,000. **C4 input** £350,000 (lf/i) (13%)
　1st tx 2 Apr 87 (FF)
　MFB May 86

BLACKOUT *see* **MOONLIGHTING**

THE BOMB
FGR/Austria/Switzerland/UK/Sweden, 105 mins, colour
Multimedia Gesellschaft for Audiovisuelle Information (Hamburg) with ZDF (Mainz), ORF (Vienna), SRG (Bern), Channel 4 and SVT (Stockholm). © ZDF 1987
　c ed KB. **no** (-)
　p MATHIAS WITTICH. **assoc p** Christoph Holch. **p man** Dieter Rauh. **unit man** Hansjörg Füting
　d HELMUT CHRISTIAN GÖRLITZ. **asst d** Meibrit Ahrens; Kai Wessel
　sc HELMUT CHRISTIAN GÖRLITZ from the novel by Lars Molin
　ph ALFRED D. EBNER; Rolf Schmitt. **2nd ph** Haral Marxen; Jochen Bärwald
　m MATTHIAS THUROW
　ed KIM PULS; Ursula Roderjan

　ad BERND GAEBLER
　cost GABRIELE ARENDT. **make-up** Erich Schmekel, Derrick Bosch
　sd HORST STROEMER; Siegfried Sellentin. **mix** Hans Gralke
　cast Michael Degen (*Paul Meyerdiercks*), Rosel Zech (*Helga Meyerdiercks*), Rolf Becker (*Jan Lessing*), Wolfgang Wahl (*Police Chief Klaus Kuhnke*), Ulrich Matschoss (*Mayor Schröder*), Dietrich Mattausch (*Interior Minister Winter*), Franz Rudnick (*Dr Tomczyck*), Gudo Hoegel (*Schmölders*), Siegfried Kernen (*Dr Richard*), Matthias Fuchs (*Lt Col Uhl*), Hartmut Reck (*von Plottnitz*), Jochen Paulmann (*MEK chief*), Christoph Felsenstein (*psychologist*), Eleonore Weisgerber, Fritz Lichtenhahn
　shooting Hamburg
　budget (?) **C4 input** £75,000 (lf)
　1st tx 29 Sep 90 (FFI)
　German release title *Die Bombe*

DIE BOMBE *see* **THE BOMB**

BORN OF FIRE
UK, 84 mins, colour
Dehlavi Films for Channel 4. © Film Four International 1986
　c ed DR/KB. **no** 74
　p JAMIL DEHLAVI, THÉRÈSE PICKARD. **assoc p** Stewart Richards
　d JAMIL DEHLAVI. **asst d** Alison Barnett, (2nd) Ali Can Gebes. **continuity** Sarah Hayward. **casting** Liz Cassidy
　sc RAFICQ ABDULLAH. **story** Jamil Dehlavi
　ph BRUCE MCGOWAN. **addit ph** Clive Tickner. **insect ph** Alistair McEwan. **stills** Douglas Dawson
　m COLIN TOWNS. **key flute** KUDSI ERGUNER. **flautist** (Poulenc, Debussy, Mayer) JAMES

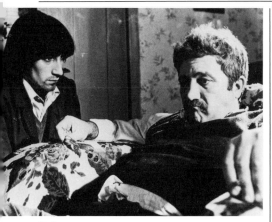

Cal

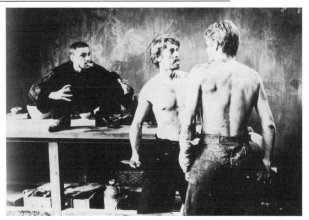

Caravaggio

GALWAY. **recitation of prayers** Abdi Coskun
  ed ROBERT HARGREAVES
  ad MICHAEL PORTER
  cost JOHN HIBBS. **artistic/sp eff make-up**
Sula Loizou
  sd rec DEREK WILLIAMS. **sd ed** Anthony
Sloman. **dub mix** Paul Carr
  cast Peter Firth (*Paul Bergson/Paul's
father*), Suzan Crowley (*the woman*), Stefan
Kalipha (*Bilal*), Oh-Tee (*the Master
Musician*), Nabil Shaban (*the Silent One*),
Jean Ainslie (*mother*), Peter Penry-Jones (*the
manager*), Morris Perry (*the director*),
Richard Bebb (*newsreader*), Ziya Derlen,
Tamer Üstel, Ismet Arasan, Cemal Uzunoglu,
Güner Gülbahar (*dervishes*), Asaf Erguner,
Bayram Özbay, Tanju Duru, Tengüz Ünsal
(*musicians*)
  shooting England; Turkey
  budget £854,000. **C4 input** £755,000 (i)
(88%)
  1st tx 14 Apr 88 (FF)
  V 28 Oct 87
  awards 1st P (genre section), Madrid 87.
Gold A (Special Jury P), Houston 87
  festivals Rio de Janeiro 86; Avoriaz,
Madrid, Houston, Hamburg, Cattolica,
Ghent, Cairo, Geneva 87; Trivandrum,
Belgrade 88; Antenna 89
  working title *The Master Musician*

CAL
UK, 102 mins, colour
Enigma Films with the Eastern Counties
Newspapers Group and the United Film
Distribution Company for Warner Bros,
Goldcrest Films & Television and Channel 4.
© Eastern Counties Newspapers Group 1984
  c ed DR. **no** 131 [formerly 61]
  p STUART CRAIG, DAVID PUTTNAM. **exec p**

TERENCE A. CLEGG. **p man** Dominic Fulford.
p co-ord Mo Coppitters
  d PAT O'CONNOR. **asst d** Bill Craske;
Christopher Thompson, John Phelan, Nick
Daubeny. **continuity** Pauline Harlow.
casting d Patsy Pollock
  sc BERNARD McLAVERTY from his own
novel
  ph JERZY ZIELINSKI. **cam op** Seamus
Corcoran. **stills** Tom Collins, David Appleby
  m MARK KNOPFLER
  ed MICHAEL BRADSELL
  pd STUART CRAIG. **ad** Josie MacAvin
  cost PENNY ROSE. **make-up** Toni Delany.
hair Joanna Lennox
  sp eff sup JOHN EVANS
  stunt co-ord ROY ALON
  graphics Howard Brown, John Gorham.
titles Richard Morrison
  sd rec PAT HAYES. **dub ed** Campbell
Askew. **dial ed** Peter Horrocks. **dub mix** Bill
Rowe
  cast Helen Mirren (*Marcella Morton*),
John Lynch (*Cal McCluskie*), Donal McCann
(*Shamie*), John Kavanagh (*Skeffington*), Ray
McAnally (*Cyril Dunlop*), Stevan Rimkus
(*Crilly*), Catherine Gibson (*Mrs Morton*),
Louis Rolston (*Dermot Ryan*), Tom Hickey
(*preacher*), Gerard Mannix Flynn (*Arty*),
Seamus Ford (*Old Mr Morton*), Edward
Byrne (*Skeffington Sr*), J. J. Murphy (*man in
library*), Audrey Johnston (*Lucy Morton*),
Brian Munn (*Robert Morton*), Daragh
O'Malley (*scarfaced policeman*), George
Shane (*2nd policeman*), Julia Dearden (*shop
assistant*), Yvonne Adams (*neighbour*),
Lawrence Foster (*soldier at roadblock*),
Scott Frederick, Gerard O'Hagan (*soldiers at
farm*)
  shooting Nov 83. Eire

The Chain

Christmas Present

budget £1,932,995 [David Puttnam]
C4 input £325,000 (lf) (17%)
1st tx 26 Feb 87 (FF)
MFB Sep 84. **V** 23 May 84
awards Best Actress (Helen Mirren),
Cannes 84
festivals Cannes 84

CARAVAGGIO

UK, 93 mins, colour
The British Film Institute with Nicholas
Ward-Jackson and Channel 4. © Derek
Jarman 1986
c ed KB. **no** 80
p SARAH RADCLYFFE. **exec p** COLIN
MACCABE. **exec i/c p** Jill Pack. **p man** Sarah
Wilson
d DEREK JARMAN. **asst d** Glynn Purcell,
(2nd) Simon Moseley. **continuity** Heather
Storr. **casting** Debbie McWilliams
sc DEREK JARMAN from an original idea by
Nicholas Ward-Jackson
ph GABRIEL BERISTAIN. **2nd cam op** Steve
Tickner. **stills** Mike Laye
m SIMON FISHER TURNER, assisted by Mary
Phillips. **musicians** Bill Badley, Steart
Butterfield, Lol Coxhill, Charlie Duncan,
Brian Gulland, Stuart Hall, Julia Hodgson,
Timothy Hugh, Neil Kelly, Chi Chi
Nwanoku, Jocelyn Pook, Rodney Skeaping,
El Tito, Veryan Weston. **singers** John
Douglas-Williams, Charles Gibbs, Mary
Phillips, Nicolas Robertson, Angus Smith
ed GEORGE AKERS
pd/paintings CHRISTOPHER HOBBS. **ad**'
Mike Buchanan
cost des SANDY POWELL. **make-up** Morag
Ross
stunt co-ord JIM DOWDALL, GARETH MILNE.
stunt perf Tracey Eddon

sd rec BILLY MCCARTHY. **dub ed** 'Budge'
Tremlett. **dub mix** Peter Maxwell
cast Noam Almaz (*boy Caravaggio*), Dawn
Archibald (*Pipo*), Sean Bean (*Ranuccio
Thomasoni*), Jack Birkett (*Pope*), Una
Brandon-Jones (*weeping woman*), Imogen
Claire (*lady with the jewels*), Robbie
Coltrane (*Cardinal Scipione Borghese*), Garry
Cooper (*Davide*), Sadie Corre (*Princess
Collona*), Lol Coxhill (*old priest*), Nigel
Davenport (*Giustiniani*), Vernon Dobtcheff
(*art lover*), Terry Downes (*bodyguard*),
Dexter Fletcher (*young Caravaggio*),
Michael Gough (*Cardinal Francis Del
Monte*), Jonathan Hyde (*Baglione*), Spencer
Leigh (*Jerusaleme*), Emil Nicolaou (*young
Jerusaleme*), Gene October (*model peeling
fruit*), Cindy Oswin (*Lady Elizabeth*), John
Rogan (*Vatican official*), Zohra Segal
(*Jerusaleme's grandmother*), Tilda Swinton
(*Lena*), Lucien Taylor (*boy with guitar*),
Nigel Terry (*Michelangelo Merisi,
Caravaggio*), Simon Turner (*Fra Fillipo*),
Derek Jarman (*priest attendant on Pope*)
shooting autumn 85. Limehouse studios
budget £475,000 [BFI]. **C4 input** £250,000
(lf) (54%)
1st tx 14 May 87 (FF)
MFB Apr 86. **V** 26 Feb 86
awards Silver Bear (visual conception),
Outstanding Single Achievement (Gabriel
Beristain), Berlin 86
festivals Berlin 86

THE CHAIN

UK, 100 mins, colour
Quintet Productions with County Bank and
Channel 4. © Quintet Productions 1984
c ed DR. **no** 51
p VICTOR GLYNN. **exec p** DAVID DEUTSCH.

The Company of Wolves

Comrades

co-p KIFFER WEISSELBERG. **assoc p** Peter Manley. **p man** Jean Walter
d JACK GOLD. **asst d** Gary White, (2nd) Nicholas Laws, (co-2nd) Patrick Kinney.
continuity Renée Glynne. **casting d** Irene Lamb
sc JACK ROSENTHAL
ph WOLFGANG SUSCHITZKY. **cam op** Gerry Anstiss. **stills** Nobby Clark
m STANLEY MYERS. **title song** Barbara Dickson, Jack Rosenthal, Stanley Myers. **singer** Barbara Dickson
ed BILL BLUNDEN
pd PETER MURTON
cost des TUDOR GEORGE. **make-up** Sandra Shepherd. **hair** Ross Carver
sd mix BRIAN SIMMONS. **sd ed** Jonathan Bates. **dub mix** Gerry Humphreys, Robin O'Donoghue
cast Denis Lawson (*Keith Hodges*), Rita Wolf (*Carrie Hodges*), Phyllis Logan (*Alison Metcalf*), David Troughton (*Dudley Metcalf*), Jade Magri (*Tasha*), Maurice Denham (*Alison's grandpa*), Nigel Hawthorne (*Mr Thorn*), Anna Massey (*Betty Thorn*), Billie Whitelaw (*Mrs Andreos*), Judy Parfitt (*Deirdre*), John Rowe (*Alex*), Matthew Blakstad (*Mark*), Charlotte Long (*Rosemary*), Leo McKern (*Thomas Jackson*), Herbert Norville (*Des*), Carmen Munroe (*Des's mother*), Ron Pember (*Stan*), Warren Mitchell (*Bamber*), Bernard Hill (*Nick*), Tony Westrope (*Paul*), Gary Waldhorn (*Tornado*), Ann Tirard (*homeless old lady*), Patsy Smart (*old lady*), Bill Thomas (*postman*), Robin Summers (*policeman*), Ben Onwukwe (*1st removal man*), James Coyle (*2nd removal man*), George Rossi (*3rd removal man*), Graham Jarvis (*Foxx*), Darliah Wood (*Bozo*), Kim Clifford (*Dingy*), Alex Tetteth-Lartey

(*Edgar, Mr Thorn's neighbour*), Paddy Joyce (*carpet layer*), Christopher Ettridge (*removal man*), Mark Dignam (*Ambrose*), Michael Mulkerrin (*clampsman*), Vicky Licorish (*Myra*), Steven Woodcock (*Gary*), Bob Holness (*newsreader*)
shooting London
budget £1,150,000. **C4 input** £363,000 (lf/i) (32%)
1st tx 12 Feb 87 (FF)
MFB Jun 85. **V** 15 May 85

CHRISTMAS PRESENT
UK, 73 mins, colour
Telekation International for Channel 4.
© Channel 4 Television 1985
c ed DR. **no** 64
p BARRY HANSON. **p man** Caroline Hewitt.
p co-ord Ginny Roncoroni
d TONY BICÂT. **asst d** Peter Jaques, (2nd) Nancy Platt. **continuity** Annie South. **casting d** Ann Fielden
sc TONY BICÂT
ph GABRIEL BERISTAIN
m NICK BICÂT. **cond** Tony Britten. **songs** Nick Bicât, Tony Bicât
ed BILL SHAPTER
des NIGEL PHELPS, JOCELYN JAMES
cost des ANDREA GALER. **make-up** Pat Hay. **hair** Meinir Brock
sd TERRY HARDY. **sd ed** Michael Connell.
dub mix Dean Humphreys
cast Peter Chelsom (*Nigel Playfayre*), Lesley Manville (*Judy Tall*), Karen Meagher (*Anne*), Hetty Baynes (*Pamela*), Richard Ireson (*Ned*), Bill Fraser (*Sir Percy Hammond*), Danny Wooder (*Viv*), Clive Parker (*Gos*), Janet Steel (*Mary*), Nadim Sawahla (*Joseph*), Mark Harvey (*Sticky*), Elizabeth Bradley (*Granny Harris*), Badi

Conquest of the South Pole

The Country Girls

Uzzaman (*Amir Mehrban*), Jamila Massey
(*Mrs Mehrban*), Harry Jones (*placard man*),
Sohan Maharaj (*Talvar*), Malser Asghar
(*Munni*), Simmi Salimi (*Tunni*), Abraham
Osuagwa (*Nigerian tourist*), Nick Brimble
(*Tom*), Amelda Brown (*Angela Benton, ITN
reporter*), Philip Herbert (*Santa Claus*),
Michael Melia (*security guard*), Christopher
Birch (*police inspector*), Jonathon Stratt
(*police constable*), Pamela Abbott (*Pamela's
mother*), Norman Adams (*Pamela's father*),
Jackie D. Broad, Debbie Mullins, Les Sharp
(*street theatre*), Stephen Bronowski, Adrian
Gilpin, Pat Gorman (*ITN crew*)
   shooting Feb–Mar 85. London
   budget £567,000. **C4 input** £567,000 (lf/i)
(100%)
   1st tx 19 Dec 85 (FF)
   V 11 Dec 85
   awards Silver Nymph (best screenplay),
Monte Carlo 86. Best Children's Production
(feature length), New Jersey 86
   festivals London 85; Monte Carlo, New
Jersey 86
   working title *An English Christmas*

THE COMPANY OF WOLVES
UK, 95 mins, colour
Palace Productions for Channel 4. © ITC
Entertainment 1984
   c ed WD. **no** 44
   p CHRIS BROWN, STEPHEN WOOLLEY. **exec
p** STEPHEN WOOLLEY, NIK POWELL. **p man**
Vivien Pottersman. **p co-ord** Norma Brusa,
(eff unit) Chris Carreras
   d NEIL JORDAN. **asst d** Simon Hinkly, (eff)
Clive Hedges, (2nd) Paul Tivers. **continuity**
Alison Thorne, (eff) Mary Holdsworth.
casting d Susie Figgis
   sc ANGELA CARTER, NEIL JORDAN. **adapt**

Angela Carter from her own story
   ph BRYAN LOFTUS, (eff) PETER
MACDONALD. **cam op** Mike Roberts, (eff) John
Campbell. **stills** Tom Collins
   m GEORGE FENTON. **synthesizers** David
Lawson
   ed RODNEY HOLLAND
   pd ANTON FURST. **ad** Stuart Rose
   cost des ELIZABETH WALLER. **sp make-up
eff des/exec** CHRISTOPHER TUCKER. **make-up**
Jane Royle. **hair** Paula Gillespie
   sp eff sup ALAN WHIBLEY. **animatronic
wolf** RODGER SHAW. **animatronics sup**
STUART ROBINSON
   stunt arr MARC BOYLE. **stunts** Terry Cade,
Gareth Milne, Graeme Crowther, Nick Hobbs,
Dinny Powell, Bill Weston, Tex Fuller
   sd mix DAVID JOHN. **eff unit sd rec** NEIL
KINGSBURY. **sup dub ed** Anthony Sloman.
dub ed Alan Bell, Bryan Tilling. **dub mix**
Paul Carr
   cast Angela Lansbury (*granny*), David
Warner (*father*), Graham Crowden (*old
priest*), Brian Glover (*amorous boy's father*),
Kathryn Pogson (*young bride*), Stephen Rea
(*young groom*), Tusse Silberg (*mother*),
Micha Bergese (*the huntsman*), Sarah
Patterson (*Rosaleen*), Georgia Slowe (*Alice*),
Susan Porrett (*amorous boy's mother*), Shane
Johnstone (*amorous boy*), Dawn Archibald
(*witch woman*), Richard Morant (*wealthy
groom*), Danielle Dax (*wolfgirl*), Vincent
McClaren (*devil boy*), Ruby Buchanan
(*dowager*), Jimmy Gardner (*ancient*), Roy
Evans (*eyepatch*), Edward Marksen (*lame
fiddler*), Jimmy Brown (*blind fiddler*),
Terence Stamp (*Prince of Darkness*), Percy
Edwards (*wolf noises*)
   shooting Jan–Mar 84. Shepperton
studios

Dance with a Stranger

The Dead

budget £2,400,000. **C4 input** £200,000 (lf) (8%)
1st tx 5 Mar 87 (FF)
MFB Sep 84. **V** 18 Jul 84
awards Best Director, Critics' Circle As (UK) 84

COMRADES
A Lanternist's account of the Tolpuddle Martyrs and what became of them
UK, 183 mins, colour
Skreba Films with the National Film Finance Corporation and Curzon Film Distributors for Channel 4. 1986
c ed DR/KB. **no** 72
p SIMON RELPH. **assoc p** Redmond Morris, (Australia) David Hannay, (addit post-p) Patrick Cassavetti. **p co-ord** (UK) Deborah Carter, (Australia) Vanessa Brown. **p man** Donna Grey, (Australia) Charles Hannah
d BILL DOUGLAS. **asst d** (UK) Redmond Morris, (2nd, UK) Nick Laws, (2nd, Australia) Christine King. **sc sup** Penny Eyles. **casting** Susie Figgis, Gail Stevens, (Australia) Michael Lynch, Rae Davidson
sc BILL DOUGLAS. **sc ed** Peter Jewell
ph GALE TATTERSALL. **stills** David Appleby
m HANS WERNER HENZE, DAVID GRAHAM.
cond Hans Werner Henze. **m perf** The London Sinfonietta. **period m advisers** George and Isobel Deacon
ed MICK AUDSLEY, (addit post-p) Mike Ellis, Simon Clayton
des MICHAEL PICKWOAD. **ad** Henry Harris, (Australia) Derek Chetwyn
cost DOREEN WATKINSON, (Australia) BRUCE FINLAYSON. **make-up** Elaine Carew.
hair Patricia Cameron
stunt co-ord (Australia) PETER ARMSTRONG

sd CLIVE WINTER. **dub ed** Jupiter Sen, Alan Bell, Richard Dunford, (addit post-p) Peter Musgrave. **re-rec mix** (UK) Hugh Strain. **eff rec** (UK) Peter Maxwell, Mick Boggis
cast [the Tolpuddle Martyrs] Robin Soans (*George Loveless*), William Gaminara (*James Loveless*), Stephen Bateman (*Old Tom Stanfield*), Philip Davis (*Young John Stanfield*), Jeremy Flynn (*James Brine*), Keith Allen (*James Hammett*), [and] Alex Norton (*the Lanternist/Sgt Bell/Diorama Showman/Laughing Cavalier/Wollaston/ Ranger/Tramp/Sea Captain/McCallum/ Silhouettist/Mad Photographer/Witch*); [guest stars] Michael Clark (*the Sailor*), Arthur Dignam (*the Fop*), James Fox (*William Moncrieff Norfolk*), John Hargreaves (*the Convict*), Michael Hordern (*Mr Pitt*), Freddie Jones (*the Vicar*), Murray Melvin (*the Clerk*), Vanessa Redgrave (*Mrs Violet Carlyle*), Robert Stephens (*Frampton*), Barbara Windsor (*Mrs Wetham*); [the Tolpuddle families] Imelda Staunton (*Betsy Loveless*), Katy Behean (*Sarah Loveless*), Amber Wilkinson (*Hetty Loveless*), Patricia Healey (*Mrs Brine*), Shane Downe (*Joseph Brine*), Sandra Voe (*Diana Stanfield*), Valerie Whittington (*Elvi Stanfield*), Harriet Doyle (*Charity Stanfield*), Patrick Field (*John Hammett*), Heather Page (*Bridget Hammett*); [in Dorset] Joanna David (*Mrs Frampton*), Trevor Ainsley, Malcolm Terris (*gentlemen farmers*), Dave Atkins (*foreman*), Collette Barker (*Frampton's servant girl*), Jack Chissick (*policeman*), Alex McCrindle (*jailor*), Mark Brown (*Edward Legg*), Sarah Reed (*blonde girl*), Nicola Hayward (*dark girl*), Sophie Randall, Emma Tuck (*Legg's children*), Jon Holman, Jan Holman (*gypsy band*), Raven James (*escapologist*), John Lee

The Disappearance of Harry

Distant Voices, Still Lives

(*juggler*); [in Australia] Shane Briant (*official*), Ralph Cotterill (*Bertie the guard*), Lynette Curran (*prostitute*), Tim Eliott (*registrar*), Simone Landis (*Flower, Norfolk's daughter*), Brian Macdermott (*auctioneer*), David McWilliams (*digger*), David Netheim (*the Fop's officer*), Symon Parsonage (*Charlie*), Anna Volska (*woman in white*), Charles Yunipingu (*lone aboriginal*)
   shooting Sep 85–Jan 86. Dorset; New South Wales
   budget £3,014,000. **C4 input** £1,000,000 (lf/i) (33%)
   1st tx 27 Apr 89 (FF)
   MFB Sep 87. **V** 10 Dec 86
   awards Most Original and Imaginative F Premiered at NFT, BFI As 86
   festivals London 86

CONQUEST OF THE SOUTH POLE
UK, 95 mins, colour/b&w
Jam Jar Films with Channel 4. © Jam Jar Films 1989
   c ed KB. **no** 133
   p GARETH WARDELL. **exec p** JOHN KELLEHER. **assoc p** Penny Thomson. **p man** Lee Leckie
   d GILLIES MACKINNON. **asst d** Darryl Collins, (2nd) Gus MacLean. **sc sup** Margaret Waldie. **casting** (London) John Hubbard
   adapt GARETH WARDELL from the play by Manfred Karge, translated by Tinch Minter, Anthony Vivis. **sc adviser** Frederic Lindsay
   ph SEAN VAN HALES. **stills** Gordon Terris
   m GUY WOOLFENDEN. **m cons** Wayne Bickerton. **song** ('Star of Scotland') Guy Woolfenden, performed by Christopher Gradwell (alto saxophone), Dave Hancock (trumpet), Colin Sheen (trombone), David Firman (keyboards), Dave Olney (bass

guitar), Eric Allen (percussion), Barry De Souza (drums)
   ed STEPHEN SINGLETON
   ad ANDY HARRIS
   cost des LYNN AITKEN. **make-up** Mari Baird
   sp eff KEVIN MOLLOY
   stunt co-ord STUART ST PAUL
   sd mix COLIN NICOLSON. **sd ed** Paul Clegg, Clive Gardener. **dub mix** Colin Martin
   archive material Norwegian Film Institute
   cast Stevan Rimkus (*Sloopianek*), Leonard O'Malley (*Butcher*), Gordon Cameron (*Brown*), Alastair Galbraith (*Frankieboy*), Ewen Bremner (*Penguin*), Laura Girling (*Louise*), Julie-Kate Olivier (*Rosie*), John Michie (*Roddy*), Michael Nardone (*job centre assistant*), Romilly Squire (*barman*), Allan Ross (*1st tramp*), Rab Christie (*2nd tramp*), Gareth Wardell (*Shackleton*), Matthew Costello (*waiter*), Andy Munro (*1st musician*), Graham McKellar (*2nd musician*), Cindy (*dog*), Max (*penguin*)
   shooting Jan–Feb 89. Leith Docks and Arthur's Seat, Edinburgh
   budget £300,000. **C4 input** £300,000 (lf) (100%)
   1st tx 26 Apr 90 (FF)
   MFB Jun 90
   festivals Edinburgh, London 89

THE COUNTRY GIRLS
UK/Eire, 108 mins, colour
London Films for Channel 4 with the Irish Film Board. © London Films International 1983
   c ed DR. **no** 30
   p AIDA YOUNG. **exec p** DAVID CONROY,

The Dive

Doc's Kingdom

MARK SHELMERDINE. **p man** Kevan Barker
d DESMOND DAVIS. **asst d** Roy Millichip,
(2nd) Martin O'Malley. **continuity** Jean
Bourne. **casting d** Dawn Robinson, Ann
Fielden
  sc EDNA O'BRIEN from her own novel
  ph DENIS LEWISTON. **stills** Tom Collins
  m FRANCIS SHAW
  ed TIMOTHY GEE
  ad ARDEN GANTLY
  cost des GWENDA EVANS. **make-up** Toni
Delany. **hair** Anne Dunne
  sp eff GERRY JOHNSTON
  sd mix PAT HAYES, TREVOR O'CONNOR. **sd
ed** Peter Horrocks. **sd re-rec** Trevor Pyke
  cast Sam Neill (*Mr P. W. Gentleman*), John
Kavanagh (*James Brady*), Niall Toibin (*Jack
Holland*), Maeve Germaine (*Caithleen
Brady*), Jill Doyle (*Bridget 'Baba' Brennan*),
John Olohan (*Hickey*), Britta Smith (*Lil*),
Patricia Martin (*Martha*), Des Nealon (*Frank
Brennan*), Sheila Flitton (*Sister Margaret*),
Anna Manahan (*Mrs Hilda Burns*), Agnes
Bernelle (*Joanna Schwarz*), Patricia Jeffares
(*Miss Moriarty*), Vincent Smith (*Harry*), Tom
Laidlaw (*Reg*), Sheila O'Sullivan (*Sister
Cecilia*), Lisa Cook (*Sister Rosario*), Jim Reid
(*priest*), Joan Harpur (*Cynthia*), Pat Power
(*Herman*), Deirdre Rafferty (*prefect*), Frank
Melia (*barman*), Paul Conway (*train
barboy*), Lorraine Barry, Christine Shiels,
Carla Purdue, Adele Monahan (*dancers*),
Majella Nolan, Laura Conway, Susan Ryan
(*schoolgirls*)
  shooting May–Jul 83. Bray, Co. Wicklow
  budget £770,000. **C4 input** £330,000 (lf/i)
(43%)
  1st tx 24 Nov 83 (FF)
  MFB May 84. **V** 9 Nov 83
  awards Best F, Cork 83

  festivals Cork, London 83

DANCE WITH A STRANGER
UK, 102 mins, colour
First Film Company for Goldcrest Films &
Television with the National Film Finance
Corporation and Channel 4. Assisted by the
National Film Development Fund and
Shooting Lodge. 1984
  c ed DR. **no** 48
  p ROGER RANDALL-CUTLER. **assoc p** Paul
Cowan. **p co-ord** Laura Julian
  d MIKE NEWELL. **asst d** Micky Finch, (2nd)
Fraser Copp. **sc sup** Annie South. **casting**
Celestia Fox
  sc SHELAGH DELANEY
  ph PETER HANNAN. **cam op** Bob Smith.
stills Diana Miller
  m RICHARD HARTLEY
  ed MICK AUDSLEY
  pd ANDREW MOLLO. **ad** Adrian Smith
  cost PIP NEWBERY. **make-up** Pat Hay. **hair**
Meinir Brock
  stunt co-ord JIM DOWDALL
  sd mix KEN WESTON. **dub ed** George Akers.
dub mix Peter Maxwell
  cast Miranda Richardson (*Ruth Ellis*),
Rupert Everett (*David Blakely*), Ian Holm
(*Desmond Cussen*), Matthew Carroll (*Andy*),
Tom Chadbon (*Anthony Findlater*), Jane
Bertish (*Carole Findlater*), David Troughton
(*Cliff Davis*), Paul Mooney (*Clive Gunnel*),
Stratford Johns (*Morrie Conley*), Joanne
Whalley (*Christine*), Susan Kyd (*Barbara*),
Lesley Manville (*Maryanne*), Sallie-Anne
Field (*Claudette*), David Beale (*man in Little
Club*), Martin Murphy (*Roy*), Tracy-Louise
Ward (*girl with David Blakely*), Michael Jenn
(*Wilf*), Alan Thompson (*Ralph*), Nicholas
McArdle (*landlord, country pub*), Miki Iveria

The Draughtsman's Contract

The Dream

(*landlady*), Lizzie McKenzie (*woman in launderette*), Ian Hurley (*1st policeman*), Charles Cork (*2nd policeman*), Patrick Field (*builder*), Colin Rix (*'Magdala' landlord*), Tony Mathews (*'Magdala' customer*), Charon Bourke (*ballroom singer*), Elizabeth Newell (*baby*)
  shooting Mar–May 84. London
  budget £1,400,000. **C4 input** £283,000 (lf/i) (20%)
  1st tx 3 Mar 88 (FF)
  MFB Mar 85. **V** 13 Mar 85
  awards Best Actress (Miranda Richardson), *Standard* F As 85

DANS LA VILLE BLANCHE *see* **IN THE WHITE CITY**

THE DEAD
USA/UK/FGR, 83 mins, colour
Liffey Films (Valencia, California) with Vestron Pictures (Stamford, Connecticut), Zenith Productions (London), Channel 4 and Delta Film (Berlin). © Zenith Productions/Liffey Films 1987
  c ed DR. **no** 104
  p WIELAND SCHULZ-KEIL, CHRIS SIEVERNICH. **exec p** WILLIAM J. QUIGLEY. **p co-ord** Anne M. Shaw. **p man** Tom Shaw. **post-p sup** Keith M. Sheridan
  d JOHN HUSTON. **asst d** Tom Shaw, (2nd) John 'Joe' Brooks, (Ireland, 2nd unit) Seamus Byrne, (Ireland, 2nd Unit, 2nd) Gay Brabazon. **sc sup** Karen Golden. **casting** Nuala Moiselle
  sc TONY HUSTON from the story by James Joyce. **literary adviser** (James Joyce estate) Clive Hart
  ph FRED MURPHY. **cam op** Randy Nolen. **Irish landscapes cam** Michael Coulter. **stills**

François Duhamel
  m ALEX NORTH. **solo harp** Ann Stockton. **orch** Richard Bronskill. **song** 'The Lass of Aughrim' performed by Frank Patterson
  choreo PAUL GLEASON
  ed ROBERTO SILVI
  pd STEPHEN GRIMES in collaboration with DENNIS WASHINGTON. **ad** (Ireland, 2nd unit) Arden Gantly
  ward des DOROTHY JEAKINS. **make-up** Fern Buchner. **hair** Anthony Cortino
  sp eff CANDY FLANAGIN. **sp eff sup** (Ireland, 2nd unit) Maurice Foley
  sd mix BILL RANDALL. **sd ed** James E. Nownes. **sup sd ed** Marvin I. Kosberg. **re-rec mix** Robert W. Glass (dial), Ken S. Polk (m), John B. Asman (eff)
  cast Helena Carroll (*Aunt Kate Morkan*), Cathleen Delany (*Aunt Julia Morkan*), Rachael Dowling (*Lily*), Katherine O'Toole (*Miss Furlong*), Bairbre Dowling (*Miss Higgins*), Maria Hayden (*Miss O'Callaghan*), Cormac O'Herlihy (*Joseph Kerrigan*), Colm Meaney (*Eamon Bergin*), Ingrid Craigie (*Mary Jane*), Dan O'Herlihy (*Mr Brown*), Anjelica Huston (*Gretta Conroy*), Donal McCann (*Gabriel Conroy*), Frank Patterson (*Bartell D'Arcy*), Marie Kean (*Mrs Malins*), Donal Donnelly (*Freddy Malins*), Seán McClory (*Mr Grace*), Maria McDermottroe (*Molly Ivors*), Lyda Anderson (*Miss Daly*), Dara Clarke (*young lady*), Paul Grant (*Mr Duffy*), Paul Carroll (*2nd young gentleman*), Patrick Gallagher (*3rd young gentleman*), Brendan Dillon (*cabman*), Redmond M. Gleeson (*nightporter*)
  shooting Valencia, California; Dublin
  budget £2,259,000. **C4 input** £175,000 (lf) (8%)
  1st tx 22 Feb 90 (FF)

The Dressmaker

Drowning by Numbers

MFB Dec 87. **V** 2 Sep 87
festivals London 87

THE DISAPPEARANCE OF HARRY
UK, 90 mins, colour
Labrahurst for Channel 4. © Labrahurst
1982
   c ed DR. **no** 3
   p JOSEPH DESPINS, CHRIS GRIFFIN
   d JOSEPH DESPINS. **asst d** Dominic Fulford;
Andrew Montgomery, Nick Daubeny.
continuity Mary Holdsworth. **casting d**
Debbie McWilliams
   sc HOWARD WAKELING, JOSEPH DESPINS
from an idea by Howard Wakeling
   ph PHIL MÉHEUX. **cam op** John Maskall.
stills Robert Marshall
   m NICK BICÂT
   ed TONY LAWSON
   pd HERBERT WESTBROOK
   ward sup DONALD MOTHERSILL. **make-up**
Freddie Williamson. **hair** Betty Glasow
   sp eff DAVID HARRIS
   sd mix CHRIS WANGLER. **dub ed** Alan Bell.
dub mixer Mike Billing
   cast Annette Crosbie (*Lizzie Webster*),
Cornelius Garrett (*Freddie Mason*), David
Lyon (*Harry Webster*), Philip Locke
(*Guthfrithson*), Leonard Preston (*Geoff*), Cora
Kinnaird (*Pat*), Dudley Sutton (*Stan Harris*),
Rosalind Knight (*Dr Abbeydale*), Peter
Dahlsen (*Edwards*), Wolfe Morris (*antique
dealer*), David Calder (*Bracey*), Roger Kemp
(*chairman*), Pat Connell, Suzan Crowley
(*reporters*), Niall Padden (*detective*), Allan
Mitchell (*desk sergeant*), Charlotte
West-Oram (*receptionist*), Mike Walling
(*library assistant*), Jean Ainslie (*Mrs Ellis*),
Anthony Douse (*factory foreman*), Ted Beyer
(*workman*), Joe Black (*old man*), Kitty

Scopes (*canvasser*), Ted Charles (*other man*),
Sue Nott (*shop assistant*), Ken Humphries
(*entertainer*), Lisa Clarke (*goose girl*), Trevor
Clarke (*suspect*), Vince Eager (*Ned Ludd*),
Carl Howard-Walsh (*teddy boy*), Bill Lund
(*workman*), Marcus Marker (*King Snot*),
Glen Marsh, Saly Anne Meese (*young
couple*), Dick Pleasant (*barman*), Cal Ross
(*Charles*), Ken Youle (*Robin Hood*), Robert
Young (*shop manager*)
   shooting Oct–Nov 81. Nottingham
   budget £413,000. **C4 input** £403,000 (lf)
(98%)
   1st tx 8 Dec 82 (FF)
   V 29 Jun 83
   festivals Edinburgh, London 82; Chicago
85

DISTANT VOICES, STILL LIVES
UK/FGR, 84 mins, colour
The British Film Institute with Channel 4
and ZDF (Mainz). © Terence Davies 1988
   c ed KB/DR. **no** 123
   p JENNIFER HOWARTH. **exec p** COLIN
MACCABE. **exec i/c p** Jill Pack. **p man** Sarah
Swords, Olivia Stewart
   d TERENCE DAVIES. **asst d** Andy Powell,
Glynn Purcell, (2nd) Marc Munden, Matthew
Evans. **continuity** Claire Hughes Smith,
Melanie Matthews. **casting** Priscilla John
   sc TERENCE DAVIES
   ph WILLIAM DIVER, PATRICK DUVAL. **stunt
ph** Arthur Wooster. **cam op** Harriet Cox. **stills**
Mike Abrahams
   m perf (harmonica) Tommy Reilly
   ed WILLIAM DIVER. **collab ed** Geraldine
Creed, Toby Benton
   ad MIKI VAN ZWANENBERG, JOCELYN JAMES
   cost des MONICA HOWE. **make-up/hair**
Lesley Rouvray-Lawson, Aileen Seaton,

Eat the Peach

Experience Preferred But Not Essential

Lesley Sanders, Gerry Jones. **stunt make-up** Jenny Shircore
  sp eff RICHARD ROBERTS
  stunt co-ord ALF JOINT. **stunts** Bill Weston
  sd rec MOYA BURNS, COLIN NICOLSON. **dub ed** Alex Mackie. **sd mix** Aad Wirtz; Ian Turner
    cast Freda Dowie (*Mrs Davies, the mother*), Peter Postlethwaite (*Tommy Davies, the father*), Angela Walsh (*Eileen*), Dean Williams (*Tony*), Lorraine Ashbourne (*Maisie*), Sally Davies (*young Eileen*), Nathan Walsh (*young Tony*), Susan Flanagan (*young Maisie*), Michael Starke (*Dave, Eileen's husband*), Vincent Maguire (*George, Maisie's husband*), Antonia Mallen (*Rose, Tony's wife*), Debi Jones (*Micky*), Chris Darwin (*Red*), Marie Jelliman (*Jingles*), Andrew Schofield (*Les*), Anny Dyson (*granny*), Jean Boht (*Aunty Nell*), Alan Bird (*baptismal priest*), Pauline Quirke (*Doreen*), Matthew Long (*Mr Spaull*), Frances Dell (*Margie*), Carl Chase (*Uncle Ted, Tommy's brother*), Roy Ford (*wedding priest*), Terry Melia, John Thomalla (*military policemen*), John Carr (*registrar*), John Michie (*soldier*), Jeanette Moseley (*barmaid*), Ina Clough (*licensee*), Chris Benson, Judith Barker, Tom Williamson, Lorraine Michaels (*Rose's family*)
    shooting Sep–Oct 85 (*Distant Voices*), Sep–Oct 87 (*Still Lives*). London; Liverpool
    budget £703,000. **C4 input** £375,000 (lf) (53%)
    1st tx 4 Aug 91 (FF)
    MFB Oct 88. **V** 18 May 88
    awards International Critics' P, Best F (outside official selection), Cannes 88. Golden Leopard (joint), Art Cinemas' Jury P (CICAE), Locarno 88. Critics' P, Toronto 88.

Golden Spike (Best F), Best Photography P, Valladolid 88
  festivals Cannes, Locarno, Toronto, Valladolid 88

THE DIVE
Norway/UK, 90 mins, colour
Filmeffekt (Oslo), Millennium Films (London) and British Screen with Channel 4.
© K/S 'Dykket' 1989
  c ed KB. **no** 142
  p DAG ALVEBERG, PATRICK CASSAVETTI. **p man** Jeanette Sundby
  d TRISTAN de VERE COLE. **asst d** Arve Figenschow. **continuity** Eva Isaksen. **casting** (UK) Mary Selway, (Norway) Eva Isaksen
    sc LEIDULV RISAN, CARLOS WIGGEN. **sc cons** Christopher Wicking
    ph HARALD PAALGARD. **stills** Mona Gundersen
    m GEIR BØHREN, BENT ÅSERUD. **oboe soloist** Brynjar Hoff
    ed RUSSELL LLOYD
    des JARLE BLESVIK
    cost ANNE HAMRE. **make-up** Siw Järbyn
    sp eff PETTER BORGLI, JARLE BLESVIK, ERIK LIE
    diving sup BJØRN GJERDE, ARVID BERTHELSEN. **stunt divers** Jon Are Hvalby, Jan Holand, Kåre Lier, Vigulf Schøll Larsen
    sd rec KARI NYTRØ; Peter A. Stoop. **sd** Jan Lindvik. **sd eff ed** John Foster
    cast Bjørn Sundquist (*Gunnar*), Frank Grimes (*Dobrolsky*), Eindride Eidsvold (*Rolf*), Michael Kitchen (*Bricks*), Sverre Anker Ousdal (*captain*), Marika Lagercrantz (*Ann*), Nils Ole Oftebro (*Akselsen*), Inger Lise Westby (*Sonja*), John Stoudt (*assistant supervisor*), Thomas G. Stoudt (*Marius*), Christopher Curtis (*Jonas*), Steinar Raaen

The Eyes of Birds

Fatherland

(*pilot*), Magnar Miljeteig (*engineer*)
  budget £1,800,000. **C4 input** £275,000 (lf)
(15%)
  1st tx 15 Sep 91 (FF)
  SS Oct 91. **V** 30 Aug 89
  Norwegian release title *Dykket*

DOC'S KINGDOM
Portugal/France/UK, 90 mins, colour
Filmargem (Lisbon) and Garance (Paris)
with Channel 4. © Garance-Filmargem
1987
  c ed DR. **no** (-)
  exec p PAULO BRANCO, DOMINIQUE
VIGNET. **American sequences p** HARVEY
WALDMAN (Ocean Films). **p admin**
Jean-Marc Vignet. **p man** Cecilia Roque;
Antonio Gonçalo
  d [ROBERT] KRAMER. **director's asst** Pedro
Ruivo. **casting** Pat Golden
  sc [ROBERT] KRAMER
  lighting [ph] RICHARD COPANS. **cam** Robert
Machover
  m BARRE PHILLIPS
  ed SANDRINE CAVAFIAN; Christine Aya
  make-up Sharon Ilson Reed
  sd OLIVIER SCHWOB. **sd ed** Guy Lecorne.
mix Jean-Pierre Laforce
  cast Paul McIsaac (*James 'Doc' Matter*),
Vincent Gallo (*Jimmy Matter*), Ruy Furtado
(*Señor Ruy*), Cesar Monteiro (*Cesar*), Roslyn
Payne (*Rozzie*)
  shooting Lisbon; New York
  budget (?) **C4 input** (?) (lf)
  1st tx 13 Oct 90 (FFI)
  V 31 Aug 88
  festivals Locarno 88

DIE DOPPELTE WELT *see*
STRAWBERRY FIELDS

THE DRAUGHTSMAN'S CONTRACT
UK, 108 mins, colour
The British Film Institute with Channel 4.
© Peter Greenaway 1982
  c ed DR/WD. **no** 6
  p DAVID PAYNE. **head of production** PETER
SAINSBURY. **production officer** Peter
Broughan
  d PETER GREENAWAY. **asst d** Andy Powell.
continuity Marie Meyrick. **casting** Lucy
Boulting
  sc PETER GREENAWAY
  ph CURTIS CLARK. **rostrum cam/titles**
Hugh Gordon. **stills** Simon Archer, James
Morrell
  m MICHAEL NYMAN. **musicians** Alexander
Balanescu, John Harle, Elisabeth Perry, Steve
Saunders, Keith Thompson, Stina Wilson,
Ben Grove, David White, Malcolm Bennett,
Edward Pillinger, Ian Mitchell, Michael
Nyman. **counter-tenor** Chris Royle
  ed JOHN WILSON
  ad BOB RINGWOOD
  cost des SUE BLANE, (co-ordinator) David
Perry. **make-up** Lois Burwell. **wig creator**
Peter Owen. **wigs/hair** Peter King
  calligraphy Kenneth Breese
  sd GODFREY KIRBY. **dub ed** Doctor Lion.
dub mix Tony Anscombe
  cast Anthony Higgins (*Mr R. Neville*),
Janet Suzman (*Mrs Virginia Herbert*), Anne
Louise Lambert (*Sarah Talmann*), Hugh
Fraser (*Louis Talmann*), Neil Cunningham
(*Thomas Noyes*), Dave Hill (*Mr Herbert*),
David Gant (*Mr Seymour*), David Meyer,
Tony Meyer (*the Poulencs*), Nicolas Amer
(*Mr Parkes*), Suzan Crowley (*Mrs Pierpoint*),
Lynda Marchal (*Mrs Clement*), Michael
Feast (*the statue*), Alastair Cummings
(*Philip*), Steve Ubels (*Mr van Hoyten*), Ben

The Final Frame

The First Kangaroos

Kirby (*Augustus*), Sylvia Rotter (*governess*), Kate Doherty (*maid*), Joss Buckley (*Mr Porringer*), Mike Carter (*Mr Clarke*), Vivienne Chandler (*laundress*), Geoffrey Larder (*Mr Hammond*), Harry van Engel, George Miller (*servants*)
  shooting Aug–Sep 81. Groombridge Place, Kent
  budget £360,000. **C4 input** £180,000 (i) (50%)
  1st tx 30 Jun 83 (FF)
  MFB Nov 82. **V** 8 Sep 82
  festivals Venice, London 82

DE DREAM *see* **THE DREAM**

THE DREAM
Netherlands/UK, 90 mins, colour
Roeland Kerbosch Filmproduktie (Amsterdam) and NOS Cultural Television Programmes (Hilversum) with Channel 4.
© Roeland Kerbosch Filmproduktie 1985
  c ed DR. **no** (-)
  p ROELAND KERBOSCH. **p man** Gerrit Martijn, Yvonne Belonje
  d PIETER VERHOEFF. **asst d** Mady Saks.
continuity Annemarie van de Putte. **casting** Pauline Durlacher
  sc DIRK AYELT KOOIMAN, PIETER VERHOEFF.
Friesian dial translator Rink van der Velde
  cam PAUL VAN DEN BOS. **lighting** Wietze Vos, Kees Kroeze. **2nd unit cam** Peter Brugman. **stills** René Höcker
  m CEES BIJLSTRA. **m perf** The Friesian Orchestra, conductor Henk Alkema
  ed EDGAR BURCKSEN
  ad HENDRIK JAN VISSER
  cost JANY VAN HELLENBERG HUBAR.
make-up Dick Naastepad, Winnie Gallis
  sp eff ROB BLOMKWIST

  direct sd PAUL VELD. **sd ed** Maurits Guépin. **mix** Ad Roest. **sd eff** Hans Walter Kramski
  cast Peter Tuinman (*Wiebren Hogerhuis*), Huub Stapel (*Police Inspector Remmelinck*), Joke Tjalsma (*Iemkje Jansma*), Freark Smink (*Pieter Jelsma*), Hans Veerman (*police commissioner*), Adrian Brine (*officer of justice*), Jan Arendsz (*Allard Dijkstra*), Rense Westra (*Paulus van Dijk*), Fije Spoelstra (*Sybold Alberda*), Geert Lageveen (*Marten Hogerhuis*), Fokke de Vries (*Keimpe Hogerhuis*), Wieger Dam (*Hendrikje Hogerhuis*), Catrien Wolthuyzen (*Mother Hogerhuis*), Rients Gratama (*Tjeerd Stienstra*), Klaasje Postma (*Grietje*), Eelco Vellema (*Sieds Jansma*), Wytze Hoekstra (*Gatze Haitsma*), Aly Bruinsma (*Neeltje*), Hessel van der Wal (*stage director*), Pierre Bokma (*lawyer*), Theo Pont (*constable's assistant*), Niels Hamel (*constable*), Romke Tysma (*village policeman*), Arend Jan Heerma van Vos (*president of Rechtbank*), Hans van Toorenburg (*police inspector's colleague*), Romke de Leeuw (*Farmer Kalma*), Byke Tichelaar, Thomas van der Goot, Sietse Postmus, Ger Sterk, Hilly Harms, Jan Jansma
  shooting Feb–Mar 85. Friesland
  budget $800,000 [Roeland Kerbosch]/ £596,000. **C4 input** £17,000 (lf) (3%)
  1st tx 15 Sep 90 (FFI)
  V 23 Oct 85
  awards Golden Calf (best actor, Peter Tuinman), Dutch F Days 85. Golden Halo, Southern California Motion Picture Council 86. Best Musical Score, Karlovy Vary 86
  festivals Utrecht 85; Karlovy Vary 86
  Dutch release title *De Dream/De Droom*

A Flame to the Phoenix

Flight to Berlin

THE DRESSMAKER
UK, 91 mins, colour
Dressmaker Productions for Channel 4 with
British Screen. © Channel 4 Television 1988
  c ed DR/KB. **no** 105
  p RONALD SHEDLO. **exec p** JOHN MCGRATH.
assoc p Steve Clark-Hall. **p co-ord** Gail
Samuelson
  d JIM O'BRIEN. **asst d** Gary White, (2nd)
Patrick Kinney, Nick Laws. **sc sup** Angela
Noakes. **casting d** Priscilla John, (US) Mary
Colquhoun
  sc JOHN MCGRATH from the novel by Beryl
Bainbridge
  ph MICHAEL COULTER. **cam op** John
Maskall. **stills** Frank Connor
  m GEORGE FENTON
  choreo ISOBEL HURLL
  ed WILLIAM DIVER
  pd CAROLINE AMIES. **ad** Chris Townsend
  cost des JUDY MOORCROFT. **make-up** Kezia
De Winne. **hair** Karen Turner
  stunt co-ord JIM DOWDALL. **stunts** Wayne
Michaels, Tom Delmar, Tom Lucy, Gareth
Milne, Nick Powell, Trevor Steedman, Mark
Stewart
  sd rec SANDY MACRAE. **dub ed** Peter Joly.
dub mix Peter Maxwell
  cast Joan Plowright (*Nellie*), Billie
Whitelaw (*Margo*), Jane Horrocks (*Rita*), Tim
Ransom (*Wesley*), Peter Postlethwaite
(*Jack*), Pippa Hinchley (*Val Manders*),
Rosemary Martin (*Mrs Manders*), Tony
Haygarth (*Cyril Manders*), Michael
James-Reed (*Chuck*), Sam Douglas (*Cpl
Zawadski*), Bert Parnaby (*Mr Barnes*),
Lorraine Ashbourne, Mandy Walsh (*factory
girls*), Margi Clarke (*shop woman*), Andrew
Moorcroft (*Tommy the butcher's boy*), Marie
Jelliman (*Mrs O'Toole*), Rita Howard

(*producer*), Pamela Austin, Gerry White
(*singers*), Dorothy Dearnley (*pianist*),
Anthony Benson (*Terrence*), Al Kossy (*Mr
Betts*), Val Elliott (*secretary*), Mandy
Humphrey, Jayne Male, Bradley Lavelle,
Andrew Woodman (*party guests*), Freda
Kelly, Terry Canning (*couple in doorway*)
  shooting Jul–Aug 87. Liverpool;
Pinewood studios
  budget £1,276,000. **C4 input** £827,000 (i)
(65%)
  1st tx 26 May 91 (FF)
  MFB Jan 89. **V** 11 May 88
  awards 2nd P Rose of Lidice, Karlovy
Vary 88. Best Actress (joint) (Billie
Whitelaw), *Standard* F As 89
  festivals Seattle, San Francisco,
Washington, Barcelona, Karlovy Vary,
Edinburgh, Toronto, Vancouver, Rimini,
Cherbourg, Cork, London, Dublin,
Braunschweig 88; New Delhi, Göteborg,
Moscow, Warsaw 89

DE DROOM *see* **THE DREAM**

DROWNING BY NUMBERS
UK/Netherlands, 119 mins, colour
Allarts Enterprises (Amsterdam) with VPRO
Television (Hilversum) and the
Co-production Fund for the Dutch
Broadcasting Corporation for Elsevier
Vendex Film and Channel 4. Assisted by
Recorded Releasing (London), The Movies
(Netherlands), Prokino (FGR), BAC Films
(France), Progrès Films (Belgium). © Allarts/
Drowning by Numbers 1988
  c ed DR. **no** 106
  p KEES KASANDER, DENIS WIGMAN. **p man**
Evelien Jansen. **p co-ord** Alison Owen,
(Netherlands) Eljo Embregts

Forever Young

A Gathering of Old Men

d PETER GREENAWAY. **asst d** Gerrit Martijn, Peter Jaques, (2nd) Chris Martin. **continuity** Marietta de Vries. **casting d** Sharon Howard-Field

sc PETER GREENAWAY. **creative adv** Walter Donohue

ph SACHA VIERNY. **cam op** Adam Rodgers. **stills** Stephen Morley

m/md MICHAEL NYMAN. **m perf** The Michael Nyman Band, Alexander Balanescu, Jonathan Carney, Miranda Fulleylove, Rosemary Furniss, Briony Shaw, Jackie Shave (violins), Kate Musker, Joe Rappaport (violas), Tony Hinnigan, Andrew Shulman (cellos), Robin McGee (double bass), David Fuest (clarinet, bass clarinet), John Harle (soprano, alto sax), David Roach (alto sax), Andrew Findon (tenor, baritone sax, piccolo), John Wilbraham (trumpet, flugelhorn), Michael Thompson (French horn), Steve Saunders (bass trombone), Michael Nyman (piano)

ed JOHN WILSON

pd BEN van OS, JAN ROELFS

cost sup HEATHER WILLIAMS. **chief make-up** Sara Meerman. **hair** Mary Sturgess

stunt co-ord PETER BRAYHAM. **stuntmen** Andy Bradford, Les Marion, Frank Kenton

sd rec GARTH MARSHALL. **addit sd** (Netherlands) Lucas Boeke. **sd ed** Chris Wyatt. **dial ed** Sarah Vicker, Bridget Reiss, Shirley Shaw, Heather Holden. **dub mix** Peter Maxwell. **sd eff ed** Trevor Holland. **addit sd eff** Tony Fish

cast Joan Plowright (*Cissie Colpitts 1*), Juliet Stevenson (*Cissie Colpitts 2*), Joely Richardson (*Cissie Colpitts 3*), Bernard Hill (*Henry Madgett*), Jason Edwards (*Smut*), Bryan Pringle (*Jake*), Trevor Cooper (*Hardy*), David Morrissey (*Bellamy*), John Rogan

(*Gregory*), Paul Mooney (*Teigan*), Jane Gurnett (*Nancy Gill*), Kenny Ireland (*Jonah Bognor*), Michael Percival (*Moses Bognor*), Joanna Dickins (*Mrs Hardy*), Janine Duvitski (*Marina Bellamy*), Michael Fitzgerald (*Mr 70 Van Dyke*), Edward Tudor Pole (*Mr 71 Van Dyke*), Natalie Morse (*skipping girl*), Arthur Spreckley (*Sid the gravedigger*), Ian Talbot (*police detective*), Roderic Leigh (*policeman*), Vanni Corbellini (*The Hare*), José Berg (*skipping girl's mother*)

shooting Oct–Nov 87. Suffolk

budget £1,023,000. **C4 input** £450,000 (lf/i) (44%)

1st tx 5 May 91 (FF)

MFB Oct 88. **V** 11 May 88

awards Best Artistic Contribution (Peter Greenaway), Cannes 88

festivals Cannes, Piccadilly (London), Barcelona, Edinburgh, Birmingham, Toronto, Mill Valley, São Paulo, Dublin, Rio de Janeiro 88; New Delhi, Göteborg, Hong Kong, Moscow, Warsaw 89

DYKKET *see* **THE DIVE**

EAT THE PEACH
Eire/UK, 95 mins, colour
Strongbow with the Irish Film Board for Channel 4. Assisted by the National Film Development Fund (London) and Kelcom (Dublin). © Strongbow 1986

c ed DR/KB. **no** 63

p JOHN KELLEHER. **exec p** DAVID COLLINS. **p sup** Kevin Moriarty. **p man** Mary Alleguen

d PETER ORMROD. **asst d** Martin O'Malley, (2nd) Mick Rowland. **continuity** Jean Skinner. **casting** Nuala Moiselle

sc PETER ORMROD, JOHN KELLEHER from an idea by Peter Ormrod. **sc assoc** Jan Ashdown

Genesis

Giro City

ph ARTHUR WOOSTER. **cam op** Malcolm Mackintosh. **2nd unit cam** Sean Corcoran, Eamon de Buitlear. **stills** Tom Collins
m DONAL LUNNY. **m sup** Ray Williams. **title song** Paul Brady, Donal Lunny. **singer** Paul Brady
ed J. PATRICK DUFFNER
pd DAVID WILSON
ward mist JANET O'LEARY. **make-up** Toni Delany. **hair** Anne Dunne
sp eff BOB NUGENT, JOE FITT
titles des Chris Wood
stunt engineers DAVE BICKERS, RAY PURVIS, DICK TODD. **Wall of Death rider** Charles Winter. **stand-ins** Seamus Collins, Barbara Halford, John Markey
sd rec PAT HAYES. **sd ed** Ron Davis. **sd mix** Robin O'Donoghue
cast Stephen Brennan (*Vinnie Galvin*), Eamon Morrissey (*Arthur*), Catherine Byrne (*Nora Galvin*), Niall Toibin (*Boots*), Joe Lynch (*Boss Murtagh*), Tony Doyle (*Sean Murtagh*), Takashi Kawahara (*Bunzo*), Victoria Armstrong (*Vicky Galvin*), Barbara Adair (*Mrs Fleck*), Bernadette O'Neill (*Nuala*), Paul Raynor (*O'Hagan*), Martin Dempsey (*Uncle Pat, quiz master*), Maeliosa Stafford (*priest*), Jill Doyle (*Aileen*), Don Foley (*journalist*), Brian J. Hogg (*Danny*), Pat Kenny (*TV reporter*), Barry Kelly (*TV cameraman*), Edmund Lynch (*TV soundman*), Jack Lynch (*man at petrol station*), Liam Sweeney (*cattle drover*), Ronan Wilmot (*Cahill*), Robert Byrne (*look-out at border bar*), Mark Shelley (*patrol leader*), Dick Keating, Jim Reid, Frank Quinlan (*Nashville Three*), John Gallagher, Fintan McKeown, David Nolan (*Murtagh's heavies*), Akiko Hoashi Kobayashi, Snu Miyoshi Hayashi (*Japanese*), Patricia Jeffares

(*hospital sister*), David Carey, Chris Dunne, Peter Gowan, Tim McConnell, Noel O'Donovan, Stephen Ryan (*locals*), Frank Melia (*man at petrol station*)
shooting Bog of Allen, Co. Kildare; Co. Dublin; Co. Meath; Co. Wicklow
budget £1,387,000. **C4 input** £517,000 (lf/i) (37%)
1st tx 7 Apr 88 (FF)
MFB Dec 86. **V** 26 Mar 86
awards Bronze A, Taormina 86
festivals Helsinki, Taormina, Quimper, Edinburgh, Vevey, Rimini, Toronto, Telluride, Cherbourg, Hof, Troia, London 86; New Delhi, Brussels, Utah, Göteborg, Vienna, Madrid, Göttingen, Reykjavík 87

AN ENGLISH CHRISTMAS *see* **CHRISTMAS PRESENT**

EXPERIENCE PREFERRED BUT NOT ESSENTIAL
UK, 75 mins, colour
Enigma Television/Goldcrest Films & Television for Channel 4. © Samuel Montagu & Co 1982
c ed DR. **no** 4
p CHRIS GRIFFIN. **exec p** DAVID PUTTNAM. **assoc p** David Bill
d PETER DUFFELL. **asst d** Dominic Fulford; Andrew Montgomery, Russell Lodge.
continuity Mary Holdsworth. **casting d** Marilyn Johnson
sc JUNE ROBERTS. **story ed** Jack Rosenthal
ph PHIL MÉHEUX. **cam op** Jimmy Turrell.
stills Robert Marshall
m RACHEL PORTMAN. **addit m** John Scott
ed JOHN SHIRLEY
ad JANE MARTIN
cost des TUDOR GEORGE. **make-up** Freddie

Good and Bad at Games

The Good Father

Williamson. **hair** Pat McDermott
  sd rec ROBIN GREGORY, KEN SCRIVENER. **sd ed** Chris Greenham
  cast Elizabeth Edmonds (*Annie*), Sue Wallace (*Mavis*), Geraldine Griffiths (*Doreen*), Karen Meagher (*Paula*), Maggie Wilkinson (*Arlene*), Ron Bain (*Mike*), Alun Lewis (*Hywel*), Robert Blythe (*Ivan*), Roy Heather (*Wally*), Peter Doran (*Dai*), Arwen Holm (*Helen*), Sion Tudor Owen (*Nin*), Robert Gwilym (*Gareth*), Mostyn Evans (*Now*), Paul Haley (*Mr Howard*), Margo Jenkins (*Mrs Howard*), Gerry Brooks (*M.C.*)
  shooting Jul–Sep 82
  budget £505,000. **C4 input** £200,000 (lf) (40%)
  1st tx 22 Dec 82 (FF: 'First Love')
  V 24 Nov 82
  festivals London 82

THE EYES OF BIRDS
France/Switzerland/UK, 80 mins, colour
Antenne 2, Plaisance Productions and
Forum Films (Paris) and Télévision Suisse
Romande (Geneva) with Channel 4 and the
French Ministry of Culture. © Antenne 2/
Plaisance Productions/Forum Films 1982
  c ed DR. **no** (-)
  p DANIEL VAISSAIRE. **p man** Raphaël
Caussimon. **p sup** Gisèle Grellet-Bouquet
  d GABRIEL AUER. **asst d** Georges Manulelis,
Claire Lusseyran. **sc sup** Agathe Sallaberry
  sc GABRIEL AUER, CARLOS ANDREU
  ph JEAN YVES ESCOFFIER; Carlo Varini,
Pascal Rabaud
  m FRANÇOIS TUSQUES. **songs** Carlos
Andreu
  ed JOËLLE HACHE
  des NOËLLE FREMONT, HUGUES TISSANDIER
  cost MARIE CLAUDE ALTOT. **make-up**

Suzanne Pisteur, Maryvonne Autret
  sd JEAN MARCEL MILAN, PHILIPPE
SENECHAL. **sd ed** Marie Christine Rougerie,
Thierry Delor. **dub mix** Maurice Gilbert
  cast Roland Amstutz (*Dr Norberto
Palacios*), Carlos Andreu (*Carlos*), Patrick
Bonnel (*officer*), Philippe Clevenot (*Enrique
Materneo*), Christian Colin (*Col Hector Del
Rio*), Caroline Coste (*Susana Materneo*),
Jean-Yves Dubois (*François Riond*), Gérard
Demond (*Walter Bacelo*), Maxime Dufeu
(*Raoul Estancia*), Philippe du Janerand
(*Victor Benavente*), Pierre Forest (*Pato
Ruiz*), Mario Gonzalez (*Dr Julio Rojas*),
Raquel Iruzubieta (*Gloria Materneo*),
Jean-Claude Jay (*Mikael Pavlokov*),
Jean-Claude Leguay (*Dr Rudolf Hoegen*),
Guy Matchoro (*Pablo Kleist*), Claudine
Mavros (*Violeta Kleist*), Bertrand Migeat
(*Luis Gómez*), Vincent Rouche (*Anibal
Ferrandis*), Georges Senechal (*Grégorio
Armendia*), Bernard Waver (*Claude Dubath*),
Philippe Auriault, Philippe Besson, Patrick
Blondel, Peter Bonke, Michel Caron, Jacky
Evrard, Thierry Ferrer, Jean Forneris, Jérôme
Forneris, Noëlle Fremont, Danièle Laroche,
Thierry Le Floch, Gérard Lester, Alain
Mottet, Alain Mueller, Annie Noël, Philippe
Papadopoulos, Pierre Van Dievoet
  shooting Maison d'Arrêt de Lorient-
Ploemeur, Morbihan
  budget ?£200,000. **C4 input** £36,000 (lf)
  1st tx 13 Mar 86 (FF from France)
  V 27 Apr 83
  awards Grand Prix, Festival of New Latin
American Cinema, Havana 82. Prix de la
Critique Populaire, '7 Days of Cinema', Hull
(Canada). Samuel G. Engel A for Best Foreign
TV Drama, Chicago 85
  festivals Havana 82; London 83;

Good Morning Babylon

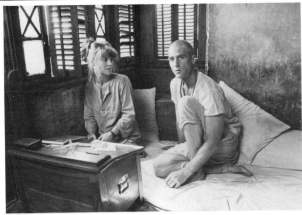

Heat and Dust

Chicago 85
  French release title *Les Yeux des Oiseaux*

FATHERLAND
UK/FGR/France, 111 mins, colour/b&w
Kestrel II (London), Clasart Film (Munich)
and MK2 Productions (Paris) for Channel 4.
1986
  c ed DR. **no** 79
  p RAYMOND DAY. **exec p** IRVING
TEITELBAUM. **co-p** MARIN KARMITZ, FRITZ
BUTTENSTEDT, HERBERT G. KLOIBER. **assoc p**
Ingrid Windisch, Catherine Lapoujade. **p
co-ord** Marita Frei, Sylvie Chevereau
Marchais
  d KENNETH LOACH. **asst d** Andrea
Buttenstedt, Gilbert Funke. **continuity**
Gabriele Mattner
  sc TREVOR GRIFFITHS
  ph CHRIS MENGES. **stills** Ronald Simoneit,
David Farrell
  m CHRISTIAN KUNERT, GERULF PANNACH
  ed JONATHAN MORRIS
  pd MARTIN JOHNSON
  cost des ANTJE PETERSEN. **make-up**
Marianne Müller
  titles David Raitt
  sd rec KARL LAABS. **dub ed** Kevin Brazier.
dub mix Colin Martin
  cast Gerulf Pannach (*Klaus Drittemann*),
Fabienne Babe (*Emma de Baen*), Sigfrit
Steiner (*James Dryden formerly Jacob
Drittemann*), Cristine Rose (*Lucy Bernstein*),
Robert Dietl (*East German lawyer*), Heike
Schrötter (*Marita*), Patrick Gillert (*Thomas
Drittemann*), Stephan Samuel (*Max*), Heinz
Diesing (*Jürgen Kirsch*), Eva Krutina (*Rosa
Drittemann*), Marlowe Shute (*US Consul
official*), Hans Peter Hallwachs (*Rainer
Schiff*), Jim Rakete (*Braun*), Winfried Tromp

(*Herr Hennig*), Bernard Bloch (*journalist*),
Thomas Oehlke (*young Klaus Drittemann*),
Ronald Simoneit (*Uwe, photographer at
checkpoint*), Julia Breit, Roy Schmucker-
meier, Florrie Buck
  shooting West Berlin; Cambridge;
Southern England
  budget £884,000. **C4 input** £459,000 (i)
(52%)
  1st tx 20 Apr 89 (FF)
  MFB Mar 87. **V** 17 Sep 86
  awards UNICEF A, Venice 86
  festivals Venice, Cork, Toronto, Dublin,
London 86; New Delhi, Utah, Belgrade, Hong
Kong, Sydney, Jerusalem, Melbourne,
Warsaw, Cairo 87; Malaga, Istanbul, Cuenca
88

THE FINAL FRAME
UK, ?95 mins, colour
Kinesis Films for Channel 4. © Channel 4
Television 1989
  c ed KB. **no** (-)
  p DEANNE EDWARDS. **assoc p** Kevin
Sampson. **p man** Marian Lacey
  d PAUL OREMLAND. **asst d** Michael Higgins,
(2nd) Trevor Puckle. **sc sup** Gillian Hazell.
casting d Dorothy Andrew
  sc HOWARD WAKELING from a story by Paul
Oremland, Howard Wakeling
  ph ALISTAIR CAMERON. **Betacam op**
Howard Smith. **Steadicam op** Steve
Bernstein. **stills** Tobi Corney
  m/m prod DAVID FERGUSON
  ed BERNARD MOSS. **VT ed** Jan Langford
  pd SOPHIE BECHER. **ad** Alison Riva
  cost des CANDIDA BUTT. **make-up** Anni
Buchanan
  sp eff sup JOHN MARKWELL. **senior sp eff
technician** Alan Whibley

Heavenly Pursuits

Hero

stunt arr ANDY BRADFORD. **stunt perf** Roy Alon

sd rec TREVOR HOTZ. **dub mix** Colin Martin

cast Graham McPherson (*East*), Nick Reding (*Hadi*), Craig Fairbrass (*Franklin*), Jan Ravens (*Thea*), Barry Eaton (*animal rights man*), Corinne Skinner-Carter (*Miss Gibson*), Andrew Tansey (*V.J.*), James Aubrey (*Paul Mandell*), Katherine Pratt (*Debbie*), The Farm (*band at concert*), Umberto (*concert MC*), Claire Toeman (*Judy*), Sheldon Lazarus (*Baz*), Nicola Stephenson (*Louise*), Liz Stooke (*receptionist*), Zoot Money (*Ronnie Campbell*), Harry Goodier (*Mr Timmins*), Lorraine Peters (*Franklin's mother*), Gillian Kearney (*Cassy*), Matthew Vaughan (*Kieron*), Joan Campion, Anni Domingo (*cleaners*), Peter Faulkner (*chef*), Christine Moore (*minicab controller*), John Jardine (*East's father*), Paula Tilbrook (*East's mother*), Marcus Lund (*1st cyclist*), David Newall (*2nd cyclist*)

shooting summer 89. Leeds; Manchester

budget ?£450,000. **C4 input** ?£450,000 (100%)

1st tx 12 Apr 90 (FF)

THE FIRST KANGAROOS

Australia/UK, 105 mins, colour
Roadshow Coote & Carroll (Sydney) for Channel 4. Co-produced under the sponsorship of the Australian Film Commission. 1988

c ed DR. **no** 93

p MOYA ICETON. **exec p** MATT CARROLL, GREGORY COOTE. **assoc p** (UK) Peter Jaques. **p man** Stephen Jones. **p co-ord** (Australia) Barbara Ring, (UK) Christine Fenton

d FRANK CVITANOVICH. **asst d** Bob

Howard, (2nd, Australia) Ian Freeman, (2nd, UK) Paul Lowin. **continuity** Sian Fatouros. **casting** (UK) Sue Whatmough

sc NIGEL WILLIAMS from an idea by Frank Cvitanovich

ph ROSS BERRYMAN. **stills** Brett Cochrane

m WILLIAM MOTZING

ed RICHARD HINDLEY

pd HERBERT PINTER. **ad** (Australia) Stewart Way

cost des ANNA SENIOR. **make-up** Judy Lovell. **hair** (Australia) Lita Bosco, (UK) Jennifer Boost

titles Fran Burke

sd rec NOEL QUINN. **dub ed** Bruce Lamshed. **sd mix** Peter Fenton

cast Wayne Pearce (*Sandy Pearce*), Alexander Brown (*Morton*), Wayne Pygram (*Albie Rosenfeldt*), Philip Quast (*Bluey Burdon*), John Dicks (*Reverend Green*), Robert Davis (*Major Thompson*), Chris Haywood (*James Giltinan*), Tony Martin (*Dan Frawley*), Dominic Sweeney (*Dally Messenger*), Clarissa Kaye Mason (*Mrs Messenger*), Nell Schofield (*Betty*), Andrew Ettingshausen (*Conlon*), Kelly Dingwall (*Devereaux*), Robert Giltinan (*reporter*), Harold Kissin (*trainer*), Alan Surtees (*George, barman*), Dennis Waterman (*Albert Goldthorpe*), Vic Rooney (*John Jackson*), Ian Gilmour (*steamship official*), Kym Lynch (*butler*), Edward Peel (*Nugent*), Patrick Monckton (*Perivale*), Kevin Dukes (*engineer*), Charles Pemberton (*large man*), Robert Austin (*mayor*), Julie Godfrey (*hotel manageress*), Charlotte Mitchell (*Mrs Oaks*), Kim Knuckey (*ticket inspector*), Jim Carter (*Arthur Hughes*), Dorothy Vernon (*Mrs Jackson*), Fred Welsh, Bob Duncan, Bob Hicks (*men in pub*), John Bird (*Jupes*), Mike

Hidden City

High Hopes

Harris (*George*), Philip Davis (*young reporter*), Frank Taylor (*Falthorpe*), Gordon Streek (*photographer*), Ross Sharp, Greg O'Donovan (*reporters*)
   shooting Apr–May 87. Australia; England
   budget £1,433,000. **C4 input** £558,000 (lf/i) (39%)
   1st tx 21 Apr 88 (FF)
   V 30 Sep 87

A FLAME TO THE PHOENIX
UK, 80 mins, colour
Granada Television for Channel 4.
© Granada TV 1983
   c ed DR. **no** 26
   p RICHARD EVERITT. **p man** Lars Macfarlane. **floor manager** David Meddick
   d WILLIAM BRAYNE. **assistant stage manager** Shirley Dynevor. **casting d** Priscilla John
   sc MURRAY SMITH
   ph MIKE POPLEY. **cam op** Douglas Hallows
   m CHRISTOPHER GUNNING
   ed ANTHONY HAM
   pd DAVID BUXTON
   cost ESTHER DEAN. **make-up** Sallie Adams
   stunt arr PETER BRAYHAM
   graphics John Leech
   sd rec KEN REYNOLDS. **dub mix** John Whitworth
   cast Frederick Treves (*Gen Mikolau Pradzynski*), Ann Firbank (*Countess Kurowicka*), Malcolm Jamieson (*Lt Florian Ozarkowski*), Benedict Taylor (*Lt Max Kurowicki*), Lucy Hornak (*Lydia Kurowicka*), Paul Geoffrey (*Stefan Kurowicki*), Andrew Burt (*David Warner*), Robin Sachs (*Gavin McCrae*), David Haig (*Sgt Mirek Grabinski*), Frances Barber (*Wanda

Grabinska), Constantine Gregory (*Waclaw Ranczowski*), Stuart Richman (*Maj Antoni Krajski*), Donald Bisset (*Janusz*), Richard Ireson (*Starzynski*), Martin Oldfield (*Father Felicjan*), John Rowe (*Sir Howard Kennard*), Gerry Cowan (*Fl Lt Spenster*), Will Tacey (*Josef Gurtner*), David Calladine (*Adam Wackerle*), Louis Hasler (*brigadier*), Jonathan Oliver (*Polish trooper*), Ian Bleasdale (*Hauptman*), Danny McCarthy (*Polish NCO*), David Riley (*Polish staff captain, front lines*), Christine Moore (*woman neighbour*), Vishanya Petulengro (*fortune teller*), David Miller (*rabbi*), Michael Shevelew (*cantor*), Stefan Brochwicz-Lewinski (*newsboy*), Nigel Cartner (*baby Grabinski*)
   shooting Aug–Sep 82
   budget £440,000 [Richard Everitt].
C4 input £300,000 (lf) (68%)
   1st tx 15 Dec 83 (FF)

FLIGHT TO BERLIN
UK/FGR, 90 mins, colour
Road Movies Filmproduktion (Berlin) with the British Film Institute for Channel 4.
© Road Movies 1983
   c ed WD. **no** 37
   p/exec p CHRIS SIEVERNICH. **assoc p** Walter Donohue, Peter Sainsbury, Lynda Myles. **p man** Gerhard von Halem. **p co-ord** Ulla Zwicker
   d CHRISTOPHER PETIT. **asst d** Martin Müller. **continuity** Angela Wecker
   sc CHRISTOPHER PETIT, HUGO WILLIAMS from the novel *Strange Days* by Jennifer Potter
   ph MARTIN SCHÄFER. **stills** Philipp Goetz
   m IRMIN SCHMIDT
   ed PETER PRZYGODDA

High Season

Hope and Glory

ad RAINER SCHAPER
cost SUE SNELL. **make-up** Karin Seebach
Lück
sd JON RALPH, KLAUS MANKEWITZ. **sd ed**
Ester Ronay. **sd re-rec** Hartmut Eichgrün
cast Tusse Silberg (*Susannah Lawrence*),
Paul Freeman (*Nicholas*), Lisa Kreuzer (*Julie
Lawrence*), Jean-François Stévenin
(*Edouard*), Ewan Stewart (*Jack*), Eddie
Constantine (*himself*), Tatjana Blacher
(*Carlotta*), Ellen Umlauf, Larry Lamb, Sema
Poyraz, Jonathan Kinsler, Udo Heiland,
Gisela Glück, Sonja Warnke, Bogdan Faluta,
Claus D. Streuber
shooting Berlin
budget £525,000. **C4 input** £332,000 (lf/i)
(63%)
1st tx 21 Jun 84 (FF)
MFB Mar 84. **V** 7 Mar 84
festivals Cannes 84
German release title *Fluchtpunkt Berlin*

FLUCHTPUNKT BERLIN *see*
FLIGHT TO BERLIN

FOREVER YOUNG
UK, 84 mins, colour/b&w
Enigma Television/Goldcrest Films &
Television for Channel 4. © Enigma
Productions 1983
c ed DR/WD. **no** 47
p CHRIS GRIFFIN. **exec p** DAVID PUTTNAM.
assoc p David Bill. **p man** Dominic Fulford
d DAVID DRURY. **asst d** Andrew
Montgomery; Russell Lodge, Callum
McDougall. **continuity** Caroline Sax. **casting
d** Simone Reynolds
sc RAY CONNOLLY. **sc ed** Jack Rosenthal
ph NORMAN LANGLEY. **cam op** Gale
Tattersall, John Maskell. **stills** Robert

Marshall
m arr ANTHONY KING. **lyrics** (title song)
Ray Connolly
ed MAX LEMON
ad JEFFREY WOODBRIDGE
cost des TUDOR GEORGE. **make-up** Jean
Richmond. **hair** Madeleine Masters
sd rec DAVID CROZIER. **sd ed** Ron Davis.
dub mix Gerry Humphreys
cast James Aubrey (*James*), Nicholas
Gecks (*Father Michael*), Karen Archer
(*Mary*), Alec McCowen (*Father Vincent*),
Liam Holt (*Paul*), Jane Forster (*Cathy*), Ruth
Davies (*Suzie*), Joseph Wright (*Luke*), Jason
Carter (*young Michael*), Julian Firth (*young
James*), Oona Kirsch (*Maureen McMahon*),
Eileen Fletcher (*Alison*), Carol MacReady
(*Brenda*), Philip McGough (*Ian*), Pamela
Miles (*Carol*), Martin Duncan (*John*),
Robin Wentworth (*Bert*), Shelley Borkum
(*Sandra*), Kate Percival (*policewoman*),
James Wynn (*brother*), Kathy Burke (*girl*),
Michael Sundin (*Peter*), Cyril Bass, Roger
James, Martin Jay, Nigel Palmer (*band*),
Robert Stagg, Peter Scott Harrison (*boys at
dance*), Paul Sims, Nick Berry (*boys at
school*)
shooting Mar–Apr 83
budget £506,000. **C4 input** £240,000 (lf)
(47%)
1st tx 6 Jun 85 (FF: 'First Love')
MFB Oct 84. **V** 31 Oct 84

A GATHERING OF OLD MEN
USA/UK/FGR, 91 mins, colour
Consolidated Productions (Los Angeles),
Jennie & Co (New York), Zenith Productions
(London), Bioskop-Film (Munich),
Hessischer Rundfunk (Frankfurt) for
CBS (New York) and Channel 4.

Hôtel du Paradis

Ill Fares the Land

© Zenith Productions 1987
  c ed DR. **no** 98
    p GOWER FROST. **exec p** MICHAEL DEELEY.
co-p EBERHARD JUNKERSDORF. **assoc p** James
Bigwood. **p man** Preston Holmes
    d VOLKER SCHLÖNDORFF. **asst d** Dwight
Williams, Paula Brody. **sc sup** Mamie
Mitchell. **casting d** Pat Golden
    sc CHARLES FULLER from the novel by
Ernest J. Gaines
    ph EDWARD LACHMAN
    m/perf RON CARTER. **addit m** Papa John
Creach
    ed NANCY BAKER, Craig McKay
    pd THOMAS A. WALSH
    cost des SUSAN GAMMIE. **make-up** Gigi
Cooker. **hair** Ted Long
    sd NEELON CRAWFORD. **re-rec sup** Dick
Vorisek
    cast Louis Gossett Jr (*Mathu*), Richard
Widmark (*Sheriff Mapes*), Holly Hunter
(*Candy Marshall*), Joe Seneca (*Clatoo*), Will
Patton (*Lou Dimes*), Woody Strode (*Yank*),
Tiger Haynes (*Booker*), Papa John Creach
(*Jacob*), Julius Harris (*Coot*), Rosanna Carter
(*Beulah*), Walter Breaux (*Charlie*), Jay Flash
Riley (*Jameson*), Danny Barker (*Chimley*),
Sandman Sims (*Uncle Billy*), P. Jay Sidney
(*Gable*), Art Shilling (*Griffin*), Lenore Banks
(*Miss Merle*), Al Shannon (*Luke*), Stocker
Fontelieu (*William Fix Boutan*), Adam Storke
(*Gil Boutan*), Richard Whaley (*Beau
Boutan*), Lucille McKay (*Bea Marshall*),
Elliott Keener (*Herman*), Carol Sutton
(*Janey*), Pat Perkins (*Aunt Glo*), Jerome
Reddick (*Snookum*), David Petitjean
(*Russell*), Dwayne Jones (*Leroy*), James
Michael Bailey (*Alcee*), Robert Earl Willis
(*Sharp*), Buddy St Amant (*Tee-Jack*), Michael
Audley (*Jack Marshall*), Randy Charamie

(*Jean*), Paul Landry (*Auguste*), Rick Duet
(*Claude*), Michael Johnson (*Sully*), Michael
Thomas (*Cal*), Rosetta Wiggs (*Corrine*),
Catundra Reese (*Minnie*), Eliska Thomas
(*Sally*), Rod Masterson (*coach*), Cindy Taylor
(*Cajun girl*), Henry Willis (*man at Glo's*)
    shooting Nov 86. Thibodaux, Louisiana
    budget $3,500,000 [Zenith Productions]/
£2,140,000. **C4 input** £50,000 (lf) (2%)
    1st tx 19 May 88 (FF)
    V 13 May 87
    festivals Cannes 87

GENESIS
France/India/Belgium/Switzerland/UK, 105
mins, colour
Scarabée Films (Paris), Mrinal Sen
Productions (Calcutta), Les Films de la Drève
(Brussels) and Cactus Film (Zurich) with
Channel 4 and Télévision Suisse Romande
(Geneva). © Scarabée Films 1986
    c ed DR. **no** (-)
    exec p (Scarabée Films) MARIE PASCALE
OSTERRIETH. **assoc p** Palaniappan Ramasamy,
Eliane Stutterheim, Jean-Jacques Andrien.
p co-ord Mukul Chaudhuri. **p man** Jitesh
Basu-Thakur
    d MRINAL SEN. **assistants** Amal Sirkar,
Supantha Bhattacharya, Umashankar Pathik
    sc MRINAL SEN from the novella by
Samaresh Basu. **sc collab** Mohit
Chattopadhya. **dial** Surendra P. Singh,
Umashankar Pathik
    ph CARLO VARINI. **stills** Subhash Nandy
    m RAVI SHANKAR, (asst) Kumar Bose.
musicians Ravi Shankar, Kumar Bose,
Kamalesh Maitra, Benoît Charvet, Jerry
Lipkin, François Auboux, Laura Patchen
    ed ELIZABETH WAELCHLI
    sets/cost NITISH ROY. **make-up** Debi

In Fading Light

The Innocent

Halder, Ramprasad Kahar
sd HENRI MORELLE, FRANK STRUYS. **sd ed**
Ludo Troch. **mix** Gérard Lamps. **sd eff**
Jérôme Lévy
cast Shabana Azmi (*the Woman*),
Naseeruddin Shah (*the Farmer*), Om Puri
(*the Weaver*), M. K. Raina (*the Trader*)
budget (?) **C4 input** (?) (lf)
1st tx 18 Mar 89 (FFI)
MFB Jul 87. **V** 21 May 86
festivals Cannes, London 86
French release title *Génésis*

GIRO CITY
UK, 102 mins, colour
Silvarealm for Rediffusion Films and
Channel 4. Project development Cine Cymru.
1982
c ed DR. **no** 10
p SOPHIE BALHETCHET, DAVID PAYNE. **exec
p** (Rediffusion Films) JOHNNY FIELDER. **p. sup**
Graham Easton
d KARL FRANCIS. **asst d** Patrick Cadell,
(2nd) Monica Hyde. **continuity** Jill Rodger.
casting d Debbie McWilliams
sc KARL FRANCIS
ph CURTIS CLARK. **2nd unit ph** Graham
Berry. **stills** Chris Parker
m/cond ALUN FRANCIS
ed NEIL THOMSON
ad JAMIE LEONARD
cost des DAVID PERRY. **make-up** Lois
Burwell. **hair** Peter King
sd mix GODFREY KIRBY. **sd ed** Martin
Evans. **dub mix** Aad Wirtz
cast Glenda Jackson (*Sophie*), Jon Finch
(*O'Mally*), Kenneth Colley (*Martin Osborne*),
James Donnelly (*James*), Karen Archer
(*Brigitte*), Graham Berry (*TV 10 cameraman*),
Chris Renty (*TV 10 soundman*), David

Quilter (*TV 10 lawyer*), Peter Halliday
(*Northern Ireland minister*), Simon Coady
(*awards compère*), Emrys James (*Tommy
Williams*), Simon Jones (*Henderson*),
Michael Lees (*GNH chairman*), Bruce
Alexander (*GNH lawyer*), David Beames
(*Joe*), Huw Ceredig (*Elwyn Davies*), Valerie
Baker (*Megan Davies*), Colette Barker (*Annie
Davies*), Gerwyn Baker (*Gerwyn Davies*),
Alun Lewis (*photographer*), James Benson
(*Dublin boy*), Dermot Crowley (*Flynne*),
Philip Compton (*Flynne's bodyguard*),
Taylor McAuley (*Irish policeman*), John
Kearney (*Murphy*), Robert Pugh (*John
Williams*), Norman Caro (*Plattinsky*),
Madhav Sharma (*doctor*), Robert Austin
(*government official*), Sophie Kind
(*O'Mally's elder daughter*), Terry Jackson
(*council official*), William Ingrams (*Arthur*),
Bob Blythe (*Welsh policeman*), Sharon
Morgan (*Miss Harding, social worker*), Roger
Nott (*Welsh bank teller*), Arthur Whybrow
(*Wilf, pickpocket*), Marion McLoughlin
(*Martin's secretary*), Elisabeth Lynne
(*newsreader*), Frank Baker (*film editor*),
Matthew Long (*vision mixer*), Jennifer Hill
(*Mrs Williams*), Celestine Randall (*James's
secretary*), Tallulah Turney (*O'Mally's
younger daughter*)
shooting Feb-Mar 82. London; Wales
budget £441,000. **C4 input** £185,000 (lf/i)
(42%)
1st tx 1 Dec 82 (FF)
MFB Dec 82. **V** 27 Oct 82
festivals Jerusalem 86; Antenna 89
US release title *And Nothing but the
Truth*

GOOD AND BAD AT GAMES
UK, 85 mins, colour

In the White City

Joyriders

Portman Quintet for Channel 4. © Portman Quintet 1983
c ed WD. **no** 32
p VICTOR GLYNN. **exec p** IAN WARREN, TOM DONALD. **p man** Malcolm Christopher
d JACK GOLD. **asst d** Roy Stevens, (2nd) Richard Dobson. **continuity** Renée Glynne. **casting** Sheila Trezise
sc WILLIAM BOYD. **sc ed** Mike Ockrent
ph WOLFGANG SUSCHITZKY. **cam op** Gerry Anstiss. **stills** Sarah Quill
m Coombe Music International
ed LAURENCE MÉRY-CLARK
pd HERBERT WESTBROOK
ward sup LAURA NIGHTINGALE. **make-up** Sandra Shepherd
sd mix BRIAN SIMMONS. **sd ed** Peter Krook. **sd re-rec** Trevor Pyke
cast Martyn Stanbridge (*Quentin 'Wog' Niles*), Anton Lesser (*John 'Animal' Cox*), Laura Davenport (*Frances Mount*), Dominic Jephcott (*Alistair Mount*), Frederick Alexander (*Jerry Joyce*), Graham Seed (*Mungo Harrop*), Ewan Stewart (*Colenso*), Ceri Jackson (*girl at dance*), Philip Goodhew (*Treagear*), Tristram Wymark (*boy*), Rupert Graves (*Guthrie*)
shooting May–Jun 83. Buckinghamshire; West London
budget £468,000. **C4 input** £355,000 (lf/i) (76%)
1st tx 8 Dec 83 (FF)
V 30 Nov 83
festivals London 83; Milan 84

THE GOOD FATHER
UK, 90 mins, colour
Greenpoint Films for Channel 4. © Film Four International 1986
c ed DR/KB. **no** 78

p ANN SCOTT. **p man** Ann Wingate. **p co-ord** Caroline Hill
d MIKE NEWELL. **asst d** Tony Hopkins, (2nd) Fraser Copp. **sc sup** Francine Brown. **casting d** Sheila Trezise
sc CHRISTOPHER HAMPTON from the novel by Peter Prince
ph MICHAEL COULTER. **cam op** Denis Kington. **stills** Sarah Quill
m RICHARD HARTLEY
ed PETER HOLLYWOOD
pd ADRIAN SMITH. **ad** Alison Stewart-Richardson. **Mary Hall's paintings** Jane Human
cost des PIP NEWBERY. **make-up** Christine Beveridge, Sally Harrison
stunt arr JIM DOWDALL. **stunt perf** Gareth Milne
titles Richard Morrison
sd DAVID STEPHENSON, TONY JACKSON. **sd ed** Richard Dunford. **dub mix** Peter Maxwell
cast Anthony Hopkins (*Bill Hooper*), Jim Broadbent (*Roger Miles*), Harriet Walter (*Emmy Hooper*), Frances Viner (*Cheryl Langford*), Simon Callow (*Mark Varda*), Miriam Margolyes (*Jane Powell*), Joanne Whalley (*Mary Hall*), Michael Byrne (*Leonard Scruby*), Jennie Stoller, Johanna Kirby (*Bill's friends*), Stephen Fry (*Creighton*), Clifford Rose (*Judge Kirby-Smith*), Harry Grubb (*Christopher, Bill's son*), Tom Jamieson (*Richard, Roger's son*), Chris Bradshaw (*punk*)
shooting Nov–Dec 85. South London
budget £764,000. **C4 input** £764,000 (lf/i) (100%)
1st tx 12 May 88 (FF)
MFB Oct 86. **V** 3 Sep 86
awards Most Original Festival Entry, BP & Shell As, Zimbabwe 87. 1st P (drama

Katinka

The King and the Queen

section), Prix Italia, Capri 88
festivals Edinburgh, Rimini, Cherbourg,
Dublin 86; New Delhi, Zimbabwe, Jerusalem,
Montreal 87

GOOD MORNING BABILONIA *see*
GOOD MORNING BABYLON

GOOD MORNING BABYLON
Italy/France/USA, 118 mins, colour
Filmtre (Rome), MK2 Productions (Paris)
and the Edward Pressman Film Corporation
(Burbank) with RAI (Rome) and Films A2
(Paris). 1986
c ed DR. **no** 99
p GIULIANI G. DE NEGRI. **French co-p**
MARIN KARMITZ. **exec p** EDWARD PRESSMAN.
assoc p Lloyd Fonvielle, Caldecot Chubb,
Milena Canonero. **general supervisor** Grazia
Volpi. **p sup** Tommaso Calevi; (US) John
Engel, (France) Catherine Lapoujade. **unit
man** Claudio Gaeta, Livia Leto
d PAOLO & VITTORIO TAVIANI. **asst d**
Mimmola Girosi. **continuity** Carla Vezzoso
Taviani. **US casting** José Villaverde
st/sc PAOLO & VITTORIO TAVIANI based on
an idea by Lloyd Fonvielle. **sc collab** Tonino
Guerra
ph GIUSEPPE LANCI. **cameraman** Fabio
Conversi. **glass shots** Franco & Stefano
Angeletti, Vincenzo Forletta. **stills** Umberto
Montiroli, (US) Jonathan Levine
m/md NICOLA PIOVANI. **m perf** Orchestre
dell'Unione Musiciste Romani
choreo GINO LANDI
ed ROBERTO PERPIGNANI
ad GIANNI SBARRA, (asst) Lorenzo
D'Ambrosio. **sculptures/models** Raffaello
Giunta, Paolo Lazzari (Viareggio)
cost LINA NERLI TAVIANI. **make-up**

Gianfranco Mecacci. **hair** Mauro Tamagnini
sd mix CARLO PALMIERI. **sd sup** Michael
Billingsley. **sd ed** Sandro Peticca. **mix
engineer** Fausto Ancillai
cast Vincent Spano (*Nicola Bonanni*),
Joaquim De Almeida (*Andrea Bonanni*),
Greta Scacchi (*Edna*), Désirée Becker
(*Mabel*), Omero Antonutti (*Bonanno
Bonanni*), Bérangère Bonvoisin (*Mrs
Griffith*), David Brandon (*Grass*), Brian
Freilino (*Thompson*), Margarita Lozano (*the
Venetian lady*), Massimo Venturiello (*Duccio
Bonanni*), Andrea Prodan (*Sean, Irish
cameraman*), Charles Dance (*D. W. Griffith*),
Dorotea Ausenda, Ugo Bencini, Daniel
Bosch, Renzo Cantini, Marco Cavicchioli,
Fiorenza D'Alessandro, Lionello Pio Di
Savoia, Maurizio Fardo, Domenico Fiore,
Mirio Guidelli, John Francis Lane, Ubaldo
Lo Presti, Luciano Machereli, Sandro
Mallegni, Elio Marconato, Michele Melega,
Mauro Monni, Lamberto Petrecca, Diego
Ribon, Antonio Russo, Giuseppe Scarcella,
Leontine Snel, Egidio Termine, Francesco
Tola, Pinon Toska
shooting Pisa, Florence and Tarquinia
budget (?) **C4 input** £125,000 (lf)
1st tx 6 Apr 89 (FF)
MFB Aug 87. **V** 13 May 87
festivals Cannes 87
Italian release title *Good Morning
Babilonia*

HEAT AND DUST
UK, 130 mins, colour
Merchant Ivory Productions. © Luroak 1982
c ed DR. **no** 43
p ISMAIL MERCHANT. **assoc p** Rita Mangat,
Connie Kaiserman. **p man** Peter Manley. **p
co-ord** Shama Habibullah.

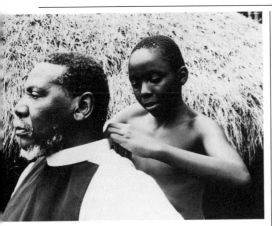

The Kitchen Toto

Ladder of Swords

d JAMES IVORY. **asst d** Kevan Barker, (2nd) David Nichols. **continuity** Jane Buck. **casting d** Susie Figgis

sc RUTH PRAWER JHABVALA from her own novel. **dial** (Urdu) Saeed Jaffrey, (Hindi) Harish Khare

ph WALTER LASSALLY. **stills** Christopher Cormack, Mary Ellen Mark

m/md RICHARD ROBBINS. **assoc md** Zakir Hussain. **musicians** Pandit Chaurasia (flute), Sultan Khan (sarangi), Nishat Khan (sitar), Zakir Hussain (percussion), Michael Reeves (piano), Mick Parker (synthesizer), Ameer Mohammed Khan (singer), Harry Rabinowitz (conductor)

ed HUMPHREY DIXON

pd WILFRID SHINGLETON. **ad** Maurice Fowler, Ram Yadekar

cost BARBARA LANE, (asst) Mary Ellis. **make-up** Gordon Kay. **hair** Carol Hemming

sd RAY BECKETT. **dub ed** Brian Blamey. **dub mix** Richard King

cast [the Nineteen Twenties in the Civil Lines at Satipur] Christopher Cazenove (*Douglas Rivers, the Assistant Collector*), Greta Scacchi (*Olivia, his wife*), Julian Glover (*Crawford, the District Collector*), Susan Fleetwood (*Mrs Beth Crawford, the Burra Memsahib*), Patrick Godfrey (*Dr Billy Saunders, the Medical Officer*), Jennifer Kendal (*Mrs Joan Saunders*); [at the Palace in Khatm] Shashi Kapoor (*the Nawab*), Madhur Jaffrey (*the Begum Mussarat Jahan, the Nawab's mother*), Nickolas Grace (*Harry Hamilton-Paul*), Barry Foster (*Major Minnies, the Political Agent*); [1982. In Satipur Town] Julie Christie (*Anne*), Zakir Hussain (*Inder Lal, Anne's landlord*), Ratna Pathak (*Ritu, Inder Lal's wife*), Tarla Mehta (*Inder Lal's mother*), Charles McCaughan

(*Chid*); [also] Sajid Khan (*dacoit chief*), Amanda Walker (*Lady Mackleworth*), Parveen Paul (*Maji*), Jayant Kirpalani (*Dr Gopal*), Sudha Chopra (*chief princess*), Dan Chatto (*Guy*), Leelabai (*Leelavati*), Humphrey Dixon (*man telling crocodile story*), Wilfrid Shingleton (*Governor General*), Richard Robbins, Zakiya Powell, Geoff Heinrich, Ishtiaq Khan, Deep Bedi, Baba Ghaus

shooting Feb–Apr, Aug 82. Hyderabad; Gulmarg, Kashmir; London

budget £1,100,000 [Merchant Ivory Productions]. **C4 input** £115,000 (lf) (10%)

1st tx 22 May 86 (FF)

MFB Jan 83. **V** 19 Jan 83

HEAVENLY PURSUITS
UK, 91 mins, colour
Island Films with Skreba Films and the National Film Finance Corporation for Channel 4. © Film Four International 1986

c ed DR/KB. **no** 65

p MICHAEL RELPH. **exec p** ANN SKINNER. **assoc p** Clive Reed. **p man** Liz Kerry

d CHARLES GORMLEY. **asst d** Clive Reed, (2nd) Gus MacLean. **continuity** Anne Coulter. **casting d** Anne Henderson

sc CHARLES GORMLEY

ph MICHAEL COULTER. **cam op** Jan Pester. **stills** Ken Mellin, (special) Oscar Marzaroli

m B. A. ROBERTSON. **md** Simon Webb

ed JOHN GOW

pd RITA MCGURN. **ad** Annette Gillies

cost des LINDY HEMMING. **make-up** Lois Burwell. **hair** Jeanette Freeman

stunt arr GERRY CRAMPTON. **stuntmen** Roy Alon, Alan Stuart

sd mix LOUIS KRAMER. **sd ed** Nicolas Gaster. **dub mix** Peter Maxwell

Lamb

Landscape in the Mist

cast Brian Pettifer (*Father Cobb*), Tom Busby (*Msgr Brusse*), Tom Conti (*Vic Mathews*), Ewen Bremner (*Stevie Deans*), Philip Maxwell (*Wee Mike*), Helen Mirren (*Ruth Chancellor*), David Hayman (*Jeff Jeffries*), James Gibb (*Macarthur*), John Mitchell (*Gibbons*), Robert Paterson (*Mackrimmond*), Dave Anderson (*headmaster*), Grace Kirby (*French teacher*), Juliet Cadzow (*teacher*), Jenny McCrindle (*Carole Adams*), Paul Nolan (*Robbie*), David McCormack (*James*), Ronnie McCann (*Eddie, boy on roof*), Ann-Marie D'Agostino, Christopher Thomas Bryant, Tony Curran, Fiona Chalmers, Louise Duncan, William Fox, John Fraser, Michael Honan, Jeni Maxwell, Sarah Miller, Susan Nisbet, Kate Sandison, Pamela Wright (*children in Vic's class*), John Sheddon (*dentist*), Margo Croan (*woman at bus stop*), Mel Donald, Sandy Neilson (*men at bus stop*), Monica Brady (*radiologist*), Sam Graham (*Dr Knox*), Jennifer Black (*sister*), Ron Donachie (*big man at bar*), Jake D'Arcy (*wee man at bar*), Kara Wilson (*registrar McAllister*), David McKail (*consultant*), Bill Denniston (*bishop*), Lawrie McNicol, Billy McElhaney (*reporters*), Jay Smith (*photographer*), Carey Wilson (*education officer*), Robert Carr (*night editor*), Doreen Cameron (*nurse*), Gordon Jackson (*himself on TV*)
   shooting Glasgow
   budget £1,150,000. **C4 input** £748,000 (lf/i) (65%)
   1st tx 17 Mar 88 (FF)
   MFB Jan 87. **V** 21 May 86
   awards Gold Polyhymnia Mask (best actor) (Tom Conti), Taormina 86
   festivals Taormina, Edinburgh, Dublin 86; New Delhi, Warsaw 87; Antenna 89

HERO
UK, 92 mins, colour
Maya Films (Scotland) for Channel 4. 1982
   c ed DR. **no** 12
   p ANDREW ST JOHN. **p man** Adam Kempton
   d BARNEY PLATTS-MILLS. **asst d** Tony Vandenende, Amynta Cardwell. **continuity** Jaqi Nellist
   sc BARNEY PLATTS-MILLS adapted from *Tales of the Western Highlands* by J. F. Campbell. **Gaelic translator/adviser** Aonghas MacNiachell
   ph ADAM BARKER-MILL
   m PAUL STEEN, with Al Fraser, Jimmy Davidson
   ed ROBERT HARGREAVES
   ad TOM PAINE
   sd ed AUSTIN MARTIN
   cast Derek McGuire (*Dermid O'Duinne*), Caroline Kenneil (*Princess Grannia*), Alastair Kenneil (*Finn MacCumhaill*), Stewart Grant (*O'Shin*), Harpo Hamilton (*Oscar*), Danny Melrose (*page*), Samuel Z. Colclough (*Moden*), Phil Ashmore (*Molug*), Bill Dunn (*Miodac*), Clare Stephen (*young girl*), Nancy Pitt (*witch*), Bryan Gourlay, Rab Hendry (*fish boys*), Billy McColm (*Irish minstrel*), Matt McKay, Hamish McNicoll, Davie Anderson (*warriors*)
   shooting Argyll
   budget £363,000. **C4 input** £363,000 (lf) (100%)
   1st tx 29 Dec 82 (FF)
   MFB Dec 82. **V** 15 Sep 82
   festivals Venice, Edinburgh, London 82

HIDDEN CITY
UK, 108 mins, colour/b&w
Hidden City Films for ZDF (Mainz) and

Last Day of Summer

Leave to Remain

Channel 4. © Channel 4 Television Company 1987
  c ed KB. **no** 94
  p IRVING TEITELBAUM. **assoc p** Ron Purdie.
p co-ord Jane Oscroft
  d STEPHEN POLIAKOFF. **asst d** Peter Jaques,
(2nd) Tony Dyer. **continuity** Lilian
Havlickova. **casting d** Gail Stevens
  sc STEPHEN POLIAKOFF
  ph WITOLD STOK. **cam op** John Gibson.
stills David Farrell
  m MICHAEL STOREY
  ed PETER COULSON
  pd MARTIN JOHNSON. **ad** Alastair Paton
  cost des DAPHNE DARE. **make-up**
Madeleine Masters. **hair** Stephanie Kaye
  title des Chris Allies
  stunt arr PETER BRAYHAM
  sd rec MALCOLM HIRST. **dub ed** Richard
Dunford. **dub mix** Hugh Strain
  cast Charles Dance (*James Richards*),
Cassie Stuart (*Sharon Newton*), Bill Paterson
(*Anthony*), Richard E. Grant (*Brewster*),
Alex Norton (*Hillcombe*), Tusse Silberg
(*Barbara*), Richard Ireson (*schoolmaster*),
Saul Jephcott (*Curtis*), Michael Mueller
(*Boyce*), Stevan Rimkus, Gerard Horan
(*young men in tunnel*), Chris Jury (*man at
incinerator*), Campbell Morrison (*man at
rubbish tip*), Robin Soans (*man in tram
tunnel*), Noreen Kershaw (*teacher*), Auriol
Goldingham (*girl at flat*), Michelle Fairley
(*cleaner*), Helena Little, Charles Millham
(*guests at dinner party*), Michele Copsey
(*manageress at hairdressing salon*), Jelena
Budimir (*woman in film library*), Barbara
Young (*woman in film-disposal office*),
Michelle Collins, Wendy Nottingham
(*applicants at hairdressing salon*), James
Trigg (*James Richards as a boy*), Laura Welch

(*Jodie*); [in the black-and-white film] Brid
Brennan (*woman*), Katy Behean (*blond
woman*), Jason Carter (*young man*), William
Hoyland (*interrogator*), Vass Anderson
(*undertaker*), Anthony May (*burned man*)
  shooting Sep–Nov 86. London
  budget £1,068,000. **C4 input** £1,068,000
(lf/i) (100%)
  1st tx 9 Mar 89 (FF)
  MFB Jun 88. **V** 27 May 87
  festivals Cambridge, Venice, San
Sebastián, Figueira da Foz, Cherbourg,
Birmingham, Ghent 87; Trivandrum, Hong
Kong, Göttingen 88

HIGH HOPES
UK, 112 mins, colour
Portman Productions for British Screen and
Channel 4. © Portman Productions 1988
  c ed DR. **no** 107
  p SIMON CHANNING-WILLIAMS, VICTOR
GLYNN. **exec p** TOM DONALD. **p co-ord** Britt
Harrison. **p man** Caroline Hill. **unit man** Sue
Hayes
  d MIKE LEIGH. **asst d** Howard Arundel,
(2nd) Marc Munden. **sc sup** Heather Storr.
casting d Sue Whatmough
  sc MIKE LEIGH
  ph/cam op ROGER PRATT. **stills** David
Appleby, Frank Connor
  m ANDREW DICKSON
  ed JON GREGORY
  pd DIANA CHARNLEY. **ad** Andrew
Rothschild
  cost des LINDY HEMMING. **make-up** Morag
Ross. **hair** Miri Ben-Shlomo
  titles Chris Allies
  sd mix BILLY MCCARTHY. **dub ed** Peter
Joly. **dub mix** Peter Maxwell
  cast Philip Davis (*Cyril Bender*), Ruth

Sheen (*Shirley*), Edna Doré (*Mrs Bender*), Philip Jackson (*Martin Burke*), Heather Tobias (*Valerie Burke*), Lesley Manville (*Laetitia Boothe-Braine*), David Bamber (*Rupert Boothe-Braine*), Jason Watkins (*Wayne*), Judith Scott (*Suzi*), Cheryl Prime (*Martin's girlfriend*), Diane-Louise Jordan (*assistant at chemist shop*), Linda Beckett (*receptionist*), Ali (*Baby the dog*)
   shooting Jan–Mar 88. London; Essex
   budget £1,276,000. **C4 input** £745,000 (lf/i) (58%)
   1st tx 1 Mar 90 (FF)
   MFB Jan 89. **V** 7 Sep 88
   awards International Critics' P (joint), Venice 88. 2nd P (joint) Best Leading Player (Ruth Sheen), 1st P (joint) Best Director, 'Stars de Demain', Geneva 89. Most Popular Feature Film, Melbourne 89. Anthony Asquith A (F Music), BFI As 89. Peter Sellers Comedy A (Mike Leigh), *Standard* F As 89. European Actress of the Year (Ruth Sheen), European Supporting Performance of the Year (Edna Doré), European Composer of the Year, European F As 89. Special Jury P (Best Cast), Golden Fleece Festival, Georgia (USSR) 90
   festivals Venice, Edinburgh, Telluride, New York, Vancouver, Mill Valley, Hof, Leeds, London 88; Göteborg, Brussels, Houston, Vienna, Hong Kong, San Francisco, Durban, Bragafest, Sydney, Geneva, Wellington, Moscow, Melbourne, Valladolid 89; Georgia 90
   working title *Winter*

HIGH SEASON

UK, 101 mins, colour
Forever Films/Marlie Productions with British Screen, Hemdale Film Corporation, Curzon Film Distributors and Michael White for Channel 4. Assisted by the National Film Development Fund. © Hemdale Film Corporation. 1987
   c ed DR. **no** 89
   p CLARE DOWNS. **exec p** MICHAEL WHITE.
co-p RAYMOND DAY. **assoc p** Mary Clow.
p sup Dimitri Dimitriades. **unit man** Haris Kontorouhas. **p co-ord** Maggie Parsons
   d CLARE PEPLOE. **asst d** Guy Travers; Andrew Wood, Thanassis Christopoulos.
sc sup Pat Rambaut. **casting d** Gail Stevens
   sc MARK PEPLOE, CLARE PEPLOE.
   ph CHRIS MENGES. **stills** David Appleby
   m/cond JASON OSBORN

   ed GABRIELLA CRISTIANI. **film ed** Peter Dansie
   pd ANDREW MCALPINE. **ad** Caroline Hanania, Petros Kapouralis
   cost des LOUISE STJERNSWARD. **make-up** Nick Forder. **hair** Mike Lockey
   sp eff YANNIS SAMIOTIS
   main title des Paul Derrick
   sd rec JUDY FREEMAN. **sd ed** Mike Hopkins, Geoff Brown. **dub mix** Andy Nelson
   cast Jacqueline Bisset (*Katherine Shaw*), James Fox (*Patrick Shaw*), Irene Papas (*Penelope*), Sebastian Shaw (*Basil Sharp*), Kenneth Branagh (*Rick Lamb*), Lesley Manville (*Carol Lamb*), Robert Stephens (*Konstantinis*), Geoffrey Rose (*Thompson*), Paris Tselois (*Yanni*), Ruby Baker (*Chloe Shaw*), Mark Williams (*Benny*), Shelly Laurenti (*June*), George Diakoyorgio (*mayor*), Father Bassili (*Pappas*), Captain Stelios (*fisherman*), Michael White (*man with lavatory chain*)
   shooting Lakhania, Rhodes
   budget £1,902,000. **C4 input** £350,000 (lf/i) (18%)
   1st tx 2 Mar 89 (FF)
   MFB Jun 87. **V** 3 Jun 87

A HISTORY LESSON *see* **REFLECTIONS**

HOPE AND GLORY

USA/UK, 112 mins, colour
Columbia Pictures with Nelson Entertainment and Goldcrest Films & Television. Filmed by Davros Production Services. © Columbia Pictures Industries 1987
   c ed DR. **no** 108
   p JOHN BOORMAN. **exec p** JAKE EBERTS, EDGAR F. GROSS. **co-p** MICHAEL DRYHURST.
p co-ord Sheila Collins
   d JOHN BOORMAN. **asst d** Andy Armstrong; Melvin Lind, Julian Wall. **2nd unit d** Michael Dryhurst. **sc sup** Elaine Schreyeck. **casting** Mary Selway
   sc JOHN BOORMAN
   ph PHILIPPE ROUSSELOT. **cam op** Mike Fox.
addit ph John Harris. **stills** Murray Close
   m/m arr/cond PETER MARTIN
   choreo ANTHONY VAN LAAST
   ed IAN CRAFFORD
   pd ANTHONY PRATT. **ad** Don Dossett
   cost des SHIRLEY RUSSELL. **make-up** Anna Dryhurst. **hair** Joan Carpenter
   sp eff des PHIL STOKES. **sp eff sup**

Rodney Fuller, Michael Collins
sd rec PETER HANDFORD. **sd ed** Ron Davis.
dial ed Paul Smith. **sd mix** John Hayward
  cast Sebastian Rice Edwards (*Bill Rohan*),
Geraldine Muir (*Sue Rohan*), Sarah Miles
(*Grace Rohan*), David Hayman (*Clive
Rohan*), Sammi Davis (*Dawn Rohan*), Derrick
O'Connor (*Mac*), Susan Wooldridge (*Molly*),
Jean-Marc Barr (*Cpl Bruce Carey*), Ian
Bannen (*Grandfather George*), Annie Leon
(*Grandma*), Jill Baker (*Faith*), Amelda Brown
(*Hope*), Katrine Boorman (*Charity*), Colin
Higgins (*Clive's pal*), Shelagh Fraser (*WVS
woman*), Gerald James (*headmaster*),
Barbara Pierson (*Miss Evans, teacher*), Nicky
Taylor (*Roger*), Jodie Andrews, Nicholas
Askew, Jamie Bowman, Colin Dale, David
Parkin, Carlton Taylor (*Roger's gang*), Sara
Langton (*Pauline*), Imogen Cawrse (*Jennifer*),
Susan Brown (*Mrs Evans*), Charley Boorman
(*Luftwaffe pilot*), Peter Hughes (*policeman*),
Ann Thornton, Andrew Bicknell (*honey-
moon couple*), Christine Crowshaw (*pianist*),
William Armstrong (*Canadian sergeant*),
Arthur Cox (*fireman*), the voice of John
Boorman
  shooting Aug–Oct 86. Wisley; Brighton;
Middlesex; Bray studios
  budget $9,100,000 [John Boorman]/
£5,564,000. **C4 input** £325,000 (lf) (6%)
  1st tx 28 Apr 91 (FF)
  MFB Sep 87. **V** 15 Jul 87
  awards Best F, Best Technical
Achievement (Anthony Pratt), *Standard* F As
88. Best Supporting Actress (Susan
Wooldridge), BAFTA F As 88

HÔTEL DU PARADIS
UK/France, 113 mins, colour
Umbrella-Portman Films (London) and
Pierson Production (Paris) for Antenne 2
(Paris), London Trust Productions and
Channel 4. © Umbrella-Portman Films 1986
  c ed DR. **no** 81
  p SIMON PERRY. **exec p** ALAN CAPPER, TOM
DONALD, CLAUDE PIERSON. **p co-ord** Marie
McFerran
  d JANA BOKÓVA. **asst d** Jean-Luc Olivier,
(2nd) Faouzi Kasri. **continuity** Dominique
Piat
  sc JANA BOKÓVA. **sc cons** Gualberto
Ferrari, Alan Passes. **French translation**
Claire Blatchley, Michelle Seawell,
Viviane Mathieu. Fernando Rey's one-
man show based on extracts from

The Fall by Albert Camus
  ph/cam op GÉRARD DE BATTISTA. **stills**
Monica Douek
  m RODOLFO MEDEROS
  ed BILL SHAPTER
  des PATRICK WEIBEL
  cost RENÉE RENARD. **make-up** Jackie
Reynal. **hair** Patrick Deloille
  title des Sid Sutton
  sd rec BRUNO CHARIER. **sd ed** Jacques
Leroide, (eff) Michael Hopkins. **re-rec mix**
Trevor Pyke
  film extract *The Third Man*
  cast Carola Regnier (*Sarah Goldman*),
Fernando Rey (*Joseph Goldman*), Marika
Rivera (*Marika*), Artus de Penguern (*Patric*),
Fabrice Luchini (*Arthur*), Sheila Kotkin
(*Sheila*), Bérangère Bonvoisin (*Frédérique*),
Gilberte Geniat (*caretaker*), Rémi Deroche
(*Harry*), Nounours (*Harry's dog*), Catherine
Mathely (*Marianne*), Hugues Quester
(*Maurice*), Raul Gimenez (*Emilio*), Max
Berto (*Max*), Irène Langer (*Irène*), Lou Castel
(*tramp*), Consuelo de Haviland (*Barbara*),
Aurelle Doazan (*dream girl*), Juliet Berto
(*prostitute*), Georges Geret (*Dr Jacob*),
Michael Medwin (*Stanley, 'the English
producer'*), Zanie Campan ('*Lucienne
Boyer*'), Sacha Briquet (*Georges*), Pascal
Aubier, Bertrand Bonvoisin, Gérard
Courant, Pascale Dauman, Alex Joffé, Arthur
Joffé, Faouzi Ramses, 'Ovide' Freddy
Lington, Roberto Lugones, Madeleine Marie,
Vincent Martin, Thierry Ravel, Carlos
Rudnickyj, Jeannine Seawell, Cyrille Spiga
  shooting Nov 85–Jan 86. Paris
  budget £704,000. **C4 input** £459,000 (lf/i)
(65%)
  1st tx 24 May 90 (FF)
  MFB Jun 89. **V** 20 May 87
  festivals Cannes, Edinburgh 87

ILL FARES THE LAND
UK, ?100 mins, colour
Portman Productions for Scottish and
Global Television Enterprises and Channel 4.
© Portman Productions 1982
  c ed DR. **no** 15
  p ROBERT LOVE. **exec p** IAN WARREN. **assoc
p** Dickie Bamber. **p man** Pat Pennelegion
  d BILL BRYDEN. **asst d** Dickie Bamber,
(2nd) Melvin Lind. **continuity** Marjorie
Lavelly. **casting d** Liz Cassidy
  sc BILL BRYDEN
  ph JOHN COQUILLON. **cam op** Lou Lavelly.

2nd unit cam Leslie Dear. **stills** Douglas Dawson

m JOHN TAMS

ed LESLEY WALKER

pd KEN BRIDGEMAN, (assoc) Ray Simm

cost des DEIRDRE CLANCY. **make-up** Karen Dawson, Yvonne Coppard. **hair** Anne McFadyen, Pearl Tipaldi

sd rec LAURIE CLARKSON. **dub ed** Paul Smith. **sd re-rec** Tony Anscombe

cast Fulton Mackay (*Finlay Gillies*), James Grant (*Donald Gillies*), George MacInnes (*Neil Gillies*), Jan Wilson (*Christian Gillies*), Jean Taylor Smith (*Widow Gillies*), James Ellis (*Neil Ferguson Sr*), Ewan Stewart (*Neil Ferguson Jr*), David Hayman (*Willie MacDonald*), J. G. Devlin (*Old MacDonald*), Andrew McCulloch (*Ewen MacDonald*), Valerie Whittington (*Rachel MacDonald*), Joan MacKenzie (*Widow MacDonald*), Joseph Brady (*Norman MacKinnon*), Ron Donachie (*Campbell MacKinnon*), William MacBain (*Archie MacKinnon*), Erica MacInnes (*Fiona MacKinnon*), Donald MacLean (*Donald MacKinnon*), Morag Hood (*Nurse Barclay*), Roy Hanlon (*Munro*), James Copeland (*Captain Craig*), Robert James (*the minister*), Brian Pettifer (*Fergie*), Neil Duncan (*Gilchrist*), John Shedden (*the heckler*), Robert Stephens (*the Under Secretary of State*)

shooting Jul–Aug 82. Wester Ross; St Kilda

budget £628,000. **C4 input** £300,000 (i) (48%)

1st tx 19 May 83 (FF)

festivals London 82

IN FADING LIGHT

UK, 107 mins, colour
Amber Films for Channel 4. Made under the auspices of the ACTT Workshop declaration with support from Northern Arts. © Amber Films 1989

c ed KB. **no** 170

Amber production team KITTY FITZGERALD, RICH GRASSICK, ELLIN HARE, SIRKKA-LIISA KONTTINEN, PAT MCCARTHY, MURRAY MARTIN, LORNA POWELL, PETER ROBERTS. **continuity** Wendy McEvoy

sc TOM HADAWAY

m ALASDAIR ROBERTSON, RAY STUBBS. **md** Alasdair Robertson. **musicians** Catherine Holmes, Alasdair Robertson, Ray Stubbs, Wendy Weatherby

ad JUDITH TOMLINSON

crew of the *Sally* Davy Butterfield, Tony Chester, Jimmy Cullen Sr, Jimmy Cullen Jr, Terry McDermott, Davy Miller

sd rec DAVE EADINGTON. **sd engineer** Frank Gibbon. **dub mix** Dave Skilton

cast Joanna Ripley (*Karen Olsen*), Dave Hill (*Alfie Olsen*), Sammy Johnson (*Dandy Mac*), Brian Hogg (*Micky Molloy*), Amber Styles (*Betty*), Mo Harold (*Irene*), Joe Caffrey (*Yopper*), Art Davies (*Peter Parkin*), Norma Day (*kitchen lady*), Mike Mason (*clerk*), Cilla Mason (*barmaid*), Ray Stubbs (*Ray*), Gavin Kitchen (*pool player*), Pete Morrison (*big man*), Steve Evans (*taxi driver*), Brendan Healey (*quay master*), Anna-Maria Gascoigne (*Tracy*), Jacqui Clairemont, Lisa Sanderson (*Tracy's mates*)

shooting Mar–Apr, Aug–Sep 1989. North Shields; North Sea

budget £310,000. **C4 input** £310,000 (lf/i) (100%)

1st tx 31 May 90 (FF)

MFB Mar 90. **V** 10 Jan 90

awards Finalist A, New York 91. Finalist A (single drama), Royal TV Soc 91. Silver Anchor, Festival of Marine and Maritime Exploration Fs, Toulon 91

festivals London 89; New York, Toulon 91

THE INNOCENT

UK, 96 mins, colour
Tempest Films for TVS and Channel 4. Assisted by the National Film Development Fund. © TVS 1984

c ed DR. **no** 40

p JACKY STOLLER. **exec p** DICKIE BAMBER. **assoc p** Sheila Trezise. **p co-ord** Ping Mudie. **p man** Michael-John Knatchbull

d JOHN MACKENZIE. **asst d** Chris Rose, (2nd) John Dodds. **sc sup** Margaret Waldie

sc RAY JENKINS from the novel *The Aura and the Kingfisher* by Tom Hart

ph ROGER DEAKINS. **cam op** Andrew Speller. **kingfisher ph** Andrew Anderson. **2nd unit cam** John Simmons. **stills** Douglas Dawson

m FRANCIS MONKMAN

ed TONY WOOLLARD

pd ANDREW MOLLO. **ad** Philip Elton

cost des JOHN FRASER. **make-up** Tom Smith. **hair** Anne McFadyen

title des Richard Morrison

sd mix BRUCE WHITE. **dub ed** Shirley

Shaw, Brigitte Arnold. **sd re-rec** Tony Anscombe, Aad Wirtz

cast Andrew Hawley (*Tim Dobson*), Kika Markham (*Mrs Dobson*), Kate Foster (*Win*), Liam Neeson (*John Carns*), Patrick Daley (*Eddie King*), Paul Askew (*Stanley*), Lorraine Peters (*Win's grandmother*), Tom Bell (*Frank Dobson*), Richard Hope (*mouth organ player*), Jack Carr (*mill owner*), Clive Wood (*Turner*), Miranda Richardson (*Mary Turner*), Richard Laxton (*Reg Reid*), Denis Lill (*doctor*), Alison Lloyd (*Edith, woolshop owner*), Bill Rodgers (*drinkbearer*)

shooting Aug–Sep 84. Settle, Yorkshire
budget £1,000,000. **C4 input** £300,000 (lf) (30%)
1st tx 19 Jun 86 (FF)
MFB Jun 85. **V** 22 May 85
festivals Cannes, Washington, Montreal, Chicago 85

IN THE WHITE CITY

Portugal/Switzerland/FGR/UK, 108 mins, colour

Metro Filme (Lisbon) and Filmograph (Geneva) with WDR (Cologne), Channel 4 and Télévision Suisse Romande (Geneva). © Metro Filme-Filmograph 1983

c ed DR. **no** 29
p PAULO BRANCO, ALAIN TANNER, JOSE MARIA VAZ DA SILVA. **exec p** PAULO BRANCO, ALAIN TANNER. **p man** José María Vaz da Silva, Antonio Gonçalo, (Rhine) Jean-Louis Porchet
d ALAIN TANNER. **asst d** Christine Chenevière, (2nd) Pedro Ruivo, João Canijo. **sc girl** Sophie Enderlin
sc ALAIN TANNER.
ph ACACIO DE ALMEIDA. **stills** Gabriel Lopes, Mario Castanheira
m JEAN-LUC BARBIER
ed LAURENT UHLER
ad MARIA JOSE BRANCO
sd JEAN-PAUL MUGEL. **mix** Laurent Barbey
cast Bruno Ganz (*Paul*), Teresa Madruga (*Rosa*), Julia Vonderlinn (*Elisa*), José Carvalho (*José the bar proprietor*), Victor Costa (*Victor the bartender*), Francisco Baiao (*thief with knife*), José Wallenstein (*2nd thief*), Lidia Franco (*woman in bar*), Pedro Efe (*friend in bar*), Cecilia Guimaraes (*woman on train*), Joana Vicente (*girl on train*), Paulo Branco (*man at station with paper and pen*)
shooting Lisbon; the Rhine

budget (?) **C4 input** £25,000 (lf)
1st tx 28 Jun 84 (FF)
MFB Oct 83. **V** 9 Mar 83
European release title *Dans la ville blanche*

JOYRIDERS

UK, 96 mins, colour
Little Bird with Walsh Smith for Granada Film Productions with British Screen and Channel 4. Assisted by the National Film Development Fund. © Granada Film Productions 1988

c ed DR/KB. **no** 109
p EMMA HAYTER. **assoc p** Jonathan Cavendish. **p exec** Sue Austen. **p man** Gemma Fallon. **p sup** David Brown. **p co-ord** Lorraine Stierle
d AISLING WALSH. **asst d** David Brown, (2nd) Mick Rowland. **sc sup** Jean Bourne. **casting d** Di Carling
sc ANDY SMITH. **st** Aisling Walsh, Andy Smith
ph GABRIEL BERISTAIN. **cam op** Des Whelan. **2nd unit cam** Patrick Duval. **stills** (unit) Paddy Monaghan, (special) David James
m HAL LINDES, TONY BRITTEN. **song** Tony Britten, Andy Smith
choreo JUNE GLAZIER
ed THOMAS SCHWALM
pd LEIGH MALONE. **ad** David Wilson
cost des NIC EDE. **make-up** Rosie Blackmore. **hair** Dee Corcoran
sd mix KIERAN HORGAN. **dub ed** 'Budge' Tremlett. **dial ed** Brigitte Arnold. **dub mix** Hugh Strain
cast Patricia Kerrigan (*Mary Flynn*), Andrew Connolly (*Perky Rice*), Billie Whitelaw (*Tammy O'Moore*), David Kelly (*Daniel Tracey*), John Kavanagh (*hotel manager*), Deirdre Donoghue (*Dolores Flynn*), Tracy Peacock (*Finbar Flynn*), Rolf Saxon (*1st American sailor*), Otto Jarman (*2nd American sailor*), Gerard Mannix Flynn, Sean Lawlor (*thugs in gents toilet*), Gina Moxley (*Mary's neighbour*), Jim Bartley (*Tony*), Stuart Dunne (*Hank the barman*), Martin Dunne (*vocalist*), Des Moore, Chris Kneavey, John Drummond, Desi Reynolds (*band*), Eanna MacLiam (*Perky's pal in pub*), Ronan Wilmot (*Tyrone*), Doreen Keogh (*nun*)
shooting Feb–Mar 88. Dublin; Co. Wicklow; Co. Clare

budget £1,300,000 [Emma Hayter].
C4 input £100,000 (lf) (8%)
1st tx 6 Oct 91 (FF)
MFB May 89. **V** 22 Feb 89
awards *Sunday Tribune* Arts A for
Cinema (Ireland) 88
festivals Montreal, Toronto, Edmonton,
Munich, Uppsala 89

KATINKA
Denmark/Sweden/UK, 96 mins, colour
Nordisk Film (Copenhagen) with Svensk
Filmindustri (Stockholm), the Danish Film
Institute (with Peter Poulsen), the Swedish
Film Institute (with Katinka Faragó) and
Channel 4. © Nordisk Film 1988
　c ed DR. **no** (-)
　p BO CHRISTENSEN. **p man** Lene Nielsen.
unit p man Inge Rask
　d MAX VON SYDOW. **asst** Tom Hedegaard.
sc sup Lotta Mothander
　sc KLAUS RIFBJERG from the novel *Ved*
Vejen (*Along the Road*) by Herman Bang
　A-ph SVEN NYKVIST, Claus Loof. **B-ph**
Birger Bohm, Søren Berthelin. **stills** Rolf
Konow, Else Kjaer Hedegaard
　m GEORG RIEDEL. **m cons** Jan Glæsel
　choreo NIELS BJORN LARSEN
　ed JANUS BILLESKOV JANSEN
　ad PETER HØIMARK
　cost ANNELISE HAUBERG, PIA MYRDAL, OLE
GLAESNER. **make-up** Kaj Grönberg
　sd sup MICHAEL DELA. **sd post-p** John
Nielsen, Nalle, Bjarne Risbjerg. **mix** Hans Eric
Ahrn
　cast Tammi Øst (*Katinka Bai*), Ole Ernst
(*Bai*), Kurt Ravn (*Wilhelm Huus*), Erik Paaske
(*Pastor Linde*), Tine Miehe-Renard (*Agnes
Linde*), Vibeke Hastrup (*Ida Abel*), Birthe
Backhausen (*Mrs Abel*), Bodil Lassen
(*Louise Abel*), Ghita Nørby (*Helene Jensen*),
Anne Grete Hilding (*Mrs Linde*), Bjarne G.
Nielsen (*Herman Bang*), Henrik Kofoed
(*Bentsen*), Kim Harris (*railway conductor*),
Birgitte Bruun (*singer, 'Stakkels Mary
Anna'*), Hanna Damian Lindquist (*singer,
'Massemorderen Thomas'*), Lizzie Schwartz,
Inge Vendelboe, Poul Erik Christensen (*in
the singing gallery*), Anna Lise Hirsch
Bjerrum, Paul Hüttel, Kjeld Nørgaard, Dick
Kaysø, Søren Sætter-Lassen, Tom Jensen,
Wilhelm Weber, Tine Stochholm
　shooting Denmark
　budget ?£800,000. **C4 input** £45,000 (lf)
　1st tx 26 May 90 (FFI)

V 18 May 88
festivals Cannes, London 88
Danish release title *Ved vejen*
Swedish release title *Vid vägen*

THE KING AND THE QUEEN
Spain/UK/Italy, 115 mins, colour/b&w
TVE (Madrid) with Channel 4, SACIS
(Rome) and RAI (Rome). © Televisión
Española 1985
　c ed DR. **no** (-)
　p FERNANDO QUEJIDO. **production** Juan
José Sánchez, Pastora Díaz, Esteban Velez,
José Delgado. **p man** Germán Quejido
　d JOSE ANTONIO PARAMO. **asst d** Carlos
Martínez, Isidro Serrano. **continuity** Carmen
Guarido. **casting** Rafael Borque
　sc JOSE A. PARAMO, LUIS ARINO based on
the novel by Ramón José Sender
　ph FRANCISCO FRAILE
　m JOSE NIETO
　ed NIEVES MARTIN
　pd FERNANDO SAENZ. **ad** Carlos
Dorremochea
　cost CARMEN MOYA. **make-up** Josefina
Flores, Juan Luis Farsack, Pilar Parrilla. **hair**
Esther Martín
　sp eff ANTONIO BUEÑO
　titles Pablo Nuñez
　sd (direct) ANTONIO CARDENAS, JOSE
LUMBRERAS, ENRIQUE VIÑUALES. **mix** Enrique
Molinero. **sd eff** Luis Castro, Jesús Peña
　cast Omero Antonutti (*Rómulo*), Nuria
Espert (*Duchess of Alquezar*), Xavier
Elorriaga (*Capt Ordóñez*), Victor Valverde
(*Duke of Alquezar*), Ramiro Oliveros
(*Esteban, Marquis of Irati*), Alvaro De Luna
(*Sergeant*), Daniel Dicenta, José Manuel
Cervino, Walter Vidarte, Francisco Algora,
Kino Pueyo, Quique San Francisco, Rafael
Izuzquiza, Antonio Gamero, Francisco
Nieto, Braulio Dorado, Paloma Pages, Helena
Fernán Gómez, Margarita Lascoitty, David
Rocha, Vicente Vega, José María Tasso
　shooting Córdoba, Madrid
　budget ?£450,000. **C4 input** £50,000 (lf)
　1st tx 27 Mar 86 (FF from Spain)
　Spanish release title *El Rey y la Reina*
　English subtitle *King and Queen*

KIPPERBANG *see*
P'TANG, YANG, KIPPERBANG

THE KITCHEN TOTO
UK, 95 mins, colour

Skreba Films for the Cannon Group, British Screen and Channel 4. © Cannon Films & Cannon International 1987

c ed DR/KB. **no** 91

p ANN SKINNER. **exec p** MENAHEM GOLAN, YORAM GLOBUS. **p sup** Ted Morley. **p co-ord** Katy Radford

d HARRY HOOK. **asst d** Guy Travers, (2nd) Andrew Wood. **continuity** Lissa Ruben.

casting Anne Henderson, Meja Mwangi

sc HARRY HOOK

ph ROGER DEAKINS. **cam op** Ronnie Fox-Rogers. **2nd unit cam** Charles Patey.

stills Peter Murphy

m JOHN KEANE. **harmonica** Tommy Reilly

sup ed TOM PRIESTLEY

pd JAMIE LEONARD

cost des BARBARA KIDD. **make-up** Sara Monzani, Maureen Stephenson. **hair** Frieda Hart

sp eff DIGBY MILNER

titles Stephen Masters

sd rec CHRISTIAN WANGLER. **sd ed** Jupiter Sen. **re-rec** Hugh Strain

cast Edwin Mahinda (*Mwangi Moses Kariuki*), Nathan Dambuza Mdledle (*the Rev Mzee Moses Kariuki*), Ann Wanjugu (*Mrs Kariuki*), Job Seda (*Kamau*), Konga Mbandu (*Kamau's henchman*), Bob Peck (*John Graham*), Leo Wringer (*Sgt Stephen*), Nicholas Charles (*Mugo the houseboy*), Abdullah Sunado (*Gikuya the cook*), Lidya Kigada (*Warimu the nanny*), Emmanuel Mnguto (*Muriuki the gardener*), Phyllis Logan (*Janet Graham*), Ronald Pirie (*Edward Graham*), Robert Urquhart (*D. C. McKinnon*), Kirsten Hughes (*Mary McKinnon*), Edward Judd (*Dick Luis*), Paul Onsongo (*oath administrator*), Lawi Leboire (*Samburu askari*)

shooting Aug–Nov 86. Kenya

budget £1,767,000. **C4 input** £332,000 (lf/i) (19%)

1st tx 29 Mar 90 (FF)

MFB Nov 87. **V** 13 May 87

awards Anthony Asquith A (*Young Composer*), BFI As 87. Most Promising Newcomer (Harry Hook), *Standard* F As 88. Grand Prix, Best Actor (Edwin Mahinda), Best Music, Festival of Youth, Paris 88

festivals Edinburgh, London 87; Paris 88

LADDER OF SWORDS

UK, 98 mins, colour

Arden Films for Channel 4 and British Screen. © Channel 4 Television Co 1988

c ed KB. **no** 110

p JENNIFER HOWARTH. **p man** Olivia Stewart. **p co-ord** Lil Stirling

d NORMAN HULL. **asst d** David Brown, (2nd) Gus MacLean. **sc sup** Libbie Barr.

casting d Priscilla John

sc NEIL CLARKE. **st** Norman Hull, Neil Clarke

ph THADDEUS O'SULLIVAN. **2nd unit ph** Peter Harvey. **stills** David Appleby, John Brown, (specials) Sven Arnstein

m STANLEY MYERS

ed SCOTT THOMAS

des CAROLINE HANANIA. **ad** Careen Hertzog

cost des SHUNA HARWOOD. **make-up** Jenny Shircore. **hair** Aileen Seaton

sd rec COLIN NICOLSON. **dub ed** Alan Knight. **dial ed** Alex Mackie. **re-rec mix** Peter Maxwell

cast Martin Shaw (*Don Demarco*), Eleanor David (*Denise Demarco*), Bob Peck (*Det Insp Geoff Atherton*), Simon Molloy (*Sgt Phil Bilby*), Pearce Quigley (*PC Lowe*), Juliet Stevenson (*Alice Howard*), Anthony Benson (*grumpy gun*), Graham Rigby (*1st gun*), Bobby Knutt (*Russell Platt*), Robert Whelan (*young gun*), Peter Martin (*John the chauffeur*), Alan Hockey (*Herbert*), Danny James (*gardener*), Les Wilde (*farmer*), Czeslaw Grocholski (*Eddie Bukowski*), Tessa Ujazdowska (*Maria Bukowski*), Anne Orwin (*woman at fortune teller's*), Paul Butterworth (*constable*), Johnny Leeze (*beach photographer*), Daley (*the bear*)

shooting Northumberland

budget £1,300,000. **C4 input** £882,000 (lf/i) (68%)

1st tx 11 Aug 91 (FF)

MFB Jan 90. **V** 31 May 89

festivals Cambridge, Edinburgh, Vancouver, Leeds, Belfast, London 89; Palm Springs, Würzburg, Hong Kong, Haifa, Aurillac, Fort Lauderdale, Polish Film Week, Cairo 90

LAMB

UK, 110 mins, colour

Flickers Productions and Limehouse Pictures for Channel 4. © Channel 4 TV Co 1988 [amended credit, shown 1985]

c ed DR/KB. **no** 66

p NEIL ZEIGER. **exec p** AL BURGESS. **assoc p** Martin Proctor. Arthur Ferriman. **p co-ord**

Faye Perkins. **p man** Christabel Albery
   d COLIN GREGG. **asst d** Gerry Gavigan,
(2nd) Terry Madden. **2nd unit d** Kevin Smith.
sc sup Diana Dill. **casting d** Simone
Reynolds
   sc BERNARD MacLAVERTY from his own
novel
   ph MIKE GARFATH. **cam op** Peter Taylor,
(2nd unit) Michael Miles. **stills** Douglas
Dawson
   m VAN MORRISON. **m soundtrack arr/
addit m** Bill Whelan
   ed PETER DELFGOU
   pd AUSTEN SPRIGGS. **ad** Val Wolstenholme
   cost des MONICA HOWE. **make-up** Vivien
Placks. **hair** Stevie Hall
   sp eff GORDON COXON
   titles Chris Allies
   stunt arr BILL WESTON
   sd rec BILL BURGESS, (2nd unit) Mervyn
Gerrard. **dub ed** John Delfgou. **dub mix**
Rupert Scrivener, Ken Somerville
   cast Liam Neeson (*Brother Sebastian,
Michael Lamb*), Harry Towb (*priest*), Hugh
O'Conor (*Owen Kane*), Frances Tomelty
(*Mrs Bernadette Kane*), Ian Bannen (*Brother
Benedict*), Ronan Wilmot (*Brother Fintan*),
Denis Carey (*Mr Lamb*), Eileen Kennally
(*neighbour*), David Gorry (*O'Donnell*),
Andrew Pickering (*Murphy*), Stuart
O'Connor (*O'Halloran*), Ian McElhinney
(*Maguire*), Bernadette McKenna (*jeweller's
assistant*), Jessica Saunders (*bank teller on
boat*), Robert Hamilton (*stranger at
Holyhead*), Roger Booth (*farmer on train*),
Marjie Lawrence (*assistant, department
store*), Nicola Wright (*hotel receptionist*),
Freddie Stuart (*1st crook*), Roy Glascock (*2nd
crook*), Doreen Keogh (*landlady of cheap
hotel*), Nick Dunning (*football spectator*),
Nigel Humphries (*policeman*), Tony
Wredden (*pharmacist*), Dudley Sutton
(*Haddock*), Larrington Walker (*Newtan*),
Walter McMonagle (*carpenter*), Colum
Convey (*plumber*), Emer Gillespie (*Avis girl*)
   shooting Mar–Apr 85. Cornwall;
London; Wales; Eire
   budget £1,260,000. **C4 input** £605,000
(lf/i) (48%)
   1st tx 24 Mar 88 (FF)
   MFB Jun 86. **V** 20 Nov 85
   awards Bronze Leopard (joint), 1st P
(youth section), 1st P (ecumenical section),
Locarno 86. Golden Butterfly (Best Film
about Children), Isfahan 91

   festivals Locarno, Montreal, Ghent 86;
Cape Town, Durban, Moscow, Bilbao, Rio de
Janeiro 87; Vienna 88; Isfahan 91

LANDSCAPE IN THE MIST
Greece/France/Italy/UK, 124 mins, colour
Theo Angelopoulos Productions for the
Greek Film Centre and ERT (Athens), Paradis
Films (Paris), Basicinematografica and RAI
(Rome) and Channel 4. 1988
   c ed DR. no (-)
   p THEO ANGELOPOULOS. **p man** Emilios
Konitsiotis
   d THEO ANGELOPOULOS. **asst d** Takis
Katselis, (2nd) Dimitris Frangoulis, Eleni
Petraki
   sc THEO ANGELOPOULOS, TONINO GUERRA,
THANASIS VALTINOS. **st** Theo Angelopoulos
   ph GIORGIOS ARVANITIS
   m ELENI KARAINDROU
   ed YANNIS TSITSOPOULOS
   ad MIKES KARAPIPERIS
   sp eff GINO DE ROSSI
   titles Cornelios Vardopoulos
   cost ANASTASIA ARSENI. **make-up** Stella
Votsou
   sd rec MARINOS ATHANASSOPOULOS. **sd
re-rec** Thanasis Arvanitis
   cast Michalis Zeke (*Alexandros*), Tania
Palaiologou (*Voula*), Stratos Tzortzoglou
(*Orestes*), Nadia Mourouzi (*service station
waitress*), Eva Kotamanidou, Aliki Georgouli,
Vangelis Kazan, Stratos Pachis, Kyriakos
Katrivanos, Grigoris Evangelatos, Yannis
Firios (*travelling players*), Vassilis Kolovos,
Vassilis Bouyouklakis, Ilias Logothetis,
Michalis Yannatos, N. Kouros, Vasia
Panagopoulou, Toula Stathopoulou,
N. Papazafiropoulou, Christoforos Nezer,
G. Skiadaressis, A. Alafouzos, D. Kamberidis,
T. Palatsidis, P. Botinis, Th. Vouyoukas,
A. Varouchas
   shooting Greece
   budget £912,000. **C4 input** £50,000 (lf)
(5%)
   1st tx 28 Apr 90 (FFI)
   MFB Aug 89. **V** 7 Sep 88
   awards Silver Lion, Best Director A,
Venice 88. Best F, European F As 89
   festivals Venice, London 88
   Greek release title *Topio stin omichli*

LAST DAY OF SUMMER
UK, 55 mins, colour
The Moving Picture Company for

Channel 4. © Channel 4 1983
c ed DR/WD. **no** 35
p NIGEL STAFFORD-CLARK. **assoc p** Peter
Jaques. **location manager** Hugh O'Donnell
d DEREK BANHAM. **asst d** Michael Finch,
(2nd) Monica Hyde. **continuity** Mary
Holdsworth. **casting d** Ann Fielden
sc IAN MCEWAN from his own short story
ph NIC KNOWLAND. **stills** Diana Miller
m RACHEL PORTMAN. **m perf** John White
ed RICHARD TREVOR
ad ANTON FURST
ward sup CARLA WILLSHER. **make-up**
Gordon Kay. **hair** Paula Gillespie
sd rec MALCOLM HIRST. **dub mix** Rod
Guest
cast Annette Badland (*Jenny*), Graham
McGrath (*Tom*), James Gaddas (*Pete*),
Christina Jones (*Kate*), John Telfer (*José*),
Steven Beard (*Sam*), Karen Scargill (*Sharon*),
Saskia Reeves (*Linda*), Rebecca Elsworth
(*Alice*), Denise Buckley (*mother*)
shooting Aug–Sep 83. Thames Valley
budget £209,000. **C4 input** £160,000 (lf)
(77%)
1st tx 7 Jun 84 (FF)
festivals London 83

LAUGHTERHOUSE *see*
SINGLETON'S PLUCK

LEAVE TO REMAIN
UK, 107 mins, colour
Spellbound Productions for Channel 4.
© Channel 4 Television Company 1988
c ed KB. **no** 111
p IRVING TEITELBAUM. **co-p** PAUL
ANTHONY HARRIS. **assoc p** Ron Purdie.
p co-ord Jane Oscroft
d LES BLAIR. **asst d** Howard Arundel, (2nd)
Sean Dromgoole. **continuity** Doreen Soan.
casting Gail Stevens
sc ROB RITCHIE, IRAJ JANNATIE ATAIE
ph IVAN STRASBURG. **cam op** Luke Cardiff.
stills Simon Mein
m SIMON BRINT, ROWLAND RIVRON
ed JON GREGORY
ad ALASTAIR PATON
cost des DAPHNE DARE. **make-up** Christine
Allsopp. **hair** Stephanie Kaye
sd rec MIKE MCDUFFIE. **dub ed** Michael
Crowley. **dub mix** Peter Maxwell
cast Meda Kidem (*Shahin Mohamadi*),
Kazuko Hohki (*Henry*), Jonathan Phillips
(*Jimmy Johnstone*), Nasser Memarzia

(*Javad*), Sahand Meshcot (*Bamdaad*), Akbar
Moein (*Akbar*), Ali Kamrani (*Ramin
Arastafar*), H. Hamid (*Guran*), Zahra Jorjani
(*Nasrin*), Georgia Clarke (*Mina*), William
Gaminara (*Nick*), Alfred Hoffman
(*Kalinowski*), Alisa Bosschaert (*Ellen*),
Linda Bassett (*woman at Home Office,
London*), David Bamber (*Dover official*),
Amir Rima (*embassy official*), Paul Bentall
(*mullah*), Mano Shada (*embassy aide*), Steve
Ashton (*Raouf*), Lavinia Bertram (*registrar*),
Anthony Milner (*lab assistant*), Michael
Hadley (*photographer*), Barry Birch (*bike
boy*), Kit Jackson, David Millet, Steve
Weston (*immigration officers*), Philippe
Giraudeau (*French waiter*), Christopher
Simon (*chicken bar assistant*), Steven
O'Donnell (*customer*)
shooting Aug–Sep 87. Spain; London;
Croydon; Dover; Lee International studios
budget £900,000. **C4 input** £900,000 (i)
(100%)
1st tx 11 May 89 (FF)
V 26 Oct 88
festivals Mill Valley 88

LETTERS TO AN UNKNOWN LOVER
UK/France, 101 mins, colour
Portman Productions (London) for Channel
4 and Antenne 2 (Paris) with the Société
Française de Production (Paris). © Portman
Productions 1985
c ed DR. **no** 75
p IAN WARREN, (SFP) JAQUES MADER, SERGE
BANY. **exec p** TOM DONALD. **assoc p** Adam
Kempton. **p co-ord** Sophie Zemrani
d PETER DUFFELL. **asst d** Alain Peyrollaz,
Nicole Larrieu, (2nd) Philippe Dufour.
continuity Agnès Thiabaudat
sc HUGH WHITEMORE from the novel *Les
Louves* by Pierre Boileau, Jean Narcejac (shot
double version, French and English)
ph CLAUDE ROBIN. **cam op** Claude Butteau.
stills Philippe Aubeges, Roger Beltramy
m/m arr RAYMOND ALESSANDRINI. **m perf**
Arcana Quartet; Raymond Alessandrini
(piano)
sup ed TEDDY DARVAS
pd MICHEL JANIAUD. **ad** Henri Lacoste
cost des LISELLE ROOS, EMMANUELLE
CORBEAU. **make-up** Nadine Fraigneau-Robin.
hair Catherine Gómez, Alain Barnasson
sp eff MARK CAUVY
stunt arr GÉRARD NAPROUS
sd mix MICHEL GUIFFAN. **sd ed** Anne

Parsons. **sd re-rec** Trevor Pyke
  cast Cherie Lunghi (*Hélène*), Mathilda
May (*Agnès*), Yves Beneyton (*Gervais*), Ralph
Bates (*Bernard*), Cadine Constan (*elderly
woman*), Gabriel Gobin (*elderly man*),
Andrea Ferréol (*Julia*), Les Clack (*lawyer*)
  shooting SFP Joinville studios, Paris;
Lyon; Tours
  budget £1,153,000. **C4 input** £600,000 (lf)
(52%)
    1st tx 5 Jun 86 (FF)
    V 27 Nov 85
    festivals London 85

LETTER TO BREZHNEV
UK, 95 mins, colour
Palace Pictures and Channel 4 with Charles
Caselton. © Yeardream 1985
  c ed KB. **no** 71
  p JANET GODDARD. **exec p** FRANK CLARKE.
assoc p Paul Lister, Caroline Spack. **p co-ord**
Christine Kerr, (Palace Pictures) Paul
Webster. **p man** Piers Player
  d CHRIS BERNARD. **asst d** Peter Cavacluti,
(2nd) Glenys Davies
    sc FRANK CLARKE
    ph BRUCE MCGOWAN. **stills** James Ridpath
    m ALAN GILL. **m scored/arr** Wolfgang
Kafer. **perf** The Royal Liverpool
Philharmonic Orchestra, leader Malcolm
Stewart, conductor Edward Warren
    ed LESLEY WALKER
    film des LEZ BROTHERSTON, NICK
ENGLEFIELD, JONATHAN SWAIN
    cost des MARK REYNOLDS. **make-up/hair**
Viv Howells
    titles/poster des Jamie Reid
    sd rec RAY BECKETT. **sd ed** Charles Ware,
(dial) Phyllida Poltock. **sd re-rec** Richard
King
    cast Alfred Molina (*Sergei*), Peter Firth
(*Peter*), Tracey Lea (*Tracy*), Alexandra Pigg
(*Elaine Spencer*), Margi Clarke (*Teresa
King*), Susan Dempsey (*girl in pub*), Ted
Wood (*Mick*), Carl Chase (*taxi driver*),
Sharon Power (*Charlie's girl*), Robbie Dee
(*Charlie*), Eddie Ross (*Rayner*), Syd
Newman (*Dimitri*), Gerry White (*1st
doorman*), Pat Riley (*2nd doorman*),
Jeanette Votel (*1st girl on bus*), Wendy Votel
(*2nd girl on bus*), Eileen Walsh (*Elaine's
mother*), Angela Clarke (*Josie Spencer*), Joey
Kaye (*Elaine's father*), Paul Beringer (*boy at
party*), Frank Clarke (*Vinny*), Iggy Navaro
(*President of Russia*), Thelma Dee (*Miss

Jones), D. J. Swain (*postman*), Ken Campbell
(*newspaper reporter*), Neil Cunningham
(*man from the Foreign Office*), John Carr
(*man in pub*)
    shooting Liverpool
    budget £379,000. **C4 input** £231,000 (lf/i)
(61%)
    1st tx 7 May 87 (FF)
    MFB Oct 85. **V** 11 Sep 85
    awards Most Promising Newcomers
(Alexandra Pigg, Margi Clarke), *Standard
F As* 85. Samuelson A, Birmingham 85
    festivals Birmingham, Venice 85

EIN LIED FÜR EUROPA *see*
A SONG FOR EUROPE

LIVING APART TOGETHER
UK, 95 mins, colour
Darkbeem/Legion Films for Channel 4.
© Channel 4 1983
  c ed DR. **no** 18
  p GAVRIK LOSEY, PADDY HIGSON. **location
manager** David Brown
  d CHARLES GORMLEY. **asst d** Malcolm
Stamp, (2nd) Terry Dalzell. **continuity** Susi
Oldroyd
    sc CHARLES GORMLEY
    ph MARK LITTLEWOOD. **cam op** Jan Pester.
stills Tom Hilton
    songs B. A. ROBERTSON
    choreo GILLIAN GREGORY
    ed PATRICK HIGSON
    ad ADRIENNE ATKINSON
    ward NADIA ARTHUR. **make-up** Tulah
Tuke
    sd mix LOUIS KRAMER. **dub ed** David
Docker. **sd re-rec** Tony Anscombe
    cast B. A. Robertson (*Ritchie Hannah*),
David Bain, Gilly Gilchrist, John McGlynn,
Kenny Potter (*Ritchie's band*), Stevie Lange,
Sylvia Mason-James (*Ritchie's singers*), Judi
Trott (*Alicia*), Barbara Kellerman (*Evie
Hannah*), Amy Walls (*Amy Hannah*), Ben
Walls (*Ben Hannah*), James Cosmo (*priest*),
Jimmy Logan (*Jake Eldridge*), David
Anderson (*Steve McNally*), William Elliott
(*Mike's brother*), Kathy Brawley (*pub singer*),
George McGowan Band (*pub band*), Peter
Capaldi (*Joe Edwards*), Anne Kristen
(*Ritchie's mother*), Douglas Sannachan
(*piano shop assistant*), Hilton Middleton
(*piano shop manager*), Doreen Cameron,
Terry Neason (*women at shop window*),
Sharon Erskine (*waitress*), Kampari (*pub

trio), Jim D'Arcy (*barman*), David McNiven, Bill Ridoch (*scaffolders*), Tim Stevens (*Eddie Gee*), John Gordon-Sinclair (*Zak's barman*), Billy Greenlees (*1st heavy*), Tom Busby (*2nd heavy*), David MacLennan (*drunk driver*), Jimmy McGregor (*2nd taxi driver*), Jeff Jackson, Samantha Brown (*audition singers*), Ida Schuster (*woman on stairs*), Peter Finlay (*sergeant*)
   shooting Oct–Nov 82. Glasgow
   budget £485,000. **C4 input** £393,000 (lf/i) (81%)
   1st tx 2 Jun 83 (FF)

LORCA – DEATH OF A POET
Spain/UK/FGR/Italy/France, 122 mins, colour
Acción Films and Uninci (Madrid) for TVE (Madrid) with Channel 4, Beta Film (Unterföhring), SACIS and RAI (Rome) and La SEPT (Paris). © TVE 1987
   c ed DR. **no** (-)
   exec p SAMUEL MENKES. **TVE assoc** Julio Sempere, Alfonso Santos. **p man** José Salcedo, Félix Rodríguez. **p admin** Miguel Alonso
   d J. A. BARDEM. **asst d** Andrés Vich. **2nd unit d** Alfonso Albacete
   sc J. A. BARDEM based on books by Ian Gibson and on the life and death of Federico García Lorca. Extracts of texts, plays, poems and songs by F. G. Lorca
   ph HANS BURMANN. **2nd op** Manuel Velasco. **2nd unit cam** W. Burmann. **stills** Felipe López. **archive selection** María Bardem
   m JUAN BARDEM AGUADO. **orch d** Javier Iturralde
   ed GUILLERMO S. MALDONADO
   ad WOLFGANG BURMANN
   cost LEON REVUELTA. **make-up** Mariano García Rey. **hair** Dolores García Rey
   sp eff FERNANDO PEREZ
   direct sd JOSE NOGUEIRA. **sd technician** Eduardo Fernández. **eff** Luis Castro
   cast Nickolas Grace (dubbing Javier Dotú) (*Federico García Lorca*), [Nuria Espert (*Margarita Xirgú*), Jesús Alcaide (*Pepín Bello*), María José Alfonso (*Catalina Bárcena*),] Alexander Allerson (*Brig Gen Don Miguel Campins Aura*), [Fernando Valverde (*Luis Buñuel*), Fernando Veloso (*Salvador Dalí*),] Eduardo Puertas (*the child*), Angel de Andrés López, Miguel Arribas, Concha Bardem, Amparo Baró, Manuel de

Benito, José Manuel Cervino, Fernando Chinarro, Luis Hostalot, Antonio Iranzo, Francisco Jarque, Montserrat Julio, Nicolas Lansky, Margarita Lozano, Chema Muñoz, Mario Pardo, Diana Peñalver, María Luisa Ponte, Teresa del Río, Mireia Ross, Manuel Sierra, Manuel Zarzo, Santiago Acera, Alberto Alonso, Hugo Blanco, José Luis Baringo, Eduardo Bea, Teófilo Calle, Alfredo Calles, José Canalejas, José Díaz Cantero, Fabián Conde, José Angel Egido, María Luisa Esteva, Sergio de Frutos, Lola Gaos, Ernesto Girela, Iñaqui Guevera, Antonio Guti, Pablo del Hoyo, Fabio León, Fernando Marín, María Jesús Mateos, Carlos Merediz, Miguel Palenzuela, David Palmer, Ignacio de Paúl, Marcos del Pino, Rodolfo Poveda, José Riesgo, José Maria del Rio, José Robles, Eufemia, Román, José María Rueda, Pearo Javier Sanchez, José Segura, Francisco Torres, Luis Valdivieso, Antonio Valverde, Frank Astor, Pilar Bardem, Carmen Bullejos, Germán Cobos, Rosalía Dans, Jesús Guzman, José María Pou, Fabiola Toledo
   shooting Madrid; Granada; Viznar; Alcalá de Henares; Getafe
   budget (?) **C4 input** £75,000 (lf)
   1st tx 4 Aug 90 (FFI)
   V 6 Jan 88
   Spanish release title *Lorca Muerte de un Poeta*

LORCA MUERTE DE UN POETA *see*
   LORCA – DEATH OF A POET

LOVING WALTER *see*
   WALTER and **WALTER & JUNE**

MASCHENKA
FGR/UK/France/Finland, 103 mins, colour
Clasart Film (Munich) and Jörn Donner Productions (Helsinki) with the Finnish Film Foundation for ZDF (Mainz), Channel 4 and FR3 (Paris). © Clasart Film 1986
   c ed DR. **no** 87
   p HERBERT G. KLOIBER, FRITZ BUTTENSTEDT. **exec p** MANFRED HEID. **p man** Horst Burkhard, (Finland) Pekka Lehto
   d JOHN GOLDSCHMIDT. **asst d** Marijan Vajda, (2nd, Finland) Eva Janikova-Pakaslahti. **continuity** Gabriele Mattner. **casting** (UK) Priscilla John, (FGR) Horst D. Scheel
   sc JOHN MORTIMER from the novel by Vladimir Nabokov

ph WOLFGANG TREU. **stills** Ronald
Simoneit, (Finland) Jussi Aalto
   m NICK GLOWNA, (asst) J. J. Gerndt
   ed TANJA SCHMIDBAUER
   pd JAN SCHLUBACH. **ad** Albrecht Konrad
cost des BARBARA BAUM. **make-up** Hasso
von Hugo. **hair** (Finland) Aune Ollila
   sd rec GUNTHER KORTWICH, (Finland) OLLI
SOINIO. **sd mix** Dieter Schwarz
   cast Cary Elwes (*Leo Ganin*), Irina Brook
(*Maschenka*), Sunnyi Melles (*Lilly*), Jonathan
Coy (*Alfyrov*), Freddie Jones (*Podtyagin*),
Michael Gough (*Leo's father*), Jean-Claude
Brialy (*Kolin*), Lena Stolze (*Klara*), Eva Lissa
(*Frau Dorn*), Vernon Dobtcheff (*the butler*),
Constantine Gregory (*Pyotr*), Carsten Hirsch
(*Anton*), Caroline Redl (*Lida*), Antonio
Messina (*tenor*), Elisabeth Degen (*Nina*),
Richard Thomas Feiner (*Alec*), Pehr-Olof
Sirén (*the guest*), Kyllikki Forssell (*the
General's wife*), Jack Witikka (*the General*),
Maximilian Ruethlein, Jean-Théo Jost, Hans
Martin Stier, Friedhelm Lehmann, Angela
Schultz Zehden, Susanna Bonasewicz,
Johanna Fraatz
   shooting Berlin; Paris; Finland
   budget £2,000,000. **C4 input** £300,000 (lf)
(15%)
   1st tx 31 Mar 88 (FF)
   V 20 May 87
   Finnish release title *Mashenka*

MASHENKA *see* **MASCHENKA**

THE MASTER MUSICIAN *see*
   BORN OF FIRE

MAURICE
UK/USA, 140 mins, colour
Merchant Ivory Productions (London) with
Cinecom Pictures (New York) and Channel
4. © Maurice Productions 1987
   c ed KB. **no** 100
   p ISMAIL MERCHANT. **assoc p** Paul Bradley.
p sup Raymond Day. **p co-ord** Joyce Turner
   d JAMES IVORY. **asst d** Michael Zimbrich,
Kevan Barker, (2nd) Lee Cleary, John Phelan.
continuity Lorely Farley. **casting** Celestia
Fox
   sc KIT HESKETH-HARVEY, JAMES IVORY'
from the novel by E. M. Forster
   ph PIERRE LHOMME. **cam op** Nigel
Willoughby, Tony Woodcock. **stills** John
Gardey, Katya Grenfell
   m RICHARD ROBBINS. **cond** Harry

Rabinowitz. **m assoc** Bob Stewart
   ed KATHERINE WENNING
   pd BRIAN ACKLAND-SNOW. **ad** Peter James,
Brian Savegar
   cost JENNY BEAVAN, JOHN BRIGHT, (co-)
WILLIAM PEIRCE. **make-up** Mary Hillman.
hair Carol Hemming
   title des Chris Allies
   stunts Harvey Kip, Adrian Ffooks
   sd MIKE SHORING. **sd ed** Tony Lenny,
(dial) Alan Killick. **sd re-rec** Richard King
   cast James Wilby (*Maurice Hall*), Hugh
Grant (*Clive Durham*), Rupert Graves (*Alec
Scudder*), Denholm Elliott (*Dr Barry*), Simon
Callow (*James Ducie*), Billie Whitelaw (*Mrs
Hall*), Ben Kingsley (*Lasker-Jones*), Judy
Parfitt (*Mrs Durham*), Phoebe Nicholls (*Anne
Durham*), Mark Tandy (*Viscount Risley*),
Helena Michell (*Ada Hall*), Kitty Aldridge
(*Kitty Hall*), Patrick Godfrey (*Simcox*),
Michael Jenn (*Archie*), Barry Foster (*Dean
Cornwallis*), Peter Eyre (*the Rev Borenius*),
Catherine Rabett (*Pippa Durham*), Orlando
Wells (*young Maurice*), Helena Bonham
Carter (*lady at cricket match*), Mark Payton
(*Arthur Chapman*), Maria Britneva (*Mrs
Sheepshanks*), John Elmes (*Hill*), Alan Foss
(*old man on train*), Philip Fox (*Dr Jowitt*),
Olwen Griffiths (*Mrs Scudder*), Chris Hunter
(*Fred Scudder*), Gerard McArthur (*3rd
undergraduate*), Breffni McKenna
(*guardsman*), Miles Richardson (*1st
undergraduate*), Phillada Sewell (*matron*),
Mathew Sim (*Fetherstonhaugh*), Andrew
St Clair (*2nd undergraduate*), Harriet Thorpe
(*barmaid*), Julian Wadham (*Hull*), Richard
Warner (*judge*), Arthur Whybrow (*Mr
Scudder*)
   shooting British Museum and Linley
Sambourne House, London; King's College
and Trinity College, Cambridge; Wilbury
Park, Wiltshire
   budget £1,577,000. **C4 input** £375,000
(lf/i) (24%)
   1st tx 5 Apr 90 (FF)
   MFB Nov 87. **V** 26 Aug 87
   awards Silver Lion, Best Actor (James
Wilby/Hugh Grant), Venice 87
   festivals Venice 87

MEANTIME
UK, 110 mins, colour
Central Productions with Mostpoint for
Channel 4. © Central Independent TV 1983
   c ed DR. **no** 25

p GRAHAM BENSON. **p man** Vivien
Pottersman
d MIKE LEIGH. **asst d** Chris Rose, (2nd)
Steve Finn. **continuity** Heather Storr. **casting
d** Sue Whatmough
devised by MIKE LEIGH
ph ROGER PRATT. **stills** Ed Buziak
m ANDREW DICKSON. **m perf** Andrew
Dickson, George Khan
ed LESLEY WALKER
ad DIANA CHARNLEY
cost des LINDY HEMMING. **make-up**
Sandra Shepherd
graphic des Mon Mohan
sd rec MALCOLM HIRST. **dub ed** Charlie
Ware. **dub mix** Trevor Pyke
cast Marion Bailey (*Barbara Lake*), Phil
Daniels (*Mark Pollock*), Tim Roth (*Colin
Pollock*), Pam Ferris (*Mavis Pollock*), Jeff
Robert (*Frank Pollock*), Alfred Molina (*John
Lake*), Gary Oldman (*Coxy*), Tilly Vosburgh
(*Hayley*), Paul Daly (*Rusty*), Leila Bertrand
(*Hayley's friend*), Hepburn Graham
(*boyfriend*), Peter Wight (*estate manager*),
Eileen Davies (*unemployment benefit clerk*),
Herbert Norville (*man in pub*), Brian Hoskin
(*barman*)
shooting Mar–Apr 83. London
budget £357,000. **C4 input** £307,000 (lf)
(86%)
1st tx 1 Dec 83 (FF)
V 30 Nov 83
awards *Zity* Magazine A, Berlin 83
festivals Berlin, London 83
working title *Smoke*

MILK AND HONEY
Canada/UK, ?90 mins, colour
J. A. Film Company (Toronto) with Zenith
Productions (London) with Téléfilm Canada,
the Ontario Film Development Corporation
and First Choice Canadian Communications
Corporation. Developed with the Sundance
Institute. © J. A. Film Company Inc 1988
c ed KB. **no** 113
p PETER O'BRIAN. **co-p** REBECCA YATES,
GLEN SALZMAN. **line p/post-p sup** Gabriella
Martinelli. **p co-ord** Sandy Pereira. **p man**
Mary Kahn, (Jamaica) Natalie Thompson.
consultant Ralph Rosenblum
d REBECCA YATES, GLEN SALZMAN. **asst d**
Mac Bradden, (2nd) Felix Gray, (2nd,
Jamaica) Jeremy Francis. **continuity** Kathryn
Buck. **casting** Maria Armstrong, Ross
Clydesdale, (UK) Leo Davis

sc GLEN SALZMAN, TREVOR RHONE
ph GUY DUFAUX. **stills** Michaelin
McDermott
m/md MICKEY ERBE, MARIBETH SOLOMON
ed BRUCE NYZNIK
ad FRANÇOIS SEGUIN
ward des DELPHINE WHITE. **make-up**
Sandra Duncan. **hair** Reginald LeBlanc
sd mix JOHN MEGILL. **sd des/sup sd ed**
Bruce Nyznik. **sd ed** Alison Clark, Marta
Nielsen Sternberg, Nick Rotundo. **sd re-rec**
Paul Massey
cast Josette Simon (*Joanna Bell*), Lyman
Ward (*Adam Bernardi*), Richard Mills
(*David*), Djanet Sears (*Del*), Leonie Forbes
(*Miss Emma*), Jane Dingle (*Maureen*), Errol
Slue (*Gordon, Mr Fixit*), Fiona Reid (*Sandy
Wineberg*), Tom Butler (*Steven Wineberg*),
Tyler Oxenholm, Brandon Botham (*Josh, 1
year old*), Christopher Doherty (*Josh, 4 years
old*), Jackie Richardson (*preacher*), David
Ferry (*night school teacher*), Lubomir
Mykytiuk (*Ellis, 1st immigration officer*),
Robert Wisden (*Flanagan, 2nd immigration
officer*), Diane D'Aquila (*David's teacher*),
Irene Pauzer (*school secretary*), Lucy
Filippone (*chicken waitress*), Richardo
Keens-Douglas (*bartender*), Gerry Mendicino
(*Mr Stefano*), David Smith (*stylish man*),
Christopher Benson (*policeman*); [Jamaican
cast] Charles Hyatt (*village preacher*),
Dorothy Cunningham (*Joanna's mother*),
Ann-Marie Fuller (*Joanna's sister*), Marjorie
Whylie (*Joanna's aunt*), Grace McGhie
(*Joanna's cousin*), Yero Magnus (*David, 7
years old*), Volier Johnson (*taxi driver*), Kevin
Wynter (*man in trunk*)
shooting Apr–May 87. Toronto; Jamaica
budget Can$2,800,000 [Zenith
Productions]/£1,299,000. **C4 input** £40,000
(lf) (3%)
1st tx 18 May 89 (FF)
V 7 Sep 88
awards Genie A (screenplay) 89

THE MIRROR
FGR/UK, 91 mins, colour
Von Vietinghoff Filmproduktion (Berlin)
with ZDF (Mainz) and Channel 4. © ZDF/
Von Vietinghoff Filmproduktion 1984
c ed DR. **no** (-)
p JOACHIM VON VIETINGHOFF. **p man** Udo
Heiland, Vasilis Katsoufis
d ERDEN KIRAL. **asst d** Konstantin
Schmidt, Odysseas Lapas

sc ERDEN KIRAL based on the story *The White Ox* by Osman Sahin. **sc sup** Agape Dorstewitz

ph KENAN ORMANLAR. **stills** Irmgard Frey

m BRYNMOR JONES. **singer** Sümeyra Çakir

ed AGAPE DORSTEWITZ

ad NIKOS PERAKIS

cost HEIDRUN BRANDT

sd LUC YERSIN. **mix** Hans-Dieter Schwarz

cast Nur Sürer (*Zelihan*), Suavi Eren (*Necmettin*), Hikmet Çelik (*the Young Aga*), Vasilis Tsaglos (*soothsayer*), Nikos Skiadas (*the Aga*), Vera Deludi (*mother*)

> **shooting** Greece
> **budget** ?£150,000. **C4 input** £50,000 (lf)
> **1st tx** 8 Mar 90 (FFI)
> **V** 12 Sep 84
> **festivals** Venice 84
> **German release title** *Der Spiegel*
> **Turkish release title** *Ayna*

MONA LISA
UK, 104 mins, colour
Palace Productions for HandMade Films. © HandMade Films (1985) Partnership 1986

c ed DR/KB. **no** 68

p PATRICK CASSAVETTI, STEPHEN WOOLLEY. **exec p** GEORGE HARRISON, DENIS O'BRIEN. **co-p** NIK POWELL, RAY COOPER, CHRIS BROWN. **p co-ord** Laura Julian. **p man** Linda Bruce

d NEIL JORDAN. **asst d** Ray Corbett, (2nd) Chris Brock. **sc sup** Pat Rambaut. **casting d** Susie Figgis

sc NEIL JORDAN, DAVID LELAND

ph ROGER PRATT. **cam op** Mike Roberts. **stills** Clive Coote

m MICHAEL KAMEN. **m perf** The National Philharmonic Orchestra

ed LESLEY WALKER

pd JAMIE LEONARD. **ad** Gemma Jackson

cost des LOUISE FROGLEY. **make-up** Lois Burwell, (sp eff) Nick Dudman. **hair** Stevie Hall

stunt arr TERRY FORRESTAL

sd rec DAVID JOHN. **sd ed** Jonathan Bates. **re-rec mix** Paul Carr, Brian Paxton

film extract *They Live by Night*

cast Bob Hoskins (*George*), Cathy Tyson (*Simone*), Michael Caine (*Dinny Mortwell*), Robbie Coltrane (*Thomas*), Clarke Peters (*Anderson*), Kate Hardie (*Cathy*), Zoe Nathenson (*Jeannie*), Sammi Davis (*May*), Rod Bedall (*Terry*), Joe Brown (*Dudley*), Pauline Melville (*George's wife*), Hossein Karimbeik (*Raschid*), John Darling (*hotel security*), Bryan Coleman (*gentleman in mirror room*), Robert Dorning (*man in hotel bedroom*), Raad Raawi (*Arab servant*), David Halliwell (*Tim Devlin*), Stephen Persaud (*black youth in street*), Maggie O'Neill (*girl in Paradise Club*), Gary Cady (*hotel waiter*), Donna Cannon (*young prostitute*), Perry Fenwick (*pimp*), Dawn Archibald (*wig girl in club*), Richard Strange (*man in porn shop*), Alan Talbot (*bath house attendant*), Geoffrey Larder (*hotel clerk*), Helen Martin (*peep show girl*), Kenny Baker, Jack Purvis, Bill Moore (*Brighton buskers*)

> **shooting** Oct–Dec 85. London; Brighton
> **budget** £2,400,000. **C4 input** £225,000 (lf) (9%)
> **1st tx** 23 Feb 89 (FF)
> **MFB** Sep 86. **V** 14 May 86
> **awards** Best Actor (Bob Hoskins), Cannes 86. Samuelson A (joint) (original treatment of city experience), Birmingham 86. Best Actor (Bob Hoskins), BAFTA F As 87. Best Dramatic Actor (Bob Hoskins), Golden Globe As
> **festivals** Cannes, Birmingham 86

A MONTH IN THE COUNTRY
UK, 96 mins, colour
Euston Films for Channel 4 with Pennies from Heaven. © Euston Films 1987

c ed DR. **no** 95

p KENITH TRODD. **exec p** JOHNNY GOODMAN, JOHN HAMBLEY. **assoc p** Dominic Fulford. **p co-ord** Pat Pennelegion

d PAT O'CONNOR. **asst d** Bill Craske; Tim Reed, Rupert Ryle-Hodges, Michael Trent. **continuity** Sarah Hayward. **casting** Michelle Guish

sc SIMON GRAY from the novel by J. L. Carr

ph KENNETH MacMILLAN. **cam op** Mike Frift

m/cond HOWARD BLAKE. **m perf** The Sinfonia of London

ed JOHN VICTOR SMITH

pd LEO AUSTIN. **ad** Richard Elton. **painting** ('The Judgment') Margot Noise

cost des JUDY MOORCROFT. **make-up** Jenny Shircore. **hair** Carole Bennett

sd mix TONY DAWE. **sd ed** Peter Horrocks

cast Colin Firth (*Tom Birkin*), John Atkinson (*old man on train*), Jim Carter (*Jack Ellerbeck*), Patrick Malahide (*Rev J. G. Keach*), Kenneth Branagh (*James Moon*), Richard Vernon (*Colonel Hebron*), Tim

Barker (*Mossop*), Vicki Arundale (*Kathy Ellerbeck*), Martin O'Neil (*Edgar Ellerbeck*), Natasha Richardson (*Alice Keach*), Tony Haygarth (*George Douthwaite*), Eileen O'Brien (*Mrs Ellerbeck*), Elizabeth Anson (*Lucy Sykes*), Barbara Marten (*Mrs Sykes*), Kenneth Kitson (*Mr Sykes*), Judy Gridley (*Mrs Clough*), Lisa Taylor (*Emily Clough*), Andrew Wilde (*shop assistant*), David Gillies (*Milburn*), David Garth (*old Birkin*)

shooting Aug–Sep 86. Buckinghamshire; Yorkshire; Bray studios

budget £1,075,000. **C4 input** £678,000 (lf/i) (63%)

1st tx 19 Apr 90 (FF)

MFB Dec 87. **V** 13 May 87

awards Silver A (Un Certain Regard), Cannes 87. Grand Prix, Brussels 88. Anthony Asquith A (F Music), BFI As 88

festivals Cannes, Bergamo, Figueira da Foz, New York, Cherbourg, Ghent, London, Rio de Janeiro, Cairo 87; Brussels, Vienna, Hong Kong, Durban 88

MOONLIGHTING

UK, 97 mins, colour
Michael White with Channel 4. Assisted by the National Film Development Fund. © Michael White 1982

c ed DR. **no** 13

p MARK SHIVAS, JERZY SKOLIMOWSKI.
assoc p Michael Guest. **location manager** Rufus Andrews

d JERZY SKOLIMOWSKI. **asst d** Peter Cotton, (2nd) Nicholas Daubeny. **continuity** Pat Rambaut. **casting d** Debbie McWilliams

sc JERZY SKOLIMOWSKI. **script assistance** Barry Vince, Boleslaw Sulik, Danuta Stok, Witold Stok

ph TONY PIERCE-ROBERTS. **cam op** Jimmy Stilwell. **stills** Murray Tulip Close, David Farrell

m STANLEY MYERS. **electronics** HANS ZIMMER

ed BARRY VINCE

pd TONY WOOLLARD

cost JANE ROBINSON. **make-up** Sheila Thomas. **hair** Marsha Lewis

sp eff ROY WHYBROW

sd mix DAVID STEPHENSON. **dub ed** Alan Bell. **dub mix** Richard King

cast Jeremy Irons (*Nowak*), Eugene Lipinski (*Banaszak*), Jiri Stanislav (*Wolski*), Eugeniusz Haczkiewicz (*Kudaj*), Dorothy Zienciowska (*Lot airline girl*), Edward Arthur

(*immigration officer*), Denis Holmes (*neighbour*), Renu Setna (*owner of junk shop*), David Calder (*supermarket manager*), Judy Gridley (*supermarket supervisor*), Claire Toeman (*supermarket cashier*), Catherine Harding (*lady shoplifter*), Jill Johnson (*haughty supermarket customer*), David Squire (*supermarket assistant*), Mike Sarne (*builders' merchant*), Lucy Hornak, Robyn Mandell (*assistants in Wrangler shop*), Ann Tirard (*lady in telephone box*), Christopher Logue (*workman*), Hugh Harper (*newspaper boy*), Julia Chambers (*chemist's assistant*), Fred Lee Own (*Chinese man*), Kenny Ireland (*timber man*), Trevor Cooper, Ian Ormsby-Knox (*men in hire shop*), David Gant (*Aquascutum assistant*), Jennifer Landor (*Aquascutum shoplifter*), Jenny Seagrove (*Anna*), Ian McCulloch (*boss lookalike*), Laura Frances Hart (*boss lookalike's woman*), Jerzy Skolimowski (*boss*)

shooting Feb–Mar 82. Kensington, West London; Luton Airport

budget £596,000. **C4 input** £298,000 (i) (50%)

1st tx 5 May 83 (FF)

MFB Sep 82. **V** 26 May 82

awards Best Screenplay, Cannes 82. Best F, *Standard* F As 82. Best F, Salsomaggiore 83

festivals Cannes 82; Salsomaggiore 83

shooting titles *Novak*; *Blackout*

MY BEAUTIFUL LAUNDRETTE

UK, 97 mins, colour
Working Title and SAF Productions for Channel 4. © Channel 4 1985

c ed KB. **no** 73

p SARAH RADCLYFFE, TIM BEVAN. **p man** Jane Frazer

d STEPHEN FREARS. **asst d** Simon Hinkly, (2nd) Waldo Roeg. **continuity** Penny Eyles. **casting d** Debbie McWilliams

sc HANIF KUREISHI

ph OLIVER STAPLETON. **stills** Mike Laye

m LUDUS TONALIS. **m prod** Hans Zimmer, Stanley Myers

ed MICK AUDSLEY

des HUGO LUCZYC-WYHOWSKI

cost des LINDY HEMMING. **make-up** Elaine Carew. **hair** Wendy Rawson

stunt co-ord ROCKY TAYLOR, JIM DOWDALL, BILL WESTON, NOSHER POWELL. **stunt perf** Tip Tipping, Tracey Eddons, Wayne Michaels

graphics Julian Rothenstein
sd rec ALBERT BAILEY. **sd ed** 'Budge'
Tremlett. **dub mix** Peter Maxwell
  cast Daniel Day Lewis (*Johnny*), Richard
Graham (*Genghis*), Winston Graham (*1st
Jamaican*), Dudley Thomas (*2nd Jamaican*),
Derrick Branche (*Salim*), Garry Cooper
(*squatter*), Gordon Warnecke (*Omar Ali*),
Roshan Seth (*Papa Hussain Ali*), Saeed
Jaffrey (*Nasser*), Shirley Anne Field
(*Rachel*), Charu Bala Choksi (*Bilquis*), Souad
Faress (*Cherry*), Rita Wolf (*Tania*), Persis
Maravala (*Nasser's elder daughter*), Nisha
Kapur (*Nasser's younger daughter*), Neil
Cunningham (*Englishman*), Walter Donohue
(*Dick O'Donnell*), Gurdial Sira (*Zaki*),
Stephen Marcus (*Moose*), Dawn Archibald
(*1st gang member*), Jonathan Moore (*2nd
gang member*), Gerard Horan (*telephone
man*), Ram John Holder (*poet*), Bhasker
(*Tariq*), Ayub Khan Din (*student*), Dulice
Leicier (*girl in disco*), Badi Uzzaman
(*dealer*), Chris Pity (*1st kid*), Kerryann White
(*2nd kid*), Colin Campbell ('*Madame
Butterfly' man*), Sheila Chitnis (*Zaki's wife*)
  shooting Feb–Apr 85. London
  budget £650,000. **C4 input** £650,000 (lf/i)
(100%)
  1st tx 19 Feb 87 (FF)
  MFB Nov 85. **V** 21 Aug 85
  awards Best F, *Standard* F As 85. Golden
Toucan, Rio de Janeiro 86. Best Original
Screenplay, Best Supporting Actor (joint)
(Daniel Day Lewis), New York F Critics' As
86. Media A, Alliance for Gay & Lesbian
Entertainment Artists 87
  festivals Edinburgh, London 85;
Göteborg, Rotterdam, Madrid, Quimper,
Durban, Jerusalem, Bergamo, Wellington,
Locarno, São Paulo, Troia, Rio de Janeiro 86;
Belgrade, Ljubljana, Istanbul 87; Moscow
Gay & Lesbian, Birmingham 91

THE NATURE OF THE BEAST
UK, 96 mins, colour
Rosso Productions for Channel 4 with
British Screen. © Channel 4 Television. 1988
  c ed KB/PA. **no** 125
  p JOANNA SMITH. **p co-ord** Diane Chittell.
p man Linda Bruce
  d FRANCO ROSSO. **asst d** Ray Corbett, (2nd)
Kieron Phipps. **sc sup** Claire Hughes Smith.
casting Doreen Jones
  sc JANNI HOWKER from her own novel
  ph NAT CROSBY. **Steadicam/2nd unit ph**

Nigel Kirton. **rostrum** Chris King. **stills**
Stephen Morley
  m STANLEY MYERS, HANS ZIMMER
  ed GEORGE AKERS
  des JAMIE LEONARD
  cost des SUSANNAH BUXTON. **make-up**
Norma Hill. **hair** Meinir Jones Lewis
  stunt double Malcolm Weaver
  sd rec MIKE SHORING. **dub ed** Jupiter Sen.
dub mix Peter Maxwell
  cast Lynton Dearden (*Bill Coward*), Paul
Simpson (*Mick Dalton*), Tony Melody
(*Charlie 'Chunder' Coward*), Freddie
Fletcher (*Ned Coward*), Dave Hill (*Oggy*),
Roberta Kerr (*Mrs Dalton*), David Fleeshman
(*Jim Dalton*), Willie Ross (*Danny*), George
Malpas (*Bill Howgill*), Howard Crossley (*Big
Man*), Jonathan Parkinson (*Hargreaves*),
Julian Walsh (*tinker lad*), Simon Molloy (*Mr
Arkwright*), Sally Edwards (*social worker*),
Gordon Wharmby (*Mr Dickson*), Nigel
Collins (*Chris Fairfield, reporter*), Dave
Dutton (*Mr Lord*), Safka Green (*camera shop
assistant*), Dickie Arnold (*shepherd*), Ted
Carroll (*poacher*), Harry Goodier (*farm
hand*), Arthur Spreckley (*shepherd*), Joan
Campion (*Jean, secretary at 'Observer'*), Joel
David (*landlord*), Danny James (*worker*),
Andrew Welch (*Clever Clogs*), Michael Holt
(*policeman*)
  shooting Jul–Aug 87. Hollins School and
Woodnook Estate, Accrington
  budget £1,022,000. **C4 input** £702,000
(lf/i) (69%)
  1st tx 30 Mar 89 (FF)
  MFB Dec 88. **V** 11 May 88
  festivals Southampton, San Sebastián,
Birmingham, London 88; Würzburg,
Moscow, Durban, Antenna, Trento 89

NELLY'S VERSION
UK, 100 mins, colour
Mithras Films for Channel 4. © Channel 4
Television Co 1983
  c ed DR. **no** 19
  p PENNY CLARK. **assoc p** Paul Sparrow
  d MAURICE HATTON. **asst d** Peter Cotton,
(2nd) Nick Daubeny. **continuity** Jean Bourne.
casting d Mary Selway
  sc MAURICE HATTON based on the novel
by Eva Figes
  ph CURTIS CLARK. **cam op** Luke Cardiff.
stills Stephen Morley
  m/cond MICHAEL NYMAN. **addit m** Alan
Leeming

ed THOMAS SCHWALM
pd GRANT HICKS. **ad** Peta Button
cost des MARIT ALLEN. **make-up** Pat Hay.
hair Meinir Brock
sd rec DIANA RUSTON. **dub mix** Andy
Nelson
extract *Spellbound*
cast Eileen Atkins (*Nelly*), Anthony Bate
(*George Wilkinson*), Barbara Jefford (*Miss
Wyckham*), Nicholas Ball (*Detective
Inspector Leach*), Brian Deacon (*David*),
Marsha Fitzalan (*Susan*), Stella Maris
(*Carmelita*), Hugh Fraser (*brush salesman*),
Hilton McRae (*vagrant*), Arthur Whybrow
(*man at vacant house*), Alec Sabin (*hotel
manager*), Jacqueline Spears (*hotel
receptionist*), Anthony Pedley (*hotel waiter*),
Nizwar Karanj (*hotel porter*), Jane Wood
(*hotel maid*), Andrew de la Tour (*station
porter*), Arabella Weir (*hospital nurse*),
William Hoyland (*Fawcett, assistant bank
manager*), Miki Iveria (*Mrs Knatchbull*),
George A. Cooper (*Douglas McKenzie*), Ann
Firbank (*Patricia McKenzie*), Eleanor David
(*Mrs Monroe*), Toby Salaman (*detective
constable*), Darcy & Lewis Hare (*twins*),
Laura & Ben Miller (*children outside shop*),
the voice of Susannah York
shooting Nov–Dec 82. Phyllis Court,
Henley on Thames; Thames Valley
budget £440,000. **C4 input** £400,000 (lf/i)
(91%)
1st tx 9 Jun 83 (FF)
V 15 Jun 83
shooting title *The Rewards of Virtue*

NO MAN'S LAND
Switzerland/France/FGR/UK, 110 mins,
colour
Filmograph (Geneva) and MK2 Productions
(Paris) with WDR (Cologne) and Télévision
Suisse Romande (Geneva), Films A2 (Paris)
and Channel 4. © Filmograph-MK2
Productions 1985
c ed DR. **no** (-)
p ALAIN TANNER, MARIN KARMITZ. **exec p**
(CAB Productions) JEAN-LOUIS PORCHET. **p
man** Gérard Ruey. **p sup** Madeleine Trisconi
d ALAIN TANNER. **asst d** Claudio Tonetti,
Agnès Guhl. **sc sup** Madeleine Fonjallaz
sc ALAIN TANNER
ph BERNARD ZITZERMANN. **stills** Carole
Kozuchowski
m TERRY RILEY. **m perf** Terry Riley,
Krishna Batt. **musicians at disco** Simon Ben

Dahan, Martin Engel, Michel Derouin. **m
compositions** Waziz Diop, Myriam Mézières,
Simon Ben Dahan
ed LAURENT UHLER
des ALAIN NICOLET
cost (Myriam Mézières) CLAUDE SABBAH
sd JEAN-PAUL MUGEL. **mix** Dominique
Hennequin
cast Hughes Quester (*Paul*), Myriam
Mézières (*Madeleine*), Jean-Philippe Ecoffey
(*Jean*), Betty Berr (*Mali*), Marie-Luce Felber
(*Lucie*), María Cabral (*woman at the
bus-stop*), André Steiger, Jacques Michel
(*French policemen*), Teco Celio
(*direction-giver*), Jean-Pierre Malo (*banker*),
Maurice Aufair (*Jean's uncle*), Adrien Nicati
(*Paul's father*), Jean-Marc Henchoz (*French
customs man*), Marcel Nagel, Roger Jendly
(*Swiss customs men*), Jacqueline Burnand
(*Jean's mother*), Michèle Gleiser (*Swiss
customs woman*)
budget (?) **C4 input** £50,000 (lf)
1st tx 15 Feb 90 (FFI)
V 4 Sep 85
festivals London 85

EL NORTE
USA/UK, 140 mins, colour
Independent Productions with American
Playhouse with funds from Public Television
stations and the Corporation for Public
Broadcasting. Additional funding Channel 4.
© Independent Productions 1983
c ed DR/WD. **no** 39
p ANNA THOMAS. **p sup** (post-production)
Amanda Gill. **p co-ord** (US) Toni-Conchita
Rios. **p man** (US) Trevor Black, (Mexico)
Berta Navarro
d GREGORY NAVA. **asst d** (US) Robert
Romero, (Mexico) Roberto Gerhard, (2nd US)
Amanda Gill. **continuity** (US) Mary
Armantrout, (Mexico) Rosa Perez Romo.
casting (US) Bob Morones
sc GREGORY NAVA, ANNA THOMAS from a
story by Gregory Nava
ph JAMES GLENNON, (additional US)
Gregory Nava
m/m perf (trad/orig) LOS FOLKLORISTAS,
(trad/orig harp) MELECIO MARTINEZ,
(marimba/atmospheric) EMIL RICHARDS,
(mariachi) MARIACHI NUEVO UCLATLAN
ed BETSY BLANKETT
set des (US) DAVID WASCO
cost (US) HILARY WRIGHT. **make-up**
(Mexico sp eff) Alfredo Bustos

stunt co-ord (US) BOB OZMAN
sd (production) ROBERT YERINGTON,
(design) MICHAEL C. MOORE. **sd ed** David
Kern, Barbara Noble, Sheila Amos, Baird
Bryant, Keva Rosenfeld. **sd re-rec** Richard
Portman
cast Ernesto Gómez Cruz (*Arturo
Xuncax*), David Villalpando (*Enrique
Xuncax*), Zaide Silvia Gutierrez (*Rosa
Xuncax*), Alicia Del Lago (*Lupe*), Miguel
Gómez Giron (*informer*), José Martin Ruano
(*foreman*), Stella Quan (*Josefita*), Eraclio
Zepeda (*Pedro*), Emilio Gómez Ozuna (*Luis*),
Daniel Lemus Valenzuela (*Encarnacion*),
Rodrigo Puebla (*El Puma, the soldier*),
Yosahandi Navarrete Quan (*Josefita's
daughter*), Rodolfo Alexandre (*Ramón
Munoz*), Emilio Del Haro (*truck driver*), Jorge
Moreno (*old man on bus*), Palomo García
(*coyote at bus station*), Mike Gómez (*Jaime
the coyote*), Ismael Gamez, Silverio Lujan,
Socorro Velazquez (*leering slumdwellers*),
John Martin (*Ed, border guard*), Ron Joseph
(*Joel, border guard*), Abel Franco (*Raimundo
Gutierrez*), Rosario Cevellos (*fruit vendor*),
Trinidad Silva (*Monty*), Lupe Ontiveros
(*Nacha*), Young Chung (*Mr Chung*), Gregory
Enton (*Len the restaurateur*), Tony Plana
(*Carlos the bus boy*), Slavitza Yhuelo, Julie
Silliman (*models in sweatshop*), Enrique
Castillo (*Jorge the dishwasher*), Momo
Yashima (*Florence the English teacher*), Jo
Marie Ward (*Helen Rogers*), Loraine Shields
(*girl who orders coffee*), Larry Cedar (*Bruce
the waiter*), Sheryl Bernstein (*Karen the
hostess*), Diana Civita (*Alice Harper*), Eulalia
Cardenas (*Curandera*), Jules Segal, Perry
Page (*INS officers*), Mary Armantrout (*nurse*),
George O'Hanlon Jr (*Dr Murphy*), Bob Cane
(*lab technician*), Pablo Velásquez (*foreman
at construction site*)
shooting Mexico; California
budget £361,000. **C4 input** £25,000 (lf/i)
(7%)
1st tx 13 Jun 85 (FF)
MFB Jul 84. **V** 7 Dec 83
festivals Cannes 84
English subtitle *The North*

THE NORTH *see* **EL NORTE**

NO SURRENDER
UK/Canada, 104 mins, colour
No Surrender Films with the Canadian
Broadcasting Corporation (Ottawa) and
Téléfilm Canada (Montreal). [Dumbarton
Films with William Johnston, Ronald Lillie,
Lauron International, the National Film
Finance Corporation and Channel 4.]
© National Film Trustee Company 1985
c ed DR. **no** 67
p MAMOUN HASSAN. **exec p** MICHAEL
PEACOCK. **assoc p** Clive Reed. **p co-ord**
Harriet Fenner
d PETER SMITH. **asst d** John Watson, (2nd)
Crispin Reece. **continuity** Jean Skinner.
casting d Priscilla John
sc ALAN BLEASDALE
ph MICHAEL COULTER. **cam op** Steven
Alcorn. **stills** Peter Kernot
m DARYL RUNSWICK. **song** Andrew
Schofield
ed RODNEY HOLLAND. **sup ed** Kevin
Brownlow
pd ANDREW MOLLO
titles Chris Wood
cost des EMMA PORTEOUS. **make-up** Lois
Burwell. **hair** Jeanette Freeman
stunt co-ord GEORGE LEECH
sd mix SANDY MacRAE, BRIAN SIMMONS.
dub ed Alan Bell. **dub mix** Hugh Strain
cast Michael Angelis (*Mike Moriarty*),
Avis Bunnage (*Martha Gorman*), James Ellis
(*Paddy Burke*), Tom Georgeson (*Leonard
Ross*), Bernard Hill (*Bernard*), Ray McAnally
(*Billy McRacken*), Mark Mulholland
(*Norman*), Joanne Whalley (*Cheryl*), J. G.
Devlin (*George Gorman*), Vince Earl (*Frank*),
Ken Jones (*Ronny*), Michael Ripper (*Tony
Bonaparte*), Marjorie Sudell (*Barbara*), Joan
Turner (*Superwoman*), Richard Alexander
(*smoking kid*), Pamela Austin (*organist*), Ina
Clough (*infirm woman*), Paul Codman
(*member of rock group*), Paul Connor
(*infirm*), Elvis Costello (*Rosco de Ville*),
James Culshaw (*Gorman's cab driver*),
Gabrielle Daye (*Winnie*), David Doyle (*Ulster
boy*), Lovette Edwards (*infirm*), Gerry
Fogarty (*moustached veteran*), Harry
Goodier (*cleanshaven veteran*), Eric
Granville (*Donald Duck*), Robert Hamilton
(*Special Branch officer*), Ian Hart (*uncertain
menace*), Gerard Hely (*senior policeman*),
Joey Kaye (*driver of Catholic party*), Vera
Kelly (*infirm*), Phil Kernot (*Stan Laurel*), Al
Kossy (*Bobby*), Penny Leatherbarrow (*Mrs
Morgan*), Stephen Lloyd (*member of rock
group*), Johnny Mallon (*French onion
seller*), Joe McGann (*2nd policeman*), Mark
McGann (*leader of rock group*), Ron Metcalf

(*veteran*), Bill Moores (*Quasimodo*), Robert Nield (*Yousee*), Doc O'Brien (*driver of Protestant party*), Steve O'Connor (*veteran*), Peter Price (*comedian*), Christopher Quinn (*warden*), Helen Rhodes (*infirm*), Linus Roache (*Ulster boy*), Tony Rohr (*Robert McArthur*), Tommy Ryan (*veteran*), Andrew Schofield (*Macker*), Tony Scoggo (*cold eyes*), Mabel Seward (*older waitress*), Georgina Smith (*Oliver Hardy*), Arthur Spreckley (*Matthew*), Mike Starke (*member of rock group*), Frank Vincent (*1st policeman*), Eileen Walsh (*waitress*), Harry Webster (*priest*), Gery White (*driver for infirm party*), Dean Williams (*real menace*), Peter Wilson (*comedian's boyfriend*)

budget £2,337,000. **C4 input** £600,000 (lf/i) (26%)

1st tx 19 Mar 87 (FF)

MFB Feb 86. **V** 18 Sep 85

NOVAK *see* **MOONLIGHTING**

OFFRET *see* **THE SACRIFICE**

ON THE BLACK HILL

UK, 117 mins, colour
The British Film Institute with British Screen for Channel 4. © British Film Institute 1987

c ed KB. **no** 114

p JENNIFER HOWARTH. **exec p** COLIN MACCABE. **co-p** ENÉ WATTS-VANAVESKI. **exec i/c p** Jill Pack. **p co-ord** Lil Stirling. **p man** Olivia Stewart

d ANDREW GRIEVE. **asst d** Chris Hall, (2nd) Jane Studd. **continuity** Libbie Barr. **casting** Priscilla John

sc ANDREW GRIEVE from the novel by Bruce Chatwin

ph THADDEUS O'SULLIVAN. **2nd unit ph** Harriet Cox. **stills** David Appleby, (set photographs) Adrian Gillard

m ROBERT LOCKHART. **m perf** Royal Regiment of Wales Territorial Army Band

ed SCOTT THOMAS

ad JOCELYN JAMES

cost des PHOEBE DE GAYE. **make-up** Jenny Shircore. **hair** Aileen Seaton

sd rec MOYA BURNS. **sd ed** Alan Knight. **dub mix** Peter Maxwell

cast [the family] Mike Gwilym (*Benjamin Jones*), Robert Gwilym (*Lewis Jones*), Bob Peck (*Amos Jones*), Gemma Jones (*Mary Jones*), Jack Walters (*Sam Jones*), Nesta Harris

(*Hannah Jones*), Rhys Baker (*Benjamin, 6 years*), Aled Baker (*Lewis, 6 years*), Huw Toghill (*Benjamin, 12 years*), Gareth Toghill (*Lewis, 12 years*), Lynn Gardner (*Rebecca*), Claire Evans (*Rebecca, 7 years*), Eryl Phillips (*Kevin*), Rhys & Aled Baker (*Kevin, 6 years*), Lillian Evans (*Mrs Redpath*), Ceri Morgan (*Eileen*); [the Welsh] Eric Wynn (*Tom Watkins*), Iona Banks (*Aggie Watkins*), Terry Jackson (*Haines*), Nicola Beddoe (*Rosie*), Ronan Vibert (*Jim Watkins*), Mark Jones (*Jim, 10 years*), Lyndon Lewis (*Jim, 16 years*), Siôn Probert (*Dai Morgan*), Jill Richards (*Ruth Morgan*), Geoffrey Hutchings (*the solicitor*), Robert Page (*draper*), James Warrior (*Mr Griffiths*), Rob Edmunds (*Thomas Philips, the conscript*), William Vaughan (*1st preacher*), Ken Caswell (*2nd preacher*), Kim Dunn (*Virgin Mary*), Huw Evans (*innkeeper*); [the English] Benjamin Whitrow (*Arkwright*), James Bree (*Colonel Bickerton*), Antonia Pemberton (*Mrs Bickerton*), Patrick Godfrey (*the auctioneer*), Tricia George (*Joy Lambert*), Mark Dignam (*the Rev Latimer*), Anthony Benson (*the vicar*), Rodney Wood (*1st doctor*), David Garfield (*2nd doctor*); Catherine Schell (*Lotte Zons*), Ben Marloe (*POW*)

shooting Mar–May 87. Wales

budget £639,000. **C4 input** £122,000 (lf) (19%)

1st tx 3 May 90 (FF)

MFB May 88. **V** 18 May 88

awards Grand Gold Shell (best feature), San Sebastián 88

festivals London 87; San Sebastián 88

THE OUTCASTS

Eire/UK, 100 mins, colour
Tolmayax with the Irish Film Board, the Arts Council of Ireland and Channel 4. © Tolmayax Company 1982

c ed DR. **no** 36

p ROBERT WYNNE-SIMMONS. **p man** Tony Dollard

d ROBERT WYNNE-SIMMONS. **asst d** Ben Gibney, (2nd) Robert Dwyer-Joyce.

continuity Jean Bourne

sc ROBERT WYNNE-SIMMONS

ph SEAMUS CORCORAN. **underwater cam** Peter Dorney. **rostrum cam** Günther Wulff

m STEPHEN COONEY. **m perf** Micheál Ó hAlmháin, Fran Breen, Kevin Glackin, Maeve Toner, Vincent Kilduff, Patrick McElwee, Nollaig Ní Cathasaigh, Audrey

Letters to an Unknown Lover

Letter to Brezhnev

Collins, Brian Dunning, Clodagh McSwiney, Maurice Lennon, Archie Collins, Paul Roche, Aisling Drury-Byrne, Tom Hayes, Stephen Cooney
ed ARTHUR KEATING
des BERTRAM TYRER
cost des CONSOLATA BOYLE. make-up Toni Delany. hair Anne Dunne
titles Aileen Casey
sd rec TOMMY CURRAN. sd ed Robert Sellick. dub mix Robert Bell
cast Mary Ryan (*Maura O'Donnell*), Mick Lally (*Scarf Michael*), Don Foley (*Hugh O'Donnell*), Tom Jordan (*Conor Farrell*), Cyril Cusack (*Myles Keenan*), Brenda Scallon (*Breda*), Bairbre Ní Chaoimh (*Janey*), Mairtín Ó Flathearta (*Eamon Farrell*), Brendan Ellis (*blacksmith*), Gillian Hackett (*Triona*), Hilary Reynolds (*Roisín*), Donal O'Kelly (*Owen*), James Shanahan (*Peadar*), Paul Bennett (*Father Connolly*)
budget £112,000. C4 input £47,000 (lf/i) (42%)
1st tx 14 Jun 84 (FF)
MFB Dec 85. V 3 Aug 83
awards Irish Arts Council F A (script) 81. Best F, Brussels Fantasy Festival 83. Best 1st Feature, Best Female Performance (Mary Ryan), San Remo 84. Special Grand Jury P, Critics' P, Fantasporto, Porto 84
festivals Brussels, London 83; San Remo, Porto 84

PARIS, TEXAS
FGR/France/UK, 148 mins, colour
Road Movies Filmproduktion (Berlin) and Argos Films (Paris), with WDR (Cologne), Channel 4 and Pro-Ject Film (Munich).
© Road Movies Filmproduktion 1984
c ed WD/DR. no 38

p DON GUEST. co-p ANATOLE DAUMAN. exec p CHRIS SIEVERNICH. assoc p Pascale Dauman. WDR c ed J. von Mengershausen. p co-ord Dianne Lisa Cheek. p man Karen Koch
d WIM WENDERS. asst d Claire Denis. sc sup Helen Caldwell. casting d Gary Chason
sc SAM SHEPARD. story adapt L. M. Kit Carson. story ed (C4) Walter Donohue
ph ROBBY MÜLLER. 2nd unit ph (addit) Martin Schär. stills Robin Holland
m RY COODER
ed PETER PRZYGODDA
ad KATE ALTMAN
cost des BIRGITTA BJERKE. make-up/hair Charles Balazs
sd mix JEAN-PAUL MUGEL. sd ed Dominique Auvray. sd processing Lothar Mankewitz. re-rec mix Hartmut Eichgrün
cast Harry Dean Stanton (*Travis Clay Anderson*), Sam Berry (*gas station attendant*), Bernhard Wicki (*Dr Ulmer*), Dean Stockwell (*Walter R. Anderson*), Aurore Clément (*Anne Anderson*), Claresie Mobley (*car rental clerk*), Hunter Carson (*Hunter Anderson*), Viva Auder (*woman on TV*), Socorro Valdez (*Carmelita*), Edward Fayton (*Hunter's friend*), Justin Hogg (*Hunter, age 3*), Nastassja Kinski (*Jane*), Tom Farrell (*screaming man*), John Lurie (*Slater*), Jeni Vici (*Stretch*), Sally Norvell (*Nurse Bibs*), Sharon Menzel (*comedienne*), The Mydolls (*rehearsing band*)
shooting Texas; California
budget £1,162,000. C4 input £250,000 (lf/i) (22%)
1st tx 29 May 86 (FF)
MFB Aug 84. V 23 May 84
awards Palme d'Or, International Critics' P (joint), Jury P, Cannes 84. Best English

Living Apart Together

Lorca – Death of a Poet

Language F, Best Actor (Harry Dean Stanton), Critics' Circle As (UK) 84. Best Direction, BAFTA F As 85
festivals Cannes 84

PASCALI'S ISLAND
UK/USA, 104 mins, colour
Initial Film and Television (London) for Avenue Pictures (Los Angeles) with Channel 4 and Dearfilm. © Avenue Pictures Release 1988
c ed KB. **no** 115
p ERIC FELLNER. **exec p** CARY BROKAW. **co-p** PAUL RAPHAEL. **p sup** Yannis Petropoulakis. **p man** Angela Petropoulakis
d JAMES DEARDEN. **asst d** Guy Travers, (2nd) Chris Thompson. **continuity** Photini Argyropoulou. **casting** Noel Davis, Jeremy Zimmerman
sc JAMES DEARDEN from the novel by Barry Unsworth
ph/cam op ROGER DEAKINS. **stills** Tom Collins
m LOEK DIKKER. **m perf** The Royal Philharmonic Orchestra of Flanders, conductor Huub Kerstens
ed EDWARD MARNIER
pd ANDREW MOLLO. **ad** Philip Elton, Petros Kapouralis
cost des PAM TAIT. **make-up** Peter Frampton. **hair** Sue Love
stuntman Paul Weston
sd rec IAN VOIGT. **dub ed** Campbell Askew. **dial ed** Roy Burge. **dub mix** Aad Wirtz
cast Ben Kingsley (*Basil Pascali*), Charles Dance (*Anthony Bowles*), Kevork Malikyan (*Mardosian*), George Murcell (*Herr Gesing*), Helen Mirren (*Lydia Neuman*), Nadim Sawalha (*Pasha*), Stefan Gryff (*Izzet*

Effendi), Vernon Dobtcheff (*Pariente*), Sheila Allen (*Mrs Marchant*), T. P. McKenna (*Dr Hogan*), Danielle Allan (*Mrs Hogan*), Nick Burnell (*Chaudan*), George Ekonomou (*Greek rebel*), Alistair Campbell (*captain*), Ali Abatsis (*boy in bath*), Brook Williams (*Turkish officer*), Josh Losey (*Turkish soldier*)
shooting Sep–Nov 87. Simi and Rhodes, Greece
budget £2,261,000. **C4 input** £275,000 (lf) (12%)
1st tx 8 Sep 91 (FF)
MFB Jan 89. **V** 18 May 88

PING PONG
UK, 100 mins, colour
Picture Palace Films for Channel 4. © Film Four International 1986
c ed KB/PA. **no** 77
p MALCOLM CRADDOCK, MICHAEL GUEST. **p man** Annie Rees. **p co-ord** Faye Perkins, (Chinese) Stanley Lau
d PO CHIH LEONG. **asst d** John O'Connor, Iain Whyte, (2nd) Trevor Puckle. **casting** John Hubbard, Ros Hubbard, (Hong Kong) Tina Liu
sc JERRY LIU from an idea by Po Chih Leong
ph NIC KNOWLAND. **stills** Sarah Quill
m RICHARD HARVEY
ed DAVID SPIERS
pd COLIN PIGOTT
ward sup SALLY CAIRNEY. **make-up** Sally Harrison. **hair** Meinir Brock
stunt arr ALAN STUART. **stuntman** Mark McBride
sd rec JOHN MIDGLEY. **sd ed** Nick Hosker. **re-rec mix** Andy Nelson
cast David Yip (*Mike Wong*), Lucy Sheen (*Elaine Choi*), Robert Lee (*Mr Chen*), Lam

Maschenka

Maurice

Fung (*Ah Ying*), Victor Kan (*Siu Loong*),
Barbara Yu Ling (*Cherry Kwan*), Ric Young
(*Dr Alan Wong*), Victoria Wicks (*Maggie,
Alan's wife*), Stephen Kuk (*Uncle Choi*),
Rex Wei (*A Chee*), Hi Ching (*Jimmy Li*),
Won Hun Tse, Chad Lee (*Siu Loong's kids*),
K. C. Leong (*Sam Wong*), David Lyon
(*Peter*), Karen Seacombe (*Susie*), Nigel Fan
(*mortician*), Jonathan Elsom (*probate
official*), Yee San Foo (*Winnie*), Olivier Pierre
(*Mr Orbach*), Eddie Yeoh, Lu Sang Wong
(*bouncers*), Susan Leong (*WPC Rainbird*),
Clive Panto, Jonathan Docker-Drysdale,
Nicholas Pritchard (*Mike's school friends*),
Errol Shaker (*West Indian bouncer*), Juliet
Hammond (*Sarah Lee*), Trevor Baxter (*priest
in church*), San Lee (*woman warrior*), Alan
Wong (*Sam Wong at 40*), Philip Voon
(*embassy official*), Ryan Yap (*young Mike*),
Pat Starr, Kate Harper, Manning Redwood,
Bruce Boa (*American tourists*), Romolo
Bruni (*maître d'*), Kim Teoh (*chef*), Linda
Datsun (*butch blonde*), Stan Young
(*doorman*), Vincent Wong (*Chinese
gambler*), Diana Choy (*young Ah Ying*)
   shooting Sep–Oct 85. London;
Shepperton studios
   budget £650,000. **C4 input** £650,000 (lf/i)
(100%)
   1st tx 23 Mar 89 (FF)
   MFB Aug 87. **V** 23 Apr 86
   festivals Hong Kong, Locarno, Edinburgh,
Venice, Birmingham 86; Utah, Los Angeles,
Madrid 87; Locarno 88

PLAYING AWAY
UK, 102 mins, colour
Insight Productions for Channel 4. 1986
c ed PA/DR. **no** 82
p BRIAN SKILTON, VIJAY AMARNANI. **assoc**

p Christopher Sutton. **p co-ord** Dee Hodgson,
(post-) Valerie Ames
   d HORACE OVÉ. **asst d** Simon Hinkly, (2nd)
Paul Frift. **continuity** Joan Marine. **casting**
Michael Barnes
   sc CARYL PHILLIPS. **sc ed** Peter Ansorge
   ph NIC KNOWLAND. **stills** Stephen Morley
   m SIMON WEBB. **theme song** Junior
   ed GRAHAM WHITLOCK
   ad PIP GARDNER
   cost ALYSON RITCHIE. **make-up** Vivien
Placks. **hair** Mark Nelson
   graphics Chris James
   sd red CHRISTIAN WANGLER. **sd ed** Chris
Godden, Stuart de Jong. **dub mix** Alan Dykes
   cast Norman Beaton (*Willie-Boy*), Robert
Urquhart (*Godfrey Matthews*), Helen Lindsay
(*Marjorie Matthews*), Nicholas Farrell
(*Derek*), Brian Bovell (*Stuart*), Gary Beadle
(*Errol*), Suzette Llewellyn (*Yvette*), Trevor
Thomas (*Jeff*), Stefan Kalipha (*Louis*),
Bruce Purchase (*Fredrick*), Joseph Marcell
(*Robbo*), Sheila Ruskin (*Viv*), Mark Barratt
(*Kevin*), Valerie Buchanan (*Pat*), Jim Findley
(*Boots*), Julian Granger (*Mick*), Ram John
Holder (*Wilf*), Patrick Holt (*the Colonel*),
Elizabeth Anson (*Sandra*), Juliet Waley
(*Julie*), Ross Kemp (*Sonny*), Gareth Kirkland
(*Tommy*), Archie Pool (*Steadroy*), Errol
Shaker (*Desert-Head*), Femi Taylor (*Maisie*),
Larry Dann (*John*), Neil Morrisey (*Ian*),
Charles Pemberton (*constable*), Roddy
Maude-Roxby (*vicar*), Zulema Dene (*Miss
Rye*), Ian Cross (*David*), Jimmy Reddington
(*tavern barman*), Mary Tempest (*Angie*),
Lucita Lijertwood (*lady in telephone box*)
   shooting Jun–Jul 86. London; Suffolk
   budget £924,000. **C4 input** £924,000 (lf/i)
(100%)
   1st tx 4 May 89 (FF)

Meantime

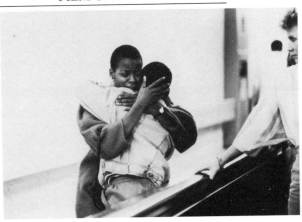

Milk and Honey

MFB Nov 87. **V** 10 Dec 86
festivals London, Sorrento 86; Utah, Berlin, Sydney, Jerusalem, New York, Bergamo, Aspen, Figueira da Foz, Aurillac, Amiens 87; Trivandrum, Vienna, Turin, Caribbean, Hamburg 88; Antenna 89; Kiev 90; Geneva 91

THE PLOUGHMAN'S LUNCH
UK, 107 mins, colour
Greenpoint Films for Goldcrest Films & Television/Michael White with Channel 4. © AC&D (Plant Hirers) 1983
 c ed DR. **no** 22
 p SIMON RELPH, ANN SCOTT. **p man** Redmond Morris
 d RICHARD EYRE. **asst d** Simon Relph, (2nd) Christopher Figg, Linda Bruce.
continuity Pat Rambaut. **casting d** Susie Figgis
 sc IAN MCEWAN. **Edward's poem** Christopher Reid
 ph CLIVE TICKNER. **sp ph** John Haynes.
stills John Brown
 m/cond DOMINIC MULDOWNEY
 ed DAVID MARTIN
 pd LUCIANA ARRIGHI. **ad** Michael Pickwoad
 cost des LUCIANA ARRIGHI, (assoc) Joy Kleiner. **make-up** Elaine Carew. **hair** Joan Carpenter
 titles des Nicholas Jenkins
 sd mix DAVID STEPHENSON. **dub ed** Richard Dunford. **dub mix** Gerry Humphreys
 cast Jonathan Pryce (*James Penfield*), William Maxwell, Paul Jesson, Andy Rashleigh (*journalists*), Christopher Fulford (*young journalist*), David Lyon (*newsreader*), David De Keyser (*Tom Gold*), Polly Abbott (*Gold's assistant*), Tim Curry (*Jeremy*

Hancock), Charlie Dore (*Susan Barrington*), Peter Walmsley (*Bob Tuckett*), Bob Cartland (*editor*), Nat Jackley (*Mr Penfield*), Pearl Hackney (*Mrs Penfield*), Simon Stokes (*Edward Long*), Anna Wing (*woman at poetry reading*), Ken Drury (*young man at poetry reading*), Richard Cottan (*student at poetry reading*), Peter Birch (*barman*), Bill Paterson (*lecturer*), Ken Shorter (*squash coach*), Orlando Wells (*Tom Fox*), Rosemary Harris (*Ann Barrington*), Frank Finlay (*Matthew Fox*), Witold Schejbal (*Jacek*), Libba Davies (*Betty*), Sandra Voe (*Carmen*), Andrew Norton (*Pete*), Cecily Hobbs (*Carol*), Clare Sutcliffe (*Jill*), Robert McIntosh (*dad in commercial*), Vivienne Chandler (*mum in commercial*), Nicole Kleeman (*daughter in commercial*), Bernard Mullins (*son in commercial*), Allan Mitchell (*junior minister*)
 shooting Nov–Dec 82. London; Brighton; Norfolk
 budget £599,000. **C4 input** £300,000 (lf/i) (50%)
 1st tx 3 Nov 83 (FF)
 MFB Jun 83. **V** 20 Apr 83
 awards Best F, Best Screenplay, *Standard* F As 83. Best Original Story (given by directors and critics), Rimini 84
 festivals Rimini 84

PRAYING MANTIS (Parts I and II)
UK, 80 mins (Part I), 80 mins (Part II), colour
Portman Productions for Channel 4. © 1982
 c ed DR. **nos** 8 and 9
 p IAN WARREN, DICKIE BAMBER. **exec p** T. L. DONALD. **p man** Andrew Warren
 d JACK GOLD. **asst d** Michael Gowans, (2nd) Adrian Bate. **continuity** Renée Glynne.
casting Irene Lamb

The Mirror

Mona Lisa

sc PHILIP MACKIE from the novel
Les Mantes Religieuses by Hubert
Monteilheit
 ph JOHN COQUILLON. **cam op** Herbert
Smith
 m CARL DAVIS
 ed KEITH PALMER
 pd ROBERT CARTWRIGHT
 ward BRIDGET SELLERS, NORMAN DICKENS.
make-up Joan Hills, Mary Hillman. **hair**
Helen Lennox
 sd rec BRIAN SIMMONS. **dub ed** John
Ireland. **sd mix** Ken Scrivener
 cast (Parts I and II) Jonathan Pryce
(*Christian Magny*), Cherie Lunghi (*Béatrice
Manceau*), Carmen du Sautoy (*Vera
Canova*), Pinkas Braun (*Professor Paul
Canova*), Anna Cropper (*Gertrude*),
Friedrich von Thun (*insurance director*),
Arthur Brauss (*Richter*), Sarah Berger
(*Madeleine*), Kevin McNally (*Bernard*),
David Schofield (*café waiter*), Margaret
Ward (*Mme Magny*), Richard Warner (*M
Magny*), Jonathan Blake (*Raymond*), John
Bryans (*Dubreuil*), Gordon Kane (*sound
technician*), Barbara Young (*solicitor's
secretary*), Derek Smith (*Maître Chardois*),
(Part II) Douglas Wilmer (*Maître Fleury*),
Peter Blake (*Dr Courant*), Joby Blanshard
(*Dr Laporte*), Clive Swift (*Dr Fauré*), Denyse
Alexander (*Alice*), Carol Gillies (*convent
sister*), Ralph Schicha (*Rudi*), Gerard Hely
(*bank cashier*)
 shooting Rouen
 budget £680,000. **C4 input** £450,000 (If/i)
(66%)
 1st tx 17 Nov 82 (Part I), 24 Nov 82 (Part
II) (FF)
 V 10 Nov 82
 festivals London 82 (combined version)

PRICK UP YOUR EARS
UK, 110 mins, colour
Civilhand/Zenith with British Screen and
Channel 4. © Zenith Productions 1987
 c ed DR/KB. **no** 85
 p ANDREW BROWN. **p co-ord** Lorraine
Goodman. **p man** Ann Wingate
 d STEPHEN FREARS. **asst d** Michael
Zimbrich, (2nd) Lee Cleary. **Morocco asst d**
Hatimi Ahmed. **sc sup** Penny Eyles. **casting**
Debbie McWilliams
 sc ALAN BENNETT from the biography by
John Lahr
 ph OLIVER STAPLETON. **cam op** David
Morgan. **stills** Sarah Quill
 m STANLEY MYERS. **md/orch** John Harle.
m perf John Harle's Berliner Band.
synthesizers Hans Zimmer. **song** ('Dancing
Hearts') Stanley Myers, Richard Myhill
 ed MICK AUDSLEY
 pd HUGO LUCZYC-WYHOWSKI. **ad** Phil
Elton
 cost des BOB RINGWOOD. **make-up** Elaine
Carew
 titles Julian Rothenstein
 sd sup TONY JACKSON. **sd rec** PETER
MAXWELL. **sd ed** Brian Trenerry, (dial)
Katrina Sheldon
 cast Gary Oldman (*Joe Orton*), Alfred
Molina (*Kenneth Halliwell*), Vanessa
Redgrave (*Peggy Ramsay*), Wallace Shawn
(*John Lahr*), Lindsay Duncan (*Anthea Lahr*),
Julie Walters (*Elsie Orton*), James Grant
(*William Orton*), Frances Barber (*Leonie
Orton*), Janet Dale (*Mrs Sugden*), Dave
Atkins (*Clifford Sugden*), Margaret Tyzack
(*Madame Ada Lambert*), Eric Richard
(*education officer*), William Job (*RADA
chairman*), Rosalind Knight, Angus Mackay
(*RADA judges*), Linda Spurrier (*RADA

A Month in the Country

Moonlighting

instructor), Charlotte Wodehouse (*Janet*), Helena Michell, Sean Pertwee (*Orton's friends*), Liam de Staic (*brickie*), Charles McKeown (*Mr Cunliffe*), Selina Cadell (*Miss Battersby*), Bert Parnaby (*magistrate*), Antony Carrick (*counsel*), Neil Dudgeon (*policeman*), Richard Wilson (*psychiatrist*), Christopher Guinee (*publisher*), Stevan Rimkus (*Kenneth*), Michael Mueller (*1st BBC actor*), Anthony Douse (*2nd BBC actor*), John Kane (*director*), Steven Mackintosh (*Simon Ward*), Garry Cooper (*1st actor, 'Entertaining Mr Sloane'*), Roger Lloyd Pack (*2nd actor*), Joanne Connelly (*stage manager*), John Moffatt (*wigmaker*), Philippa Davies (*Peggy Ramsay's secretary*), David Cardy (*Brian Epstein*), Julie Legrand (*gallery owner*), Noel Davis (*Philip*), Jane Blackburn (*1st woman in gallery*), Stella Richman (*2nd woman in gallery*), Neville Phillips (*man in gallery*), Jonathan Philips (*youth outside lavatory*), Richard Ireson (*man outside lavatory*), Ahmed El Jheur (*1st Moroccan boy*), Moktar Dagmouni (*2nd Moroccan boy*), Sian Thomas (*Marilyn Orton*), Stephen Bill (*George Barnett*), Karl Johnson (*Douglas Orton*), David Bradley (*undertaker*), Simon Adams (*undertaker's boy*), James Duggan (*labourer*), Max Stafford-Clark (*awards chairman*), Mark Brignal (*Beatles' chauffeur*), Joan Sanderson (*Anthea's mother*), Neville Smith (*police inspector*), Spencer Leigh (*constable*), John Salthouse (*chauffeur*), Robin Hooper (*mortuary attendant*), Derek Jarman (*painter*)

shooting Jul–Sep 86. London; Jacob Street studios; Tangier

budget £1,900,000. **C4 input** £300,000 (lf) (16%)

1st tx 16 Mar 89 (FF)
MFB May 87. **V** 4 Mar 87
awards Best Artistic Contribution (Stanley Myers), Cannes 87. Best Screenplay, *Standard* F As 88
festivals Cannes 87

P'TANG, YANG, KIPPERBANG
UK, 80 mins, colour
Enigma Television/Goldcrest Films & Television for Channel 4. © Enigma Television 1982

  c ed DR. **no** 2
  p CHRIS GRIFFIN. **exec p** DAVID PUTTNAM.
assoc p David Bill. **location manager** Peter Elford
  d MICHAEL APTED. **asst d** Dominic Fulford, (2nd) Andrew Montgomery, Russell Lodge.
continuity Mary Holdsworth. **casting** Joyce Gallie
  sc JACK ROSENTHAL
  ph TONY PIERCE-ROBERTS. **cam op** Nick Beeks-Sanders. **stills** Robert Marshall
  m DAVID EARL
  ed JOHN SHIRLEY
  ad JEFF WOODBRIDGE
  cost design SUE YELLAND. **make-up** Freddie Williamson. **hair** Betty Glasow
  sd rec DEREK BALL. **sd ed** Chris Greenham.
dub mix Hugh Strain
  cast John Albasiny (*Alan Duckworth*), Abigail Cruttenden (*Ann Lawton*), Maurice Dee (*Geoffrey Whitaker*), Alison Steadman (*Estelle Land*), Mark Brailsford (*Abbo*), Chris Karallis (*Shaz Willoughby*), Frances Ruffelle (*Eunice*), Robert Urquhart (*Henry, the headmaster*), Garry Cooper (*Tommy*), Maurice O'Connell (*gym teacher*), Tim Seeley (*French master*), Richenda Carey (*botany teacher*), Peter Dean (*policeman*),

My Beautiful Laundrette

The Nature of the Beast

Dave Atkin (*fish shop owner*), Eric Richard, Arthur Whybrow (*workmen*), Nicola Prince (*Maureen*), Sara Godbold, Lisa Maresca, Nicola Strong, Sian Dunlop, Cathy Cleere, Lisa De Cosimo, Lisa Lancashire, Samantha Creed, Johan Hendrie, Kathleen Logue, Natalie Akers, Stephanie Jane Collins (*schoolgirls*), Thomas Austin, Stephen Bovill, Anthony Byrne, Daniel Devitt, Niall Devitt, Philip Edkins, Cassion Harrison, Dominic Holland, Christopher John, Martin Kelly, Wladislaw Lodzinski, Laurence O'Brien, Malcolm Springett (*schoolboys*), the voice of John Arlott
   shooting Wimbledon Chase Middle School and Cardinal Vaughan School, London
   budget £395,000. **C4 input** £200,000 (lf) (51%)
   1st tx 3 Nov 82 (FF: 'First Love')
   MFB Sep 84. **V** 15 Feb 84
   US release title *Kipperbang*

RED MONARCH
UK, 100 mins, colour
Enigma (Red Monarch)/Goldcrest Films & Television for Channel 4. © AC&D (Plant Hirers) 1983
   c ed DR. **no** 20
   p GRAHAM BENSON. **exec p** DAVID PUTTNAM. **p man** Robin Douet
   d JACK GOLD. **asst d** Gary White, (2nd) Adrian Rawle. **continuity** Renée Glynne. **casting d** Irene Lamb
   sc CHARLES WOOD based on the stories of Yuri Krotkov
   ph MIKE FASH. **cam op** Chic Anstiss. **stills** David Appleby
   ed LAURENCE MÉRY-CLARK
   pd NORMAN GARWOOD. **ad** Keith Pain

cost design EVANGELINE HARRIS. **make-up** Sandra Shepherd. **hair** Sally Harrison
   sd mix BRIAN SIMMONS. **sd ed** Jonathan Bates. **dub mix** Trevor Pyke
   cast Colin Blakely (*Stalin*), David Suchet (*Beria*), Carroll Baker (*Ellen Brown*), Ian Hogg (*Shaposhnikov*), David Kelly (*Sergo*), Jean Heywood (*Sopha*), David Threlfall (*Vasily*), Lee Montague (*Lee*), Glynn Edwards (*Vlasek*), Nigel Stock (*Molotov*), Wensley Pithey (*Voroshilov*), Brian Glover (*Khrushchev*), George A. Cooper (*Kaganovitch*), Peter Woodthorpe (*Malenkov*), Freddie Earlle (*Mikoyan*), Gawn Grainger (*Zamorsky*), Oscar Quitak (*Mekhlis*), Bernard Gallagher (*Vovka*), Jane Galloway (*Svetlana*), Tim Preece (*Lukov*), George Costigan (*projectionist*), Fred Lee-Own (*Mao Tse-tung*), Malcolm Terris (*physical education chairman*), Eileen Helsby (*Nina*), Susan Carpenter (*Seraphima*), Paddy Joyce (*Akhmet*), Virginia Balfour (*housekeeper*), Ceri Jackson (*Olga*), Darren Gordon (*Young Josef*), Flora Page (*Little Masha*)
   shooting Nov–Dec 82. Royal Mint and County Hall, London
   budget £811,000. **C4 input** £350,000 (lf/i) (43%)
   1st tx 16 Jun 83 (FF)
   V 13 Jul 83
   awards Best Actor (David Suchet), Best Gag (Mao sequence), Marseille Festival of Comedy 83
   festivals Cannes, Marseille 83

REEFER AND THE MODEL
Eire/UK, 93 mins, colour
Berber Films with the Irish Film Board, RTE and Channel 4. © Berber Films 1987

Nelly's Version

No Man's Land

c ed DR. **no** 117
p LELIA DOOLAN. **co-p** (development) Tom Hayes. **p man** Darryl Collins. **co-ord** (Dublin) Jane Gogan
d JOE COMERFORD. **asst d** Dave Murphy, (2nd) Mick Rowland. **continuity** Deirdre O'Brien
sc JOE COMERFORD. **sc assoc** Lelia Doolan. **st ed** Eoghan Harris
ph BREFFNI BYRNE. **stills** Peter Harkin, Jonathan Hession
m JOHNNY DUHAN. **songs** Johnny Duhan, Seán McCarthy. **musicians** Aiveen Anderson, Frankie Colohan, Johnny Duhan, Tony Maher, Eamon Murphy, Gerald O'Donoghue, Davy Spillane
ed SÉ MERRY
pd JOHN LUCAS
ward mist JACQUELINE YOUNG. **make-up** Ailbhe Lemass. **hair** Eileen Doyle
sp eff MAURICE FOLEY, OWEN MacCARTHAIGH
stunt co-ord MICK ROWLAND. **stunts** Bronco McLoughlin, Patrick Condren, Susan Foreman
sd rec KIERAN HORGAN. **sd ed** Martin Evans. **dub mix** David Old
cast Ian McElhinney (*Reefer*), Eve Watkinson (*Reefer's mother*), Carol Scanlan (*Teresa Flaherty, the Model*), Birdy Sweeney (*Instant Photo*), Sean Lawlor (*Spider*), Ray McBride (*Badger*), Fionn Comerford (*messenger boy*), John Lillis (*porter*), Henry Comerford (*waiter*), Paraic Breathnach (*quays fisherman*), Máire Chinsealach (*island woman*), Dave Duffy (*sergeant*), Rosena Brown (*the blonde*), Little John Nee (*boy soldier*), Seán Ó Coistealbha ('*Rossaveal' skipper*), Noel Spain (*boatman*), Peter Fitzgerald (*bank guard*), Dick

Donaghue, Márie Ní Mháille (*bank tellers*), Mick Rowland (*older bank guard*), Patrick Blackaby (*1st tinker guard*), Uinseann MacThómais (*2nd tinker guard*), Deirdre Lawless (*policewoman*), Gary McMahon (*young guard*), Sabina Higgins (*restaurant woman*), Henry Waters (*pub musician*)
shooting Apr–Jun 87. Co. Galway
budget £1,052,000. **C4 input** £250,000 (lf) (24%)
1st tx 25 Aug 91 (FF)
MFB Dec 89. **V** 24 Feb 88
awards Arts Council F Script A (joint) (first-draft screenplay) 83. Main Feature P, Celtic Film Festival, Caernarfon 88. Europa P for Best F, Barcelona 88
festivals Berlin, Caernarfon, Hamburg, Barcelona, Bergamo, Cambridge, Montreal, Edinburgh, Birmingham, Cherbourg, Leeds, São Paulo 88; New Delhi, Antenna, Moscow, Reykjavík 89; Sense of Ireland 90

REFLECTIONS

UK, 100 mins, colour
Court House Films for Channel 4. © Court House Films 1983
c ed DR/WD. **no** 31
p DAVID DEUTSCH, KEVIN BILLINGTON.
p man Ann Wingate
d KEVIN BILLINGTON. **asst d** Tony Hopkins, (2nd) Crispin Reece. **continuity** Heather Storr, Peggy Spirito, Marjorie Lavelly. **casting d** Patsy Pollock
sc JOHN BANVILLE from his novella *The Newton Letter*
ph MIKE MOLLOY. **cam op** Peter Macdonald, Gerry Anstiss. **stills** Dave Morse
m RACHEL PORTMAN
ed CHRIS RIDSDALE
ad MARTIN JOHNSON

El Norte

No Surrender

cost des JANE BOND. **make-up** Jeanne
Richmond. **hair** Sally Harrison
   sd rec TONY JACKSON. **dub ed** Edward
Marnier. **dub mix** Aad Wirtz
   cast Gabriel Byrne (*William Masters*),
Donal McCann (*Edward Lawless*), Fionnula
Flanagan (*Charlotte Lawless*), Harriet Walter
(*Ottilie Grainger*), Gerard Cummins (*Michael
Lawless*), Niall Toibin (*Mr Prunty*), Paedar
Lamb (*doctor*), Des Nealon (*Tom Mittler*),
Margaret Wade (*Diana 'Bunny' Mittler*),
Larry O'Driscoll, Noel O'Flaherty (*rat men*)
   shooting Jun–Jul 83. Dripsey Castle and
Blarney Castle, Co. Cork
   budget £502,000. **C4 input** £462,000 (lf/i)
(92%)
   1st tx 5 Jul 84 (FF)
   MFB May 84. **V** 25 Jul 84
   festivals Cambridge 84; San Remo,
Antwerp 85; Reggio nell'Emilia 86; Antenna
87
   working title *A History Lesson*

REMEMBRANCE
UK, 117 mins, colour
Colin Gregg Film Productions for Channel 4.
Assisted by the National Film Development
Fund. © Colin Gregg Film Productions 1982
   c ed DR. **no** 7
   p COLIN GREGG. **assoc p** Selwyn Roberts.
p man John Davies
   d COLIN GREGG. **asst d** Selwyn Roberts,
(2nd) Nigel Goldsack. **continuity** Melinda
Rees. **casting d** Simone Reynolds
   sc HUGH STODDART from a story by Hugh
Stoddart, Colin Gregg
   ph JOHN METCALFE. **cam op** John
Simmons. **stills** Gordon Moore
   ed PETER DELFGOU
   ad JAMIE LEONARD

ward sup PHILIPPE PICKFORD. **make-up**
Lindy Shaw. **hair** Ross Carver
   stunt arr FRANK MAHER
   sd mix DAVID STEPHENSON. **dub mix** Clive
Pendry
   cast Roger Adamson (*provost driver*), John
Altman (*Steve*), Dawn Archibald (*Gill*), Sean
Arnold (*landlord 'Antelope'*), Al Ashton
(*John*), Dicken Ashworth (*Frank*), Sheila
Ballantine (*Marie*), Martin Barrass (*Malcolm
White*), John Barrett (*Jimmy*), Derek Benfield
(*Vincent's father*), Jesse Birdsall (*matelot*),
Roger Booth (*Mark's father*), Jon Croft (*Stan*),
Alison Dowling (*student*), Mark Drewry
(*Harry, matelot*), Nick Dunning (*Chris*), Nick
Ellesworth (*naval provost*), Peter Ellis
(*policeman*), Myra Frances (*teacher at party*),
Michael Godley (*father at party*), Kenneth
Griffith (*Joe*), Dave Hill (*Paul*), Sally Jane
Jackson (*Sue*), David John (*Mark*), Peter
Jonfield (*Dave*), Wolf Kahler (*Dutch matelot*),
Marjie Lawrence (*Mark's mother*), Peter
Lee-Wilson (*Vincent*), Doel Luscombe
(*landlord 'White Swan'*), Tony Mathews
(*naval surgeon*), Lisa Maxwell (*girl at disco*),
Don Munday (*doorman*), Gary Oldman
(*Daniel White*), Eileen Page (*mother at party*),
Robert Pitman (*landlord 'Two Trees'*), John
Price (*naval officer*), Lawrie Quayle (*TV
interviewer*), Anna Rees (*girl at disco*), John
Rutland (*Alf*), Timothy Spall (*Douglas*),
Ewan Stewart (*Sean*), Kim Taylforth
(*Christine*), Flip Webster (*barmaid at disco*),
Michele Winstanley (*Gail*), Nicola Wright
(*student*)
   shooting Oct–Nov 81. Plymouth
   budget £338,000. **C4 input** £338,000 (lf)
(100%)
   1st tx 10 Nov 82 (FF)
   MFB July 82. **V** 2 Oct 85

On the Black Hill

The Outcasts

awards Golden Cyclops, Taormina 82.
Special Jury P, Chicago 82
festivals Taormina, Chicago 82

THE REWARDS OF VIRTUE *see*
NELLY'S VERSION

EL REY Y LA REINA *see*
THE KING AND THE QUEEN

RITA, SUE AND BOB TOO
UK, 93 mins, colour
Umbrella Entertainment Productions for
British Screen and Channel 4. Assisted by the
National Film Development Fund. © Film
Four International 1986
  c ed KB. **no** 92
  p SANDY LIEBERSON. **exec p** OSCAR
LEWENSTEIN. **co-p** PATSY POLLOCK. **p sup**
Garth Thomas. **p co-ord** Laura Grumitt
  d ALAN CLARKE. **asst d** Mike Gowans,
(2nd) Jon Older. **continuity** Francine Brown.
casting Beverley Keogh
  sc ANDREA DUNBAR from her plays *The
Arbour* and *Rita, Sue and Bob too*. **sc cons**
Jennifer Howarth
  ph IVAN STRASBURG. **Steadicam op** John
Ward
  m MICHAEL KAMEN. **m sup** Daniel Secunda
  ed STEPHEN SINGLETON
  pd LEN HUNTINGFORD
  cost des CATHY COOK. **make-up** Alan
Boyle. **hair** Barbara Sutton
  stunt co-ord ROY ALON, JOHN LEES
  sd rec MIKE MCDUFFIE. **sd ed** Allan
Morrison. **dub mix** Alan Dykes
  cast Willie Ross (*Sue's father*), Michelle
Holmes (*Sue*), Danny O'Dea (*Paddy*), David
Britton, Mark Crompton, Stuart Goodwin,
Max Jackman, Andrew Krauz, Simon Waring

(*Rita's brothers*), Maureen Long (*Rita's
mother*), Siobhan Finneran (*Rita*), Joyce
Pembroke (*Lawn-Mower Lil*), Lesley Sharp
(*Michelle*), George Costigan (*Bob*), Patti
Nicholls (*Sue's mother*), Jane Atkinson
(*Helen*), Bryan Heeley (*Michael*), Paul
Oldham (*Lee*), Bernard Wrigley (*teacher*),
Kulvinder Ghir (*Aslam*), Dennis Conlon (*taxi
driver*), Joanna Steele (*Sylvia*), Joanne
Barrow (*Judy*), Rachel Shepherd (*schoolgirl*),
Paula Jayne (*2nd schoolgirl*), Alison
Goodman (*Hilda*), Marie Jelliman (*gym
mistress*), Black Lace (*themselves*), Nancy
Pute (*Mavis*), Ken Hainsworth (*Billy*), Niall
Costigan (*Simon*), Sinead Parkinson (*Jenny*),
Paul Hedges (*Hosepipe Harry*), Laura Devon
(*neighbour on balcony*), Charles Meek (*taxi
driver*), Kailash Patel (*Aslam's sister*), Usma
Islam, Naeela Jaben Sabir, Shabar Hussain
(*Aslam's nieces*), Claude Powell, Alexander
Cruise, Nelson Fletcher (*West Indians in
taxi office*), Mel Fredricks (*white man in taxi
office*), Blake Roberts (*West Indian in cab*)
  shooting Buttershaw Estate, Bradford
  budget £993,000. **C4 input** £726,000 (lf/i)
(73%)
  1st tx 10 May 90 (FF)
  MFB Sep 87. **V** 11 Mar 87
  festivals Cannes, Bergamo, Barcelona,
Edinburgh, Haifa, Troia, São Paulo, Rio de
Janeiro 87; Vienna, Hamburg 88

THE ROAD HOME
UK/Poland, 95 mins, colour
Zed Productions (London) with Film Polski
(Warsaw) for Channel 4. © Zed, Film Polski
and Channel 4 Television Company 1987
  c ed DR/KB. **no** 88
  p SOPHIE BALHETCHET, GLENN WILHIDE
and Production Unit Tor. **artistic dir for**

Paris, Texas

Pascali's Island

Production Unit Tor Krzysztof Zanussi.
p sup Andrzej Janowski. **p co-ord** Krystyna
Dwornik. **p man** Wojciech Bednarek
  d JERZY KASZUBOWSKI. **asst d** Maria
Kuzemko, (2nd) Danuta Spychalska.
continuity Miroslawa Sada
    sc JERZY KASZUBOWSKI
    ph WIT DABAL. **cam op** Bogdan Stachurski
    m ZYGMUNT KONIECZNY. **m perf** The Lodz
Philharmonic Orchestra, conductor Zdzislaw
Szostak
      ed MAREK DENYS
      pd ANDRZEJ KOWALCZYK
      cost des IRENE BIEGANSKA. **make-up**
Iwona Karpinska. **hair** Malgorzata
Gniedzijko
      sd mix ALEKSANDER GOLEBIOWSKI. **sd eff**
sup Zygmunt Nowak
      cast Rafal Synowka (*Jerzy Ostrowski*),
Jerzy Binczycki (*Josef*), Marzena Trybala
(*Maria*), Slawa Kwasniewska (*Marta*),
Boguslaw Linda (*Edward*), Eugeniusz
Kujawski (*pastor*), Zuzanna Helska (*pastor's
wife*), Lech Alexandrowicz (*American
soldier*), Mieczyslaw Janowski, Sylvester
Zawadzki (*British soldiers*), Emilia
Przeminska (*girl in convent*), Beata Maj,
Beata Redo-Dober (*nuns*), Jerzy Kaszubowski
(*father's ghost*), Miroslaw Skupin (*Russian
soldier*), Igor Kujawski (*German soldier*),
Halina Skoczynska (*schoolteacher*),
Wojcech Grzywaczewski (*Buras*), Cezary
Karpinski (*Edward's friend*), Elias
Kuziemski (*priest*), Zygmunt Bielawski
(*organist*)
      shooting Poland; Wroclaw studios
      budget £800,000. **C4 input** £400,000 (i)
(50%)
      1st tx 15 April 89 (FFI)
      V 27 Apr 88

  festivals Haifa, Vancouver, Cherbourg,
Mill Valley 88; New Delhi, Hong Kong 89

A ROOM WITH A VIEW
UK, 117 mins, colour
Merchant Ivory Productions for Goldcrest
Films & Television with the National Film
Finance Corporation, Curzon Film
Distributors and Channel 4. © A Room with
a View Productions 1985
  c ed DR. **no** 58
  p ISMAIL MERCHANT. **assoc p** Paul Bradley,
(Italy) Peter Marangoni. **p co-ord** Caroline
Hill. **p man** Ann Wingate, Lanfranco
Diotallevi
    d JAMES IVORY. **asst d** Kevan Barker, (2nd)
Daniel Sonnis, Simon Moseley. **continuity**
Renée Glynne. **casting** Celestia Fox
    sc RUTH PRAWER JHABVALA based on the
novel by E. M. Forster
    ph TONY PIERCE-ROBERTS. **2nd unit cam**
Sergio Melaranci. **stills** Sarah Quill, Katya
Grenfell
    m RICHARD ROBBINS. **orch/cond** Francis
Shaw, Barrie Guard
      ed HUMPHREY DIXON
      pd GIANNI QUARANTA, BRIAN
ACKLAND-SNOW. **ad** Brian Savegar, Elio
Altamura
      cost des JENNY BEAVAN, JOHN BRIGHT.
make-up Christine Beveridge. **hair** Carol
Hemming
      title des Chris Allies. **title background**
Folco Cianfanelli
      sd RAY BECKETT. **sd ed** Tony Lenny, Peter
Compton, Alan Killick. **sd re-rec** Richard
King
      cast [in Florence] Maggie Smith (*Charlotte
Bartlett, a chaperon*), Helena Bonham Carter
(*Lucy Honeychurch, Miss Bartlett's cousin*

Ping Pong

Playing Away

and charge), Denholm Elliott (*Mr Emerson, an English tourist*), Julian Sands (*George Emerson*), Simon Callow (*the Rev Arthur Beebe*), Patrick Godfrey (*the Rev Mr Eager, Chaplain of the Anglican Church in Florence*), Judi Dench (*Eleanor Lavish, a novelist*), Fabia Drake, Joan Henley (*the Misses Catharine and Teresa Alan*), Amanda Walker (*the Cockney Signora*); [in England] Daniel Day Lewis (*Cecil Vyse*), Maria Britneva (*Mrs Vyse, Cecil's mother*), Rosemary Leach (*Mrs Honeychurch*), Rupert Graves (*Freddy Honeychurch*), Peter Cellier (*Sir Harry Otway, a landlord*), Mia Fothergill (*Minnie Beebe*); Kitty Aldridge (*new Lucy*), Isabella Celani (*Persephone*), Luigi Di Fiori (*murdered youth*), Matyelock Gibbs (*new Charlotte*), Mirio Guidelli (*Santa Croce guide*), Freddy Korner (*Mr Floyd*), Patty Lawrence (*Mrs Butterworth*), Elizabeth Marangoni (*Miss Pole*), Lucca Rossi (*Phaeton*), Brigid Erin Bates, Peter Munt, Stefano Serboli, Phillada Sewell, Margaret Ward

shooting May–Jul 85. Florence; London; Kent

budget £2,259,000. **C4 input** £235,000 (lf) (10%)

1st tx 13 Apr 89 (FF)

MFB Apr 86. **V** 29 Jan 86

awards Best F, Best Technical Achievement (Tony Pierce-Roberts), *Standard* F As 86. Best Supporting Actress (Maggie Smith), Golden Globe As 86. Best Supporting Actor (joint) (Daniel Day Lewis), New York F Critics' As 86. Best Supporting Actress (Maggie Smith), Variety Club of GB. Best F, Best Actress (Maggie Smith), Best Supporting Actress (Judi Dench), Best Production Design, Best Costume Design,

BAFTA F As 87. Anthony Asquith A (F Music), BFI As 87. Best Screenplay Adaptation, Best Art Direction, Best Costume Design, Academy As 87

festivals Venice 86

RUNNERS

UK, 106 mins, colour

Hanstoll Enterprises for Goldcrest Films & Television. © Samuel Montagu & Co 1983

c ed KB. **no** 34

p BARRY HANSON. **p co-ord** Norma Hazelden. **p man** Bill Kirk

d CHARLES STURRIDGE. **asst d** Steve Lanning, (2nd) Peter Waller, Waldo Roeg.

continuity Jean Skinner. **casting d** Celestia Fox

sc STEPHEN POLIAKOFF from his own story

ph HOWARD ATHERTON. **cam op** Jerry Dunkley. **stills** Sarah Quill, Diana Miller

m/cond GEORGE FENTON

ed PETER COULSON

pd ARNOLD CHAPKIS. **ad** Mark Nerini

cost des DAVID PERRY. **make-up** Lois Burwell. **hair** Paula Gillespie

sd rec CHRIS MUNRO. **dub ed** Sarah Vickers. **dub mix** Richard King

cast Kate Hardie (*Rachel Lindsay*), James Fox (*Tom Lindsay*), Jane Asher (*Helen Turner*), Eileen O'Brien (*Gillian Lindsay*), Ruti Simon (*Lucy Lindsay*); [the road] Max Hafler, Peter Turner (*policemen*); [the school] Bridget Turner (*teacher*), Lisa Howard, Deborah Hawley, Hazel Berry, Charla Haughton, Nicola Glew (*schoolgirls*); [the swimming pool] Robert Lang (*Martin Wilkins*), Shay Gorman (*Irishman*), Anna Wing (*old lady*), Ursula Camm (*lady*), Laurin Kaski (*steward*); [the radio station] Paul Angelis (*Tony Gavin*), Julian Firth

The Ploughman's Lunch

Praying Mantis

(*researcher*); [the hostel] Patrick O'Connell (*warden*), Sarah London (*Deborah*); [the train] Bridget Meade (*schoolgirl*), John Holmes (*boy*), Norman Lumsden (*ticket collector*), Ashley Harvey (*guard*); [the hotel] Johnny Shannon (*desk porter*), Holli Hoffman (*girl*), Tim Faulkner (*manager*), Ian East (*waiter*), Sidney Johnson (*man*), Judith Nelmes (*old lady*); [the station] Bernard Hill (*Trevor Field*), Victor Romero Evans (*Robert*), Chris Tummings (*Conrad*), Victoria Williams (*girl at kiosk*), Jane Palmer (*prostitute*), Myrtle Devenish (*lady on telephone*); [the children] Sarah Doyle, Claudia Curran, Levan Doran, Mark Ellington, Emma Fernando, Clark Flanagan, Frankie Gould, Siobhan King, Justine Orme, Mark Rahaman (*children*)
   shooting Nov−Dec 82. Nottingham; Paddington and Victoria stations and the Great Western Hotel, London
   budget £913,000. **C4 input** £354,000 (lf/i) (39%)
   1st tx 17 May 84 (FF)
   MFB Sep 83. **V** 18 May 83
   awards 1st P, Karlovy Vary 84
   festivals Karlovy Vary 84

SACRED HEARTS
UK, 89 mins, colour
Reality Productions for Channel 4. 1984
   c ed KB. **no** 52
   p DEE DEE GLASS. **p man** Rebecca O'Brien
   d BARBARA RENNIE. **asst d** John C. Wilcox, (2nd) Nancy Platt. **continuity** Heather Storr.
casting d Anne Henderson
   sc BARBARA RENNIE
   ph DIANE TAMMES. **stills** Sarah Quill
   m DIRK HIGGINS
   ed MARTIN WALSH

   ad HILDEGARD BECHTLER
   cost des MONICA HOWE. **make-up** Mary Hillman. **hair** Wendy Rawson
   sd rec MOYA BURNS, MANDY ROSE.
sd ed Christopher Ackland. **dub mix** Peter Maxwell
   cast Anna Massey (*Sister Thomas Aquinas*), Katrin Cartlidge (*Doris Miller*), Oona Kirsch (*Maggie McLean*), Fiona Shaw (*Sister Felicity*), Anne Dyson (*Sister Perpetua*), Gerard Murphy (*Father Larkin*), Annette Badland (*Sister Mercy*), Sadie Wearing (*Mary*), Ann-Marie Gwatkin (*Lizzie*), Kathy Burke (*Tillie*), Jenna Russell (*Kate*), Murray Melvin (*Father Power*), John Bett (*Dr Taylor*), Nicholas Donovan (*Major Manley*), Fred Bryant (*Warden Rodgers*), Catherine Terris (*Miss Blundell*), Alan Renwick (*1st tommy*), Kevin Quarmby (*2nd tommy*), Cyril Appleton (*plumber*), Ian Staples (*German soldier*), Trudy Howson (*1st nun*), Elizabeth Rider (*2nd nun*), Richard Bebb (*radio announcer*)
   shooting Jul−Aug 84. St Martha's Convent, Barnet; St Edmund's College, Ware; West London; Frinton; Clacton on Sea
   budget £601,000. **C4 input** £559,000 (lf/i) (93%)
   1st tx 16 May 85 (FF)
   V 26 Dec 84
   awards Performance A (joint) (Anna Massey), Royal TV Soc As 86. Blue Riband, American F & Video Festival 86
   festivals London 84; Montreal, Mill Valley, Haifa 85; Göteborg, Madrid, Créteil, Vancouver, American F & Video 86; Genoa 87; Milan 88; Antenna 89

SACRIFICATIO *see* **THE SACRIFICE**

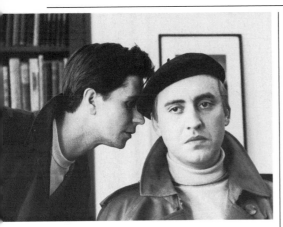

Prick Up Your Ears

P'Tang, Yang, Kipperbang

THE SACRIFICE
Sweden/France/UK, 149 mins, colour/b&w
The Swedish Film Institute (Stockholm) and
Argos Films (Paris) with Channel 4 (London)
and Josephson & Nykvist, SVT and Sandrew
Film & Teater (Stockholm) and the
participation of the French Ministry of
Culture. © Svenska Filminstitutet 1986
  c ed DR. **no** 62
  p ANNA-LENA WIBOM (Swedish Film
Institute). **p man** Katinka Faragó (Faragó
Film), Göran Lindberg. **collaborators** Jan
Lindeström, Peter Schildt, Caterina
Åhlander, Stig Björkman, Harald Stjerne
  d ANDREI TARKOVSKY. **asst d** Kerstin
Eriksdotter, (post-p) Michal Leszczylowski.
continuity Anne von Sydow. **casting**
Priscilla John, Claire Denis, Françoise
Menidrey
  sc ANDREI TARKOVSKY. **translations** Lars
Erik Blomqvist, Håkan Lövgren
  ph SVEN NYKVIST. **stills** Arne Carlsson
  m Bach's St Matthew Passion, 'Erbarme
dich', Wolfgang Gönnenwein, Julia Hamari;
calling chants from Dalarna and Härjedalen,
Elin Lisslass, Karin Edwards Johansson,
Tjugmyr Maria Larsson; syakuhachi music
from the Watazumido-Ryuso, hotchiku flute,
'Shingetsu' [New Moon], 'Nezasa no
Shirabe' [Sound of Small Bamboo], 'Dai
Bosatsu' [Buddha]
  ed ANDREI TARKOVSKY, MICHAL
LESZCZYLOWSKI
  ad ANNA ASP
  ward INGER PEHRSSON. **make-up/wigs**
Kjell Gustavsson, Florence Fouquier
  sp eff (Svenska Stuntgruppen) LARS
HÖGLUND, LARS PALMQVIST
  sd/mix OWE SVENSSON; Bo Persson, Lars
Ulander, Christin Loman, Wille

Peterson-Berger
  cast Erland Josephson (*Alexander*), Susan
Fleetwood (*Adelaide*), Allan Edwall (*Otto*),
Gudrún S. Gísladóttir (*Maria*), Sven Wollter
(*Victor*), Valérie Mairesse (*Julia*), Filippa
Franzén (*Marta*), Tommy Kjellqvist (*little
boy*), Per Källman, Tommy Nordahl
(*ambulance men*); Tintin Andersson,
Helena Brodin, Birgit Carlstén, Jane
Friedmann, Martin Lindström, Jan-Olof
Strandberg (*voices*)
  shooting Gotland; Swedish Film Institute
studio, Stockholm
  budget £1,831,000. **C4 input** £275,000 (lf)
(15%)
  1st tx 18 Feb 89 (FF)
  MFB Jan 87. **V** 14 May 86
  awards Special Jury P, Best Artistic
Contribution (Sven Nykvist), International
Critics' P, Cannes 86. Best Foreign Language
F, BAFTA F As 88
  festivals Cannes, London 86
  Swedish release title *Offret* (subtitled
Sacrificatio)

SAMMY AND ROSIE GET LAID
UK/USA, 101 mins, colour
Working Title (London) for Cinecom
(New York), British Screen and Channel 4.
© Sammy and Rosie 1987
  c ed KB. **no** 101
  p TIM BEVAN, SARAH RADCLYFFE. **p co-ord**
Sarah Cellan-Jones. **p man** Jane Frazer
  d STEPHEN FREARS. **asst d** Guy Travers,
(2nd) Andrew Wood. **sc sup** Penny Eyles.
casting d Debbie McWilliams, (US) Bonnie
Finnegan
  sc HANIF KUREISHI
  ph OLIVER STAPLETON. **stills** Mike Laye
  m STANLEY MYERS. **m co-ord** Ray

Red Monarch

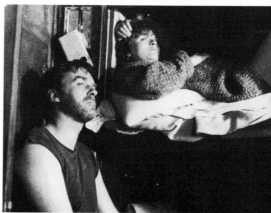

Reefer and the Model

Williams, (source) Charlie Gillett. **solo trumpet** Guy Barker
 ed MICK AUDSLEY
 pd HUGO LUCZYC-WYHOWSKI. **ad** David McHenry
 cost des BARBARA KIDD. **make-up** Elaine Carew. **hair** Paolo Mantini
 title des Julian Rothenstein
 stunt co-ord GARETH MILNE
 sd rec ALBERT BAILEY. **sd ed** 'Budge' Tremlett, (dial) Jupiter Sen. **dub mix** Peter Maxwell
 cast Shashi Kapoor (*Rafi Rahman*), Frances Barber (*Rosie*), Claire Bloom (*Alice*), Ayub Khan Din (*Sammy*), Roland Gift (*Danny*), Wendy Gazelle (*Anna*), Badi Uzzaman (*ghost*), Suzette Llewellyn (*Vivia*), Meera Syal (*Rani*), Tessa Wojtczak (*Bridget*), Emer Gillespie (*Eva*), Lesley Manville (*Margy*), Mark Sproston (*young policeman*), Cynthia Powell (*woman in kitchen*), Dennis Conlon (*Asian shopkeeper*), Megumi Shimanuki (*Japanese woman*), Buster Bloodvessle (*Angerman*), Peter Kelly (*property developer*), Carol Frazer (*property developer's wife*), Nicholas Pritchard (*Tory MP*), Valerie Buchanan (*Danny's girlfriend*), Allister Bain (*father*), Cleo Sylvestre (*mother*), Freddie Brooks (*son*), Maurice D. Iley (*gardener's boy*), Tariq Alibai (*Asian accountant*), Patrick David (*deaf young man*), Paul Daley (*Danny's boy*), Agnes Laye (*Eva's baby*), Adé Supara (*Michael*), Gerard Horan (*restaurant manager*), Anne Wood, Anna Hemery (*Pizzicata Sisters*), Allan Adebisi (*drag artiste*), Danny Brown, David Williamson, Brian Edwards, Kevin Dunkley (*Ghetto Lites*), Rudi Davies, Delphi Newman, Seamus Fulcher, Leroy Franklin Dublin, Jason Gerald Myers, James Brent Harris, Peter

Gilbert, Sara Brookes, Lawrence Speyer, Olivia Guerin, Roy O'Shea, Lydie Drouillet, Jer & Wanda Gurzynska (*straggly kids*), Jude Alderson, Judith Scott, Jane Gurnett, Paulette Randall, Siddig El Fadil, Winston Crooke, Ella Wilder, Ronan Vibert, Shaheen Khan, Elena Loizedes, George Dillon, Bev Willis (*party guests*), Colin MacCabe (*semiotics lecturer*)
 shooting Mar–Apr 87. London; Twickenham studios
 budget £1,370,000. **C4 input** £400,000 (lf) (29%)
 1st tx 8 Mar 90 (FF)
 MFB Jan 88. **V** 16 Sep 87
 festivals Toronto, Vancouver, London 87

SANS TOIT NI LOI *see* **VAGABONDE**

SECRETS
UK, 75 mins, colour
Enigma Television/Goldcrest Films & Television for Channel 4. © Samuel Montagu & Co 1982
 c ed DR. **no** 14
 p CHRIS GRIFFIN. **exec p** DAVID PUTTNAM. **assoc p** David Bill
 d GAVIN MILLAR. **asst d** Dominic Fulford; Andrew Montgomery, Russell Lodge.
 continuity Pat Rambaut. **casting d** Joyce Gallie
 sc NOELLA SMITH. **sc ed** Jack Rosenthal
 ph CHRISTOPHER CHALLIS. **cam op** Freddie Cooper. **stills** Douglas Dawson
 m/cond GUY WOOLFENDEN
 ed ERIC BOYD-PERKINS
 ad JEFFREY WOODBRIDGE
 cost des TUDOR GEORGE. **make-up** Elaine Carew. **hair** Maureen Hannaford-Nesbitt
 sd rec CHRIS MUNRO, OTTO SNEL. **sd ed**

Reflections

Remembrance

Chris Greenham

  cast Helen Lindsay (*Gwen Gibbs*), John Horsley (*Dr Jefferies*), Anna Campbell-Jones (*Louise Gibbs*), Daisy Cockburn (*Sidney*), Rebecca Johnson (*Jane 'Trottie' Barrington*), Lucy Goode (*Jane Williams*), Richard Tolan (*Paul*), Carol Gillies (*Miss Quick*), Jane Briers (*Miss Strickland*), Judith Fellows (*elderly teacher*), Georgine Anderson (*matron*), Cynthia Grenville (*Miss Johnson*), Elizabeth Choice (*Miss Jones-Wallace*), Matyelock Gibbs (*Miss Lane*), Nancy Manningham (*Miss Lightfoot*), Peter Scott Harrison, Craig Stokes, Robert Stagg, Paul Gamble (*boys on train*), Sarah Bennet, Lisa Hawkins, Michelle Hooper, Dawn Andrews, Kelly Conway, Victoria Griffiths, Tara Rodway, Louisa Howard, Lucinda Platt, Antonia Clanchy, Caroline Downer, Rosalind Archer, Katherine Franklin Adams, Jennifer Toksvig, Rachel Gassin, Vanessa Jeffcoat, Ann Roberts, Abalene Gould, Justine Page, Cipriana Da Silva, Tina De Bono, Ann Mansard, Amelia Dipple, Lisa Mareca, Jacqui Cryer, Frances Geary (*schoolgirls*)

  shooting Oct–Dec 82

  budget £486,000. **C4 input** £200,000 (lf) (41%)

  1st tx 12 May 83 (FF: 'First Love')

  V 15 Aug 84

SHADEY
UK, 106 mins, colour
Larkspur Films. © Film Four International 1985

  c ed DR/KB. **no** 49

  p OTTO PLASCHKES. **p co-ord** Kelly Howard-Garde. **p man** Paul Sparrow

  d PHILIP SAVILLE. **asst d** Guy Travers, (2nd) Chris Thompson. **sc sup**

Francine Brown

  sc SNOO WILSON

  ph ROGER DEAKINS. **cam op** Andrew Speller. **stills** Peter Kernot

  m COLIN TOWNS. **orchestra cond** Alan H. Wilson. **song** Jonathan Perkins

  ed CHRIS KELLY

  pd NORMAN GARWOOD. **ad** Keith Pain

  cost des TUDOR GEORGE. **make-up** Sandra Exelby. **hair** Michael Lockey

  sp eff GEORGE GIBBS, TERRY COX

  sd mix SANDY MACRAE. **dub ed** Anthony Sloman. **re-rec mix** Dean Humphreys

  cast Anthony Sher (*Oliver Shadey*), Billie Whitelaw (*Dr Cloud*), Patrick Macnee (*Sir Cyril Landau*), Katherine Helmond (*Lady Constance Landau*), Leslie Ash (*Carol Landau*), Bernard Hepton (*Captain Amies*), Larry Lamb (*Dick Darnley*), Jesse Birdsall (*Carl*), Olivier Pierre (*Manson*), Jon Cartwright (*Paul Shulman*), Stephen Persaud (*Winston*), Basil Henson (*bishop*), Peter Kelly (*Russian chauffeur*), Madhav Sharma (*male orator*), Susan Engel (*female orator*), Zohra Segal (*Indian cleaning lady*), Jenny Runacre (*diamond dealer*), Jane Myerson (*Penelope*), Gillian de Tourville (*hotel girl*), Zabou (*hotel maid*), Bill Bingham (*TV interviewer*), Andrew Bradford (*thief*), Rita Keegan (*minder*), Simon Prebble (*hotel manager*), Jonathan Scott-Taylor (*Arthur*), Melody Howe (*hoola-hoop girl*), Jonathan Perkins, Silver Spurs (*video pop group*)

  shooting Oct–Nov 84. London

  budget £959,000. **C4 input** £959,000 (lf/i) (100%)

  1st tx 28 Apr 88 (FF)

  MFB May 86. **V** 11 Dec 85

  festivals London 85; Göteborg, Brussels, Durban, Sorrento 86; Antenna 89

Rita, Sue and Bob too

The Road Home

SHARMA AND BEYOND
UK, 80 mins, colour
Enigma Television/Goldcrest Films &
Television for Channel 4. © Goldcrest
Television 1984
　c ed DR. **no** 27
　p CHRIS GRIFFIN. **exec p** DAVID PUTTNAM.
p man David Barron
　d BRIAN GILBERT. **asst d** Andrew
Montgomery; Russell Lodge, Richard
Coleman. **continuity** Susi Oldroyd. **casting
d** Joyce Gallie
　sc BRIAN GILBERT. **sc sup** [**sc ed**] Susan
Richards
　ph ERNEST VINCZE. **cam op** Michael
Anderson. **stills** Stephen Morley
　m RACHEL PORTMAN
　ed MAX LEMON
　ad MAURICE CAIN
　ward sup PHILIPPE PICKFORD. **make-up**
Madeleine Masters. **hair** Alison Hall
　sd rec DAVID CROZIER. **sd ed** Mark
Auguste. **dub mix** Hugh Strain
　cast Michael Maloney (*Stephen Archer*),
Suzanne Burden (*Natasha Gorley-Peters*),
Robert Urquhart (*Evan Gorley-Peters*),
Benjamin Whitrow (*Anton Heron*), Tom
Wilkinson (*Vivian Archer*), Antonia
Pemberton (*Myrna*), Bernice Stegers
(*Gabriella*), Takashi Kawahara (*Mr Sung*),
Francisco Moralles (*Francisco*), Daniel
Wozniak, Yasher Adem, Lutfi Oguz, Sofia
Walkiewicz, Swee Hoe Lim (*students*),
Katherine Best (*punk girl*), Hugh Quarshie
(*man on stairs*)
　shooting Oct 83. Warwick; W London
　budget £529,000. **C4 input** £240,000 (lf)
(45%)
　1st tx 24 May 84 (FF: 'First Love')
　V 15 Jan 86

SHE'LL BE WEARING PINK PYJAMAS
UK, 90 mins, colour
Pink Pyjama Productions for Channel 4.
© Channel 4 TV Co 1984
　c ed KB/DR. **no** 50
　p TARA PREM, ADRIAN HUGHES. **assoc p**
David McFarlane. **p man** Gregory Dark
　d JOHN GOLDSCHMIDT. **asst d** Gregory
Dark; Terry Pearce, Tim Coddington. **2nd
unit d** Richard Key. **continuity** Sarah
Hayward. **casting d** Ann Fielden
　sc EVA HARDY
　ph CLIVE TICKNER. **2nd unit cam** John
Davey. **stills** David Morse
　m/cond JOHN DU PREZ. **m perf** The
Philharmonia Orchestra
　ed RICHARD KEY
　pd COLIN POCOCK
　cost des SUE SNELL. **make-up** Maureen
Stephenson. **hair** Patti Smith
　stunt double Dorothy Ford
　sd rec PAUL FILBY. **sd mix** Terry Hardy.
dub ed Graham Whitlock. **dub mix** Tony
Anscombe
　cast Julie Walters (*Fran*), Anthony Higgins
(*Tom*), Jane Evers (*Catherine*), Janet Henfrey
(*Lucy*), Paula Jacobs (*Doreen*), Penelope
Nice (*Ann*), Maureen O'Brien (*Joan*), Alyson
Spiro (*Anita*), Jane Wood (*Jude*), Pauline
Yates (*Diane*), Bill Lund (*Bill*), Paul
Butterworth, Nicky Putnam (*instructors*),
Paul Atkinson, Gail Herring (*kids on bikes*)
　shooting Eskdale Green, Cumberland
　budget £1,005,000. **C4 input** £955,000
(lf/i) (95%)
　1st tx 12 Mar 87 (FF)
　MFB Jun 85. **V** 15 May 85
　festivals Filmotsav India, Antwerp,
Madrid, Durban, Cherbourg, Boario Terme
86; Antenna 89

A Room with a View

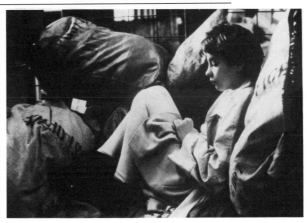

Runners

SHOOTING STARS
UK/FGR, 90 mins, colour
Viva Pictures with Granada Television and
NDR (Hamburg) for Channel 4. © 1990
  c ed KB. **no** 136
  p DAVID JONES. **exec p** JOHN
GOLDSCHMIDT. **assoc p** William Sargent.
p man Liam Foster
  d CHRIS BERNARD. **asst d** Chris Newman,
(2nd) Keith Young. **continuity** Helen
Emerson. **casting** Janet Goddard
  sc BARRY HINES from an idea by Dixie
Williams. **st ed** Sue McGregor
  ph WITOLD STOK. **cam op** Rodrigo
Gutierrez
  m GILLIAN GILBERT, STEPHEN MORRIS
  ed ANTHONY HAM
  pd MIKE GRIMES
  graphic des Keith Aldred
  cost des INEZ NORDELL. **make-up** Jane
Hatch
  sd rec PHIL SMITH. **sd ed** Peter Deakin. **dub
mix** Andy Wyatt
  cast Helmut Griem (*Karl Gutke*), Sharon
Duce (*Paula Gibson*), Jane Hazlegrove
(*Alison Connor*), Fiona Allen (*Christine*),
Caroline Joynt (*Sue, Alison's mum*), Chris
Hargreaves (*Gary Gibson*), Frank Lauder
(*Sean Gibson*), John Brobbey (*Vic*), Keith
Allen (*Bob Southgate*), David Ross (*Jim
Price*), Gary McDonald (*Calvin Clarke*),
Thomas Craig (*Paul Reid*), Vinnie Adams,
Paul Byron (*City players*), Stephen Lord
(*Simmons*), Richard Cole (*City director*),
Simon Bleackley (*shop manager*), Stratford
Johns (*Mr Groves*), Pat Mills (*cleaner*), Denis
Conlon (*'Millionaire' club owner*), Louise
Duprey (*Zoe*), Jeremy Phillips (*Tony*), Roger
Phillips-Davis (*drunk*), Gary Brown (*Robert*),
Kim Johnson (*hotel receptionist*), June Hoy

(*woman in pub*), Fiona Purvis, Devika
Wilson, Kamara Wynter (*girls at bus
station*), John Pickles (*lost-property man*),
Marie Jelliman (*reporter*), Anthony Hall (*Mr
Ali*), Ian Mercer (*Detective Stone*), Mark
Moraghan (*Detective Miller*), Ozzie Yue
(*chip shop owner*), Metin Yenal (*Hamburg
coach*), Michael Mellinger (*Hamburg
chairman*), Tricia Penrose (*'Millionaire' club
woman*)
  shooting Nov–Dec 89. Manchester
  budget £800,000. **C4 input** £350,000 (lf/i)
(44%)
  1st tx 17 May 90 (FF)

SINGLETON'S PLUCK
UK, 93 mins, colour
Greenpoint Films for Channel 4. 1984
  c ed DR. **no** 45
  p ANN SCOTT. **exec p** SIMON RELPH. **p
co-ord** Roxy Glassford. **p man** Paul Sparrow
  d RICHARD EYRE. **asst d** Ian Madden, (2nd)
Gus MacLean. **sc sup** Angela Allen. **casting
d** Susie Figgis
  sc BRIAN GLOVER
  ph CLIVE TICKNER. **stills** Sophie Baker
  m DOMINIC MULDOWNEY
  ad JAMIE LEONARD
  ed DAVID MARTIN
  cost des LINDY HEMMING. **make-up** Pat
Hay. **hair** Liz Michie
  title des Richard Morrison
  sd rec DAVID STEPHENSON. **dub ed** Richard
Dunford. **dub mix** Alan Dykes
  cast Ian Holm (*Ben Singleton*), Penelope
Wilton (*Alice Singleton*), Richard Hope
(*Hubert*), Bill Owen (*Amos*), C. J. Allen
(*Len*), Norman Fisher (*Derek*), Cherie Laine,
Denise Summers (*chicken factory girls*),
Stephanie Tague (*Emma Singleton*), Kenneth

Sacred Hearts

The Sacrifice

MacDonald (*Peter Armitage*), Barbara
Burgess (*Hubert's granny*), Ben White
(*Rollo*), Tim Seely (*landowner*), Johnny
Golde (*cowman*), Patrick Drury (*David
Wolmer*), Rosemary Martin (*continuity girl*),
Stephen Moore (*Howard*), Stephen Phillips
(*TV presenter*), Gillian Barge (*Gwen*), Steve
Vicker (*Telecom driver*), Aran Bell
(*Tristram*), Tim Sterne (*car driver*), Ken Ives
(*TV editor*), Patrick Connor (*policeman*),
Tommy Wright, Dave Atkins (*Smithfield
poultry dealers*), Eric Richard (*Basil*), Pearl
Hackney (*pub landlady*)
   shooting Feb–Mar 84. Norfolk; Suffolk;
London
   budget £750,000. **C4 input** £715,000 (lf/i)
(95%)
   1st tx 12 Dec 85 (FF)
   MFB Aug 84. **V** 11 Jul 84
   awards 1st P (joint), TV F section, Venice
84
   festivals Venice 84; Toronto 85;
Vancouver 86
   UK release title *Laughterhouse*

SMACK AND THISTLE
UK, 90 mins, colour
WTTV [Working Title Films] for Channel 4.
© Channel 4 1990
   c ed KB. **no** 162
p SARAH CELLAN-JONES, ALISON JACKSON.
p co-ord Winnie Wishart
   d TUNDE IKOLI. **asst d** Waldo Roeg, (2nd)
Max Keene. **sc sup** Glenys Davies. **casting d**
Suzanne Crowley, Gilly Poole
   sc TUNDE IKOLI
   ph PETER SINCLAIR. **stills** Christine Parry
   m/m arr COLIN TOWNS
   ed ANGUS NEWTON
   pd HUGO LUCZYC-WYHOWSKI.

ad Frank Walsh
   cost des SHEELAGH KILLEEN. **make-up des**
Fae Hammond
   sp eff sup ALAN WHIBLEY
   stunt co-ord JIM DOWDALL
   title des Tracy Drew
   sd rec ALBERT BAILEY. **sd ed** Andrew Glen.
dub mix Peter Maxwell
   cast Charlie Caine (*Abel Rose*), Rosalind
Bennett (*Elizabeth Wimbol*), Patrick
Malahide (*Terence Dirk-Brown*), Connie
Booth (*Ms Kane*), Rudolph Walker
(*Churchill*), John Elmes (*Edward Tulip*),
James Saxon (*Henry Wilks*), Geoffrey Palmer
(*Sir Horace Wimbol*), Trevor Laird (*Baron
Greenback*), Thomas Craig (*Spikey*), Robin
Summers (*Bill*), Peter McNamara (*Ben*),
Steve Sweeney (*Ariel*), Walter Sparrow
(*Waggy*), Yemi Ajibade (*Pedro*), Gina McKee
(*Lucy Lisle*), Jane Wood (*Mildred*), Lloyd
Anderson (*Walter*), Ann Morrish (*Lady
Wimbol*), Paul Stacey (*Justin*), Cindy
O'Callaghan (*Marlene*), Jim Barclay (*man in
wine bar*), Paul Arlington (*drunk*), Brian Hall
(*detective*), Ron Davies (*desk sergeant*), Ade
Ikoli, Nicola Ikoli (*Mildred's children*)
   shooting Oct–Nov 89. London
   budget £978,000. **C4 input** £873,000 (lf/i)
(89%)
   1st tx 19 May 91 (FF)
   SS May 91

SMOKE *see* **MEANTIME**

A SONG FOR EUROPE
UK/FRG/Austria/Switzerland, 95 mins,
colour
Stern TV (Hamburg) for Channel 4 and
ZDF (Mainz), ORF (Vienna) and SRG (Bern).
© Channel 4 UK/ZDF/ORF/SRG 1985

Sammy and Rosie Get Laid

Secrets

c ed DR. **no** 54
exec p JOHANN HINRICH GERHARD. **assoc p**
Renee Goddard. **p sup** Klaus D. Zeisberg.
p man Andrä Kubaile
d JOHN GOLDSCHMIDT. **asst d** Caspar
Heidelbach. **sc sup** Trudy von Trotha
 sc PETER PRINCE
 ph WOLFGANG TREU. **stills** Eduard Rieben
 m/cond CARL DAVIS
 ed RICHARD KEY
 ad INGO TÖGEL, MATHIAS MATTHIES,
(Switzerland) MAX STUBENRAUCH
 cost REGINA BÄTZ. **make-up** Gerlinde
Kunz
 sd rec TERRY HARDY
 cast David Suchet (*Steven Dyer*), Maria
Schneider (*Madeleine Dyer*), Anne-Marie
Blanc (*grandmother*), Reinhard Glemnitz
(*Dieter Weigel*), Georges Claisse (*François
Dutourd*), Dietmar Schönherr (*Dr Christian
Junger*), Robert Freitag (*Commissioner
Moser*), Michael Gempart (*Ehrli*), Jürgen
Brügger (*Dr Bauer*), Giovanno Vettorazzo
(*Giuseppe Soncini*), Manfred Reddemann
(*Henze*), Inigo Gallo (*captain*), Ernst
Schröder (*Herr Director*), Laura Jansen,
Vincent Jansen (*Dyer children*), Brigitta
Furgler, Frank Lenart, Sebastian C.
Schröder, Rudolf Ruf, Siegfried Kernen, Fritz
Hammer
 shooting Basle and Lonhof Prison, Basle;
Milan; Belgium; London
 budget £898,000. **C4 input** £454,000 (i)
(51%)
 1st tx 23 May 85 (FF)
 V 4 Sep 85
 awards Performance A (joint) (David
Suchet), Royal TV Society As 86
 festivals Vancouver, Chicago 85
 European release title *Ein Lied für Europa*

SPEAKING PARTS
Canada/Italy/UK, 92 mins, colour
Ego Film Arts (Toronto) with Academy
Pictures (Rome) and Channel 4 and the
participation of Téléfilm Canada and the
Ontario Film Development Corporation
(Toronto). © Speaking Parts 1989
 c ed KB. **no** 160
 line p/p man CAMELIA FRIEBERG. **exec p**
(Europe) DON RANVAUD. **p co-ord** Bill
Sweetman
 d ATOM EGOYAN. **asst d** David Webb, (2nd)
Cynthia Gillespie. **sc sup** Monika Gagnon.
casting (co-ord) Rose Gutierrez
 sc ATOM EGOYAN. **sc ed** Allen Bell
 ph PAUL SAROSSY. **stills** Johnnie Eisen. **24
frame video op** Cliff Lopes. **video co-ord** Bill
Sweetman
 m MYCHAEL DANNA
 ed BRUCE MCDONALD. **co-ed** Atom Egoyan
 ad LINDA DEL ROSARIO
 ward co-ord MAUREEN DEL DEGAN.
make-up Nicole Demers. **hair** Moira Verwijk
 sd rec JOHN MEGILL. **sd ed** Steven Munro.
dial ed Michael Werth. **re-rec mix** Daniel
Pellerin
 cast Michael McManus (*Lance*), Arsinée
Khanjian (*Lisa*), Gabrielle Rose (*Clara*), Frank
Tata (*Clara's brother*), Tony Nardi (*Eddy*),
David Hemblen (*the producer*), Patricia
Collins (*the housekeeper*), Gerard Parkes
(*the father*), Jackie Samuda (*Trish, the bride*),
Peter Krantz (*Ronnie, the groom*), Patrick
Tierney (*man in video store*), Robert Dodds
(*the doctor*), Leszek Lis (*the housekeeper's
pet*), Sharon Corder (*voice of hotel
management*), David MacKay (*man at party*)
 shooting Toronto
 budget £600,000. **C4 input** £75,000 (lf)
(13%)

Shadey

Sharma and Beyond

1st tx 1 Sep 91 (FF)
MFB Sep 89. **V** 10 May 89
festivals Cannes, Edinburgh, Shonan,
London 89; Calcutta, Hong Kong 90

DER SPIEGEL *see* **THE MIRROR**

SQUARING THE CIRCLE
UK/USA, 105 mins, colour
TVS with Metromedia Producers
Corporation and Britannic Film & Television
for Channel 4. © TVS 1984
    c ed DR. **no** 28
    p FREDERICK BROGGER. **exec p** PETER
SNELL, STEPHEN SCHLOW. **assoc p** Ted Lloyd
    d MIKE HODGES. **asst d** Roy Stevens, (2nd)
Kieron Phipps. **continuity** Angela Allen.
casting Debbie McWilliams
    sc TOM STOPPARD
    ph MICHAEL GARFATH. **cam op** Gerry
Dunkley. **stills** Graham Attwood
    m ROY BUDD
    ed JOHN BLOOM, ERIC BOYD-PERKINS
    pd VOYTEK. **ad** Bryan Graves
    ward sup DEREK HYDE. **make-up** Graham
Freeborn. **hair** Barbara Ritchie
    sp eff MARTIN GUTTERIDGE
    sd rec CHRISTOPHER MUNRO. **sd ed** Chris
Greenham. **eff ed** Norman Cole. **dub mix**
Graham V. Hartstone
    cast Bernard Hill (*Lech Walesa*), Alec
McCowen (*Rakowski*), Roy Kinnear (*Kania*),
John Woodvine (*Gierek*), Richard Kane
(*Jaruzelski*), Don Henderson (*Kuron*), Frank
Middlemass (*Brezhnev*), John Bluthal
(*Babiuch*), Richard Crenna (*the Narrator*),
Vovka Ashkenazy (*the Pianist*), Bob
Cartland (*Szydiak*), Peter Bayliss
(*Barcikowski*), Gary Waldhorn (*Jagielski*),
Matthew Long (*Szozopanski*), Gordon

Costelow (*Mazowiecki*), Bill McCabe
(*Finanski*), Philip Raymond (*Geremek*),
Martin Wyldeck (*Olszowski*), Henry Moxon
(*Cardinal Wyszynski*), Janet Dale (*Danuta*),
John Rogan (*Jurczyk*), Michael N. Harbour
(*Lis*), George Waring (*Aristov*), Colin Jeavons
(*Glemp*), Robert Percival (*Jablonski*), Tom
Wilkinson (*Rulewski*), Jonathan Adams
(*Gwiazda*), Robin Summers (*Bujak*), Robert
Bridges (*Kulikov*), John Antrobus (*1st
witness*), Mark Dignam (*2nd witness*), Leon
Lissek (*3rd witness*), Anthony May (*4th
witness*), James Warrior (*5th witness*)
    shooting Oct–Nov 83. Pinewood studios
    budget £1,029,000. **C4 input** £330,000 (lf)
(32%)
    1st tx 31 May 84 (FF)
    awards Gold A, New York 84
    festivals New York 84

STRAWBERRY FIELDS
FGR/UK/Austria, 95 mins, colour
Marten Taege Productions (Wiesbaden) for
ZDF (Mainz), Channel 4 and ORF (Vienna).
1984
    c ed KB/DR. **no** (-)
    p MARTEN TAEGE
    d KRISTIAN KÜHN
    sc STEPHEN POLIAKOFF, KRISTIAN KÜHN
adapted from the play by Stephen Poliakoff
    ph MARTIN SCHÄFER; Peter Harvey
    m EBERHARD WEBER
    des ALEXANDER MEISEL
    cast Beate Jensen (*Charlotte*), Rolf Zacher
(*Karl Gellert*), Thomas Schücke (*Nicki*), Lisa
Kreuzer (*Frau Ruprecht*), Wolfgang Wahl
(*long-distance driver*), Iris Disse, Dieter
Traier, Hans Hildebrandt, Thomas Stiller,
Jutta Winkelmann, Andy Danz, Angelika
Huber

She'll Be Wearing Pink Pyjamas

Shooting Stars

shooting summer 84
budget £125,000. **C4 input** £25,000 (lf)
(20%)
1st tx 20 Mar 86 (FF from Germany)
V 28 Aug 85
German release title *Die doppelte Welt*

SUCCESS IS THE BEST REVENGE
UK/France, 91 mins, colour
De Vere Studio (London) and Gaumont
(Neuilly-sur-Seine) for Channel 4. © The
Emerald Film Partnership 1984
c ed DR. **no** 46
p JERZY SKOLIMOWSKI. **assoc p** Simon
Bosanquet, Barry Vince. **p man** Simon
Bosanquet, (Paris) Jean-Louis Piel
d JERZY SKOLIMOWSKI. **asst d** Chris Rose,
(2nd) John Dodds. **2nd unit d** Andrzej
Kostenko. **continuity** Ené Watts. **casting d**
Debbie McWilliams, Michelle Guish
sc JERZY SKOLIMOWSKI, MICHAEL LYNDON.
addit script material Michel Ciment, Harriet
Pacaud, Barbara Elster
ph MIKE FASH. **cam op** John Golding. **stills**
Clive Coote
m STANLEY MYERS, HANS ZIMMER. **piano**
soloist Margaret Stachiewicz. **bass soloist**
Barry Guy
ed BARRY VINCE
pd VOYTEK. **ad** David Minty. **drawings**
Feliks Topolski
cost des SUSAN YELLAND. **make-up** Connie
Reeve. **hair** Marsha Lewis
sp eff sup JOHN EVANS
sd rec CLIVE WINTER. **sd ed** Mike Crowley,
(dial) Jim Roddan. **dub mix** Richard King
cast Michael York (*Aleksander Rodak*),
Joanna Szczerbic (*Alicja Rodak*), Michael
Lyndon (*Adam Rodak*), Jerry Skol (*Tony
Rodak*), Michel Piccoli (*government official*),

Anouk Aimée (*Monique des Fontaines*),
John Hurt (*Dino Montecurva*), Ric Young
(*Chinese waiter*), Claude Le Sache (*M
Conio*), Malcolm Sinclair (*deputy stage
manager*), Hilary Drake (*stage manager*),
Jane Asher (*bank manager*), Adam French
(*Martin*), Sam Smart (*Mallett*), Tim Brown
(*teacher*), Maribel Jones (*Maribel*), Mike
Sarne (*shop attendant*), Maureen Bennett
(*BA girl*), Martyn Whitby (*amusement arcade
attendant*), Bill Monks (*1st theatre
workman*), Rory Edwards (*2nd theatre
workman*), Archie Pool (*Casius Banghali*),
Robert Whelan (*mounted policeman*), Suzan
Crowley (*1st building inspector*), Tristram
Jellinek (*2nd building inspector*), Ralph
Nossek (*magistrate*), Colin Bennett (*usher*),
Felicity Dean (*TV director*), Guy Deghy
(*angry old man*), Eugeniusz Hackiewicz
(*Genio*), Stella Maris (*Spanish woman*), Luis
Pinilla (*Spanish man*), Witold Bujak, Robert
Gac, Jerzy Maslak, Marek Olbrycht, Marek
Szularz, Tadeusz Dembinski, Slawomir
Kowalski, Jerzy Muszka, Pawel Skibinski,
Marek Wilkus, Jaroslaw Sobik (*Polonia
Kensington football team*), Gabor Vernon,
Perry Fenwick, Hatti Riemer
shooting Jan–Feb 84. London; Paris
budget £983,000. **C4 input** £280,000 (lf)
(28%)
1st tx 26 Jun 86 (FF)
MFB Dec 84. **V** 23 May 84
festivals Cannes, London 84

SUMMER LIGHTNING
UK/Eire, 90 mins, colour
RTE with Channel 4. © The Film Services
Partnership 1984
c ed DR. **no** 56
p MICHAEL GARVEY. **p man** Eamon Hayes

Singleton's Pluck

Smack and Thistle

d PAUL JOYCE. **asst d** Val Griffin.
continuity Laura McAuley
  sc DEREK MAHON, PAUL JOYCE from the
novel *First Love* by Ivan Turgenev
  ph PETER DORNEY. **cam op** Ronan Lee
  m DONAL LUNNY, KEITH DONALD
  ed MARTIN DUFFY
  pd JAY CLEMENTS
  cost des INEZ NORDELL. **make-up** Marese
Smyth, Shelagh Cullen
  graphic des Anne Chamberlain
  sd rec PAT MURRAY. **dub mix** Tony
McHugh
  cast Paul Scofield (*Sir Robert Clarke*),
Edward Rawle-Hicks (*young Robert*), Tom
Bell (*William Clarke*), Dearbhla Molloy
(*Elizabeth Clarke*), Leonie Mellinger (*Louise
St Leger*), Maureen Toal (*Dolly St Leger*),
David Warner (*George Millington*), Donal
McCann (*Dr Lestrange*), Jonathan Ryan
(*Noel Sheridan*), Simon Chandler (*Captain
Taylor*), Bosco Hogan (*John Mitchel*), Marie
Conmee (*Mrs Walsh*), Joe Pilkington (*Davy
Grogan*), Christopher Casson (*Paddy*), Don
Foley (*beggar*), Fiona MacAnna (*Bridie*), Pat
Leavy (*Mrs Quinn*), Kathleen Barrington
(*nun*)
  shooting Eire
  budget £201,000. **C4 input** £126,000 (lf)
(63%)
  1st tx 30 May 85 (FF)

TAXIDI STA KITHIRA *see*
VOYAGE TO CYTHERA

THOSE GLORY GLORY DAYS
UK, 90 mins, colour
Enigma Television/Goldcrest Films &
Television for Channel 4. © Goldcrest
Television 1983

c ed DR. **no** 24
  p CHRIS GRIFFIN. **exec p** DAVID PUTTNAM.
assoc p David Bill. **p man** Dominic Fulford
  d PHILIP SAVILLE. **asst d** Guy Travers,
(2nd) Russell Lodge, Richard Coleman.
continuity Francine Brown. **casting d**
Simone Reynolds
  sc JULIE WELCH. **sc ed** Jack Rosenthal
  ph PHIL MÉHEUX. **cam op** Gale Tattersall.
stills Stephen Morley
  m TREVOR JONES
  ed MAX LEMON
  ad MAURICE CAIN
  cost des TUDOR GEORGE. **make-up** Mo
Haynes. **hair** Debbie Scragg
  sd rec DAVID CROZIER. **sd ed** Rusty
Coppleman. **dub mix** Hugh Strain
  cast Zoe Nathenson (*Julia 'Danny'
Herrick*), Sara Sugarman (*Marlene 'Toni'
Salt*), Cathy Murphy (*Tub*), Liz Campion
(*Meriel 'Jailbird' Fishlock*), Amelia Dipple
(*Petrina*), Elizabeth Spriggs
(*schoolmistress*), Julia McKenzie (*Mrs
Herrick*), Peter Tilbury (*Mr Herrick*), Julia
Goodman (*Julia, journalist*), Stephen Chase
(*Petrina's dad*), Alexei Sayle (*newsagent*),
Danny Blanchflower (*himself*), Bryan Pringle
(*Reg*), John Salthouse (*young Danny
Blanchflower*), Eva Lohman (*Petrina's mum*),
Frances Barber (*woman*), Rachel Meidman
(*young Julia*), Bob Goody (*doorman*), John
Joyce (*ticket seller*), Lucy Hornak (*plummy
girl*); [the journalists] Roddy Maude-Roxby
(*Brian*), Dudley Sutton (*Arthur*), Richard
Wilson (*Arnold*), Chris Jury (*Ken*); Dai
Bradley, Patrick Bergin, Ron Donachie,
Stephen Bent, Glen Murphy, Stuart Organ,
John Judd, Jon Iles, Philip Rowlands, David
Straun (*1961 Spurs team*), Robert Armstrong,
Ronald Atkin, Peter Batt, Steve Curry, Bob

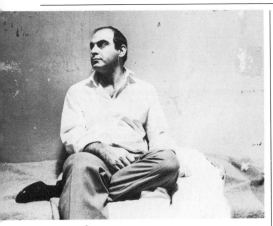

A Song for Europe

Speaking Parts

Houston, David Lacey, Colin Malam
(*gentlemen of Fleet Street*)
shooting Jun–Jul 83. London; Westfield
School, Hertfordshire
budget £581,000. **C4 input** £200,000 (lf)
(34%)
1st tx 17 Nov 83 (FF: 'First Love')
MFB Sep 84. **V** 30 Nov 83
festivals London 83

TOPIO STIN OMICHLI *see*
LANDSCAPE IN THE MIST

TREE OF HANDS
UK, 89 mins, colour
Greenpoint Films for Granada Film
Productions with British Screen and Channel
4. Assisted by the National Film
Development Fund. © Granada Film
Productions 1988
c ed KB. **no** 128
p ANN SCOTT. **assoc p** Ann Wingate.
p co-ord Pat Bryan
d GILES FOSTER. **asst d** Guy Travers, (2nd)
Chris Thompson. **sc sup** Francine Brown.
casting (UK) Sue Whatmough, (US) Deborah
Brown
sc GORDON WILLIAMS from the novel by
Ruth Rendell
ph KENNETH MACMILLAN. **cam op** Malcolm
Vinson. **stills** Sophie Baker, Simon Mein
m RICHARD HARTLEY
ed DAVID MARTIN
pd ADRIAN SMITH. **ad** Henry Harris,
Alison Stewart-Richardson
cost des BARBARA KIDD. **make-up** Jenny
Shircore. **chief hair** Meinir Jones-Lewis
graphic des Jim Stanes
stunt co-ord GARETH MILNE, ANDY
BRADFORD. **stunts** Tip Tipping, Tracey Eddon

sd rec DAVID STEPHENSON. **sd ed** Richard
Dunford. **dub mix** Peter Maxwell. **eff ed**
Jacques Leroide
cast Helen Shaver (*Benet Archdale*),
Lauren Bacall (*Marsha Archdale*), Malcolm
Stoddard (*Dr Ian Raeburn*), Peter Firth
(*Terence*), Paul McGann (*Barry*), Kate Hardie
(*Carol Stratford*), Tony Haygarth (*Kostas*),
Phyllida Law (*Julia*), David Schofield
(*detective inspector*), Amanda Dickinson
(*Molly*), Elvi Hale, Fiona McAlpine
(*neighbours*), Julie Jupp (*neighbour's
daughter*), Sean Blowers (*detective*), Allan
Mitchell (*consultant*), Simon Prebble
(*newscaster*), Barnaby Brown (*Jason*),
Charles Pountney (*James Archdale*)
shooting Feb–Apr 89. London; Cannon
Elstree studios
budget £2,000,000 [Ann Scott]. **C4 input**
£275,000 (lf) (14%)
1st tx 2 Jun 91 (FF)
MFB May 89. **V** 10 May 89

VAGABONDE
France/UK, 106 mins, colour
Ciné-Tamaris and Films A2 (Paris) with the
French Ministry of Culture, CMCC (Vitrolles)
and Channel 4. © Agnès Varda,
Ciné-Tamaris, Films A2 1985
c ed DR. **no** 69
[**p** AGNÈS VARDA.] **unit man** Oury
Milshtein. **admin** Michèle Cretel
d AGNÈS VARDA. **assts to the d** Jacques
Royer, Jacques Deschamps. **continuity**
Chantal Desanges
sc AGNÈS VARDA
ph PATRICK BLOSSIER, (asst) Pierre
Gordower. **still photographs** Y. de Fareins,
Z. Jancso, G. Le Fauconnier, E. Simard, Ph.
Terrancie (École Nationale of Arles)

Squaring the Circle

Strawberry Fields

m JOANNA BRUZDOWICZ
ed AGNÈS VARDA, PATRICIA MAZUY
sets JEAN BAUER, ANNE VIOLET
sd JEAN-PAUL MUGEL. **mix** Jean-François Auger. **sd eff** Gilbert Nottin
cast Sandrine Bonnaire (*Simone Bergeron, Mona sans toit ni loi*), Setti Ramdane (*the Moroccan who finds her*), Francis Balchère (*a policeman*), Jean-Louis Perletti (*another*), Urbain Causse (*a peasant who is questioned*), Christophe Alcazar (*another, a ditch-burner*), Dominique Durand (*the 1st motorcyclist*), Joël Fosse (*the other, Paulo, Yolande's lover*), Patrick Schmit (*the truckdriver*), Daniel Bos (*the demolition man*), Katy Champaud (*the girl at the pump*), Raymond Roulle (*the old man with matches*), Henri Fridiani (*the gravedigger*), Patrick Sokol (*the young man with a sandwich*), Pierre Imbert (*the garage-keeper*), Richard Imbert (*his son*), Marthe Jarnais (*old Aunt Lydie*), Yolande Moreau (*Yolande, her maid*), Gabriel Mariani (*Yolande's uncle Aimé B-I-O-N-N-E-T*), Patrick Lepczynski (*David, the wandering Jew*), Sylvain, Sabine (*shepherds*), Michèle Doumèche (*the p . . . by the roadside*), Pierrette Soler (*the woman talking to her husband*), Macha Méril (*Mme Landier the specialist in plane trees*), Pierre Emonnot (*the angry foreman*), Stéphane Freiss (*Jean-Pierre, the agronomist*), Laurence Cortadellas (*his wife Eliane*), Emmanuel Protopopoff (*the donor at the mobile blood bank*), Vincent Sanchez (*the nurse*), 'Garibaldi' Fernandez (*the bricklayer with the woolly hat*), Michel Constantial (*the man dispensing cash*), Alain Roussel (*the violent man in the wood*), Yahiaoui Assouna (*Yahiaoui Assouna, the vine-cutter*), Aimé

Chisci (*the farm manager*), Marguerite Chisci (*his wife, watching telly and doing the washing*), Geneviève Bonfils (*the suspicious traveller*), Christian Chessa (*the vagrant pimp at the station*), Setina Arhab (*the vagrant girl*), Jacques Berthier (*the short well-dressed man*), Olivier Jongerlinck (*the photobooth conman*), Rémi Leboucq (*the conned customer*), Jean Dambrin (*Jean the acid sniffer*), Bébert Samcir (*Bébert the harmonica player*), the voice of Agnès Varda; the people of the villages Bellegarde, Boulbon, St Étienne-du-Grès, Générac, Jonquières-St Vincent, Uchaud, Moncalm, Tresques; the people of Mas Laval, Mas Tamerlet, St André-la-Côte
shooting Feb–Apr 85. Nîmes
budget £500,000. **C4 input** £36,000 (lf) (7%)
1st tx 4 Jun 87 (FFI)
MFB April 86. **V** 4 Sep 85
awards Golden Lion, International Critics' P, Italian Critics' P, Catholic P, Venice 85
festivals Venice, London 85
French release title *Sans toit ni loi*

VED VEJEN see **KATINKA**

VERTIGES
France/UK, 107 mins, colour
Les Films du Passage with Channel 4 and the French Ministry of Culture. © Les Films du Passage. 1985
c ed WD. **no** (-)
p PAULO BRANCO. **exec p** ANTONIO VAZ DA SILVA. **p man** Eric Lambert
d CHRISTINE LAURENT. **asst d** Suzel Galliard, (2nd) José María Vaz da Silva. **trainee sc sup** Pascale Bailly

Success Is the Best Revenge

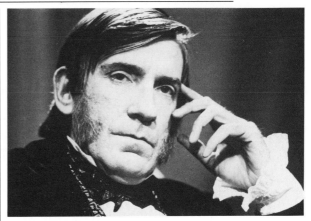

Summer Lightning

sc CHRISTINE LAURENT. **adapt** Patrick
Laurent, Christine Laurent
  ph ACACIO DE ALMEIDA
  ed FRANCINE SANDBERG
  sd PIERRE BEFVE, PIERRE LORRAIN. **sd ed**
Marie-Catherine Miqueau. **mix** Jean-François
Auger
  cast Magali Noël (*Constance*), Krystyna
Janda (*Maria*), Paulo Autran (*Eric
Hardmour*), Hélène Lapiower (*Anne*), Henri
Serre (*Marius Poudesoie*), Thierry Bosc
(*Frantz Kirkmayer*), Luis Miguel Cintra
(*Herbert Ardown*), María de Medeiros
(*Blanche*), Jorge Silva Melo (*Urbain*),
Manuel Mozos (*violinist*), Figueira Cid
(*electrician*), José Alegria (*2nd electrician*),
Fernando Moura Ramos (*thug*), Rui Madeira
(*2nd thug*), Carlos Wallenstein
(*receptionist*), José Wallenstein (*2nd
receptionist*), Vasco Segueira (*electrician,
fado singer*), the Orchestre de l'Academie de
Musica, Eborense, director Maestro Correia,
the pupils and actors of Teatro García de
Resende
  shooting Portugal
  budget (?) **C4 input** (?) (lf)
  1st tx 15 Mar 90 (FFI)
  V 15 May 85

VID VÄGEN *see* **KATINKA**

VOYAGE TO CYTHERA
Greece/FGR/Italy/UK, 136 mins, colour
Theo Angelopoulos Productions for the
Greek Film Centre, ZDF (Mainz), RAI (Rome),
ERT (Athens) and Channel 4. 1984
  c ed DR. no (-)
  p NIKOS ANGELOPOULOS. **p man**
G. Samiotis, P. Xenakis, F. Stavropoulou,
V. Lycouressi

  d THEO ANGELOPOULOS. **asst d** Takis
Katselis, Charis Papadopoulos, Nikos
Sekeris. **script** Stelanos Danilidis, Eleni
Varela
  sc THEO ANGELOPOULOS, THANASIS
VALTINOS, TONINO GUERRA based on an idea
by Theo Angelopoulos, Pierre Baudry
  ph GIORGIOS ARVANITIS
  m ELENI KARAINDROU
  ed GIORGIOS TRIANTAFYLLOU
  ad MIKES KARAPIPERIS
  cost GIORGIOS ZIAKAS. **make-up/wigs**
Giorgios Skendros
  sd THANASIS ARVANITIS, N. KITTOU,
N. ACHLADIS. **sd mix** Thanasis Arvanitis
  cast Julio Brogi (*Alexandros*), Manos
Katrakis (*Spyros, the old man*), Mary
Chronopoulou (*Voula*), Dionyssis
Papayannopoulos (*Antonis*), Dora Volanaki
(*Katerina, the old woman*), Giorgios Nezos
(*Panayotis*), Athinodoros Proussalis (*police
captain*), Michalis Yannatos (*Coast
Guard officer*), Akis Kareglis (*Spyros*),
Vassilis Tsaglos (*President of the Dock
Workers' union*), Despina Geroulanou
(*Alexandros's wife*), Tassos Saridis
(*German soldier*), Achilles Ampazis,
Irene Koumarianou
  shooting Dec 82–Apr 83; Oct 83–Feb 84.
Athens; Piraeus; Thessaloniki; northern
Greece
  budget £350,000. **C4 input** £50,000 (lf)
(14%)
  1st tx 18 Jun 87 (FFI)
  V 16 May 84
  awards International Critics' P (joint),
Cannes 84. Greek Ministry of Culture A, Best
Screenplay A 85
  festivals Cannes, London 84
  Greek release title *Taxidi sta Kithira*

Those Glory Glory Days

Tree of Hands

VROOM
UK, 89 mins, colour
Motion Pictures for British Screen and
Channel 4. © Channel 4 Television Company
1988
  c ed KB. no 130
  p PAUL LISTER. co-p RAYMOND DAY.
p co-ord Sarah Cellan-Jones
  d BEEBAN KIDRON. asst d Tony Hopkins,
(2nd) Andrew Wood. sc sup Pamela Walshe.
casting d Sheila Trezise
  sc JIM CARTWRIGHT
  ph GALE TATTERSALL. stills Frank Connor
  m ADAM KIDRON, MICHAEL MCEVOY
  ed STEPHEN SINGLETON, (addit) Simon
Clayton
  ad CAROLINE HANANIA
  cost des ANN HOLLOWOOD. make-up Sally
Harrison. hair Sarah Grundy
  stunt co-ord PETER BRAYHAM. stunt
performers Abby Collins, Simon Crane, Dave
Holland, Tom Lucy
  sd rec JOHN MIDGLEY, (addit) Ian Voigt.
dub ed Allan Morrison, (dial) Kevin Brazier.
dub mix Paul Carr, Clive Pendry
  cast Clive Owen (Jake), David Thewlis
(Ringe), Richard Henders (Abe), Bill Rodgers
(Bluto), Tim Potter (Harry), Moya Brady
(Tess), Rosalind Bennett (Lyn), Melanie
Kilburn (Kate), James Duggan (scrapman),
Diana Quick (Susan), Tricia Penrose
(supermarket girl), Dicken Ashworth (Huff),
Louis Mellis (Flanny), Jackie D. Broad (Fat
Sam), Christine Cox (Susan's sister), Martin
Oldfield (Susan's brother-in-law), Michael
Irving (Len), Maggie Lane (Ringe's mother),
Nev Goodwin (compère), Jim Broadbent
(Donald Crosby), Philip Tan (Shane), Ron
Tarr (Mr 'Fat Man' Roach)
  shooting Jun–Jul 87. Lake District;

Lancashire
  budget £1,356,000. C4 input £949,000 (lf)
(70%)
  1st tx 22 Mar 90 (FF)
  V 11 May 88
  festivals Piccadilly (London), Gijón,
Cambridge, Montreal, Birmingham, Mill
Valley, London, Leeds 88; New Delhi,
Angers, Mostra del Film d'Autore,
Southampton, Washington, Los Angeles,
Seattle, Moscow 89

WALTER
UK, 65 mins, colour
Central Productions for Channel 4 with
Randel Evans Productions. © Central
Independent Television 1982
  c ed DR. no 1
  p NIGEL EVANS. assoc p Patrick Cassavetti.
p man Redmond Morris
  d STEPHEN FREARS. asst d Raymond Day,
(2nd) Chris Rose. continuity Penny Eyles.
casting d Susie Figgis
  sc DAVID COOK from his novel Walter
  ph CHRIS MENGES. stills Tom Hilton
  m GEORGE FENTON
  ed MICK AUDSLEY
  ad MICHAEL MINAS
  cost des MONICA HOWE. make-up Elaine
Carew. hair Anne McFadyen
  titles Julian Rothenstein
  sd rec TONY JACKSON. dub ed Nicolas
Gaster. dub mix Peter Maxwell
  cast Ian McKellen (Walter), Barbara
Jefford (Sarah, Walter's mother), Arthur
Whybrow (Walter's father), Tony Melody
(Mr Hingley), David Ryall (Mr Richards),
Linda Polan (Miss Rushden), Keith Allen
(Mike, stockroom), Lesley Clare O'Neill (Jean,
stockroom), Paula Tilbrook (Mrs Ashby),

Vagabonde

Vertiges

Marjorie Yates (*social worker*), Jim Broadbent (*Joseph, orderly*), Kenny Ireland (*Angus, orderly*), Donald McKillop (*Mr Lipman*), Nabil Shaban (*Ben Gunn*), Bob Flag (*Harold*), Robert Walker (*staff nurse*), John Surman (*male nurse*), Trevor Laird (*Errol, nurse*), Robin Hooper (*washroom orderly*), Stephen Petcher (*Dave, stockroom*), Garry Cooper (*Roger, stockroom*), Frankie Connolly (*young Walter*), John Czeslaw (*Clifford*), Lol Coxhill (*shaving supervisor*), Gareth Owen, Jimmy Fagg, José Nava, Ian Hinchliffe, Neil Wintle (*patients*), Charles Lewsen (*man in next bed*)
   shooting Feb–Mar 82
   budget £325,000. **C4 input** £250,000 (lf) (77%)
   1st tx 2 Nov 82 (FF)
   V 6 Aug 86
   awards 1st P, International Rehabilitation F Festival, USA 83. Special Mention, International Magazine and TV Critics As, Monte Carlo 83. Performance A (Ian McKellen), Royal TV Society As 83. Best Original TV Music, BAFTA TV As 84. 3rd P (documentary section), World Congress of Rehabilitation Fs, Lisbon 84
   festivals International Rehabilitation F Festival, Monte Carlo, Locarno 83; World Congress of Rehabilitation Fs, Lisbon 84
   combined US release title [*Walter* and *Walter & June*] *Loving Walter*

WALTER & JUNE
UK, 65 mins, colour
Central Productions for Channel 4 with Randel Evans Productions. © Central Independent Television 1982
   c ed DR. no 17
   [**p** RICHARD CREASEY.] **assoc p** Patrick

Cassavetti. **p man** Redmond Morris
   d STEPHEN FREARS. **asst d** Raymond Day, (2nd) Chris Rose. **continuity** Penny Eyles.
casting d Susie Figgis
   sc DAVID COOK from his novel *Winter Doves*
   ph CHRIS MENGES. **stills** Tom Hilton
   m GEORGE FENTON
   ed MICK AUDSLEY
   ad MICHAEL MINAS
   cost des MONICA HOWE. **make-up** Elaine Carew. **hair** Anne McFadyen
   titles Julian Rothenstein
   sd rec TONY JACKSON. **dub ed** Nicolas Gaster. **dub mix** Peter Maxwell
   cast Ian McKellen (*Walter*), Sarah Miles (*June*), Gordon Sinclair (*Graham*), Tony Doyle (*Clive*), Jim Broadbent (*Joseph, orderly*), Christine Hargreaves (*Rita*), Catherine Schofield (*Carole*), Debbie Bishop (*black nurse*), Rowan Wylie (*white nurse*), Trevor Ray (*POA officer*), Tim Potter (*squatters' adviser*), Peter Oliver (*Tom, man in hostel*), Bob Copping (*other man in hostel*), Gary Olsen (*shower room attendant*), Jesse Birdsall (*youth in park*), John Czeslaw (*Clifford*)
   shooting Feb–Mar 82
   budget £325,000. **C4 input** £250,000 (lf) (77%)
   1st tx 26 May 83 (FF)
   awards Best Original TV Music, BAFTA TV As 84
   combined US release title [*Walter* and *Walter & June*] *Loving Walter*

WETHERBY
UK, 98 mins, colour
Greenpoint Films with Zenith Productions for Channel 4. © Greenpoint Films 1985

Voyage to Cythera

Vroom

c ed DR. **no** 53
p SIMON RELPH. **assoc p** Patsy Pollock.
p man Linda Bruce. **p co-ord** Laura Julian
d DAVID HARE. **asst d** Ian Madden, (2nd)
Gus MacLean. **continuity** Valerie Booth.
casting d Patsy Pollock, Gail Stevens
 sc DAVID HARE
 ph STUART HARRIS. **cam op** Shaun O'Dell.
stills Sophie Baker, Nobby Clark
 m NICK BICÂT. **m arr/cond** Tony Britten
 ed CHRIS WIMBLE
 pd HAYDEN GRIFFIN. **ad** Jamie Leonard
 cost des JANE GREENWOOD, LINDY
HEMMING. **make-up** Jeanne Richmond. **hair**
Gwenda Aziz Levy
 sd rec CLIVE WINTER. **sd ed** Ian Fuller. **dub
mix** Gerry Humphreys, Robin O'Donoghue
 cast [the Wetherby characters] Vanessa
Redgrave (*Jean Travers*), Ian Holm (*Stanley
Pilborough*), Judi Dench (*Marcia
Pilborough*), Marjorie Yates (*Verity
Braithwaite*), Tom Wilkinson (*Tom
Braithwaite*), Penny Downie (*Chrissie*),
Brenda Hall (*landlady*), Marjorie Sudell
(*Lilly*), Patrick Blackwell (*Derek, Chrissie's
husband*); [in the past] Joely Richardson
(*young Jean Travers*), Robert Hines (*Jim
Mortimer*), Katy Behean (*young Marcia*),
Bert King (*Mr Mortimer*), Paula Tilbrook (*Mrs
Mortimer*), Christopher Fulford (*Arthur*),
David Foreman (*young Malay*); [the school]
Stephanie Noblett (*Suzie Bannerman*),
Richard Marris (*Sir Thomas*), Jonathan
Lazenby (*boatman*), Nigel Rooke (*1st page*),
John Robert (*2nd page*), Norman Mills
(*drama teacher*), Vanessa Rosenthal, Trevor
Lunn (*pretentious parents*), Guy Nicholls (*Mr
Varley*), Ian Bleasdale (*neurotic teacher*),
Peter Martin (*helpful parent*); [Miss Travers'
class] Mouth, Dave, Dob, Flash, Johnny,

Lebanon, Tracey, Bez, Jen, Jessica, Rhianon,
Maddy, Paul, Toby, Marcus, Masher, Andy,
Janet, Peter, Ram, Liz, Ed, Suzanne, Lesley,
Shaun; [the police] Stuart Wilson (*Mike
Langdon*), Diane Whitley (*policewoman*),
Mike Kelly (*CID policeman*), Howard
Crossley (*policeman*), Matthew Guinness
(*Randall, police doctor*), Ted Beyer (*police
sergeant*); [from the University of Essex] Tim
McInnerny (*John Morgan*), Suzanna
Hamilton (*Karen Creasy*)
 shooting Jun–Aug 84. Yorkshire;
Rickmansworth; Twickenham studios
 budget £1,125,000. **C4 input** £750,000
(lf/i) (67%)
 1st tx 12 Jun 86 (FF)
 MFB Mar 85. **V** 20 Feb 85
 awards Golden Bear (joint), Berlin 85
 festivals Berlin, Haifa 85; Filmotsav India,
Belgrade, Madrid, Hong Kong, Wellington,
Troia 86; Istanbul, Moscow 87; Berlin,
Cherbourg 90

WE THINK THE WORLD OF YOU
UK/USA, 94 mins, colour/b&w
Gold Screen Films with Cinecom
Entertainment Group (New York) for British
Screen and Channel 4. © Film Four
International 1988
 c ed KB/DR. **no** 120
 p TOMMASO JANDELLI. **co-p** PAUL COWAN.
p co-ord Fran Triefus
 d COLIN GREGG. **asst d** Gary White, (2nd)
Nick Laws. **sc sup** Cheryl Leigh. **casting d**
Simone Reynolds
 sc HUGH STODDART based on the novel by
J. R. Ackerley
 ph MIKE GARFATH. **cam op** Malcolm
Vinson. **stills** Simon Mein
 m/m cond JULIAN JACOBSON. **orch** Jeremy

Walter

Walter & June

Sands
  ed PETER DELFGOU
  pd JAMIE LEONARD. **ad** Chris Edwards
  cost des DOREEN WATKINSON. **make-up**
Jennifer Boost. **hair** Karen Turner
  sd mix TONY DAWE. **dub ed** John Delfgou.
dub mix Hugh Strain
  cast Alan Bates (*Frank Meadows*), Max
Wall (*Tom Burney*), Liz Smith (*Millie
Burney*), Frances Barber (*Megan Burney*),
Gary Oldman (*Johnny Burney*), Ryan Batt
(*Dickie*), Kerry Wise (*Rita*), Sheila Ballantine
(*Margaret*), David Swift (*Bill*), Pat Keen (*Miss
Sweeting*), Ivor Roberts (*Harry*), Paula Jacobs
(*Deirdre*), Barbara New (*Mrs Grant*), Edward
Jewesbury (*judge*), Nick Stringer (*butcher*),
Danny Macdonald (*boy*), Nicola Wright (*post
girl*), Barbara Hicks, Irene Sutcliffe
(*residents' association ladies*), Betsy (*Evie*)
  shooting Jan–Mar 88. London
  budget £1,357,000. **C4 input** £550,000
(lf/i) (41%)
  1st tx 12 May 91 (FF)
  MFB Oct 89. **V** 21 Sep 88
  festivals Toronto, Cherbourg, Leeds,
London 88; Southampton, Moscow,
Edinburgh 89; Calcutta, Dinard, Denmark
Gay/Lesbian, Polish Film Week 90

WILD FLOWERS
UK, 69 mins, colour
Frontroom Films for Channel 4. © Channel
4 Television Co 1989
  c ed KB. **no** 134
  p CHRIS HARVEY. **p co-ord** John Booth.
p man Peter McAleese
  d ROBERT SMITH. **asst d** Eric Coulter, (2nd)
Hugh Boyle, Tommy Gormley. **continuity**
Margaret Waldie. **casting consultant** Lucy
Boulting

  sc SHARMAN MACDONALD
  ph WITOLD STOK. **cam op** Rodrigo
Gutierrez. **stills** Tom Hilton, Gordon Terris
  m KENNY CRADDOCK, COLIN GIBSON
  ed JOHN DAVIES
  pd CAROLINE HANANIA. **ad** Cas Stewart
  cost des MARY-JANE REYNER. **make-up**
Robert McCann. **hair** Meg Speirs
  titles Ros Boon
  sd rec LOUIS KRAMER. **dub mix** Colin
Martin
  cast Beatie Edney (*Sadie*), Sheila Keith
(*Marguerite*), Colette O'Neil (*Annie
Macfarlane*), Stevan Rimkus (*Angus
Macfarlane*), Amanda Walker (*Ina, woman in
panama hat*), Kay Gallie (*Maisie*), Calum
Miller (*Tom Macfarlane*), Charles Kearney
(*father*), John McGlynn (*lutanist*), Gerard
Slevin (*minister*), Anne Lacey (*1st woman*),
Gaylie Runciman (*2nd woman*), Alistair
Galbraith (*1st coffin bearer*), David Meldrum
(*2nd coffin bearer*), Anne Marie Timoney
(*Sadie's friend*)
  shooting Jun–Jul 89. Gourock; Glasgow;
Iona
  budget £560,000. **C4 input** £560,000 (lf/i)
(100%)
  1st tx 15 Mar 90 (FF)
  festivals London 89

WINTER *see* **HIGH HOPES**

WINTER FLIGHT
UK, 105 mins, colour
Enigma Television/Goldcrest Films &
Television for Channel 4. © Goldcrest Films
& Television 1984
  c ed DR/KB. **no** 60
  p ROBIN DOUET, SUSAN RICHARDS. **exec p**
DAVID PUTTNAM. **p co-ord** Mary Richards

Wetherby

We Think the World of You

d ROY BATTERSBY. **asst d** Christopher Newman, (2nd) Peter Chadwick. **continuity** Pauline Harlow. **casting d** Marilyn Johnson
sc ALAN JANES
ph CHRIS MENGES. **cam op** Mike Roberts. **stills** David Appleby
m RICHARD HARVEY
ed LESLEY WALKER
ad ADRIENNE ATKINSON
cost des SUE YELLAND. **make-up** Sheila Mann. **hair** Sally Harrison
titles Brian Eley
sd rec TONY JACKSON. **dub ed** Mark Auguste. **dub mix** Jon Blunt
cast Reece Dinsdale (*Mal Stanton*), Nicola Cowper (*Angie Bowyer*), Gary Olsen (*Dave*), Sean Bean (*Hooker*), Beverley Hewitt (*Lara*), Shelagh Stephenson (*Kel*), Michael Percival (*doctor*), Anthony Trent (*Sgt Bowyer*), Tim Bentinck (*Jack*), Michael Hughes (*Los*), Mark Penfold (*Fl Lt Maynard*), Annette Ekblom (*Jill*), Martin Gower (*Murph*), Robert Pugh (*military policeman*), Raymond Armstrong (*warrant officer*), Christopher Muncke (*USAF controller*), James Sport (*air tower supervisor*), Suzie Fairfax (*female controller*), Nicholas Day (*army officer*), Stuart Barren (*Sgt Reece*), Phil Smeeton (*dog-handler guard*), Terence Harvey (*SATCO*), Arbel Jones (*midwife*), Ling Tai (*Malay nurse*), Marcia Tucker (*black nurse*), Nicholas Lumley (*Robert*), Tony Peers (*ambulance man*), Carol Harvey (*nurse*), Annie Bruce (*reception nurse*), Clare McIntyre (*Mrs Maynard*), Ian Staples (*1st airman*), Gary Whelan (*2nd airman*), Douglas Sannachen (*young airman*), T. Welch-Willius (*Angie's baby*)
shooting Mar–May 84. Cambridgeshire; Bedfordshire; London

budget £606,190 [David Puttnam].
C4 input £275,000 (lf) (45%)
1st tx 20 Dec 84 (FF: 'First Love')
V 5 Dec 84
festivals London 84
shooting title *The Big Surprise*

WISH YOU WERE HERE
UK, 92 mins, colour
Zenith Productions with Working Title for Channel 4. © Zenith Productions 1987
c ed KB. **no** 90
p SARAH RADCLYFFE. **p co-ord** Ginny Roncoroni. **p man** Caroline Hewitt
d DAVID LELAND. **asst d** Steve Finn, (2nd) Nick Laws. **continuity** Libbie Barr. **casting d** Susie Figgis
sc DAVID LELAND
ph/cam op IAN WILSON. **Steadicam op** John Ward. **stills** Ian Pleeth
m STANLEY MYERS. **m co-ord** Gerry Butler. **original songs** (m) Stanley Myers, (l) David Leland
ed GEORGE AKERS
des CAROLINE AMIES. **ad** Nigel Phelps
cost SHUNA HARWOOD. **make-up** Jenny Shircore. **hair** Jan Archibald
stunt co-ord JIM DOWDALL
sd rec BILLY MCCARTHY. **sd ed** 'Budge' Tremlett. **dub mix** Peter Maxwell
film extract *Love Story* (1944)
cast Trudi Cavanagh (*tap-dancing lady*), Emily Lloyd (*Lynda Mansell*), Clare Clifford (*Mrs Parfitt*), Barbara Durkin (*Valerie*), Geoffrey Hutchings (*Hubert Mansell*), Charlotte Barker (*Gillian*), Tom Bell (*Eric*), Chloe Leland (*Margaret Mansell*), Charlotte Ball (*Lynda, 11 years*), Pat Heywood (*Aunt Millie*), Abigail Leland (*Margaret, 7 years*), Susan Skipper (*Lynda's mother*), Geoffrey

Wild Flowers

Winter Flight

Durham (*Harry Figgis*), Sheila Kelley (*Joan Figgis*), Neville Smith (*cinema manager*), Lee Whitlock (*Brian*), Jesse Birdsall (*Dave*), Frederick Hall (*passenger with brolly*), Bob Flag (*mental patient*), Heathcote Williams (*Dr Holroyd*), William Lawford (*Uncle Brian*), Pamela Duncan (*Mrs Hartley*), David Hatton (*customer, fish-and-chip van*), Ben Daniels (*policeman*), Val McLane (*Maisie Mathews*), Kim McDermott (*Vickie*), Barrie Houghton (*café manager*), Jim Dowdall (*cook*), Danielle Phelps (*the baby*), George (*Mitch the dog*)

shooting Sep–Nov 86. Worthing; Bognor Regis

budget £1,132,000. **C4 input** £849,000 (lf/i) (75%)

1st tx 15 Feb 90 (FF)

MFB Dec 87. **V** 13 May 87

awards International Critics' P, Best F (outside official selection), Cannes 87. François Truffaut A (Best 1st F), Valladolid 87. Silver Dolphin (Best 1st Work), Troia 87. Best Actress (Emily Lloyd), National F Critics' A (USA) 87. Best Actress (Emily Lloyd), Peter Sellers Comedy A (David Leland), *Standard* F As 88. Best Original Screenplay, BAFTA F As 88

festivals Cannes, Sydney, Melbourne, Moscow, Locarno, Edinburgh, Toronto, Boario Terme, Tokyo, Haifa, Valladolid, Hof, Troia, London, Cairo 87; Belgrade 88

A WORLD APART
UK/Zimbabwe, 113 mins, colour
Working Title (London) and Hippo Films (Zimbabwe) for British Screen and Atlantic Entertainment Group with Channel 4.
© Working Title-A World Apart 1987
c ed KB. **no** 121

p SARAH RADCLYFFE. **exec p** TIM BEVAN, GRAHAM BRADSTREET. **assoc p** Shawn Slovo. **p man** Caroline Hewitt. **p co-ord** Sue Sheldon

d CHRIS MENGES. **asst d** Guy Travers, (2nd) Chris Thompson, (2nd, crowd) Rupert Ryle-Hodges. **sc sup** Penny Eyles. **casting** Susie Figgis. **dialect d** Nora Dunfee

sc SHAWN SLOVO. **cam op** Mike Proudfoot, (2nd) Craig Haagensen. **stills** David Appleby

m HANS ZIMMER. **m perf** Senior Choir, St Paul's Girls' School, conductor Hilary Davan Wetton. **orch** Brian Gulland

ed NICOLAS GASTER

des BRIAN MORRIS. **ad** Mike Philips

cost des NIC EDE. **make-up** Elaine Carew, Maureen Stephenson. **wigs** Peter Owen

sd rec JUDY FREEMAN. **dub ed** 'Budge' Tremlett. **dial ed** Bob Risk. **dub mix** Hugh Strain

cast Jodhi May (*Molly Roth*), Jeroen Krabbé (*Gus Roth*), Barbara Hershey (*Diana Roth*), Nadine Chalmers (*Yvonne Abelson*), María Pilar (*Spanish dance teacher*), Kate Fitzpatrick (*June Abelson*), Tim Roth (*Harold*), Phyllis Naidoo (*Saeeda*), Linda Mvusi (*Elsie*), Carolyn Clayton-Cragg (*Miriam Roth*), Yvonne Bryceland (*Bertha Abrahams*), Mackay Tickey (*Milius*), Merav Gruer (*Jude Roth*), Albee Lesotho (*Solomon Mbusa*), Clement Muchachi (*Sipho Dlamini*), Paul Freeman (*Kruger*), Esma Levend (*Whitworth*), Rosalie Crutchley (*Mrs Harris*), Toby Salaman (*Gerald Abelson*), Theresa Memela (*Peggy*), Stephen Williams (*arresting officer*), Adrian Dunbar (*Le Roux*), David Suchet (*Muller*), Jo-Anne Huckle (*Debbie*), Margaret Hogan (*history teacher*), Nomaziko Zondo (*Thandile*), André Proctor

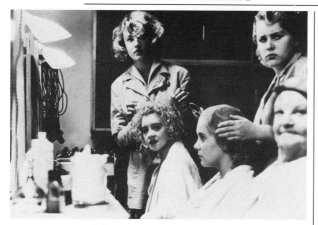

Wish You Were Here

A World Apart

(*arresting officer*), Andrew Whaley (*interrogating officer*), Cont Mhlanga (*Mtutuzeli Nzekwu*), Jude Akuwidike (*priest*), the Messias Choir (choirmaster Henry Mlauzi), Lovemore Majaivana and the Zulu Band, the Jack Buckell Band
  shooting Jun–Aug 87. Bulawayo
  budget £2,675,000. **C4 input** £275,000 (lf) (10%)
  1st tx 21 Apr 91 (FF)
  MFB Aug 88. **V** 11 May 88
  awards Special Jury P, Best Actress A (Barbara Hershey/Jodhi May/Linda Mvusi), Cannes 88. Best Original Screenplay, BAFTA F As 89
  festivals Cannes 88

YERMA
Hungary/FGR/UK, ?106 mins, colour
Hunnia Filmstudio and Hungarian Television (Budapest), Macropus-Film, Starfilm Produktion (Munich) and Sefel Pictures International for Channel 4.
© Mafilm 1985
  c ed DR. **no** 61
  p ANTAL GOTTMANN, ERIC MOSS. **co-p** JOSEF SEFEL, ÁKOS RAVASZ. **p co-ord** (Starfilm Produktion) Martin Moszkowicz. **studio man** (Hunnia Filmstudio) Miklós Köllö
  d IMRE GYÖNGYÖSSY, BARNA KABAY
  sc IMRE GYÖNGYÖSSY, BARNA KABAY, KATALIN PETÉNYI from the play by Federico García Lorca. **sc cons** Ákos Ravasz
  ph GÁBOR SZABÓ. **cam** László Ramm. **stills** Miklós Gáspár
  m PESKO ZOLTÁN
  des TAMÁS VAYER. **ad** Michaela von Andrenyi, Thomas Hohenacker
  ed KATALIN PETÉNYI, ANNA KORNIS
  cost des MÁRTA JÁNOSKUTI. **make-up**

Attila Ungvári, István Szücs
  sd ISTVÁN SIPOS. **engineers** Anja Schmidt-Zaringer, Antonio Orell, Ádám Némenyi, Tamás Villanyi
  cast Gudrun Landgrebe (*Yerma*), Titusz Kovács (*Juan*), Matthieu Carrière (*Victor*), Mareike Carrière (*María*), Hédi Temessy (*Elvira*), Róbert Gergely (*Leonardo*), Ildikó Bánsági, Sándor Szakácsi, Juli Basti, María Sulyok, Martin Halm, Erzsi Pasztor, Peter Rudolf, Éva Szabó, Péter Blaskó, Olga Antal, László Sefel, Márta Egri, Éva Tóth, Iván Angelusz, Éva Regenhart, Sándor Gáspár, Réka Gyöngyössy, Klári Bodza, Kornélia Hárs, György Gonda, Vilmos Kun, Rita Tallos
  shooting Spain
  budget (?) **C4 input** £26,000 (lf)
  1st tx 8 Apr 89 (FFI)

LES YEUX DES OISEAUX *see* **THE EYES OF BIRDS**

A ZED & TWO NOUGHTS
UK/Netherlands, 115 mins, colour
The British Film Institute (London), Allarts Enterprises (Amsterdam), Artificial Eye Productions (London) and VPRO Television (Hilversum) for Channel 4. © 1985
  c ed DR. **no** 76
  p KEES KASANDER, PETER SAINSBURY. **p co-ord** Karin Spiegel. **p man** Denis Wigman
  d PETER GREENAWAY. **asst d** Gerrit Martijn, (2nd) Marietta de Vries. **continuity** Els Rastelli. **casting d** Sharon Howard-Field
  sc PETER GREENAWAY. **st ed** Walter Donohue
  ph SACHA VIERNY. **addit ph** Mike Coles. **natural history ph** Survival Anglia. **time-lapse ph** David Spears Ltd. **cam op**

Yerma

A Zed & Two Noughts

David Claessen. **stills** Steve Pyke, Hayo
Piebenga, Luke Kelly
m MICHAEL NYMAN. **m perf** Sarah
Leonard, Elisabeth Perry, Alexander
Balanescu, Michael Nyman, Gerard
Bouqhuis, Arno Bons, John Helstone, Gerrit
Oloeman, Sofia Kiss, Beverly Lund, Jorn
Schroeder, Rob Hageman, Marien van
Staalen, Lene te Voortwis, Pieter
Gouderjaan, Jan Jansen, Bas Dekker, Wim
Steinmann, Jelle Schouten, Henk Leether,
Leo van Oostrom, Peter Stan, Adri van
Velsen, Frans Vreugdenhil, Peter
Veenhuizen, Gerbrand Westveen
  ed JOHN WILSON
  pd BEN van OS, JAN ROELFS
  cost PATRICIA LIM. **make-up** Sara
Meerman, Nicole Mora. **hair** Yvonne
Minderman
  sd rec GARTH MARSHALL. **sd ed** Charles
Ware, (dial) Matthew Whiteman. **dub mix**

Tony Anscombe
  cast Andrea Ferréol (*Alba Bewick*), Brian
Deacon (*Oswald Deuce*), Eric Deacon (*Oliver
Deuce*), Frances Barber (*Venus de Milo*), Joss
Ackland (*Van Hoyten*), Jim Davidson (*Joshua
Plate*), Agnes Brulet (*Beta Bewick*), Guusje
van Tilborgh (*Caterina Bolnes*), Gerard
Thoolen (*Van Meegeren*), Ken Campbell
(*Stephen Pipe*), Wolf Kahler (*Felipe
Arc-en-Ciel*), Geoffrey Palmer (*Fallast*),
David Attenborough (*narrator of wild-life
footage*)
  shooting Amsterdam Zoo
  budget £635,000. **C4 input** £250,000 (lf)
(39%)
  1st tx 30 Apr 87 (FF)
  MFB Dec 85. **V** 4 Dec 85
  festivals London 85; Rotterdam, Hong
Kong, Montreal, New York, Toronto, São
Paulo 86; Rio de Janeiro 87; Haifa 88; Banco
National 91

ACKNOWLEDGMENTS

I AM GRATEFUL to the following for their assistance in the preparation of this book: David Rose, Colin Leventhal, Caroline Thomson, Christopher Griffin-Beale, Karin Bamborough, David Aukin, Julie Hearn, Alison S. Carter, Emma Shepherd, Victoria Evans, Philippa Wood, Melanie Lindsell, Susanna Yager, Dawn Stanley, Bridget Pedgrift, Caroline D'Arcy, Olga Budham, David Hayward and Laurie Chapman (Channel 4); Roma Gibson, John Smoker, Dawn King, Bridget Kinally, Elaine Burrows, Jackie Morris, Clive Truman, Peter Rutland, Mark Richardson, Imdad Hussain and Deac Rossell (British Film Institute); Theo Angelopoulos, Simon Relph, Ann Scott, John Boorman, Simon Perry, David Puttnam, Roeland Kerbosch, Simon Cox, Emma Hayter, Aisling Walsh, Joe Comerford, John Kochman, Jacky Stoller, Sarah Quill, Ceri Norman, Richard Everitt, Emeric Molnar, Cruz Trickey, Neil Egerton, Torgny Wärn, Merchant Ivory Productions, Granada Television and Artificial Eye.

The Broadcasters' Audience Research Board (BARB) kindly permitted me to reprint from its records. Photographs were supplied by Channel 4 and the British Film Institute (Stills, Posters and Designs); the individual photographers being listed where known in Appendix B. Much useful information came from Longman's *Annual Register* and the weekly bulletins of the Channel 4 press office. I am indebted to Hope Pym for suggesting improvements to the text and to Celia and William Pym for copying credits; to Edwin Taylor for consenting to design the book and Chloe Taylor for laying out the jacket; to my editors Edward Buscombe and David Wilson; and to Colin MacCabe for commissioning the research. I wish to thank Markku Salmi, my former colleague at the BFI, for his advice and, in particular, for his scrutiny of the credits.

INDEX